A MICHAEL NEUGEBAUER BOOK

Text and photographs copyright © 1992 by Michio Hoshino.
First published in Switzerland under the title DAS BÄREN-KINDER-BUCH by Michael Neugebauer Verlag AG, Gossau Zurich, Switzerland.
English translation copyright © 1993 by North-South Books Inc.
The Animal Family series is supervised by biologist Sybille Kalas.
All rights reserved. No part of this book may be reproduced or utilized in any form or by any means, electronic or mechanical, including photocopying, recording, or any information storage and retrieval system, without permission in writing from the publisher.
First published in the United States and Canada in 1994 by North-South Books, an imprint of Nord-Süd Verlag AG, Gossau Zürich, Switzerland.
First published in Great Britain, Australia, and New Zealand in 1993 by Picture Book Studio Ltd., London. Reprinted in 1994 by North-South Books.
First paperback edition published in 1997.
Distributed in the United States by North-South Books Inc., New York.
Library of Congress Cataloging-in-Publication Data
Hoshino, Michio, 1952-
[Bären-Kinder-Buch. English]
The grizzly bear family book / Michio Hoshino ; translated by Karen Colligan-Taylor.
(The Animal family series)
"A Michael Neugebauer book"
1. Grizzly bear—Alaska—Juvenile literature. 2. Natural history—Alaska—Outdoor books—Juvenile literature. I. Title. II. Series.
QL737.C27H673 1993 599.74′446—dc20 92-36648

A CIP catalogue record for this book is available from The British Library.

ISBN 1-55858-350-5 (trade binding) 10 9 8 7 6 5 4 3 2 1
ISBN 1-55858-351-3 (library binding) 10 9 8 7 6 5 4 3 2
ISBN 1-55858-701-2 (paperback) 10 9 8 7 6 5 4 3 2 1
Printed in Belgium

For more information about our books, and the authors and artists
who create them, visit our web site: http://www.northsouth.com

Ask your bookseller for these other North-South Animal Family books:
THE CROCODILE FAMILY BOOK
THE DESERT FOX FAMILY BOOK
THE ELEPHANT FAMILY BOOK
THE LION FAMILY BOOK
THE PENGUIN FAMILY BOOK
THE POLAR BEAR FAMILY BOOK
THE WILD HORSE FAMILY BOOK

Michio Hoshino **The Grizzly Bear Family Book**

Translated by Karen Colligan-Taylor

NORTH-SOUTH BOOKS / NEW YORK / LONDON

Imagine meeting a grizzly bear in the wild. Not at the zoo, not in a book, but out in the open—a chance encounter with the real thing. Just you and the bear, face to face.

It happened to me once, when I was camping near Mount McKinley in Alaska. For more than half of each year, I hike through the mountains and plains of Alaska, the Great Land, with my tent on my back, taking pictures of the land which has attracted me since my teens.

Around four o'clock one morning I was awakened by something brushing against my tent. Wondering what it was, I rubbed my eyes and opened the tent flap. There, right in front of me, was a bear's face. I was startled, but the bear must have been even more surprised. It took one look at me and clumped hastily away.

I had never before been so close to a bear. And I knew then that I wanted to use my camera to record one year in the lives of the Alaskan grizzlies.

In midwinter the temperature here may fall to fifty degrees below zero. During this harsh time, a grizzly bear will sleep in a snug underground den, the entrance covered by a blanket of snow.

While the mother bear sleeps, her tiny cubs are born. They nurse and snuggle next to her until longer days and warmer temperatures signal the arrival of spring.

One day in April, as I hiked through the mountains called the Alaska Range, I noticed fresh bear tracks on the snowy slope. Following them with my binoculars, I spotted a mother bear and her cub walking through the snow.

The cold, biting wind was already giving way to spring breezes. When the bears come out of their dens, it's a sure sign that the long winter is over.

As the snow melts and shrinks into patches of crusty ice, wildflowers push their faces towards the sky. In the far north, the flowers are very small. But each blossom possesses tremendous strength. I am moved when I come upon these tiny shapes, living their lives to the fullest extent.

In early spring, grizzly bears also enjoy life to its fullest. Once I watched as a mother and her cub played tag on a slope across from me. The mother chased her cub across the grassy hillside. When she caught the youngster, she took it in her arms and hugged it to her gently, and they began to roll down the slope together. They seemed to be having such a wonderful time, I couldn't help but burst out laughing.

A nursing bear will often lie on her back and offer milk to her cub. If she has two, she will cradle one in each arm. I'm not sure that nursing tires her out, but afterwards the mother often spread-eagles on the ground, sound asleep.

People have such fearful images of bears. But is the affection and care of a human mother for her children so different from the love and tenderness the mother bear shows her cubs?

Grizzlies just emerging from their winter dens are as thin as they will be all year. They have not eaten for months, and in the snow-covered landscape, their first meal may be the carcass of a moose or caribou that did not survive

the winter. Near the sea, bears may find a beached whale, or a dead sea lion or walrus.

After the snow melts and the earth turns green, bears begin to eat roots and grasses. Sedges—grasses that grow in wetlands—are particularly important, because they grow rapidly in the early spring and are rich in protein.

Arctic ground squirrels are a popular food for bears, but it takes real work to catch one. An 850-pound bear chasing a 2-pound squirrel is a truly comical sight. When the squirrel dives into its hole, the bear begins digging

furiously with its front paws. But there may be many holes, all connected underground. Sometimes the squirrel will pop out of a hole behind the bear and watch it dig away.

Of course, many squirrels do get caught and eaten by bears. Scientists at Denali National Park in Alaska found that each grizzly bear eats about 400 ground squirrels a year.

Caribou, wolves, Dall sheep, moose, and many other animals give birth in the spring. They must keep constant watch over their newborns to protect them from danger.

One June afternoon I was sitting on a mountain slope looking down at a moose with her two young calves. For some reason the moose was uneasy, her ears pulled far back to the sides. A bear suddenly appeared from the bushes and rushed towards the calves.

The moose turned to confront the powerful bear. The bear stopped and the two faced off, staring at each other intently. A moment later the moose charged. The startled bear took off, with the moose close behind.

The moose had risked her life to protect her calves. And the bear retreated rather than risk being injured by the slashing hooves of the determined cow.

The bear will try again, of course, and next time it may be successful. But I have come to understand that when a bear catches a moose calf, it is not a sad event. The bear may have cubs of her own who will share in the meal. There will be new moose calves and new bear cubs next year, and life in the wilderness will go on. In nature, all living things, including humans, depend on other lives for their existence.

As summer nears, the daylight hours lengthen quickly until the nights are completely gone.

Imagine having no night at all. The sun moves around the sky in a big circle, always staying just above the horizon. Without a watch, it's hard to know when one day ends and the next begins. You may forget what day of the week it is, and even what month. And all the while, the sun's energy feeds the trees, grasses, and shrubs of the Alaskan wilderness.

In June salmon swim upstream in Alaska's rivers and streams, and bears are drawn to choice fishing spots. Grizzlies avoid contact with other bears during most of the year, but fishing season brings them shoulder to shoulder along the streams. With food temporarily abundant, they seem to tolerate one another more, but first a dominance order—an understanding of who bosses whom—must be established.

The stronger, more aggressive bears, usually males, command the best places. When a new bear joins a group, a brief struggle for dominance is often the result. Bears avoid fighting if at all possible, but two bears of nearly equal strength may wage a fierce battle. When two bears who have already fought meet again, the loser will automatically give up its place to the victor, avoiding another fight.

Bears use body language to express dominance or subservience within the temporary community at the river. By observing bears as they fish, I have learned some useful clues about the safest way to behave around bears in the wild.

One time I watched a mother bear with one cub, and another mother with two cubs, approach a river. While the mothers fished for salmon in the river, the cubs waited on the riverbank. Curiosity drew all three cubs together.

Suddenly the mother of the two cubs rushed up the bank. Would she kill the stranger? But the mother bear simply sniffed the cub that was not her own. Then the mother of the single cub realized what was happening, and charged out of the water to defend her young. Again it seemed as if there might be trouble. The cubs looked on nervously, staying near their mothers. In the end, the two families parted peacefully. Mother bears are usually quite tolerant of the cubs of others, even to the point of adopting strays and orphans.

I was surprised the first time I saw a bear catch a salmon, hold it briefly as if examining it, and then release it in the river. When salmon are rare, grizzlies will hungrily devour every one they catch. But at the height of the salmon

season, a bear may capture ten salmon an hour and can afford to be selective. Sometimes bears eat just the head and eggs, discarding the rest. The uneaten portion of the fish doesn't go to waste, however, because gulls swarm nearby, ready to grab the leftovers.

When a bear catches a salmon with its paws and mouth, it can probably smell the difference between a male fish and a female fish. The bear I saw

catching and releasing salmon may have been selecting only the female fish with their delicious eggs.

First-year cubs wait on the riverbank for their mothers to bring freshly caught salmon. By their second year, cubs wade in to fish for themselves. Although rarely successful at first, they learn by watching and imitating their mothers.

With the end of the salmon run, the bears' temporary society breaks up, each bear returning to its own mountain territory, where autumn food sources are now maturing.

The bugling of sandhill cranes
sweeping south in great ragged Vs
announces autumn across Alaska.
The animals of the Arctic grow lovely,
thick winter coats. Moose and caribou
antlers are now very large. Aspen and
birch forests turn golden, and the
tundra blazes red.

Blueberry, cranberry, and crowberry bushes blanket the ground, offering a rich harvest for bears.

"Don't bump heads with a bear when you go blueberry picking!" This frequently heard advice is no joke in Alaska. Both humans and bears become so engrossed in berry picking that they scarcely take a moment to lift their heads and look around. While you probably won't actually bump heads with a bear, it's wise to check your surroundings now and then.

Bears seem to like soapberries best of all. Wondering how they taste, I picked a ripe red one and popped it in my mouth. It didn't taste very good to me, but then I don't like fish heads, either.

It's wonderful to observe a huge bear holding a thin soapberry branch, gently stripping it of the delicate fruit.

As the days shorten, bears must put on a large store of fat to take them through winter. Berries are high in sugar, and the autumn feast can be critical to a bear's survival. With their shiny coats rippling as they move across the tundra, grizzlies consume an enormous amount of berries.

How many berries would you guess a grizzly can eat in one day? The bears in Denali National Park eat berries for twenty hours a day in late summer, hardly stopping to sleep. One bear may consume 200,000 berries in a single day! Bear droppings at this time of year consist mainly of partially digested berries. From the seeds in these droppings new bushes will grow to feed a new generation of bears.

One autumn day as I was hiking through the Brooks Range near the Arctic Circle, I suddenly noticed two bears running towards me from a riverbank. Were they coming at me on purpose, or did they not realize I was there? They appeared to be siblings, just old enough to leave their mother's care, but already powerful. Closer and closer they came, loping gracefully. My heart beat like a drum. When they were about twenty yards away, I raised my arms and shouted, *"Stop!"*

The two bears skidded to a halt as if in complete surprise. They stood up on their hind legs, wagging their heads from side to side, sniffing the air. I was so excited, I thought my heart would burst.

Then, as if they had finally become aware of my existence, they turned and raced off in the direction they'd come from. It had been a pretty frightening experience for me, but it must have been equally startling for the bears.

That night I couldn't fall asleep. The two grizzlies might be close by. Very few bears are interested in pursuing people, but still I felt somewhat uneasy. Unable to sleep, I thought about bears, about people, and about Alaska.

If there wasn't a single bear in all of Alaska, I could hike through the mountains with complete peace of mind. I could camp without worry. But what a dull place Alaska would be!

Here people share the land with bears. There is a certain wariness between people and bears. And that wariness forces upon us a valuable sense of humility.

People continue to tame and subjugate nature. But when we visit the few remaining scraps of wilderness where bears roam free, we can still feel an instinctive fear. How precious that feeling is. And how precious these places, and these bears, are.

Trophy hunters from the lower United States and from Europe come to Alaska to shoot grizzlies. They smile for the camera and stand, gun in hand, over the body of a dead bear. They hang their trophy on the wall—the head of a bear with its fangs bared, as if it was killed while attacking the heroic hunter. In truth, a high-powered rifle was fired from a great distance at a bear that was peacefully eating berries.

Just imagine: You're alone and unarmed on the arctic plain with a bear. You and the bear feel the same breeze pass over your faces. You—a human being—are on an equal footing with the bear.

How wonderful that would be. No matter how many books you read, no matter how much television you watch, there is no substitute for experiencing nature firsthand. If you cannot meet a bear in the wild, then you must try to imagine it—for even if you only imagine it, the feeling can be real. And it is the feeling that is important.

Today's snowfall marks the advent of winter. The daylight hours are shorter now. The aurora dances in the clear night sky. A mother bear and her half-grown cubs trace footprints in the new snow as they climb up the mountain to their den. The cubs will spend the long winter with their mother snug beneath the snow.

The snow continues to fall, and finally the tracks are gone. Alaska, the Great Land, settles down for a quiet winter sleep.

Car Repair Manual

MINI

Compiled and Written by

Andy Hugh

HOE 56S

Austin Morris Mini   from 1959

Austin 7	Clubman 1100	Riley Elf
Morris Mini-Minor	Clubman 1275 GT	Mini-Van
Mini 850	Countryman	Mini Pick-Up
Mini 1000	Traveller	Automatic versions
Clubman 1000	Wolseley Hornet	Export models

The Editor would like to acknowledge the help from the following companies in the preparation of this repair manual:

British Leyland UK Ltd
Champion Sparking Plug Co. Ltd
Radiomobile Ltd
KL Automotive Products Ltd
Sound Service (Oxford) Ltd
Car Mechanics Magazine

Autodata Car Repair Manual for the Mini

Compiled and Written by Andy Hugh
Edited by Jack Hay
Layout and paste-up: Eddie Kent/Anne White
Composing: Sajan Neal/Simer Bharji

Published by Autodata Ltd
St. Peter's Road, Maidenhead, Berkshire, SL6 7QU. England

WSM 250

ISBN 0-85666-052-3

Printed in England by Page Bros (Norwich) Ltd

Introduction

You are reading one of the best accessories that you could purchase for your car. Whether you are a keen do-it-yourself enthusiast or just eager to cut the cost of motoring, this repair manual will guide you through all the stages of various mechanical repairs - from a simple oil and filter change; fitting new brake shoes; checking the hydraulics; tuning the engine; dealing with the electrics; or even removing and overhauling the engine - all the knowledge and information you are likely to need are here!

The easy-reference contents page and individual chapter headings will guide you to the appropriate section dealing with the part of your car to be checked or repaired. The clear line-drawings will show you what fits where giving you all the confidence to tackle a job for the first time. Each chapter contains easy-to-follow repair sequences with a comprehensive Technical Data section included at the end. If problems occur that can't be solved easily then turn to the special Trouble-shooting chart to be found at the end of the appropriate section.

A large proportion of this manual is devoted to routine and preventative maintenance with a complete chapter covering the servicing of your car - indeed, a money saver in itself!

Tools are of obvious importance to the do-it-yourself car owner and, like this repair manual, can be termed as a good investment. Purchase wisely, not over-spending but just purchasing good quality tools needed for a certain job and building up your equipment as you go. Tools required for general servicing aren't that many but it will be the wise do-it-yourself motorist who invests in a good jack and axle stands or wheel ramps. Some of the operations shown in this book require special tools and, in many cases, they can be hired locally. If specialist knowledge is required then we state as much. If it is possible to manage without special aids then we tell you how. Sometimes a little ingenuity can save a lot of time and money.

Now you can be the expert and the cost of this repair manual will be easily recovered the first time that you use it.

Jack Hay

Editor

Quick Reference Data

GENERAL DIMENSIONS

Overall length
  Mini Clubman
    Saloon . . . . 10 ft 4.6 in (3160 mm)
    Estate . . . . 11 ft 2 in (3400 mm)
  Mini 1275 GT . . . . 10 ft 4.65 in (3160 mm)
Overall width
  Others . . . . 4 ft 7.5 in (1410 mm)
Overall height
  Saloon . . . . 4 ft 5 in (1350 mm)
  Estate & Pick-up . . . . 4 ft 5.5 in (1360 mm)
  Van . . . . 4 ft 6.5 in (1380 mm)
Ground clearance
  Mini 1275 GT . . . . .6 in (152.4 mm)
  Others . . . . 6.15 in (156.3 mm)
Wheelbase
  Saloon . . . . 6 ft 8.15 in (2036 mm)
  Estate, Van & Pick-up . . . . 7 ft 0.15 in (2138 mm)

CAPACITIES

Engine/transmission unit, inc. Filter:
  with manual gearbox, refill . . . . .8½ pints (4.83 litres)
  with automatic transmission, refill . . . . .9 pints (5 litres)
  total . . . . 13 pints (7.38 litres)
Cooling system:
  with heater . . . . .6¼ pints (3.55 litres)
  without heater . . . . .5¼ pints (3 litres)
Fuel tank:
  Saloon . . . . 5½ galls (25 litres)
  Estate, Van & Pick-up . . . . 6 galls (27.3 litres)
  1275 GT
    Up to 1974 . . . . 5½ galls (25 litres)
    1974 on . . . . 7½ galls (34 litres)

For specified lubricants see Service data

VALVE CLEARANCES

All, inlet and exhaust . . . . .0.012 in (0.30 mm), cold

IGNITION

Spark plugs
  Make/type . . . . Champion N9Y*
  Electrode gap . . . . 0.025 in (0.65 mm)

**N5 plugs can be used in pre '72 850/1000 manual models, and
pre '74 automatic models*

Firing order . . . . 1 - 3 - 4 - 2
Cylinder numbering . . . . .From front (radiator end of engine)
Distributor rotor rotation . . . . .Anti-clockwise
Contact breaker gap . . . . 0.014 - 0.016 in (0.35 - 0.40 mm)
Dwell angle
  DM2 & 25D4 Distributors . . . . .60° ± 3°
  43D4 & 45D4 Distributors . . . . .51° ± 5°

For ignition timing details see Tune-Up data

TYRE PRESSURES

For tyre pressures see Front Suspension data

Pass the MoT

Once a year the MoT test falls due for the vehicle three years old or more (UK only). The test fee paid to the garage covers the cost of carrying out the inspection whether the car passes the test or fails, so it makes sense to ensure that you get maximum value out of the inspection by carrying out your own pre-test check beforehand. This way you can save yourself a failure certificate by putting right any likely reasons for failure. Bear in mind that an official tester will more than likely follow a different criterion when examining the same component as the DIY owner, but just being aware of the checks that the tester will make could avoid the DIY owner a needless failure certificate, perhaps for example, because a simple item like a brake warning lamp is not working or the windscreen washers are out of action. All the items that come under the testers scrutiny are included in this repair manual in one way or another although obviously not compiled specifically for passing the test. However, if you go through the check list below and turn to the appropriate page number(s) referred to, you will have the information required to either check or service the appropriate components.

LIGHTING EQUIPMENT, STOP LAMPS, REFLECTORS, FLASHERS . . . . **Pages 20,152**
All lights must be working (including headlamp main beam and dip) and visible from a reasonable distance. Lamp lenses must not be damaged or missing. Indicators must flash at the correct rate - between one and two flashes a second and dash warning lamp(s) must be functioning. Headlamps must be correctly aligned.

STEERING . . . . **Pages 14,128**
Check for excessive play in all steering components and security of nuts, bolts and retaining devices. Check for unnatural stiffness in steering operation. Check rack gaiter for security and condition.

FRONT WHEEL BEARINGS . . . . **Page 108**
Check for roughness, excessive play or insufficient clearance in wheel bearings.

SUSPENSION . . . . **Pages 14,106,110**
Check all suspension joints (especially pivot points), bushes and bearings. Check condition of all shock absorbers. Check for deterioration of the bonding between metal and flexible material of support bearings. Check condition of coil springs - incomplete or fractured. Check condition of displacer units (Hydrolastic) and interconnecting pipes.

BRAKES . . . . **Pages 16,18,135**
Check for excessive play in brake pedal and handbrake operation. Check for brakes pulling to one side. Check security and condition of all brake lines and flexible hoses. Check that servo (where fitted) is functioning. The testing station will use a 'roller brake tester' to test the braking efficiency of each wheel.

WHEELS AND TYRES . . . . **Page 20**
Check condition of tyres - tread, wall, pressures. Check tyre 'mix' - radial tyres to rear and crossplies to front. Check road wheels for damage or distortion.

SEAT BELTS . . . . **Page 165**
Check condition and security of all seat belts, including mountings (see CORROSION also).

GENERAL - WIPERS, WASHERS, HORN AND EXHAUST . . . . **Pages 20,149,60**
Windscreen washers and wipers should be working efficiently. Check that exhaust system is intact and not emitting noise above normal.

CORROSION . . . . **Pages 124, 165**
Check for damage or corrosion in or on vehicle likely to render it unsafe.

NOTE: The above check list is only a guide so that the keen DIY car owner can check his Mini before having an MoT inspection carried out. Although it is based on the official MoT check list at the time of publication it is only a guide and should be treated as such.

Contents

Routine Maintenance

ENGINE OIL & FILTER . . . . [1]

Oil Level

The engine and transmission unit (both manual and automatic) use a common oil supply, the transmission casing acting as the oil sump.

It is essential that the engine transmission oil is maintained at the correct level. The oil level should be checked at least once a week and always before a long run.

If the engine has just been run, wait a few minutes after switching off to allow the oil to drain back into the sump. The car must be on level ground when checking the oil.

The oil level should be maintained at the 'MAXI' mark on the dipstick and must never be allowed to fall below the 'MIN' mark (Fig. A:2).

If the level is low, add oil of the appropriate grade through the filler aperture in the rocker cover after removing the filler cap. See Service Data at the end of this Section for list of specified lubricants.

The approximate quantity of oil required to raise the level from the 'MIN' to the 'MAX' mark on the dipstick is 1.0 pint (0.6 litres).

Do NOT over-fill as this may result in oil leaks and increased oil consumption.

NOTE: If oil is required more often than normal suspect engine wear or an oil leak. Check first around the engine for oil leaks and then the exhaust for excessive 'smoking'.

Oil Change

The engine transmission oil must be changed at least every 6,000 miles or twice a year and the oil filter changed at the same time.

If the vehicle is used under severe operating conditions the oil should be changed more frequently, but in this case it will suffice to change the filter every second oil change.

Drain the oil when the engine is still warm by unscrewing the drain plug from the sump. Tighten the plug firmly, but do not use excessive force.

If the oil filter is being changed, renew it as detailed later. Refill the engine with the appropriate quantity of oil, dependent on whether or not the oil filter has been renewed. Run the engine for a few minutes then check the oil level and top up if necessary.

The oil filter should be changed at the same time as the engine oil if the oil is renewed every 6,000 miles, or at every alternate oil change if the oil is changed more frequently.

Some early models are fitted with a differential pressure switch on the oil filter head which functions to indicate the need for an oil change. If the warning light on the instrument panel illuminates and continues to stay lit with the engine at or above idling speed, then both the engine oil and filter element should be changed as soon as possible, within a maximum of the next 300 miles (500 km).

The oil filter assembly is attached to a horizontal mounting flange on the front of the engine and may be either a replaceable element type or a disposable cartridge type on later models. In either case, the element should be changed at the same time as the engine oil, if the oil is renewed every 6,000 miles, or at every alternate oil change if the oil is changed more frequently.

The replaceable type filter element is contained in a detachable pressed steel bowl which is secured in position by a centre-bolt (Fig. A:3). Place a drip pan directly under the filter and unscrew the centre-bolt at the base of the filter bowl. Detach the bowl from the mounting flange, keeping it upright as it will still contain oil. Empty out the oil and filter element and wash the interior of the bowl thoroughly with petrol. Examine the rubber sealing washers on the centre-bolt and replace if necessary.

Service Schedule

The maintenance operations listed below should be carried out at the mileage shown or at the equivalent monthly intervals, whichever occurs first

EVERY 3,000 MILES (5,000 KM) OR 3 MONTHS - OPTIONAL INTERMEDIATE INSPECTION

- Check engine/transmission oil level
- Check coolant level
- Check windscreen washer level
- Check brake and clutch fluid levels
- Check fan belt condition and tension
- Check engine/transmission unit for oil/water/fuel leaks
- Check battery electrolyte level
- Check visually all brake, clutch and fuel pipes, hoses and unions for chafing, leaks or corrosion.
- Check exhaust system for leakage and security
- Check steering unit for oil leaks and gaiter condition

- Check steering, suspension and drive shaft joints for security, backlash and gaiter condition
- Check brake pedal travel and handbrake operation
- Check tyres visually for wear or damage
- Check tyre pressures, including spare
- Check tightness of road wheel nuts
- Check condition of windscreen wiper blades
- Check function of all lamps, horns, indicators and wipers
- Check headlamp beam alignment
- Check condition and security of seats and seat belts
- Check rear view mirrors for looseness, cracks or crazing

EVERY 6,000 MILES (10,000 KM) OR 6 MONTHS - STANDARD SERVICE

As for Intermediate Inspection above, plus the following additional items

- Change engine/transmission oil. Renew oil filter element
- Clean spark plugs. Reset electrode gap
- Inspect/renew distributor points. Adjust points gap or dwell angle
- Lubricate distributor
- Check ignition timing
- Lubricate accelerator control linkage and pedal fulcrum
- Top up carburettor piston damper
- Check carburettor idle settings
- Lubricate dynamo rear bearing (where applicable)
- Check clearance at clutch lever return stop

- Examine cooling and heating systems for leaks
- Check battery condition. Clean and grease battery connections
- Check tightness of steering column clamp bolt (from inside car)
- Inspect brake pads for wear and discs for condition
- Lubricate handbrake mechanical linkage and cables
- Lubricate all grease nipples (8)
- Check front wheel alignment
- Lubricate all door, bonnet and boot locks and hinges
- Check all body and door drain holes
- Road test

EVERY 12,000 MILES (20,000 KM) OR 12 MONTHS - MAJOR SERVICE

As for Standard Service above, plus the following additional items:

- Check valve rocker clearances
- Renew oil filler cap and filter element
- Renew air cleaner element

- Renew spark plugs
- Clean brake servo filter element (where applicable)
- Inspect brake linings for wear and drums for condition. Clean out dust

OTHER ITEMS - PREVENTATIVE MAINTENANCE

- Every 18,000 miles (30,000 km) or 18 months, whichever is sooner, change brake fluid completely
- Every 36,000 miles (60,000 km) or 3 years, whichever is sooner, renew all fluid seals in hydraulic system, and examine all flexible hoses and renew if necessary. Brake servo filter element should also be renewed at this time
- Every 2 years, cooling system should be drained, flushed and refilled with fresh anti-freeze mixture

NOTE: On models fitted with Emission Control Equipment, certain additional maintenance operations must be carried out. These items are listed in a separate Service Schedule at the end of the 'Emission Control' section.

Extract the large rubber sealing ring from its groove in the filter head and discard it. Ensure that the groove is clean, then fit a new sealing ring (supplied with the filter element) in position. Be careful to ensure that the ring is correctly located in the groove as otherwise an oil leak will occur once the filter bowl is refitted.

Fit the new filter element into the bowl. Locate the bowl assembly on the mounting flange, then rotate the bowl while tightening the centre-bolt to ensure it is correctly positioned on the sealing ring. Tighten the centre-bolt securely, but do NOT over-tighten, otherwise the sealing ring may be damaged.

Where the disposable cartridge type filter element is fitted, it should be possible to unscrew the filter by hand (Fig. A:4). In extreme cases it may be necessary to use a filter strap wrench to release it, if tight. An alternative method of releasing a tight filter is to drive a screwdriver blade through the filter and use this to obtain extra leverage. This is, however, a rather messy business as oil will then spill out through the holes made.

A drip tray should be placed under the filter prior to removal as a quantity of oil will be released when it is unscrewed. Discard the oil filter cartridge. Clean the mounting face on the filter head. Check that the rubber sealing ring on the new cartridge is correctly located, then wet it with clean engine oil. Screw the cartridge onto the threaded adaptor by hand until the seal just contacts the mounting face, then tighten a further half to three-quarters of a turn - BUT NO MORE.

After refilling the engine with fresh oil, start the engine and check the filter for any signs of leakage - stop the engine IMMEDIATELY if any signs are present as this indicates that the filter is not sealing correctly.

Oil Filter - Automatic Models

On models with automatic transmission, the oil filter assembly is attached to a vertical mounting flange on the front of the engine (Fig. A:5). The filter is of the replaceable element type and the element should be changed in a similar manner to that described above for the manual transmission models. However, on all models except the 'Clubman', the front grille must first be removed to allow access to the filter. The grille is secured in place by 16 screws. On 'Clubman' models sufficient clearance exists for filter bowl removal.

CRANKCASE BREATHER SYSTEM....... [2]

Most Mini models are fitted with a closed crankcase ventilation system which should be inspected and serviced periodically to ensure correct functioning of the system, as otherwise a pressure build-up in the crankcase can occur, causing subsequent oil leaks in the engine with an increase in oil consumption.

The system comprises an inlet filter in the oil filler cap on the rocker cover, an oil separator and a vent tube to the inlet manifold or air cleaner. On some early models a spring-loaded regulator valve is also incorporated in the system (Fig. A:6).

Fresh air enters the system through the filter in the filler cap, then passes down the push rod bores to the crankcase. The crankcase fumes are exhausted through a breather outlet pipe on the engine side cover at the front of the engine, and the oil droplets and mist are trapped by the oil separator before the fumes pass into the inlet manifold, via the regulator valve where fitted.

Intake Filter

The air intake filter is incorporated in the oil filler cap, and the complete cap assembly should be renewed at least every 12,000 miles.

At the same time, the hoses in the system should be checked for blockages or leaks.

Regulator Valve

The operation of the system control valve can be tested by removing the oil filler cap from the rocker cover with the engine at normal operating temperature and running at idle speed. If the valve is functioning correctly the engine speed will increase by approximately 200 rev/min. as the cap is removed. The change in speed will be audibly noticeable. If no change occurs, the valve must be serviced as described below.

Release the spring clip and remove the components of the valve from the housing (Fig. A:6). Clean all metal parts with petrol. If deposits are difficult to remove, immerse the parts in boiling water first. Clean the diaphragm with detergent or methylated spirits. Examine the components carefully and renew any which show signs of wear or damage. Ensure that the system connecting hoses are clear before reassembling the valve. Reassemble the components as shown in the illustration, making sure that the spigot on the metering valve engages in the cruciform guides and the diaphragm is seated correctly.
NOTE: The early type regulator valve assembly without the cruciform guides must be renewed as an assembly.

COOLING SYSTEM .... [3]

General Check

All hoses and connections in the cooling and heating system should be checked carefully for leaks.

Check particularly the joints at the water pump, water control valve, cylinder head gasket, cylinder block core plugs, drain plugs, radiator and all hoses and connections.

Examine the hoses for perishing, swelling, or other damage. Inspect the radiator fins to ensure they are not damaged, or clogged with dirt.

Fan Belt

Check the tension and condition of the fan belt as detailed later under the appropriate heading.

Coolant Level

The coolant level in the radiator should be checked at least weekly, and topped up as necessary. Check the level when the engine is cool. If the system is at normal operating temperature, allow it to cool first. Muffle the cap with a thick cloth to protect the hands against scalding and turn the cap slowly anti-clockwise to the first stop to release the pressure in the system through the over-flow tube before completely removing the cap.

The coolant level should be up to the 'level indicator' plate inside the radiator filler neck, or to the bottom of the filler neck where no plate is fitted. If the level in the system has fallen appreciably, suspect a leak in the system; check the hoses and hose connections first.

NOTE: When the system contains anti-freeze, ensure that the strength of the mixture is maintained when topping up.

Anti-freeze

Because of the properties of anti-freeze in raising the boiling point of the coolant, as well as lowering the freezing point, it is recommended that an 'All-Season' type anti-freeze be used permanently in the cooling system to afford maximum protection against both freezing and over-heating. The presence of a corrosion inhibitor in most anti-freezes will also help to prevent corrosion and the formation of scale in the system.

During the winter months an anti-freeze mixture MUST be used in the system to protect against frost damage. The concentration of the solution will depend on the degree of protection required, and dilution should be carried out in accordance with the manufacturer's instructions. As a guideline a 25% solution of anti-freeze by volume will remain fluid down to -13°C (9°F), and a 45% solution will give protection down to approximately -32°C (-26°F).

Before filling the system with anti-freeze solution, inspect all hoses, hose connections and cooling system joints. Tighten or renew where necessary. After adding the anti-freeze, run the engine up to normal operating temperature and check for leaks. A label should be attached to the radiator to record the date of filling.

The anti-freeze concentration in the system should be checked periodically and in any case before the beginning of the winter season. The specific gravity of the mixture can be checked using a suitable hydrometer. The specific gravity of a 45% concentration solution should be 1.065 providing no other additive is in the cooling system.

Flushing

The cooling system should be completely drained, flushed and refilled with a fresh mixture of anti-freeze and water at least every two years or as recommended by the anti-freeze manufacturer.

BATTERY . . . . [4]

The battery is located in a well in the floor of the luggage compartment on Saloon models, beneath the rear seat cushion of the Estate Car, and behind the right hand seat on Van and Pick-up variants. It should be noted that while most Mini models will have a NEGATIVE earth electrical system, on early models prior to approximately October 1969, the system had POSITIVE earth polarity and it is important to observe the correct polarities for the respective systems as the various electrical components are affected by the earthing arrangements.

Electrolyte Level

The level of the battery electrolyte in each cell should be checked periodically, and distilled water added if the level is below the separators, or the bottom of the filling tube on through-fill type batteries. Do not over-fill the battery.

In some cases the battery case is translucent to allow the level to be checked without the need for lifting the vent cover.

It is good practice to run the car immediately after topping-up the battery, especially in cold weather, to ensure thorough mixing of the acid and water and so prevent freezing.

If the battery is found to need frequent topping-up, steps should be taken to discover the reason. For example, the battery may be receiving an excessive charge from the alternator, in which case the charging system charge rate should be checked.

If one cell in particular needs topping-up more than the others, check the condition of the battery case. If there are signs of acid leakage, the source should be traced and corrective action taken.

NOTE: The electrolyte level should not be topped-up within half an hour of the battery having been charged from an external source, lest it floods.

State of Charge

The state of charge of the battery can be determined by checking the specific gravity of the electrolyte in each cell with a Hydrometer and measuring the voltage under load across the battery terminals with a heavy discharge tester. It is unlikely that the normal owner-driver will possess the latter piece of equipment, but a suitable hydrometer to test the specific gravity can be obtained quite cheaply from a motor accessory shop.

A specific gravity reading of at least 1.275 should be obtained if the battery is fully charged, or 1.120 if discharged. It is more important that the readings in each cell be equal, as a low s.g. in one cell indicates an internal fault and this will affect its ability to hold its charge.

If a heavy discharge tester is available, the output voltage of the battery can be tested as follows: The acid level in the battery must be correct before attempting to measure the voltage. Press the probes of the discharge tester firmly onto the battery terminals for about 5 to 10 seconds and read off the voltage indicated on the instrument scale. A reading of 12.6 should be obtained from a fully charged battery. If less than 8 volts, this indicates an internal fault in the battery.

Connections

The battery terminals and leads should be kept clean to ensure good connections. Remove the battery if necessary to clean the terminals, but always detach the earth lead first.

If the battery posts or cable terminals are corroded, this can normally be removed by pouring boiling water over them, then brushing them with a wire brush.

When reconnecting the cables, apply a thin film of petroleum jelly or grease to both the terminals and posts. Tighten the terminals securely.

The battery earth strap and the engine earth strap should also be checked for proper connection and condition.

DYNAMO/ALTERNATOR. . . . . [5]

Dynamo Bearing

On vehicles fitted with a dynamo, the dynamo rear bearing should be lubricated periodically. Add two or three drops of engine oil to the bearing through the central hole in the rear end bearing plate (Fig. A:7). Do NOT over-oil the bearing, otherwise the commutator may become contaminated.

An alternator does not require periodic lubrication.

Drive Belt

Check the tension and condition of the drive belt as detailed under 'FAN BELT' heading below.

FAN BELT . . . . [6]

Tension Adjustment

Correct tensioning of the fan belt is important to ensure efficient operation of the cooling and charging systems. Excessive strain will cause rapid wear of the belt, and place undue strain on the water pump and dynamo or alternator bearings.

When correctly tensioned, a total deflection of ½ inch (13 mm) should possible under normal finger-tip pressure at the midway point on the longest belt run between the two pulleys.

If adjustment is required, slacken the dynamo (alternator mounting bolts) and the adjusting link nut, and move the dynamo/alternator towards or away from the engine as necessary to achieve the correct tension. Avoid over-tightening the belt. Apply any leverage necessary to the drive end bracket only, and not to any other part of the alternator, the lever used should preferably be of

wood or soft metal. Recheck the belt tension after tightening the adjusting link nut and the mounting bolts.

Belt Replacement

The condition of the belt should be checked periodically. If nicked, cut, excessively worn, or otherwise damaged, the belt should be replaced. If the belt is noisy in operation, check for misaligned pulleys.

To replace the belt, proceed as for adjusting, but press the dynamo/alternator fully towards the engine, and detach the belt from the pulleys. Manoeuvre the belt between the fan blades and the right-hand top of the radiator cowling. On models with the sixteen bladed fan, feed the belt between the individual blade tips and the cut-outs in the cowling flange (Fig. A:9).

Fit the new belt in the same manner, ensuring that it is not twisted, and adjust the tension, as described above. Do NOT attempt to lever a new belt onto the pulleys as this can easily cause damage to the belt or pulleys.

The tension of a new belt should be checked after approximately 100 miles (160 km) use.

CLUTCH. . . . . [7]

Fluid Level

The fluid level in the clutch master cylinder reservoir should be checked periodically and topped up if required. The master cylinder is situated on the 'step' on the engine compartment bulkhead, and is the right-hand cylinder looking from the front of the car; the left-hand cylinder is the brake master cylinder (Fig. A:10).

The filler cap should be wiped clean before unscrewing it to prevent the possibility of dirt entering the system. The fluid level must be maintained at the bottom of the filler neck. Use only the specified type of hydraulic fluid for topping up - see Service Data for details.

Before refitting the filler cap, check that the vent hole in the cap is clear of obstruction.

Release Lever Clearance

It is important that a clearance should exist between the clutch release bearing and its thrust plate. As wear of the driven plate friction linings takes place, this clearance will diminish, and if neglected clutch slip will result.

To check the clearance, pull the clutch operating lever outwards away from the stop bolt on the clutch end cover and measure the gap between the lever and the stop with a feeler gauge (Fig. A:11). This should be 0.020 in (0.5 mm), or 0.060 in (1.5 mm) on very early models without the shouldered throw-out stop at the central boss on the clutch housing.

Adjust if necessary by slackening the stop bolt locknut and screw the bolt in or out as necessary to obtain the correct clearance. Tighten the locknut and recheck the gap.

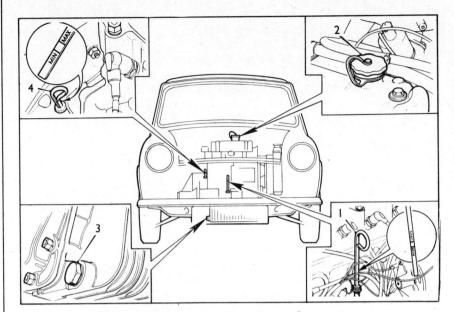

1. Oil level check (manual)
2. Oil filler cap
3. Oil drain plug
4. Oil level check (automatic)

Fig. A:2 Engine/transmission oil

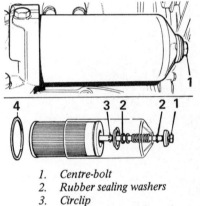

1. Rubber sealing washer
2. Rubber or felt sealing washer
3. Rubber sealing ring

Fig. A:3 Replaceable element type filter

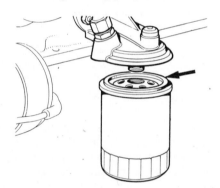

Fig. A:4 Disposable cartridge type filter

1. Centre-bolt
2. Rubber sealing washers
3. Circlip
4. Rubber sealing ring

Fig. A:5 Filter assembly on automatic models

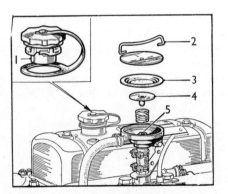

1. Oil filler cap & filter
2. Spring clip
3. Diaphragm
4. Metering valve
5. Cruciform guides

Fig. A:6 Engine breather control valve

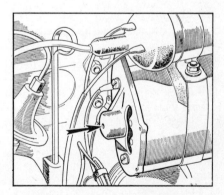

Fig. A:7 Dynamo lubrication point

SUSPENSION AND DRIVE SHAFTS......[8]

Front Suspension

The front suspension upper and lower swivel joints should be checked for excessive free play, indicating wear, by raising each front wheel in turn clear of the ground and rocking the wheel from the top and bottom. Be careful not to confuse excessive wheel bearing play with free play in the joints. The point of play is best determined by observing the suspension assembly from behind the wheel while a second person rocks the wheel to and fro. Wear in the wheel bearings will be noticeable as movement of the brake drum or disc in relation to the backplate, whereas wear in the swivel joints will be indicated by movement of the swivel hub in relation to the upper or lower suspension arm.

In almost every case, wear in the swivel joints is due to lack of regular lubrication, and overhaul of the joints will be necessary.

The inner pivot points of both the upper and lower suspension arms should be checked for any signs of play, indicating wear, but this is pretty unusual - especially if the upper arm pivot is lubricated regularly. The rubber mounting bushes at the front end of the lower arm tie-rod are another point to check for any signs of wear or perishing.

At the same time, the ball joint at the outer end of the track rod should be checked for wear by rocking the wheel back and forwards with a hand at the front and rear edge of the wheel. Wear will be obvious by the movement of the steering arm in relation to the track rod joint housing. If the joint appears in good condition check the joint boot for any signs of tears or other damage, and renew if necessary.

Drive Shafts

The large rubber boot at the drive shaft constant velocity joint (where the drive shaft enters the suspension swivel housing) should be examined carefully for any signs of splits or tears as this would allow dirt and water to enter the joint. If either the boot or the retaining clips are damaged, they should be renewed.

Wear in the C/V joint is usually indicated by 'knock-on-lock' knocking when the car is going round a corner. The knocking will usually be coming from the wheel on the outside of the corner.

Several different types of joints are used at the inner end of the drive shaft and these may be either of the rubber coupling type (early models), needle bearing universal joint type (automatic models) or offset sphere type joint (later models). With the rubber coupling type, the metal 'X' inside the joint pulls away from the rubber insulators and, if left, will eventually start contacting the transmission casing and wear away the joint U-bolts, with dire consequences. Check these joints carefully for any signs of wear or play.

The needle bearing universal joint is similar to the type normally used on propshafts and wear can be checked by observing any signs of play between the inner and outer yokes of the joint.

The later offset sphere type joint is similar to the C/V type joint at the outer end of the shaft, and wear will be indicated by excessive backlash in the joint when the centre section of the shaft is twisted. The rubber boot at this joint should also be checked carefully for any signs of damage, and renewed if necessary.

Rear Suspension

The main points to check on the rear suspension are the radius arm pivot shafts and the wheel bearings. Both these can be easily checked once the car has been jacked up with the wheels clear of the ground.

To check the radius arm pivots, grasp the wheel at the front and rear edge and rock the whole suspension assembly in and out. Wear of the pivot shaft will be indicated by movement of the arm casting in relation to the subframe at its outer pivot point. The outer pivot point is most prone to wear as a metal bush is used here as opposed to the needle bearing used at the inner pivot point. Regular lubrication goes a long way to preventing premature wear at this point - see 'GREASE POINTS' heading.

Wear at the wheel bearings can be checked by simply rocking the wheel at the top and bottom and noting any excessive movement.

STEERING...........................[9]

Track Rod Ends

The track rod end outer ball joints should be checked for wear as described in the heading above. Wear at the inner ball joints (inside the rack boots) is less usual, except where the rack gaiter has become damaged and allowed the ingress of dirt. This is normally evident as excessive ease of articulation of the inner joint, and in extreme cases outward movement of the track rod in relation to the steering rack is sometimes possible.

Steering Unit

The steering unit itself should be inspected carefully for any signs of oil leaks. These are normally due to a damaged gaiter, and the gaiters on both ends of the housing should be checked for signs of tears or other damage and renewed if necessary.

The steering unit does not require periodic maintenance, lubrication only being required when the unit has been overhauled or a new gaiter fitted.

Steering Column Clamp

The clamp at the base of the steering column where it joins with the rack pinion shaft should be checked for tightness. The clamp is easily accessible from inside the car once the carpets and rubber cover on the column have been pulled back.

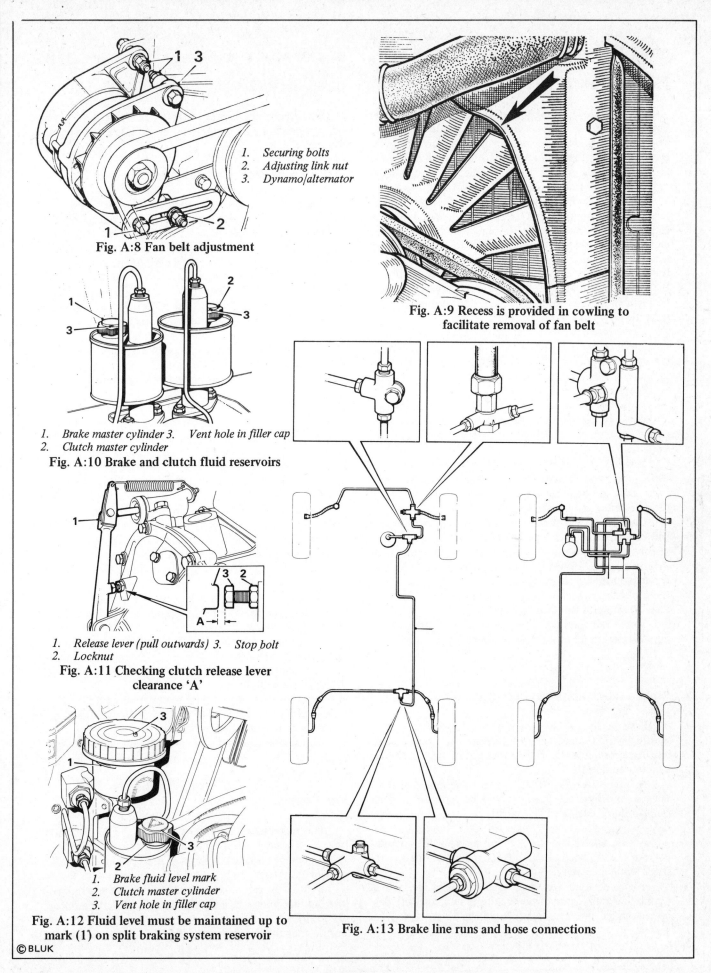

1. Securing bolts
2. Adjusting link nut
3. Dynamo/alternator

Fig. A:8 Fan belt adjustment

Fig. A:9 Recess is provided in cowling to facilitate removal of fan belt

1. Brake master cylinder 3. Vent hole in filler cap
2. Clutch master cylinder

Fig. A:10 Brake and clutch fluid reservoirs

1. Release lever (pull outwards) 3. Stop bolt
2. Locknut

Fig. A:11 Checking clutch release lever clearance 'A'

1. Brake fluid level mark
2. Clutch master cylinder
3. Vent hole in filler cap

Fig. A:12 Fluid level must be maintained up to mark (1) on split braking system reservoir

Fig. A:13 Brake line runs and hose connections

© BLUK

Fluid Level

The fluid level in the brake master cylinder reservoir should be checked periodically and topped up if required. The master cylinder is located on the 'step' on the engine compartment bulkhead, adjacent to the clutch master cylinder. The brake master cylinder is the left-hand cylinder looking towards the rear of the car (Fig. A:10).

Several different types of master cylinder and fluid reservoir are employed, requiring different checking procedures. Where the reservoir is of the same type as for the clutch, the filler cap must be removed to check the fluid level. Some models have a translucent extension fitted to the filler aperture and the fluid level can be seen through the wall of the tube. Where a split braking system is used, the tandem master cylinder has a translucent reservoir with the level marked on the side (Fig. A:11).

In all cases, the filler cap should be wiped clean before unscrewing it to prevent the possibility of dirt entering the system. The fluid level must be maintained at the bottom of the filler neck, or up to the 'Fluid Level' mark on the translucent type reservoir.

Use only the specified type of hydraulic fluid for topping up - see Service Data for details. Before refitting the filler cap, check that the vent hole in the cap is clear of obstruction.

It should be noted that brake fluid will damage paintwork if allowed to come into contact with it. Any spilt fluid must be wiped (or washed off with cold water) from the affected area immediately.

On 1275 GT models, the fluid level in the reservoir will drop slightly over a period of time as the disc caliper pistons move outwards to compensate for pad lining wear - this is normal. However, if the fluid level falls excessively, or requires frequent topping up, this indicates a leak in the hydraulic system and steps should be taken immediately to establish and deal with the cause.

The brake fluid should be changed completely every 18,000 miles or 18 months, whichever is sooner.

Brake Lines, Hoses and Cylinder Seals

Periodically, all hydraulic pipes, hoses and unions should be checked visually for chafing, leaks and corrosion. Any component which is damaged or suspect should be renewed immediately.

As preventive maintenance, at 36,000 miles, all fluid seals in the braking system should be renewed, and all flexible hoses examined thoroughly and renewed if necessary.

At the same time, the working surfaces of the cylinder bores and pistons should be examined and new parts fitted where necessary.

The procedures for renewing the seals in the various hydraulic components of the braking system are fully described under the appropriate headings in the BRAKES section.

Disc Front Brakes

The disc front brakes fitted to 1275 GT models are self-compensating and consequently do not require periodic adjustment.

Drum Front Brakes - Single Leading Shoe Type

Early Mini models (pre Sept 1964) were fitted with leading and trailing shoe type front brakes, and these have a single square headed adjuster on each brake back plate which effects adjustment of both brake shoes (Fig. A:14).

With the front wheels raised clear of the ground, turn the adjuster clockwise, using a suitable spanner or brake key, until the drum is locked, but do NOT strain the adjuster. Back off the adjuster just sufficiently to allow the wheel to rotate freely without dragging or binding.

Spin the wheel in its normal direction of forward rotation, apply the foot brake hard to centralise the brake shoes, and recheck the adjustment.

Adjust the other front brake in a similar manner.

Drum Front Brakes - Twin Leading Shoe Type

All later models, with the exception of the disc-braked 1275 GT, are equipped with the more efficient twin-leading shoe type front brakes. These have two square-headed adjusters, one for each shoe, on the backplate (Fig. A:15).

It should be noted that, due to the location of the upper adjuster behind the steering arm, it is difficult to get a proper brake spanner to fit on it and an open-ended spanner will probably be required to turn the adjuster. In this case, take great care to avoid rounding-off the corners of the adjuster if it is stiff.

With both the front wheels raised clear of the ground, turn the upper adjuster in the opposite direction to that of the forward rotation of the wheel to bring the shoe away from the drum. Now turn the lower adjuster in the same direction as normal wheel rotation until the drum is locked, then back it off sufficiently to allow the wheel to rotate freely without dragging or binding.

Spin the wheel in its normal direction of forward rotation, apply the footbrake hard to centralise the shoe, and recheck the adjustment.

Adjust the upper adjuster in the same manner as the lower one, then repeat the complete sequence for the other front brake.

Rear Brakes

The rear brakes are of the leading and trailing shoe type and a single square-headed adjuster, which effects adjustment of both brake shoes is provided at each backplate (Fig. A:16).

With both rear wheels raised clear of the ground, adjust the rear brakes in a similar manner to that described previously for the single leading shoe type front brakes. Ensure that the handbrake is fully released before attemp-

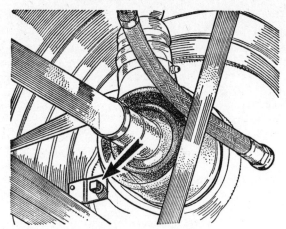

Fig. A:14 Shoe adjuster on early type front drum brakes with single leading shoe

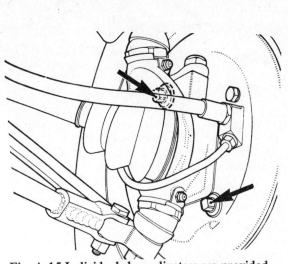

Fig. A:15 Individual shoe adjusters are provided on twin leading shoe type front brakes

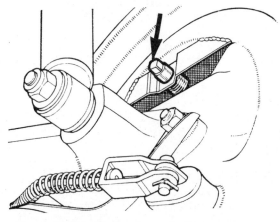

Fig. A:16 Rear brakes have single square-headed adjuster

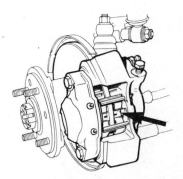

Fig. A:17 Brake pads can be inspected for wear without removing them from caliper

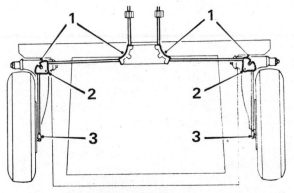

1. *Grease cable guide channels*
2. *Oil swivel sector pivots*
3. *Grease operating lever clevis pin and cable at spring anchor brackets*

Fig. A:18 Handbrake linkage lubrication points. Later models have one-piece cable with equaliser bracket

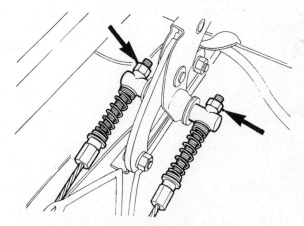

Fig. A:19 Handbrake cable adjustment point - Twin cable type linkage

ting to adjust the brakes.

Handbrake

The handbrake is correctly adjusted when it operates efficiently on the third notch of the ratchet. Braking effect should be equal on both rear wheels and it should just be possible to turn them by heavy hand pressure.

Free play in the handbrake linkage is normally taken up automatically when the rear brakes are adjusted. However, if even with the rear brakes correctly adjusted the handbrake does not hold properly, it can be adjusted as follows:

First, with the rear wheels raised clear of the ground, check that the cable or cables, dependent on model year, are operating both rear brakes properly and are not seized or stiff at the pivot sections on the radius arms, or in the cable guide channels. Also check that the handbrake levers at the backplate are operating freely.

With the handbrake lever pulled on to the third notch on the ratchet, adjust the cables at the lever trunnion immediately behind the handbrake lever (Fig. A:19). Screw the adjusting nuts along the cables until the correct braking effect is achieved at each rear wheel.

On later models a single cable linkage with a compensator bracket is used and only a single adjustment point is provided (Fig. A:20). If unequal braking effect is obtained, check that the cable is free to move through the compensator at the front of the rear subframe.

After adjusting the handbrake, release the lever then check that both rear wheels turn freely without dragging or binding.

BRAKE PADS & LININGS............[12]

Disc Front Brakes

The front wheels must be removed to allow inspection of the disc brake pads. Check the thickness of lining material left on the pads (Fig. A:17). If this is worn down to approximately 1/8 in (3 mm), and never less than 1/16 in (1.5 mm), the pads must be renewed.

Brake pads should always be renewed in sets of four to maintain braking balance.

If the pads are not being renewed, ensure that sufficient lining material remains to allow the car to run until the next service check.

The procedure for replacing the brake pads is fully detailed in the BRAKES section of the manual.

Drum Front Brakes

The front wheels and drums must be removed to allow inspection of the brake linings. The drum is secured by two cross-headed retaining screws, and it may be necessary to release the brake shoe adjustment to allow the drum to be withdrawn.

Clean out the drum, shoes and backplate using a soft brush. Take care not to inhale the asbestos dust from the linings as this can be injurious to health.

Inspect the shoe linings for wear. If the lining material has worn down to the minimum permissible thickness of 1/16 in (1.5 mm) on bonded type shoes, or within 0.040 in (1 mm) of the rivet heads on riveted type shoes, or will have done so before the next check is called for, the brake shoes should be renewed.

Brake shoes should be replaced in sets of four. On no account replace a single shoe or only one pair of shoes.

Also inspect the surface of the brake linings for oil, grease or brake fluid contamination. If present, the linings should be renewed once the cause has been established and dealt with. This should be attended to immediately.

Inspect the wheel cylinders for signs of fluid leakage. If present, the cylinder should be replaced or the seals renewed.

Full details of brake shoe replacement are included in the BRAKES section of the manual.

If the linings are satisfactory, refit the brake drum and road wheel and adjust the brake shoes as detailed previously.

Rear Brakes

The linings for the rear brakes should be inspected in similar manner to the drum front brakes above.

BRAKE SERVO.....................[13]

A brake servo unit is fitted as standard equipment only on 1275 GT models up to 1974. The only periodic maintenance required is attention to the servo air filter.

Air Filter

The filter element is located under the plastic dome on the underside of the servo unit cylinder (Fig. A:21). The filter should be removed for cleaning every 12,000 miles (20,000 km), and renewed every 36,000 miles (60,000 km).

To remove the filter, lever the dome off the valve cover with a screw-driver and lift out the filter. Clean the filter element with a low-pressure air line. Do NOT use cleaning fluid or lubricant of any description on the filter.

When refitting the filter element, ensure that the air valve spring is securely located onto the valve. Snap fit the plastic dome onto the valve cover.

HANDBRAKE ....[14]

Lubrication

The handbrake linkage must be lubricated regularly and conscientiously if it is to remain in efficient working order as it is very prone to seizing, particularly at the sector pivots on the rear radius arms. The specific points which require attention are clearly shown in Fig. A:18.

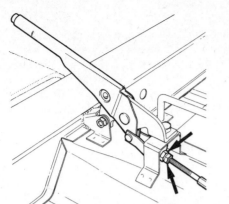

Fig. A:20 Single adjustment point is provided on later type handbrake linkage

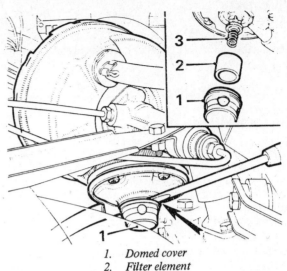

1. *Domed cover*
2. *Filter element*
3. *Valve spring*

Fig. A:21 Details on brake servo filter assembly

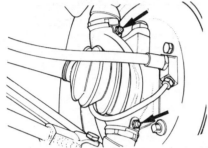

Fig. A:22 Grease points for front swivel hub ball joints

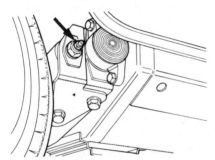

Fig. A:24 Rear suspension grease point is at outer end of radius arm pivot shaft

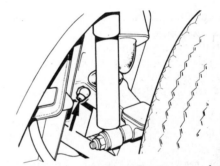

Fig. A:23 Grease nipple on front suspension upper arm

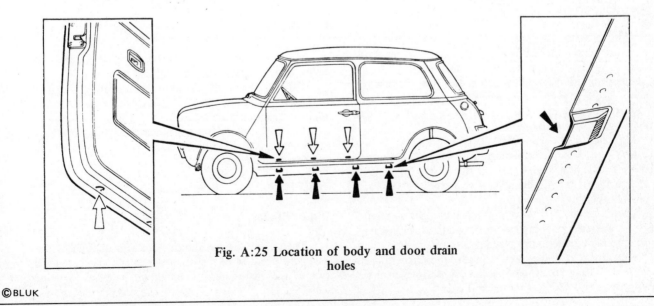

Fig. A:25 Location of body and door drain holes

Routine Maintenance

Adjustment

The procedure for adjusting the handbrake is fully detailed in 'BRAKE ADJUSTMENT' previously.

WHEELS & TYRES . . . . [15]

Tyre Pressures

The inflation pressures of all tyres, including the spare, should be checked at least once a week and adjusted if necessary. The recommended pressures are given in 'Service Data' at the end of this section. Check the pressures when the tyres are cold as tyre pressures may increase by as much as 6 psi (0.4 kg/cm^2) when hot.

Incorrect inflation pressures will cause abnormal tyre wear and may result in premature failure. There is an average loss of 13% tread mileage for every 10% reduction in inflation pressures below the recommended figure.

After checking the pressures, always ensure that the dust cap is refitted on each valve as this excludes any dirt and provides an additional seal for the valve.

Tyre Condition

The condition of the tyres should be checked periodically as a safety measure.

Measure the depth of tread of each tyre, preferably with a proper tread depth gauge. Tyres should be replaced, at the latest, when the tread depth has reached 1 mm all round and on full tread width, as this is the absolute limit for safe driving. However, it is highly recommended that tyres be replaced before this as they will be more susceptible to punctures and have greatly reduced grip, especially in the wet.

Check the tyre casing visually for cuts in the casing fabric, exposure of ply or cords, or the presence of lumps or bulges. If any of these conditions are present, the tyre should be discarded.

Abnormal tyre wear may be caused by improper inflation pressures, wheel imbalance, suspension misalignment, or mechanical irregularities. When rapid or uneven tyre wear becomes apparent, the cause should be established and dealt with.

Fins or feathers on the tread surface are an indication of severe wheel misalignment. This condition takes the form of a sharp 'fin' on the edge of each pattern rib, and the position of this indicates the direction of misalignment. Fins on the outboard edges are caused by excessive toe-out, whereas fins on the inboard edges of the pattern ribs are caused by excessive toe-in.

Finning on the near-side front tyre only may be due to severe road camber conditions and cannot be eliminated by mechanical adjustment. In this event, frequent interchanging of the affected wheel to even out tyre wear is the only solution.

Some mechanical defects which should be a cause of abnormal tread wear are: loose or worn wheel bearings, uneven braking due to dragging brakes, seized wheel cylinders or distorted brake discs, excessive looseness or damage in the suspension, loose steering connections, bent steering arms, or defective shock absorbers.

Tyre Replacement

Either radial or cross-ply tyres may be fitted as standard equipment and replacements should be of the same type. It is also recommended that only the specified size and type is fitted. Only tyres of the same type and tread pattern should be used on one vehicle. Do NOT mix cross-ply and radial ply tyres, or textile and steel cord tyres.

GREASE POINTS. . . . . [16]

Eight grease points are present on Mini models, six at the front suspension and two at the rear. It is most important that all these points are lubricated regularly to minimise wear and thus reduce the need for expensive overhaul work. The points to be lubricated are as follows:

Front Suspension Swivel Hub Joints: Two grease nipples are provided at each swivel hub, one for the top swivel joint and a second one for the lower joint (Fig. A: 22). To ensure full penetration of the grease, lubrication is best carried out with the car jacked up. Use a grease gun filled with a suitable good quality multi-purpose grease. If the nipples are already filled with grease, no further grease can usually be forced in. In the case of a dry joint, it will sometimes help the entry of grease if the steering is turned from lock to lock after each stroke of the gun.

Front Suspension Upper Arm Inner Pivots: One nipple is provided at each upper arm pivot and should be charged with grease until it is seen to exude from the end of the arm pivot (Fig. A:23).

Rear Suspension Radius Arm Pivot Shafts: One nipple is provided at the outer end of each rear arm pivot shaft (Fig. A:24). Charge the nipple until excess grease appears from the bush at the inner end of the shaft.

Gear Change Remote Control: On earlier vehicles a grease nipple was also provided at the front of the remote control housing on the right-hand side for the gearchange shaft. However, this point requires attention at major overhaul periods only. Later cars are fitted with the single rod change mechanism and a lubricating nipple is not fitted.

LIGHTS, CONTROLS & INSTRUMENTS . . [17]

The operation of all lights should be checked periodically and any defective bulbs replaced as necessary.

The operation of all controls, including the horn, wipers, washers, steering lock, heated rear window, etc. as applicable, should be checked periodically.

The function of the instruments is best carried out under road test conditions. Instrument fitment will depend on model application.

WIPERS & WASHERS . . . . [18]

Wiper Blades

The wiping speeds, intermittent wipe action (if fitted) and park position of the wiper blades as well as the condition of the blades and rubbers should be checked periodically.

Blades which are contaminated with insect or oil deposits should be removed and cleaned with a hard brush and detergent solution.

Worn blades will cause streaks and unsatisfactory cleaning of the glass. The wiping edge of the blades must not be perished or torn. Wear of the blades will increase under conditions of dust, air pullution and when used on a frozen or dry screen.

New blades should be fitted at least once a year according to condition.

The wiper blade is a straight push-fit type and is secured in position by two locating dimples on the arm. To remove the blade, depress the spring lever on the underside of the blade to disengage the lower locating dimple. Tilt the blade assembly outwards away from the arm to disengage the upper locating peg and pull the blade up and off the arm. Push the new blade onto the arm until the locating peg and dimple engage in their locations.

Check the operation of the wipers after fitting new blades.

Washers

The windscreen washer reservoir is located in the engine compartment, and the level should be checked regularly and topped up as required.

The addition of a proprietary brand of windscreen washer additive is recommended to ensure quick and efficient cleaning of the windscreen. In winter, the addition of up to 25% methylated spirits will prevent the washer fluid from freezing.

BODY . . . . [19]

Drain Holes

The drain holes in the car body and doors should be checked periodically to ensure that they are clear. There are four drain holes in the door sill panel on each side of the car, and three in the bottom of each door (Fig. A:25). Use a piece of wire to probe the apertures and remove any obstruction.

It is most important that these drain holes be unobstructed to allow a flow of fresh air through the body side members and door panels and prevent the accumulation of moisture, otherwise corrosion will quickly begin to form.

Service Data

CAPACITIES

Engine/transmission unit, inc. filter:
    with manual gearbox, refill . . . . .8½ pints (4.83 litres)
    with automatic transmission, refil . . . . .9 pints (5 litres)
    total . . . . .13 pints (7.38 litres)

Cooling system:
    with heater . . . . .6¼ pints (3.55 litres)
    without heater . . . . .5¼ pints (3 litres)

Fuel tank:
    Saloon* . . . . 5½ galls (25 litres)
    Estate, Van & Pick-up . . . . 6 galls (27.3 litres)
    1275 GT
        Up to 1974 . . . . 5½ galls (25 litres)
        1974 on. . . . . 7½ galls (34 litres)

      * Some Clubman 1100 saloon models have 7½ galls capacity

SPECIFIED LUBRICANTS

Engine/transmission unit* . . . . .HD motor oil to B.L.S. OL.02 or
                                               MIL-L-2104B or API SE quality

Steering rack . . . . EP 90 Gear Oil, or E 80 below - 15°C (10°F)
                                                     (to MIL-L-2105)

Grease points . . . . .Multipurpose Lithium Base Grease
                                              (NLG 1 consistency No. 2)

Brake & clutch systems. . . . . Brake fluid conforming to
                                   specification SAE J1703c, with
                           minimum boiling-point of 260°C (500°F)

Cooling system . . . . Anti-freeze conforming to BS 3151
                                                 or BS 3152

*In no circumstances must any additive be introduced into the lubricants
recommended for the automatic gearbox*

For tyre pressures see end of 'Front Suspension' section
For Engine Tune-up specifications see end of 'Tune-Up' section

Tune-up

INTRODUCTION . . . . [1]

Difficult starting, poor performance and excessive fuel consumption are some of the problems associated with an engine which is badly worn or out of tune. This is why, at every major service, the engine components should be checked and adjusted in accordance with the SERVICE SCHEDULE given on page 9.

Engine Tune-Up has deliberately been presented as a separate section independent of the ROUTINE MAINTENANCE so that if trouble occurs between services the engine can be tackled on its own.

Often it is the condition or adjustment of only one component which is at fault and consequently it will not be necessary to carry out a complete engine tune-up. Unfortunately it is usually only by gradual elimination that the fault can be traced and rectified. To assist in pin-pointing the source of any trouble a comprehensive 'Trouble-Shooting' chart is included at the end of this section.

The following checks and adjustments have been arranged in logical sequence and it is advised that they be followed in the order given when carrying out a complete engine tune-up. However, if attention to only one particular item is required - the spark plugs or contact breaker points for instance - then simply refer to the appropriate heading. This way either individual components or a complete engine tune can be tackled.

COMPRESSION TEST . . . . [2]

Valuable time can be wasted trying to tune an engine which is badly worn. This is particularly applicable in the case of an engine which has covered considerable mileage. It is therefore always worthwhile checking the cylinder compression pressures first to determine the general state of the unit.

A compression tester will be required for this operation, and one of these can be purchased quite cheaply from most motor accessory shops, or even hired.

The specified compression pressures for the various models are given in 'Tune-Up Data' at the end of this section, but it should be noted that the engine must be at

normal operating temperature to get reliable readings.
1. First run the engine up to normal operating temperature.
2. Remove all the spark plugs. When disconnecting the leads grasp the moulded cap and pull it off the plug. Do not pull on the lead itself otherwise the core inside the lead may be damaged or broken.
3. Push or screw the connector of the compression tester into the No. 1 plug hole and, with the throttle held in the wide open position, crank the engine over with the starter. If the compression tester has to be held in position by hand hold it firmly ensuring that there is no leakage of compression.
4. As the engine turns, the gauge reading will increase in steps until the maximum pressure is reached. Note this reading carefully. The number of compression strokes, indicated by the 'pulses' on the gauge, required to reach the maximum pressure should also be noted.
5. Repeat this procedure for the other cylinders, noting in each case the reading obtained and the number of 'pulses'.
6. Compare the readings with the specified figure. If all the readings are high and within about 10% of each other this indicates that the engine is in good order, provided that the readings are close to the specified figure.
7. If one or more readings are low, the test should be repeated after injecting a small quantity of engine oil into the cylinder through the plug hole to form a seal between the piston and the cylinder wall. If a marked increase in pressure is then obtained, this shows that the leakage is mainly via the piston rings.
8. If no increase in compression is obtained, the fault must be due to leakage past the valves or gaskets. However, it should be noted that if a cylinder has a badly scored bore, or damaged piston, the oil will fail to seal the leak and no improvement in compression will be obtained.
9. In any case, low readings will necessitate further investigation to determine the cause, and remedial action taken to correct it.

VALVE CLEARANCES . . . . [3]

The valve clearances should be checked, and adjusted if necessary, as detailed in the ENGINE section.

1. NORMAL – Core nose will be lightly coated with grey-brown deposits. Replace after 10,000 miles.

2. HEAVY DEPOSITS – Condition could be due to worn valve guides. Plug can be used again after servicing.

3. CARBON FOULING – Caused by rich mixture through faulty carburettor, choke or a clogged air cleaner.

4. OIL FOULING – Caused by worn valve guides, bores or piston rings. Hotter plug may cure.

5. OVERHEATING – Reasons could be over-advanced ignition timing, a worn distributor or weak fuel mixture.

6. PRE-IGNITION – This problem is caused through serious overheating. This could result in engine damage.

Fig. B:1 Typical spark plug conditions

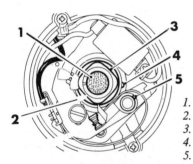

1. Cam spindle
2. Centrifugal weights
3. Cam surface
4. Base plate bearing
5. Pivot post

Fig. B:2 Distributor lubrication points (45D4 type distributor shown)

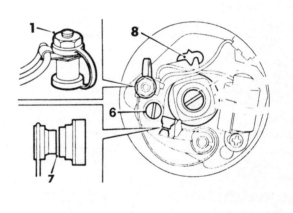

1. Nut
2. Top insulating bush
3. LT lead
4. Condenser lead
5. Lower insulating bush
6. Securing screw and washers
7. Points gap
8. Adjustment slot

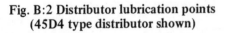
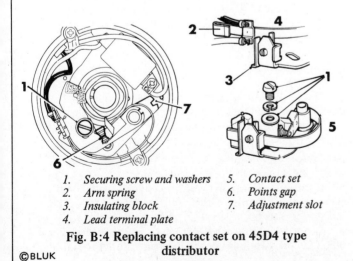

1. Securing screw and washers
2. Arm spring
3. Insulating block
4. Lead terminal plate
5. Contact set
6. Points gap
7. Adjustment slot

Fig. B:4 Replacing contact set on 45D4 type distributor

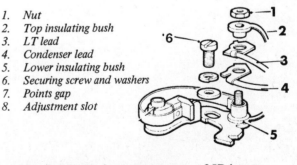

Fig. B:3 Replacing contact set on 25D4 type distributor

SPARK PLUGS . . . . [4]

Inspection

The spark plugs should be removed and examined periodically. When disconnecting the HT leads from the plugs, grasp the moulded cap and pull it off the plug. Do not pull on the plug lead itself otherwise the core inside the lead may be damaged or broken.

Blow or brush any dirt away from around the plug base before removing the plug from the cylinder head.

Inspect the condition of the insulator tip and plug electrode as this can give a good indication as to the general state of the engine.

Typical examples of spark plug conditions are shown in Fig. B:1, and should be interpreted as follows:

Normal (Fig. B:1.1)

Ideally the plugs should look like the condition shown in this photograph. The colour of the electrodes should appear greyish-brown or tan-coloured. White to yellow deposits usually mean that the car has been used for long periods at high, constant speeds. Provided that the sparking plugs have not covered a large mileage they can be cleaned, re-set and refitted.

Heavy Deposits (Fig. B:1.2)

The sparking plug in this condition will probably look worse than it is. Heavy deposits could mean worn valve guides. When deposits have been cleaned off the sparking plug should be fit to use again providing it is not worn.

Carbon Fouled (Fig. B:1.3)

This is identified by dry, fluffy deposits which result from incomplete combustion. Too rich an air/fuel mixture or faulty action of the automatic choke can cause incomplete burning. The mixture being too rich can often be traced to a dirty or blocked air cleaner.

Defective contact breaker points or high tension cables can reduce voltage supplied to the sparking plug and cause misfiring. If fouling is evident in only one of two cylinders, sticking valves may be the problem. Excessive idling, slow speeds or stop/start driving can also keep plug temperatures so low that normal combustion deposits are not burned off.

Oil Fouled (Fig. B:1.4)

These are identified by black wet sludge deposits and is traceable to oil entering the combustion chamber either past the pistons and bores or through the valve guides. Hotter sparking plugs may cure the problem temporarily, but in severe cases an engine overhaul is called for.

Overheated (Fig. B:1.5)

Sparking plugs are usually identified by a white or blistered insulator nose and badly eroded electrodes. The engine overheating or improper ignition timing could be responsible for this problem. If only a couple of sparking plugs are affected the cause may be uneven distribution of the coolant. Abnormal fast driving for sustained periods can also cause high temperatures in the combustion chambers and, in these circumstances, colder sparking plugs should be used.

Adjusting

Spark plugs which are in good condition and with low mileage can be cleaned, preferably with a proper sand-blast cleaner. Clean the electrode surfaces and file them flat with a points file.

Check the electrode gap with a gap setting gauge or feeler gauges. The gap should be 0.025 in (0.65 mm).

If necessary, adjust the gap by bending the outer electrode - NEVER attempt to bend the central electrode, otherwise the ceramic insulator may be cracked or broken.

When fitting new spark plugs, the electrode gaps should be checked before installing them in the engine. Ensure the replacement plugs are of the correct grade - see Service Data for specified types.

Great care should be taken to avoid overtightening the plug in the cylinder head. They should be tightened a maximum of 1/4 turn (90°) past finger tight.

DISTRIBUTOR . . . . [5]

Two different types of Lucas distributor are used on Mini models; the 25D4 type and the 45D4, the latter being the more recent fitment. Although both of the same basic design, they differ slightly in some details and thus require slightly different maintenance procedures.

The 25D4 type can be identified by the cast housing on the distributor body for the vacuum unit spindle. It also has the terminal for the low tension lead mounted in an insulated block on the side of the body, whereas on the 45D4 unit the LT lead comes directly out of the distributor body and has a remote Lucas connector on the end of the lead. This latter type distributor has a detachable vacuum unit which is secured to the body by two screws.

Some Mini 1000 export models may be fitted with a 43D4 type distributor which is a variation of the 45D4, but without a vacuum advance unit.

Lubrication

The distributor should be lubricated at the specified intervals and when renewing the contact breaker points.

Remove the rotor arm and apply one or two drops only of light oil to the felt pad (45D4) in the end of the distributor cam spindle, or around the spindle centre-screw (25D4). Fig. B:2 refers. Similarly, apply a few drops of oil through the gap between the contact plate and the cam spindle to lubricate the centrifugal weights. On the 45D4 type distributor, do NOT oil the cam wiping pad.

Every 24,000 miles (40,000 km), add a further drop of oil to the two holes in the base plate to lubricate the centre bearing.

Smear the contact surface of the distributor cam lightly with suitable high melting-point grease or petroleum jelly. Also apply a very light smear to the breaker arm pivot post.

Do not over-lubricate any part of the distributor. Take great care to avoid getting oil or grease onto the contact points as this will cause burning of the points surface with consequent bad starting. Wipe away any surplus lubricant and ensure the contact points are clean and dry.

Contact Breaker Points - Lucas 25D4 Type Distributor

Remove the ignition shield, where fitted. Remove the distributor cap and rotor arm and examine the distributor points. Points which are worn or badly burned should be renewed. If contact breaker points are badly worn and have a 'blue' appearance then it is likely that the condenser needs replacing.

In most cases it will be more expedient to fit new contact breaker points rather than attempt to clean up the existing ones.

To renew the points, first remove the nut from the top of the terminal post and lift off the top insulating bush and both electrical leads (Fig. B:3). Remove the screw, spring and plain washer securing the contact set to the base plate and lift out the contact set. Take great care to ensure that none of the components are dropped down inside the distributor body as, if this happens, the distributor must be removed to retrieve them.

Before installing the new contact set, clean out the inside of the distributor thoroughly. Wipe clean the contact surface on the breaker cam. Also wipe clean the contact faces of the points on the new set as these are normally coated with preservative. Methylated spirits is ideal for this purpose. Do not use petrol, as this is oil-based.

Position the new contact set on the base plate and secure with the locking screw and washers. Tighten the screw only lightly at this stage. Locate the condenser and LT lead terminals onto the top insulating bush and fit the bush over the terminal post so that the terminals make contact with the breaker arm spring. Refit the retaining nut and tighten securely. Ensure that the lead terminals are properly positioned so that they are insulated from the terminal post.

Lubricate the distributor cam, cam spindle and points pivot as detailed above.

Check that the contact face of the fixed and moving contacts are parallel to each other, aligning them correctly if necessary.

Turn the engine over by hand until the rubbing block on the breaker arm is resting on the top of the cam lobe. Adjust the position of the fixed contact by moving the contact breaker bracket until the specified gap of 0.014 - 0.016 in (0.35 - 0.40 mm) is obtained between the contact points. The fixed contact bracket can be moved by inserting a screwdriver into the notched hole at the opposite side of the plate and turning the screwdriver clockwise to decrease the gap, or anti-clockwise to increase the gap (Fig. B:3). The feeler gauge should be a neat sliding fit between the contacts.

When fitting new points it is advisable to set the gap to 0.019 in (0.48 mm) to allow for initial bedding in of rubbing block.

When the gap is correct, tighten the locking screw. Turn the engine over until the rubbing block is on the opposite cam (180°) and recheck the clearance.

After fitting new points or adjusting the points gap, the dwell angle and ignition timing should be checked as described below.

Contact Breaker Points - Lucas 45D4 Type Distributor

The contact breaker points on the 45D4 distributor should be inspected in a similar manner to that described for the 25D4 type above. However, the procedure for replacing the contact set is slightly different as the condenser and LT lead are connected to the set by means of a common terminal plate (Fig. B:4). To release the plate, press the breaker arm spring away from the insulating block and unclip the plate from the hooked end of the spring.

When reconnecting the terminal plate, slide it into the end of the spring, then position the spring on the insulated block between the two locating shoulders.

To adjust the contact gap, insert the screwdriver into the notched hole on the contact plate and lever against the pip provided on the back plate. In this case, turn the screwdriver clockwise to increase the gap, or anti-clockwise to decrease it.

Dwell Angle

For maximum efficiency and economy the contact breaker points setting should be checked with a dwell meter. Its use is particularly important in the case of used points where metal transfer has taken place between the points making accurate checking difficult using feeler gauges.

Relatively inexpensive units are available from most good accessory shops, and in some cases can even be hired.

The dwell angle of the ignition points is the angle of point closure. The wider the points gap the smaller will be the dwell angle, and vice-versa.

The specified limits for checking the dwell angle are:-
25D4 distributor . . . . .60° ± 3°
45D4 distributor . . . . .51° ± 5°

If the reading is outside these limits, it should be reset as near as possible to the mean.

With new points it is good practice to set the dwell angle to the lower limit as the angle will increase (gap will reduce) as the points rubbing block beds-in.

Connect the dwell meter in accordance with the manufacturer's instructions. Start the engine and run it at idle, then read off the dwell angle indicated on the meter. If the reading is outside the checking limits above, remove the distributor cap and rotor arm and adjust the contact breaker points to obtain the correct setting, while cranking the engine over on the starter.

As a check on the distributor condition, make a second reading with the engine speed increased to about 2,000 rpm. The needle of the dwell meter should then not deviate from the previous figure by more than ± 1°. A larger deviation indicates that the distributor shaft is worn worn.

When the dwell angle has been adjusted, the ignition timing must be reset as detailed below.

Distributor Cap & Rotor Arm

Thoroughly clean the distributor cap, inside and out, with a clean cloth, paying particular attention to the spaces between the metal electrodes inside the cap. Check that the electrodes are not excessively eroded, and that there are no signs of tracking. Tracking is visible as hairlines on the surface of the cap and is caused by the HT voltage shorting between the electrodes or the central brush and an electrode. Once tracking is present it cannot be eliminated and the cap must be discarded. Also check that the small carbon brush in the centre of the cap is undamaged.

Similarly, clean the rotor arm and inspect for damage or excessive erosion of the electrode. Also check that the rotor is a neat sliding fit on the distributor spindle without excessive side-play.

Clean the outside surface of the central tower on the ignition coil and check for signs of damage or tracking.

Wipe all grease and dirt from the HT leads and check the leads for signs of cracking, chafing, etc. Ensure that all connections at the spark plugs, ignition coil and distributor cap are secure, and the moisture seals at each end of the HT leads are firmly in place.

IGNITION TIMING . . . . [6]

The contact breaker points gap or dwell angle must be correctly set before attempting to check or adjust the ignition timing. Conversely, the ignition setting should be checked after cleaning, renewing or resetting the contact breaker points.

Static Check

During this procedure the engine can be turned over by engaging reverse gear and pushing the car backwards, or by jacking one of the front wheels clear of the ground and rotating the wheel. In this latter case, top gear should be engaged. On automatic models, use a screwdriver inserted through the aperture in the converter housing to rotate the converter by levering on the starter ring gear (Figs. B:7 and B:8 refers). Crankshaft rotation is clockwise, viewed from the radiator end of the engine.

It will facilitate rotation of the crankshaft if the spark plugs are first removed from the engine.

Remove the cover plate from the inspection hole in the clutch housing (rubber plug from the converter end cover on automatic transmission models) to allow observation of the timing scale on the flywheel or torque converter. (Fig. B:6). A mirror will be required to enable the timing marks to be seen.

Remove the distributor cap and connect a 12 volt test lamp between the distributor LT terminal and a good earthing point.

Rotate the crankshaft in its normal direction of rotation until the rotor arm is pointing approximately midway between the No. 2 and No. 1 segments in the distributor cap. The rotor arm rotation is anti-clockwise viewed from above.

With the ignition switched on, rotate the crankshaft slowly until the test lamp just lights, indicating the points have opened. This gives the firing point for No. 1 cylinder. If the ignition setting is correct, the appropriate mark on the timing scale will now be aligned, with the reference pointer in the inspection hole. Refer to 'Tune-Up Data' at the end of this section for the specified ignition settings.

The setting can be checked by gently pressing the rotor arm in the opposite direction to its normal rotation, when the test lamp should go out until the arm is released again.

It should be noted that late models have a timing scale more sensibly situated on the timing gear cover adjacent to the crankshaft pulley (Fig. B:9).

If the timing setting is incorrect, it should be adjusted as described below.

Adjustment

The 25D4 type distributor is fitted with an ignition timing adjusting device and if only a small correction is required this can be achieved by rotating the knurled adjuster nut on the end of the vacuum unit spindle (Fig. B:10). One graduation on the vernier scale is equal to about 5° of crankshaft movement and fifty five clicks of the adjuster nut. Turn the adjuster nut in the direction of the cast 'A' mark if the timing mark is past (to the left of) the reference pointer, or towards the 'R' if the mark is before the pointer.

If a large correction is required, the complete distributor body must be turned to obtain the correct setting. This is the method which must be used with the 45D4 type distributor as it does not have an adjuster nut. In the case of the 25D4 unit, first turn the knurled adjuster nut until the vernier scale is in the central position.

Turn the crankshaft until the correct mark on the timing scale is aligned with the pointer in the inspection hole. Slacken the distributor clamp bolt nut and rotate the distributor body anti-clockwise past the point where the test lamp illuminates, then carefully rotate it back clockwise until the lamp just goes out. Tighten the clamp bolt without disturbing the body setting. Finally, recheck the setting as described above.

Dynamic Check

If possible the ignition timing should be checked with the engine running using a stroboscopic timing light, as this will ensure optimum engine performance and economy. With later models, it really is essential that the ignition be set dynamically. The timing light should be used in accordance with the equipment manufacturers instructions.

It will facilitate the timing operation if both the reference pointer and the appropriate mark on the timing scale are emphasised with white paint to make them more

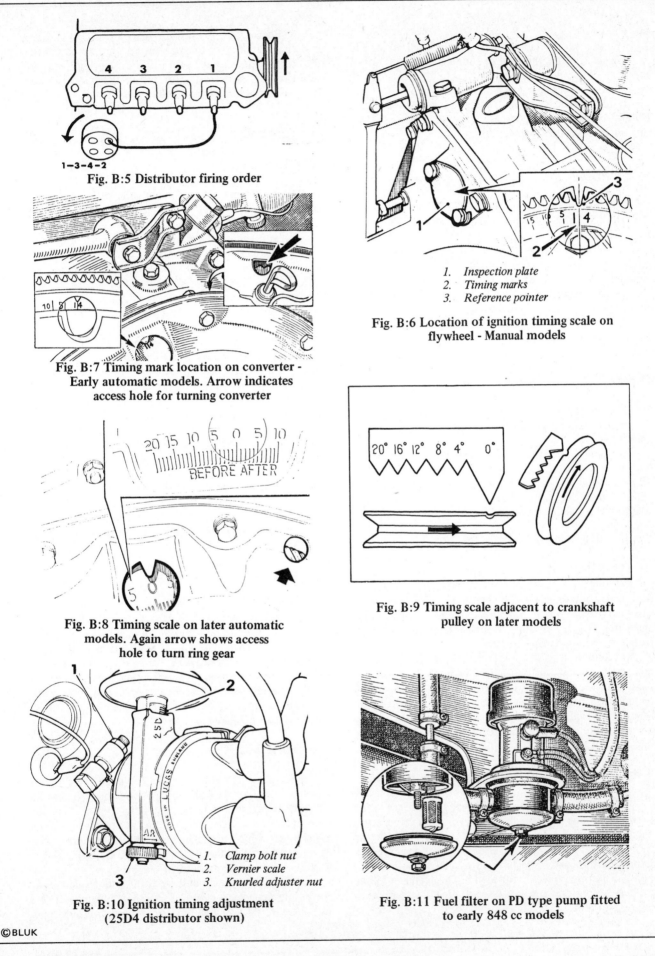

Fig. B:5 Distributor firing order

1—3—4—2

Fig. B:7 Timing mark location on converter -
Early automatic models. Arrow indicates
access hole for turning converter

1. Inspection plate
2. Timing marks
3. Reference pointer

Fig. B:6 Location of ignition timing scale on
flywheel - Manual models

Fig. B:8 Timing scale on later automatic
models. Again arrow shows access
hole to turn ring gear

Fig. B:9 Timing scale adjacent to crankshaft
pulley on later models

1. Clamp bolt nut
2. Vernier scale
3. Knurled adjuster nut

Fig. B:10 Ignition timing adjustment
(25D4 distributor shown)

Fig. B:11 Fuel filter on PD type pump fitted
to early 848 cc models

easily observed.

The distributor vacuum pipe should be disconnected and plugged. With the engine running at the specified speed, the appropriate timing mark should be in line with the reference pointer.

If adjustment is required, proceed as described above. Rotate the distributor body clockwise to advance the setting, or anti-clockwise to retard it.

FUEL PUMP . . . . [7]

Up to the replacement of the Mini Mk I & II models with the 850/1000/Clubman/1275 GT models, all models were fitted with an electric fuel pump, mounted on the rear sub-frame. Later models were equipped with a mechanical pump, mounted on the left-hand side of the cylinder block and driven from the crankshaft. This change took place round about October 1969 with the change in the electrical system to negative earth.

Several different types of electrical pump were used and the differing procedures for cleaning the filter are detailed below.

Filter - PD Type Electrical Pump

The PD type pump was only fitted to very early 848 cc models and probably most of these have been replaced by now.

To remove the filter for cleaning, unscrew the retaining nut and detach the bottom cover plate (Fig. B:11). Withdraw the gauze filter from the pump body and clean with a brush and petrol. Use a new gasket, if necessary, when refitting the cover plate.

Filter - SP & AUF 201 Type Electrical Pump

On the SP type pump the tubular filter is located at the fuel inlet nozzle which must first be unscrewed from the pump body to gain access (Fig. B:12). The gauze filter can then be withdrawn. Again clean the filter with a brush and petrol. Use a new fibre washer, if necessary, when refitting the inlet nozzle.

On the AUF 201 type pump the inlet and outlet nozzles are retained in position by a clamp plate which is secured to the pump body by two screws. Once the clamp plate is detached, the inlet nozzle can be removed and the filter withdrawn. After cleaning the filter, refit it in position and secure the nozzles with the clamp plate. Ensure that the seating rings are correctly located at the nozzles.

Filter - AUF 700 and 800 Type Mechanical Pump

The mechanical pump fitted to later models is rather inaccessible due to the proximity of the carburettor, exhaust manifold, etc. However, if necessary, the pump filter screen can be removed after removing the three retaining screws and detaching the top cover from the pump. The filter screen is retained in the top cover by the rubber sealing ring and is easily withdrawn once the sealing ring is removed.

In this case, clean both the filter screen and all traces of sediment from the chamber in the pump body before refitting the top cover. Ensure the sealing ring is in good condition and is correctly located in the cover. Tighten the cover screws evenly to obtain a good seal.

AIR CLEANER . . . . [8]

Filter Element

The air cleaner may be one of three different types; a metal case type, a small plastic case type or a large plastic case type.

Replacement of the filter element in the former type is simplest, merely being a matter of disconnecting the breather hose (when fitted), unscrewing the wing nut and lifting off the top cover. The filter element can then be lifted out and the case cleaned out with a piece of rag. Fit the new element and top cover and secure with the wing nut.

On the plastic case type cleaners, the top cover is secured by locating lugs as well as the one or two wing nuts, and it will be necessary to lever up the cover using a screwdriver inserted into the slots in the side before it can be lifted off (Figs. B:13 and B:14). Again clean out the inside of the casing before fitting the new filter element.

On the small plastic case type cleaner, ensure that the rubber seal is correctly positioned in the groove in the underside of the cover, then engage the locating lug into the top cover and snap-fit the cover onto the container (Fig. B:13). Refit and tighten the wing nut.

With the large plastic type cleaner, align the arrow marked on the top cover with the locating lug on the container and snap-fit the cover (Fig. B:14). Refit and tighten the two wing nuts.

Air Temperature Control Valve

On later models, where an air temperature control valve is incorporated in the air intake, the function of the control valve should be checked by depressing and releasing it (Fig. B:15). The valve should return easily to its original position. The valve seat should also be inspected for any signs of damage or deterioration. When the engine is cold, the valve should be in the closed position, so that only hot air from around the exhaust manifold is drawn into the cleaner intake.

CARBURETTOR . . . . [9]

Some later Mini models are equipped with special emission carburettors which have plastic seals fitted at the adjustment points to render them 'tamperproof'. The purpose of this is to prevent unqualified persons from making adjustments which could increase emissions above a predetermined level, either through lack of understanding or unsuitable measuring equipment.

These seals must be destroyed in order to gain access to the idle speed screw and/or mixture adjusting nut. The idle speed screw is sealed by a small plastic push-fit plug,

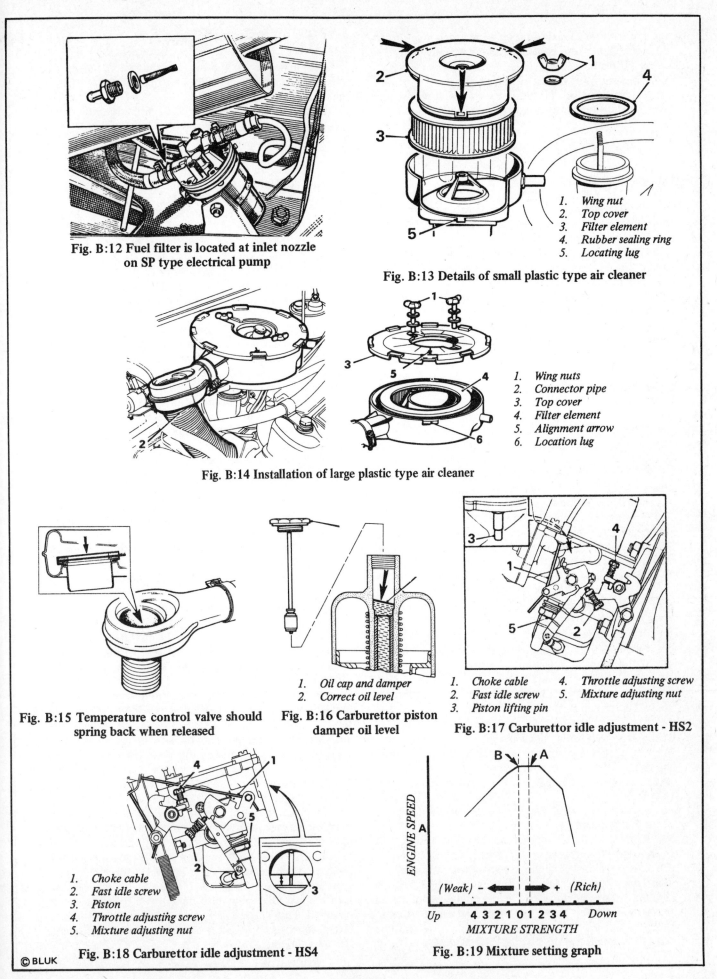

Fig. B:12 Fuel filter is located at inlet nozzle on SP type electrical pump

Fig. B:13 Details of small plastic type air cleaner

1. Wing nut
2. Top cover
3. Filter element
4. Rubber sealing ring
5. Locating lug

1. Wing nuts
2. Connector pipe
3. Top cover
4. Filter element
5. Alignment arrow
6. Location lug

Fig. B:14 Installation of large plastic type air cleaner

Fig. B:15 Temperature control valve should spring back when released

1. Oil cap and damper
2. Correct oil level

Fig. B:16 Carburettor piston damper oil level

1. Choke cable
2. Fast idle screw
3. Piston lifting pin
4. Throttle adjusting screw
5. Mixture adjusting nut

Fig. B:17 Carburettor idle adjustment - HS2

1. Choke cable
2. Fast idle screw
3. Piston
4. Throttle adjusting screw
5. Mixture adjusting nut

Fig. B:18 Carburettor idle adjustment - HS4

ENGINE SPEED

(Weak) − ← → + (Rich)

Up   4 3 2 1 0 1 2 3 4   Down

MIXTURE STRENGTH

Fig. B:19 Mixture setting graph

© BLUK

and the mixture adjusting nut by a two-piece snap-fit plastic cover. With these carburettors it is advised that no attempt be made to remove the sealing plugs or covers or alter the settings of the sealed adjusters.

On carburettors of the conventional type, without seals, the idle adjustment is carried out in the normal manner.

Damper Oil Level

The oil level in the carburettor damper reservoir must be maintained approximately 0.5 in (13 mm) above the top of the hollow piston rod (Fig. B:16).

To check the level, unscrew the damper cap from the top of the suction chamber and withdraw the cap and damper. Top up if necessary with light oil (preferably SAE 20 grade). Push the damper assembly back into position and screw the cap firmly into place.

Failure to maintain the oil at the correct level will cause the piston to flutter and reduce acceleration.

Slow Running Adjustment

Before attempting to adjust the carburettor slow-running setting, ensure that all other items relevant to good engine performance are in good condition and/or correctly adjusted (e.g. contact breaker points, ignition timing, spark plugs, valve clearances, etc.). Also check the air cleaner to ensure that the element is clean, and check that the throttle operation is free and unrestricted.

Carburettor tuning should be confined to setting the idling and fast idling speeds and the mixture at idle speed. A reliable tachometer should be used if possible - make use of the car's tachometer if one is fitted.

On vehicles fitted with emission control equipment, refer to the EMISSION CONTROL SYSTEMS section before attempting to carry out any tuning or servicing operations on the carburettor.

Where a vehicle must conform to exhaust emission control regulations, adjustments should only be carried out if the use of a reliable tachometer and exhaust gas analyser (CO meter) are available.

1. Check the oil level in the piston damper, as detailed above, and top up if necessary.
2. Check that the throttle moves freely without signs of of sticking and returns fully when released.
3. Check that the mixture control returns fully when the choke cable is pushed fully home. Also check that the cable has about 1/16 in (2 mm) free-play before it starts to pull on the lever.
4. Check that a small clearance exists between the end of the fast idle screw and the fast idle cam.
5. Raise the carburettor piston and check that it falls freely onto the carburettor bridge with a distinct metallic click when released. The piston can be raised for this purpose either with the piston lifting pin at the side of the carburettor, or directly with a finger at the air intake. In this latter case the air cleaner must first be removed to gain access. If the piston fails to fall freely, the jet must be centred as detailed in the FUEL SYSTEM section.

6. Connect a suitable tachometer to the engine, if available.
7. On models with automatic transmission, move the selector into the 'N' position and fully apply the handbrake.
8. Start the engine and run it at fast idle until it has attained its normal running temperature. Continue to run it for a further five minutes.
9. Temporarily increase the engine speed to approximately 2,500 rpm, and maintain this speed for about half a minute to clear the inlet manifold of excess fuel. Repeat this procedure at three minute intervals if the remainder of the adjustments cannot be completed within this period of time.
10. Check the idle speed and adjust if necessary by turning the throttle adjusting screw. The idle speed should be about 750 - 800 rpm for most later models, or 500 - 650 for models up to 1972. Refer to 'Tune-Up Data' at the end of the section for a list of the precise specified figures, if required.
11. Now adjust the idle mixture by turning the jet adjusting nut one flat at a time, up or down, until the fastest idle speed consistent with smooth running is achieved (Point A on graph in Fig. B:19). Turning the nut up will weaken the mixture, and down will enrich it. Now turn the nut up slowly (weakening) until the engine speed just starts to fall (point B on graph). This should give the weakest position for maximum speed.
12. Recheck the idle speed and adjust if necessary to obtain the specified idle speed.
13. The mixture strength can be checked by lifting the piston approximately 1/32 in (0.8 mm) with the lifting pin.
a) If the engine speed momentarily increases very slightly, the mixture is correct.
b) If the engine speed increases, and continues to do so, the mixture is too rich.
c) If the engine speed decreases, the mixture strength is too weak.
14. When the mixture is correct, the exhaust note should be regular and even. If it is irregular, with a splashy type of misfire and colourless exhaust, the mixture is too weak. If there is a regular or rhythmical type of misfire in the exhaust beat, together with a blackish exhaust, then the mixture is too rich.
15. On models which must conform to emission control regulations, check that the reading is within the specified limits - normally 3.0 to 4.5% CO - using the exhaust gas analyser. If the reading falls outside the specified limits, reset the jet adjusting nut by the minimum amount necessary to bring the reading just within the limits. If more than half a turn of the adjusting nut is required, the carburettor should be removed for servicing.
16. To check the fast idle speed, pull out the choke knob until the linkage is just about to move the mixture jet and lock the knob in this position. The fast idle speed should be about 1100 - 1200 rpm, or slightly less for pre '72 models. Again refer to 'Tune-Up Data' for the precise specified figures, if required. If adjustment is necessary, turn the fast idle screw until the correct fast idle speed is obtained. Push the choke knob fully in and check that a clearance exists between the end of the fast idle screw and the fast idle cam.

Tune-up Data

COMPRESSION PRESSURE

850/1000 (inc. Clubman) (59-76).	8.3:1 cr	150 psi (10.5 kg/cm^2)
850/1000 (inc. Clubman) (76 on).	8.3:1 cr	170 psi (11.9 kg/cm^2)
850/1000 (inc. Clubman) - Auto (65-74)	8.9:1 cr	160 psi (11.25 kg/cm^2)
850/1000 (inc. Clubman) - Auto (74-76)	8.3:1 cr	150 psi (10.5 kg/cm^2)
850/1000 (inc. Clubman) - Auto (76 on)	8.3:1 cr	170 psi (11.9 kg/cm^2)
Clubman 1100 (74 on).	8.5:1 cr	165 psi (11.6 kg/cm^2)
1275 GT (69 on)	8.8:1 cr	175 psi (12.3 kg/cm^2)

VALVE CLEARANCES

All, inlet and exhaust . . . . .0.012 in (0.30 mm), cold

IGNITION

Spark plugs
    Make/type . . . . Champion N9Y*
    Electrode gap . . . . 0.025 in (0.65 mm)

> * N5 plugs can be used in pre '72 850/1000 manual models, and
> pre '74 automatic models

Firing order . . . . 1 - 3 - 4 - 2
Cylinder numbering. . . . . From front (radiator end of engine)
Distributor rotor rotation . . . . .Anti-clockwise
Contact breaker gap . . . . 0.014 - 0.016 in (0.35 - 0.40 mm)
Dwell angle
    DM2 & 25D4 Distributors . . . . .60^0 ± 3^0
    43D4 & 45D4 Distributors . . . . .51^0 ± 5^0

IGNITION TIMING

Model	Year	Static	Stroboscopic
850.	59 - 72	TDC	3^0 BTDC/600 rpm VD
850 (Van & Pick-up with regular fuel distributor)	59 - 72	7^0 BTDC	10^0 BTDC/600 rpm VD
850.	72 - 74	TDC	19^0 BTD/1000 rpm VD
850 (limited number of engines, '74 on).	72 - 74	9^0 BTDC	14^0 BTDC/1000 rpm VD
850 (ECE 15).	74 - 76	6^0 BTDC	11^0 BTDC/1000 rpm VD
850 (ECE 15).	76 on	—	7^0 BTDC/1000 rpm VD
850 - Auto.	65 - 69	3^0 BTDC	6^0 BTDC/600 rpm VD
1000/Clubman 1000	67 - 72	5^0 BTDC	8^0 BTDC/600 rpm VD
1000/Clubman 1000 Van & Pick-up with regular fuel distributor	67 - 72	7^0 BTDC	10^0 BTDC/600 rpm VD
1000/Clubman 1000	72 - 74	5^0 BTDC	11^0 BTDC/1000 rpm VD
1000/Clubman 1000 (limited number of engines '74 on).	72 - 74	10^0 BTDC	13^0 BTDC/1000 rpm VD
1000/Clubman 1000 (ECE 15).	74 - 78	4^0 BTDC	7^0 BTDC/1000 rpm VD
1000/Clubman 1000 (ECE 15).	78	—	8^0 BTDC/1000 rpm VD
1000/Clubman 1000 - Auto.	67 - 74	4^0 BTDC	6^0 BTDC/600 rpm VD
1000/Clubman 1000 - Auto (ECE 15). .	74 - 78	4^0 BTDC	7^0 BTDC/1000 rpm VD
1000/Clubman 1000 - Auto (ECE 15). .	78	—	8^0 BTDC/1000 rpm VD
Clubman 1100 (ECE 15).	74 - 76	9^0 BTDC	12^0 BTDC/1000 rpm VD
Clubman 1100 (ECE 15).	76 - 78	—	12^0 BTDC/1000 rpm VD
1275 GT	69 - 72	8^0 BTDC	10^0 BTDC/600 rpm VD
1275 GT (ECE 15)	72 - 76	8^0 BTDC	13^0 BTDC/1000 rpm VD
1275 GT (ECE 15)	76 - 77	—	13^0 BTDC/1000 rpm VD

NOTE: Engine idle speeds can be found in FUEL Technical Data

NON-START
Trouble Shooter

FAULT	CAUSE	CURE
Starter will not turn engine (headlights dim)	1. Battery low 2. Faulty battery 3. Corroded battery cables or loose connections 4. Starter jammed 5. Seized engine	1. Charge battery and check charging system. 2. Fit new battery. 3. Clean battery connections or replace battery leads. Tighten battery and starter-motor connections. 4. Free starter. 5. Remove spark-plugs to confirm.
Starter will not turn engine (headlights bright)	1. Faulty starter solenoid 2. Faulty starter engagement (starter-motor whine) 3. Faulty starter 4. Faulty ignition switch	1. Replace solenoid. 2. Clean or replace starter bendix. 3. Repair or replace starter motor. 4. Fit new switch.
Engine turns slowly but will not start	1. Battery low 2. Faulty battery 3. Corroded battery leads or loose connections 4. Faulty starter	1. Charge battery and check charging system. 2. Replace battery. 3. Clean battery connections or replace battery leads. Tighten connections. 4. Repair or replace starter motor.
Engine turns but will not fire	1. Ignition fault 2. No spark at plug lead 3. Spark at plug lead 4. Fuel reaching carburettor 5. No fuel to carburettor 6. Car with electric fuel pump 7. Car with mechanical pump	1. Check for spark at plug lead. 2. Check coil output to confirm high or low-tension fault. If spark from coil, check HT leads, distributor cap and rotor arm, particularly for cracks, tracking or dampness. If no spark from coil, check ignition-coil connections and contact-breaker points for short circuits or disconnection. 3. Remove air cleaner from carburettor and check choke operation. Loosen petrol-pipe union at carburettor. Turn engine by starter for a mechanical pump, or switch on ignition for electric pump. Check if petrol is being delivered. 4. Look into carburettor mouth. Operate throttle and observe whether damp or dry. If dry, clean jets and needle valve. If damp, remove spark-plugs, dry, clean and check gaps. 5. Remove petrol-tank cap and check for fuel. 6. Check pump has a good earth and give pump a sharp tap. If it starts pumping, which will be heard, replace pump. If not fuel lines may be blocked. 7. Remove pump-top cover, clean pump filter and make sure the cover, when re-fitted, is airtight. Check flexible pipe to pump for air leaks.
Engine backfires	1. Ignition timing faulty 2. Damp distributor cap and leads	1. Check and reset ignition timing. 2. Dry thoroughly and check firing order.

Engine

Due to the relatively inaccessible situation of the power unit in the Mini, few repair operations can be easily and successfully carried out while the unit is still in the car. The obvious exception is any work concerning the cylinder head. The timing cover, timing chain and gears can be replaced with the engine in place, but only with difficulty.

Clutch replacement can be carried out once the right-hand end of the engine/transmission unit has been raised, and involves removal of the clutch cover and the flywheel assembly to gain access.

Once the unit has been lifted out of the car it is a relatively simple job to separate the engine from the gearbox casing. The clutch cover, clutch and flywheel assembly and flywheel housing however must first be removed.

VALVE CLEARANCES . . . . [1]

The rocker cover must first be removed. Where fitted, release the three clips and remove the ignition shield from the front of the engine. If necessary, remove the air cleaner assembly after disconnecting the breather hose (when fitted). Remove the two retaining nuts together with their cup washers and seals and lift off the rocker cover and gasket (Fig. C:3).

It will facilitate turning over the engine if the spark plugs are removed at this point. Suitably label the plug leads to ensure they will be reconnected correctly.

For this operation the engine can be turned over by engaging reverse gear and pushing the car backwards, or by jacking one of the front wheels clear of the ground and rotating the wheel. In this latter case, top gear should be engaged. On automatic models use a screwdriver inserted through the aperture in the converter housing to rotate the converter by levering on the ring gear. Crankshaft rotation is clockwise, viewed from the radiator end of the engine.

Rotate the crankshaft until each valve in turn listed in the left-hand column below is fully open (spring compressed), then check the clearance of the valve listed opposite in the right-hand column. Valve numbering is from the radiator end of the engine.

Valve No. 1 open		check valve No. 8
Valve No. 3 open		check valve No. 6
Valve No. 5 open		check valve No. 4
Valve No. 2 open		check valve No. 7
Valve No. 8 open		check valve No. 1
Valve No. 6 open		check valve No. 3
Valve No. 4 open		check valve No. 5
Valve No. 7 open		check valve No. 2

The valve rocker clearance should be 0.012 in (0.305 mm) for both the inlet and exhaust valves (cold). The clearance is correct when the appropriate thickness of feeler gauge is a neat sliding fit between the end of the valve stem and the pad on the rocker arm.

If adjustment is necessary, slacken the adjusting screw locknut with a ring spanner, and turn the adjusting screw on the push rod end of the rocker arm until the correct gap is obtained (Fig. C:2). Turn the screw clockwise to reduce the clearance, or anti-clockwise to increase it. Retighten the locknut while holding the adjusting screw with the screwdriver to prevent it turning, then recheck the gap.

When adjustment is complete, refit the rocker cover. Use a new cork gasket if necessary. Ensure that all traces of old gasket have been removed from the cover and cylinder head mating faces before fitting. Tighten the cover retaining nuts evenly to ensure a good seal.

Refit the spark plugs, if removed, and reconnect the plug leads. Finally, refit the air cleaner, if removed.

CYLINDER HEAD . . . . [2]

Removal (Fig. C:5)

1. Disconnect the earth strap from the battery.
2. Remove the bonnet, after first marking the fitted position of the hinges to facilitate alignment when refitting.
3. Drain the cooling system by removing the cylinder block drain plug and/or disconnecting the bottom hose at the radiator.

B

4. Disconnect the HT leads from the plugs, after suitably labelling them to ensure correct positioning on re-assembly. Also disconnect the lead from the water temperature gauge sender unit at the thermostat housing.

5. Disconnect the breather hose (where fitted) from the rocker cover, and remove the air cleaner assembly.

6. Disconnect the distributor vacuum pipe, fuel hose and engine breather pipe (where fitted) from the carburettor. On automatic models, also disconnect the kick-down linkage rod from the carburettor.

7. Disconnect the throttle return spring from the carburettor. Remove the two nuts securing the carburettor to the inlet manifold, detach the carburettor from the studs and place it to one side. Where a cable abutment plate is fitted between the carburettor and the inlet manifold, the plate should be removed with the carburettor.

8. Remove the two nuts securing the heater water control valve, detach the valve and place it to one side with the hose and cable still attached.

9. Remove the nuts securing the radiator upper support bracket to the thermostat housing, and the bolts securing it to the radiator cowl, and remove the bracket (Fig. C:6).

10. Slacken the clip securing the small by-pass hose to the cylinder head connection, this is located on the underside of the cylinder head, above the water pump (Fig. C:6).

11. Remove the two nuts, together with their cup washers and seals, retaining the rocker cover, and lift off the cover and gasket (Fig. C:3).

12. On 1275 GT models, remove the additional securing bolt 'A' and nut 'B' at the ends of the cylinder head (Fig. C:7).

13. Remove the cylinder head and rocker shaft pedestal nuts, releasing them evenly until the valve spring load on the rocker shaft assembly is released.

14. On models where the ignition coil mounting bracket is attached to one of the cylinder head studs, remove the coil and place to one side.

15. Lift off the rocker shaft assembly, then withdraw the push rods, keeping them in their installed order.

16. Disconnect the radiator top hose from the thermostat housing.

17. Lift off the cylinder head, complete with the exhaust manifold. If difficulty is encountered in removing the head, tap each side of the head with a hide-faced mallet to free it.

18. Remove the cylinder head gasket and discard it.

Installation

Installation is a reversal of the removal procedure, with special attention to the following points.

a) Ensure that all joint surfaces, especially the mating surfaces of the cylinder head and block, are perfectly clean and free from old gasket material.

b) If the cylinder head was removed to replace a leaking or blown head gasket, check the mating faces on both the head and block for distortion before reassembly.

c) Use new gaskets where appropriate. A cylinder head gasket set should be obtained, as this will contain all the necessary gaskets.

d) Do not use grease or jointing compound of any type on the cylinder head gasket when fitting.

e) Ensure the head gasket is correctly positioned. The gasket is normally marked 'TOP' and 'FRONT'.

f) Ensure that the push rods are installed in their original positions. Dip the ends of the rods in clean engine oil prior to installing them.

g) When fitting the rocker shaft assembly, ensure that the rocker arm adjusting screws locate correctly in the cupped end of their respective push rods. If any work has been carried out on the valves (e.g. recutting the valve seats) the rocker arm adjusting screws should be released slightly before installing the rocker shaft assembly. Lubricate the rocker assembly with clean engine oil.

h) Tighten the cylinder head and rocker shaft pedestal nuts evenly, following the sequence shown in Fig. C:7. The cylinder head nuts should be tightened in stages to 50 lb ft (7.0 kg m), and the rocker pedestal nuts to 24 lb ft (3.2 kg m).

i) On models which have the ignition coil bracket attached to one of the cylinder head studs, do not forget to refit the bracket before fitting and tightening the head nuts.

j) On 1275 GT models, the additional securing bolt 'A' and nut 'B' must be tightened last. These should be tightened to 25 lb ft (3.5 kg m).

k) Check the valve clearances, as described previously, and adjust if necessary.

l) When installation is complete, refill the cooling system, then run the engine and check for oil, water or exhaust leaks.

m) Finally, with the engine at normal operating temperature, check the ignition timing and engine idle settings as detailed in the TUNE-UP section at the beginning of this manual.

Dismantling

1. Unscrew the spark plugs from the cylinder head.

2. Remove the inlet and exhaust manifolds, together with the hot air intake box (Fig. C:8).

3. Remove the water outlet housing and lift out the thermostat from the recess in the head.

4. Remove all carbon deposits from the combustion chambers, valve heads and valve ports using a suitable scraper, such as a screwdriver, and a wire brush. Take care to avoid damaging the machined surface of the cylinder head.

5. Similarly, clean all deposits from the cylinder block face and piston crowns, but leave a ring of carbon around the outside of each piston and the top of each bore. Ensure that carbon particles are not allowed to enter the oil or water ways in the block. This can be prevented by plugging the passages with small pieces of cloth while the carbon is being removed.

6. At each valve in turn, remove the spring clip from the collets (early models only). Compress the valve spring, using a suitable spring compressor tool, and extract the two split tapered collets from around the valve stem. Take care to ensure the valve stem is not damaged by the spring retainer when pressing it down. Release the compressor tool and remove the spring retainer, shroud (early models only) and valve spring (Fig. C:9). Remove the rubber oil seal (where fitted) from the valve stem and withdraw the valve from the cylinder head. Suitably mark the valve and

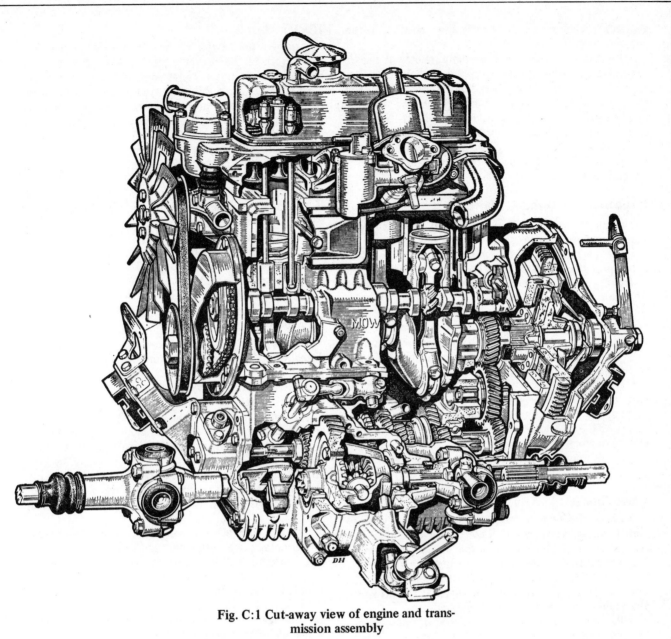

Fig. C:1 Cut-away view of engine and transmission assembly

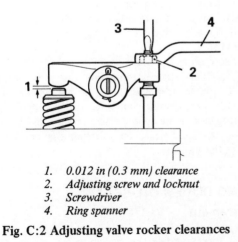

1. 0.012 in (0.3 mm) clearance
2. Adjusting screw and locknut
3. Screwdriver
4. Ring spanner

Fig. C:2 Adjusting valve rocker clearances

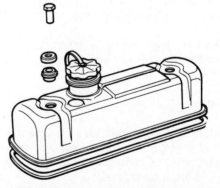

Fig. C:3 Details of rocker cover assembly

associated components to identify their position in the cylinder head.

7. To dismantle the rocker assembly, remove the shaft locating screw from the No. 2 rocker shaft bracket. Remove the split pins from each end of the rocker shaft, and slide the washers, springs, rocker arms and support brackets off the shaft (Fig. C:10 and C:11). Note the relative position of the components for reassembly. If necessary, the blanking plug can be unscrewed from the front end of the shaft to enable the oilways of the shaft to be cleaned out.

Inspection & Overhaul - Valves

Clean the valves and seatings and examine them for signs of pitting, burning or other damage.

A simple method of removing carbon from the valves is to insert the valve stem in the chuck of an electric drill and, using as slow a speed as possible, scrape the deposits off with a file or screwdriver. The valve can then be finished off with emery cloth.

Inspect the valve face and edges for pits, grooves, scores, or other damage. Valves in reasonable condition may be resurfaced on a valve grinding machine, but only sufficient metal to true up the face should be removed. If the thickness of the valve head is reduced to 0.020 in (0.5 mm) or less after grinding, then the valve should be discarded as it will run too hot in use.

Examine the valve stem for excessive or abnormal wear, and renew the valve if necessary.

If the valves are in poor condition, they should be renewed.

Valve Guides

Check the stem to guide clearance of each valve in turn in its respective guide. Raise the valve slightly from its seat and rock the head from side to side, as shown in Fig. C:12. If the movement across the seat is excessive, this indicates a worn guide and/or valve stem. Repeat the check using a new valve. If the movement is still excessive, the guide is worn and should be renewed.

Remove the old guide by drifting it downwards into the combustion chamber (Fig. C:13). Ensure the bore in the cylinder head is clean, then drive the new guide into position in the head so that its top end protrudes 0.540 in (13.72 mm), or 0.594 in (15.09 mm) on 1100 engines, above the machined face of the valve spring seating. The inlet valve guide must be fitted with the largest chamfer at the top, and the exhaust guide with the counterbore at the bottom.

NOTE: The valve seats should be recut after fitting new valve guides to ensure the seat is concentric with the guide bore.

Valve Seats

Inspect the seating surface on each valve seat in the cylinder head for signs of pitting, burning or wear. Where necessary, the seat can be recut as long as the seat width and correction angle are maintained.

The seating surface must be recut when fitting a new valve, or after fitting new valve guides.

Rocker Gear

Inspect the bearing surface on the rocker shaft and the bushes in the rocker arms for wear. Two types of rocker arm are used; a pressed-steel type and a forged type (Fig. C:12). If the latter type is fitted, the arm can be rebushed if worn, but the pressed-steel type must be renewed as an assembly. The installation of the new bushes should be left to a Specialist Machine Shop as they must be burnish-reamed to size after fitting.

Inspect the contact pad at the valve end of each rocker arm for indications of scuffing or excessive or abnormal wear. If the pad is grooved, replace the arm. Do NOT attempt to true the surface by grinding. Check that all oil passages are clear. Replace any damaged or worn adjusting screws or locknuts.

Inspect each push rod for straightness. If bent, the push rod must be replaced - do NOT attempt to straighten it. Also inspect the ends of the rods for nicks, grooves or signs of excessive wear.

Reassembly

Reassemble the cylinder head in the reverse order of dismantling, with special attention to the following points:-

a) Assemble the rocker shaft assembly in the reverse order of dismantling. The plugged end of the shaft must be located at the front of the engine. On 1275 GT models ensure that a shim is fitted behind the No. 2 (tapped) rocker shaft bracket, and another in front of the No. 3 rocker shaft bracket (Fig. C:11). Shims must also be fitted on either side of the No. 1 and No. 8 (end) rocker arms. On all other models, ensure that the double coil spring washers are fitted at either end of the rocker shaft (Fig. C:10).

b) Lap in each valve in turn using coarse, followed by fine grinding paste until a gas-tight seal is obtained at the seat. This will be indicated by a continuous matt-grey ring around the valve face and seat. When this has been achieved, clean all traces of paste from the cylinder head and valves - this is most important.

c) Lubricate the valve guides and valves with clean engine oil before installing the valves.

d) Fit new valve stem oil seals over the valve stem and onto the valve guide, where applicable. Lubricate the seal with oil to make fitting easier. On very early models with the valve spring shroud and collet spring, the oil seal is located on the valve stem at the bottom of the collet groove (Fig. C:9).

e) Ensure that the valve stem is not damaged by the spring retainer when compressing the valve spring, and that the split tapered collets engage correctly in the valve stem and spring retainer when the spring is released. Refit the spring clip to the collet, where applicable.

f) Use new gaskets when refitting the manifolds and water outlet housing.

TIMING COVER OIL SEAL. . . . .[3]
Replacement

On most models the timing cover can be removed

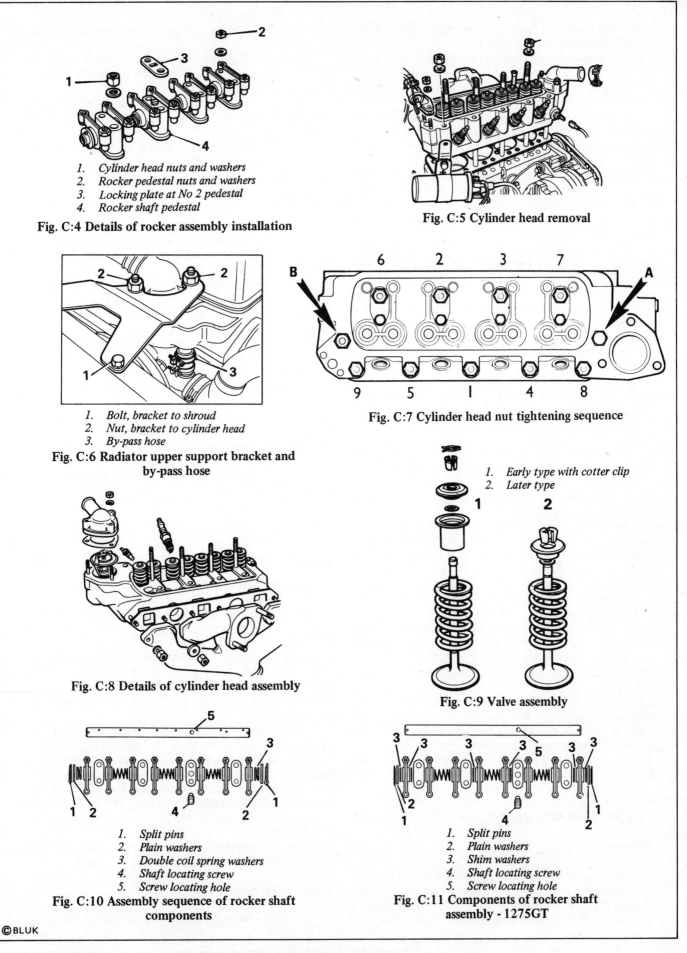

1. Cylinder head nuts and washers
2. Rocker pedestal nuts and washers
3. Locking plate at No 2 pedestal
4. Rocker shaft pedestal

Fig. C:4 Details of rocker assembly installation

Fig. C:5 Cylinder head removal

1. Bolt, bracket to shroud
2. Nut, bracket to cylinder head
3. By-pass hose

Fig. C:6 Radiator upper support bracket and by-pass hose

Fig. C:7 Cylinder head nut tightening sequence

Fig. C:8 Details of cylinder head assembly

1. Early type with cotter clip
2. Later type

Fig. C:9 Valve assembly

1. Split pins
2. Plain washers
3. Double coil spring washers
4. Shaft locating screw
5. Screw locating hole

Fig. C:10 Assembly sequence of rocker shaft components

1. Split pins
2. Plain washers
3. Shim washers
4. Shaft locating screw
5. Screw locating hole

Fig. C:11 Components of rocker shaft assembly - 1275GT

©BLUK

while the engine is in the car, as these have a split-type fan cowling. However, early models had a one-piece fan cowling, and where this is fitted the engine must first be removed.

1. Remove the radiator as described in the COOLING SYSTEM section.

2. Slacken the dynamo/alternator mounting bolts, release the fan belt tension and remove the fan belt.

3. Remove the front retaining bolts and detach the fan blades and drive pulley from the water pump hub.

4. Bend back the locking washer tab and unscrew the crankshaft pulley retaining bolt, then carefully lever the pulley off the crankshaft.

5. On 1275 GT models, disconnect the engine breather hose from the timing cover.

6. Remove the bolts securing the timing cover flange to the engine front plate and detach the timing cover and gasket (Fig. C:14).

7. Extract the old oil seal from the timing cover and check that the bore in the timing cover is clean and undamaged.

8. Lubricate the bore and outside diameter of the new seal with grease and press the seal squarely into place in the cover. It should be possible to press the seal in by hand, but if necessary the seal can be driven home by bearing on the metal outside diameter of the seal (Fig. C:15). In this case the timing cover should be firmly supported around the seal location to avoid disturbing the cover.

9. Ensure that the mating faces on both the timing cover and engine front plate are clean and free of old gasket material.

10. Locate a new gasket on the face on the engine front plate, using grease to hold it in position.

11. Ensure that the oil thrower on the crankshaft is fitted with the face marked 'F' away from the engine. On early type engines the thrower is unmarked and should be fitted with its concave face away from the engine.

12. Refit the timing cover and centralise the oil seal using the crankshaft pulley. It will avoid damage to the new seal if the sealing lips are first lubricated with oil or grease.

13. Fit and tighten the cover retaining bolts, then fit the crankshaft pulley bolt with a new lock washer. Tighten the pulley bolt to its specified torque of 75 lb ft (10.3 kg m) and secure by bending over the lock washer tab.

14. Refit the fan belt and adjust the belt tension so that a free-play of approximately 1/2 in (13 mm) exists at the midway point along its longest run, then tighten the dynamo/alternator mounting bolts.

15. Finally, refit the radiator and refill the cooling system.

TIMING CHAIN & GEARS. . . . . [4]

Removal

Remove the timing cover as described above. Remove the oil thrower from the crankshaft, noting that the face marked 'F' faces outwards away from the engine. Release the tab on the camshaft lock washer, unscrew the cam-shaft sprocket retaining nut and remove the nut and lock-washer.

On 1275 GT models, remove the two retaining screws and detach the timing chain tensioner from the engine front plate (Fig. C:16).

Rotate the crankshaft to bring the timing marks on the crankshaft and camshaft sprockets opposite each other (Fig. C:16).

Remove both the sprockets, together with the timing chain, by easing each wheel forward a fraction at a time with suitable small levers.

Installation

If moved, turn the crankshaft to bring the keyway to the top (TDC position) and the camshaft to bring the keyway to approximately the 2 o'clock position (Fig. C:16).

Assemble the sprockets in the timing chain with their alignment marks opposite each other. Keeping the gears in this position fit the sprocket in the crankshaft then rotate the camshaft as necessary to align the key with the keyway in the sprocket. Push both gears as far onto the shafts as they will go, and secure the camshaft sprocket with the lock washer and nut.

Check the alignment of the sprockets by placing a straight-edge across the teeth of both gears and measuring the gap between the straight-edge and the crankshaft sprocket with feeler gauges. Adjust, if necessary, by altering the thickness of the shim pack behind the crankshaft sprocket. The key must be removed from the crankshaft keyway to allow the shims to be removed.

On 1275 GT models, refit the timing chain tension on the engine front plate.

Refit the oil thrower and timing cover, as detailed previously.

ENGINE MOUNTINGS. . . . . [5]
Left-Hand Side

To replace the left-hand engine mounting the radiator must first be removed as detailed in the COOLING SYSTEM section.

Support the engine assembly with a jack placed under the sump. Remove the two long through-bolts securing the mounting bracket to the gearbox casing (Fig. C:17). Remove the two nuts and bolts securing the mounting to the sub-frame.

On models with the one-piece radiator cowl, if the cowl was left in position on the car, remove the two bolts securing the bottom of the cowl to the engine mounting bracket and lift the cowl out of the engine compartment.

Remove the engine mounting bracket assembly, complete with the engine mounting. The mounting can now be unbolted from the bracket, and the new mounting fitted in its place.

Refit the mounting bracket assembly and radiator in the car, following the reverse sequence of removal.

Right-Hand Side

To replace the right-hand engine mounting, the clutch

Fig. C:12 Pressed-steel type rocker arm (left), and forged type arm fitted with replaceable bush

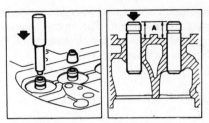

A   Protrusion after installation. Note oil seal fitted over guide on some models

Fig. C:13 Replacing valve guides

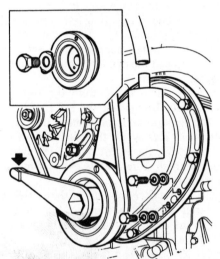

Fig. C:14 Removing timing gear cover

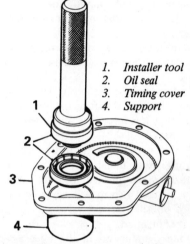

1. Installer tool
2. Oil seal
3. Timing cover
4. Support

Fig. C:15 Installing new oil seal in timing cover

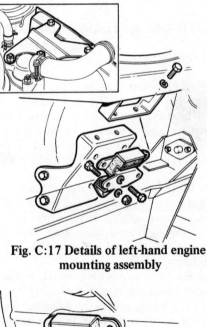

Fig. C:17 Details of left-hand engine mounting assembly

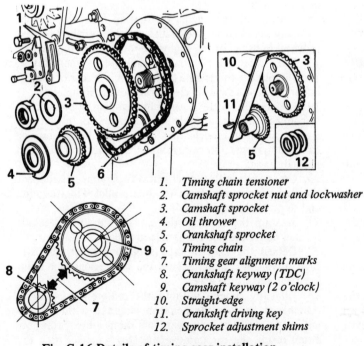

1.   Timing chain tensioner
2.   Camshaft sprocket nut and lockwasher
3.   Camshaft sprocket
4.   Oil thrower
5.   Crankshaft sprocket
6.   Timing chain
7.   Timing gear alignment marks
8.   Crankshaft keyway (TDC)
9.   Camshaft keyway (2 o'clock)
10. Straight-edge
11. Crankshft driving key
12. Sprocket adjustment shims

Fig. C:16 Details of timing gear installation - 1275 GT shown

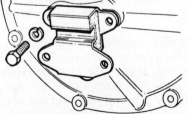

Fig. C:18 Right-hand engine mounting assembly at clutch cover

© BLUK

Engine

cover should be detached from the engine assembly as detailed for clutch replacement. The engine mounting can then be unbolted from the clutch cover and the new mounting fitted in its place (Fig. C:18).

OIL PRESSURE RELIEF VALVE . . . . [6]

The oil pressure relief valve is located under the hexagonal domed nut on the front face of the cylinder block, directly above the starter motor (Fig. C:19).

If the valve plunger is not seating correctly, or the spring is weak, this will prevent the correct oil pressure (60 psi/4.2 kg/cm^2) being maintained in the engine lubrication system.

To examine the valve, unscrew the domes nut with its folded copper washer and withdraw the coil spring and valve plunger.

Check the length of the spring. This should be 2.86 in (72.64 mm). Inspect the face of the valve plunger for pitting, and that the valve is seating correctly. Renew the valve if necessary.

If the valve is only lightly pitted, it can be lapped in on its seating using metal polish. A wooden dowel of appropriate diameter pushed into the open end of the plunger can be used to rotate it while lapping it in. Clean all traces of polish from the valve and seating when this operation is completed.

Refit the components of the valve assembly in the reverse order of removing.

ENGINE/TRANS. AXLE UNIT (MANUAL) . [7]

Removal (Fig. C:21)

1. Disconnect the earth strap from the battery.
2. Remove the bonnet, after first marking the fitted position of the hinges to facilitate alignment when refitting. On some models it will also be necessary to remove the front grille to obtain access to some of the engine components. The grille is secured in position by self-tapping screws.
3. Where fitted, release the heater air intake tube from the front grille and wing valance and secure it clear of the engine. Some later models have a plastic air intake assembly at the right-hand front wing valance and this should be removed after releasing the flexible pipe from beneath the wing.
4. Where the horn is mounted on the bonnet locking platform, disconnect and remove the horn.
5. Drain the cooling system by removing the cylinder block drain plug and/or disconnecting the bottom hose at the radiator.
6. Where required, remove the sump plug and drain the oil out of the engine/transmission unit.
7. Disconnect the heater hose from the adaptor on the radiator bottom hose. Detach the heater water control valve from the rear of the cylinder head and secure it clear of the engine with the hose and cable still attached.
8. Remove the air cleaner assembly. Disconnect the distributor vacuum pipe, fuel supply hose and engine breather pipe (where fitted) from the carburettor. Disconnect the throttle return spring from the carburettor. Remove the carburettor and position it to one side with the throttle and choke cables still attached. Where a cable abutment plate is fitted between the carburettor and the inlet manifold, the plate should be removed with the carburettor.
9. Remove the windscreen washer bottle and bracket, if necessary.
10. Disconnect the exhaust down pipe from the exhaust manifold flange.
11. On early 1275 GT models which have a brake servo unit, disconnect the servo unit vacuum pipe and detach the servo from the right-hand wing valance. It should not be necessary to disconnect the brake pipes as these can be carefully bent to position the unit out of the way once the pipe securing clip has been detached.
12. Disconnect the clutch operating lever return spring at the slave cylinder and detach the slave cylinder from the flywheel housing. It is not necessary to disconnect the hydraulic hose. Suspend the cylinder from a suitable point on the bulkhead.
13. Remove the ignition shield from the front of the engine, where fitted. Disconnect the HT leads from the spark plugs and ignition coil and remove the distributor cap and rotor arm. This avoids the possibility of damage to the cap or arm while the engine is being removed. Label the plug leads with their respective cylinder numbers to facilitate reassembly.
14. Disconnect the starter cable from the starter motor. Where the starter solenoid is mounted on the flywheel housing, detach the solenoid and place it in some suitable position out of the way.
15. Disconnect all other electrical connections from the engine (coil, temperature sender, oil pressure switch, etc). Label the leads if necessary to ensure correct connection on reassembly.
16. Disconnect the engine earth strap from the engine; normally attached to one of the clutch cover bolts at the flywheel housing, or the engine tie-rod on later models.
17. Disconnect the oil pressure gauge pipe, where fitted.
18. Disconnect the engine tie-rod from the rear of the cylinder block and swing it clear or remove it completely.
19. On models with a centrally situated speedometer, disconnect the speedo cable from the rear of the instrument. On other models, the cable must be disconnect from the transmission casing once the power unit has been partially raised.
20. On models with a mechanical fuel pump, disconnect the fuel supply pipe from the pump inlet. Plug the pipe end to prevent loss of fuel.
21. Jack up the front of the car and support on stands located under the sub-frame side-members.
22. Detach the exhaust pipe support bracket from the final drive unit casing. Secure the pipe against the bulkhead and out of the way.
23. On early models without the remote control type gearchange, remove the hexagon plug and withdraw the anti-rattle spring and plunger from the gearbox extension. From inside the car, remove the two bolts securing the gear lever retaining plate and pull the lever out of the casing into the car.

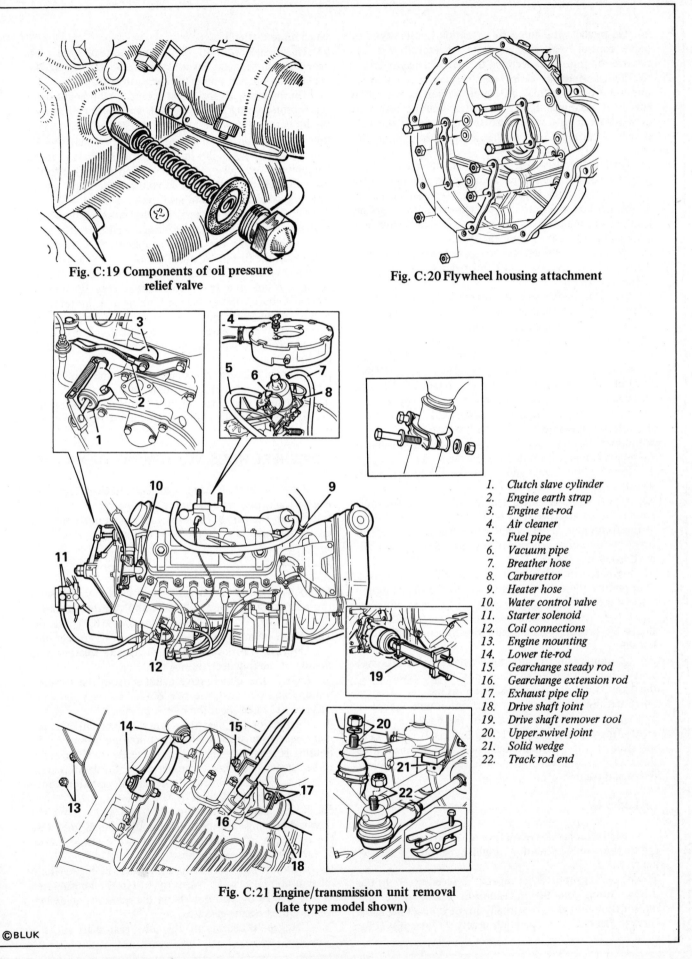

Fig. C:19 Components of oil pressure relief valve

Fig. C:20 Flywheel housing attachment

1. Clutch slave cylinder
2. Engine earth strap
3. Engine tie-rod
4. Air cleaner
5. Fuel pipe
6. Vacuum pipe
7. Breather hose
8. Carburettor
9. Heater hose
10. Water control valve
11. Starter solenoid
12. Coil connections
13. Engine mounting
14. Lower tie-rod
15. Gearchange steady rod
16. Gearchange extension rod
17. Exhaust pipe clip
18. Drive shaft joint
19. Drive shaft remover tool
20. Upper swivel joint
21. Solid wedge
22. Track rod end

Fig. C:21 Engine/transmission unit removal
(late type model shown)

Engine

24. On models with the early extension housing type remote control gear change; from underneath the car, remove the four bolts securing the gear change extension to the transmission casing and separate the extension housing from the final drive unit casing. It will allow sufficient clearance if the extension housing is merely allowed to hang down under the car. Retain the half-moon rubber plug fitted at the extension housing mating face.

25. On later models with rod type remote control gearchange, drift out the roll-pin securing the remote control extension rod to the selector shaft and separate the extension rod from the selector shaft. Remove the through-bolt securing the remote control steady rod fork to the final drive unit housing and release the steady rod.

26. On later models, detach the engine lower tie-rod from the rear of the gearbox casing and swing the tie-rod clear of the power unit.

27. On early models with the rubber coupling type drive shafts, disconnect the drive shafts from the final drive unit by removing the coupling 'U' bolts.

28. On later models with the offset sphere type inboard joint on the drive shaft, disconnect both drive shafts from the final drive unit housng as detailed in the 'FRONT SUSPENSION' section. This involves removing the road wheel, disconnecting the track rod end from the steering arm and separating the upper swivel joint ball pin from the upper suspension arm. The drive shafts can then be withdrawn from the inboard joints, then reconnect the swivel joints and track rods and refit the road wheels.

29. Remove the stands and lower the car back onto its wheels.

30. Attach a suitable lift bracket to the engine. The most common type attaches to two of the cylinder head studs at the front edge of the engine and obviates the need for removing the rocker cover which some other types of lifting bracket require.

31. Support the weight of the engine with lifting tackle, then remove the bolts and nuts securing the engine mountings to the sub-frame at each end of the power unit.

32. Lift the engine sufficiently to ensure that the drive shafts are properly disengaged from the final drive unit housing.

33. At this point, if the speedometer cable has not already been disconnected, it can now be unscrewed from the drive housing on the transmission casing.

34. Carefully lift the engine/transmission unit, complete with the radiator assembly, out of the engine compartment. Where a two position lifting bracket is being used, the straight -lift position should now be used instead of the angled-lift one which should have been used to clear the final drive unit of the bulkhead.

Installation

Installation is basically a reversal of the removal procedure, but special attention should be paid to the following points:-

a) Where appropriate, reconnect the speedo cable to the drive housing on the transmission casing while the transmission unit is only partially lowered into the engine compartment. If this operation is left till later it will be much more difficult.

b) On models without the remote control type gearchange, pull the gear lever up into the car before the engine/transmission unit is lowered into position.

c) On models with the offset sphere type inboard drive shaft joints, ensure the drive shafts are positioned clear of the inboard joints while lowering the engine/transmission unit into position. When assembling the drive shafts to the inboard joints the circlip in the end of the shaft must be compressed and the drive shaft pushed smartly into the joint to lock it in position. Reconnect the upper swivel joint and track rod end and refit the road wheel.

d) On models with the earlier rubber coupling type drive shafts, keep the sliding joints pushed well on to the drive shaft splines while the rubber couplings are moved into position at the final drive unit flanges.

e) On models with the early type remote control gearchange, ensure the half-moon rubber plug is correctly located between the extension housing and the transmission casing when reconnecting the extension housing. Also ensure that the gearchange rod on the transmission engages correctly with the primary shaft in the extension housing.

f) When installation is complete, refill the cooling system, and engine/transmission unit where required. Start the engine and check for oil, water, fuel or exhaust leaks.

g) Finally, check the ignition and idle settings and adjust if necessary.

FLYWHEEL HOUSING/PRIMARY GEAR .. [8]

The flywheel housing can be detached from the engine/transmission unit while the power unit is still installed in the car, but is more easily performed once the engine/transmission unit has been removed.

Removal

1. Detach the flywheel and clutch assembly, following the relevant steps given under the appropriate heading in the 'CLUTCH & MANUAL TRANSMISSION' section. The engine oil must also be drained out of the power unit.

2. On 1275 GT models, unbolt the engine breather from the top of the flywheel housing.

3. Unbolt the clutch slave cylinder from the flywheel housing and place to one side out of the way. It is not necessary to disconnect the hydraulic pipe.

4. Fit tape or foil over the splines of the crankshaft primary gear to protect the flywheel housing oil seal as the housing is removed. This will be unnecessary if the seal is to be renewed anyway. A proper protector sleeve is available as a special tool, but the makeshift solution above will do the same job if a bit of care is used.

5. Knock back the locking plate tabs and remove the flywheel housing securing bolts and nuts (Fig. C:20). Note the respective positions of the nuts and bolts to ensure correct fitment on reassembly.

6. Withdraw the flywheel housing from the engine/transmission unit. It may be necessary to tap the housing free as it is located by two dowels on the transmission casing. Remove the housing gasket.

7. The needle bearing of the idler gear shaft and the

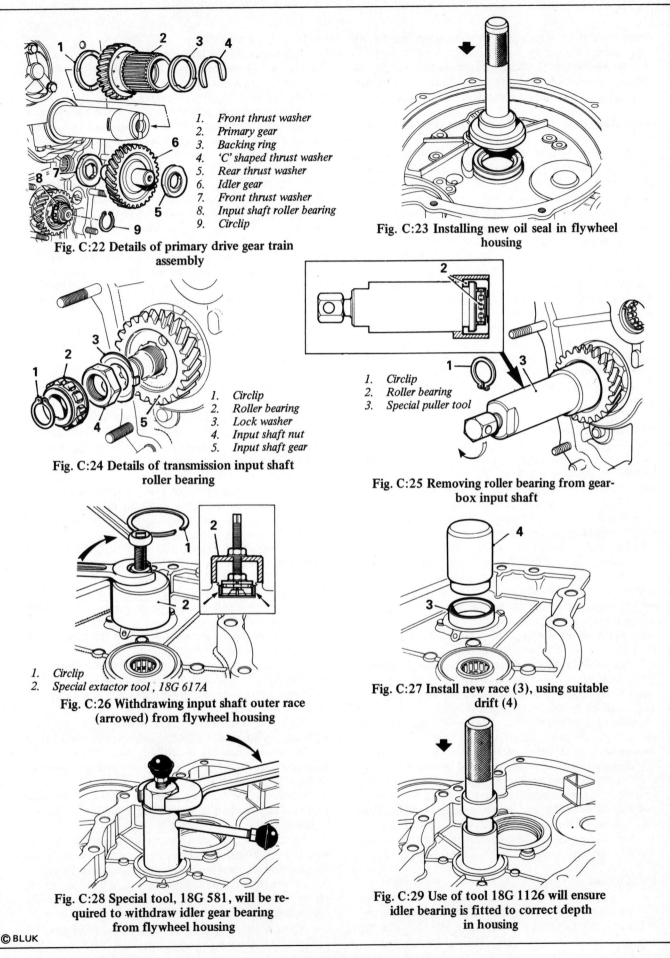

1. Front thrust washer
2. Primary gear
3. Backing ring
4. 'C' shaped thrust washer
5. Rear thrust washer
6. Idler gear
7. Front thrust washer
8. Input shaft roller bearing
9. Circlip

Fig. C:22 Details of primary drive gear train assembly

Fig. C:23 Installing new oil seal in flywheel housing

1. Circlip
2. Roller bearing
3. Lock washer
4. Input shaft nut
5. Input shaft gear

Fig. C:24 Details of transmission input shaft roller bearing

1. Circlip
2. Roller bearing
3. Special puller tool

Fig. C:25 Removing roller bearing from gear-box input shaft

1. Circlip
2. Special extactor tool , 18G 617A

Fig. C:26 Withdrawing input shaft outer race (arrowed) from flywheel housing

Fig. C:27 Install new race (3), using suitable drift (4)

Fig. C:28 Special tool, 18G 581, will be required to withdraw idler gear bearing from flywheel housing

Fig. C:29 Use of tool 18G 1126 will ensure idler bearing is fitted to correct depth in housing

© BLUK

outer race of the gearbox input shaft roller bearing will come away with the flywheel housing.

8.   Withdraw the 'C' shaped thrust washer locating the primary gear on the crankshaft, and slide off the backing ring, primary gear and inner thrust washer (Fig. C:22).

Inspection and Overhaul - Primary Gear Oil Seal

The primary gear oil seal in the flywheel housing should be renewed if it shows any signs of wear, damage or oil leakage. If the engine has covered a large mileage, a new seal should be fitted as a matter of course.

Lever the old seal out of its location in the housing, taking great care to avoid damaging the housing bore.

Lubricate the new seal with grease or engine oil and press it into position in the housing. The proper seal installer tool is shown in Fig. C:23, but it should be possible to press the seal into position by hand or by tapping it carefully on its outer edge. In this latter case, support the underside of the housing beneath the seal aperture while installing the seal.

It should be noted that the flywheel housing oil seal can be renewed while the housing is still in position on the engine/transmission unit. The procedure for this operation is fully detailed under the appropriate heading later in this section.

Flywheel Housing

As noted during the removal procedure, the needle bearing of the idler gearshaft and the outer race of the gearbox input shaft roller bearing are located in the flywheel housing and will come away with the housing when removed. If either of these bearings require to be renewed, they should be replaced as follows:-

To remove the gearbox input shaft outer race from the housing, first extract the circlip retaining the race in the housing. Expand the housing by immersing it in very hot water, then withdraw the race from the bore. A special extractor tool, such as that shown in Fig. C:26, will be required to remove the race. Press the new race into position in the housing, using a suitable size of drift (Fig. C:27). Refit the bearing retaining clip.

The roller bearing itself can be pulled off the gearbox input shaft after removing the retaining circlip. In most cases it should be possible to lever the bearing off the shaft, but the proper puller tool is shown in Fig. C:25. Fit the new bearing onto the shaft and tap into position, bearing only on the inner diameter of the bearing. Secure the bearing with the retaining circlip.

A suitable extractor tool, such as that shown in Fig. C:28, will also be required to withdraw the idler gear shaft bearing from the housing. Tap the new needle bearing into position, bearing only on the outer diameter of the bearing. The use of the proper installer tool, shown in Fig. C:-29, will ensure that the bearing is installed to the correct depth in the bore.

Installation

1.   Ensure that the mating faces on the flywheel housing, cylinder block and transmission casing are clean and free from old gasket material.

2.   If the idler gear or idler gear thrust washers have been changed, it will be necessary to check the idler gear end-float and adjust if necessary as detailed under the 'TRANSMISSION CASING' heading later in this section.

3.   If the crankshaft primary gear or thrust washers have been changed, the gear end-float should be checked and adjusted, if needed, as detailed below. It should be noted that the primary gear end-float can be checked with the flywheel housing in position on the engine/transmission unit as shown in Fig. C:30, but if the end-float requires adjustment the flywheel housing oil seal must be removed together with the primary gear to change the front thrust washer. A new housing oil seal must be fitted on reassembly.

a)   Fit the primary gear front thrust washer onto the crankshaft with its chamfered side against the crankshaft register (See Fig. C:30). Fit the primary gear and backing washer and secure in position with the 'C' shaped rear thrust washer.

b)   Measure the primary gear end-float with feeler gauges between the backing washer and the end of the gear (Fig. C:31).

c)   The gear end-float should be 0.0035 - 0.0065 in (0.089 - 0.165 mm). If the end-float is outside these figures, select a thrust washer to bring the end-float within the specified limits. Thrust washers are available in five thicknesses from 0.110 to 0.120 in (2.80 - 3.05 mm) in 0.002 in (0.05 mm) stages. The thickness of the existing thrust washer should be measured with a micrometer to determine its size for comparison.

d)   Very early engines were fitted with a primary gear which had an oil feed provided to the bushes. These are identifiable by the additional oil seal fitted to the flywheel. The running clearance is slightly less for this type of gear, being 0.003 - 0.006 in (0.076 - 0.152 mm). Thrust washers in this case are available only in three sizes, from 0.125 to 0.131 in (3.17 - 3.32 mm).

e)   Refit the primary gear assembly with its selected thrust washer and recheck that the end-float is now within the specified tolerance.

4.   Fit the protector sleeve or tape over the primary gear splines to protect the flywheel housing oil seal.

5.   Two pilot bars, made up and screwed into two bottom tapped holes in cylinder block as shown in Fig. C:32, will help locate the flywheel housing in position and take the weight off the primary gear oil seal.

6.   Pack the transmission input shaft bearing rollers with high melting point grease to help prevent them tilting as the flywheel housing is refitted. Also ensure that the idler gear thrust washer is correctly in position on the end of the idler gear shaft (Fig. C:22).

7.   Position a new housing gasket on the engine/transmission face and ensure that both locating dowels are fully in their holes.

8.   Lubricate the primary gear oil seal and fit the flywheel housing into position. Tap it fully home onto the locating dowels, then remove the two pilot bars if used.

9.   Secure the housing in position with the retaining nuts and bolts, using new locking plates. Ensure that the bolts are refitted in their original locations - this is most important as the oil gallery in the cylinder block may be

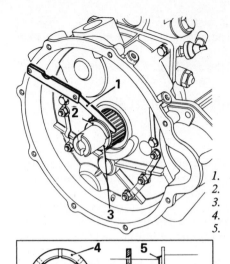

1. Feeler gauges
2. 'C' shaped thrust washer
3. Backing ring
4. Front thrust washer
5. Crankshaft register

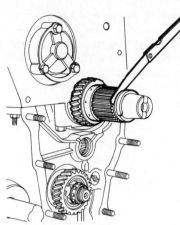

Fig. C:31 Checking crankshaft primary
gear end-float

Fig. C:30 Primary gear end-float can be
checked with flywheel housing in
position, as shown

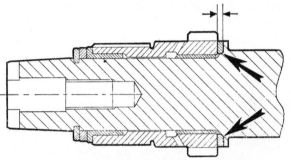

Fig. C:33 Crankshaft primary gear end-float.
Chamfered side of thrust washer (arrowed)

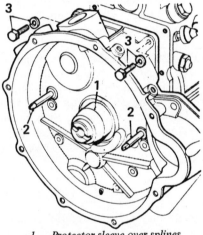

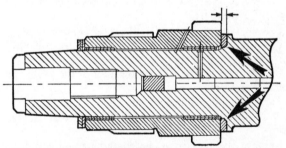

Fig. C:34 Early models have primary gear with
lubricated bushes. Note oil feed drilling
in crankshaft

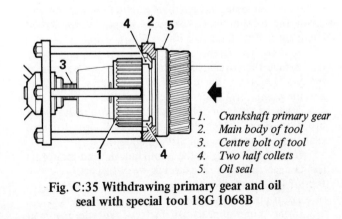

1. Protector sleeve over splines
2. Pilot bars
3. Retaining bolts

Fig. C:32 Installing flywheel housing

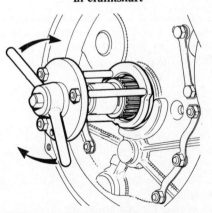

1. Crankshaft primary gear
2. Main body of tool
3. Centre bolt of tool
4. Two half collets
5. Oil seal

Fig. C:35 Withdrawing primary gear and oil
seal with special tool 18G 1068B

Fig. C:36 Use remover tool with adaptor
ring 18G 1043 to install new oil seal
in flywheel housing

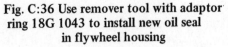

damaged if a long bolt is fitted in the right-hand upper position.

10. Tighten the flywheel housing nuts and bolts to their specified torque of 18 lb ft (2.5 kg m), then secure with the locking plate tabs.

11. On 1275 GT models, refit the engine breather to the flywheel housing.

12. Refit the clutch/flywheel assembly as detailed in the CLUTCH & MANUAL TRANSMISSION section.

13. Finally, refill the engine/transmission unit with oil as detailed in the ROUTINE MAINTENANCE section.

PRIMARY GEAR OIL SEAL . . . . [9]

The crankshaft primary gear oil seal is located in the flywheel housing and if worn or damaged can be replaced with the power unit in position in the car. However, a special tool is required to withdraw the primary gear and oil seal and unless this tool is available it will be necessary to remove the flywheel housing as detailed previously in order to renew the seal.

Replacement

1. Remove the clutch cover and the clutch and flywheel assembly as detailed in the CLUTCH & MANUAL TRANSMISSION section.

2. Remove the 'C' shaped thrust washer and backing ring securing the primary gear on the crankshaft.

3. Withdraw the primary gear and oil seal from the flywheel housing, using the special puller tool (18G 1068B), as follows:-

a) Screw the centre-bolt of the tool securely into the end of the crankshaft.

b) Pull the primary gear outwards as far as possible.

c) Pull the body of the tool over the centre-bolt until the groove in the primary gear is visible inside the tool.

d) Fit the two half collets of the tool in the groove in the gear (Fig. C:35).

e) Turn the winged nut of the tool anti-clockwise to withdraw the primary gear and oil seal clear of the housing.

f) Remove the tool from the crankshaft and withdraw the primary gear and oil seal.

4. Fit the special adaptor (tool 18G 1043) over the primary gear.

5. Lubricate the new oil seal liberally with engine oil.

6. Fit the seal protector sleeve or tape over the splines of the primary gear to protect the lips of the new seal and slide the seal onto the primary gear. Remove the protector sleeve or tape once the seal is in place.

7. Smear the primary gear front thrust washer with grease and fit it onto the crankshaft with its chamfered edge against the shoulder on the crankshaft.

8. Slide the primary gear with the oil seal onto the crankshaft until the gear teeth start to engage with those of the idler gear. The oil seal should now be contacting the housing bore while still being seated on the sealing surface of the gear.

9. Fit the tool over the crankshaft and screw the winged nut in a clockwise direction down the centre-bolt to press the seal into the housing (Fig. C:36). The seal is correctly fitted when the base of the tool contacts the lip of the housing bore. Remove the tool and adaptor.

10. Refit the backing ring and 'C' shaped thrust washer on the crankshaft.

11. Finally, refit the clutch and flywheel assembly.

OIL PUMP (MANUAL MODELS) . . . . [10]

Removal

The oil pump is easily removed once the flywheel housing has been detached from the engine/transmission unit as detailed previously.

Knock back the locking plate tabs and remove the pump retaining bolts and locking plate. The pump can now be withdrawn together with its gasket (Figs. C:37, or C:38).

On 1275 GT models, the pump is of the 'star-drive' type and the splined coupling will either be removed with the pump or left in the end of the camshaft. In the latter case, the coupling can be easily withdrawn if required. Other models have a 'pin-drive' type pump and no separate coupling is used.

Installation

Install the pump in the reverse order of removing. Use a new gasket and locking plate. Ensure that the pump inlet and delivery ports are not obstructed by the gasket when fitting.

On models with the 'pin-drive' type pump, align the slot in the end of the pump drive shaft with the pin on the camshaft before positioning the pump on the cylinder block. Ensure the pin engages correctly with the camshaft.

On 1275 GT models, fit the coupling on the pump drive spindle before positioning the pump on the cylinder block. Again ensure that the coupling engages correctly with the camshaft.

Overhaul

The oil pump may either be of Hobourne-Eaton or Concentric Pumps manufacture. The overhaul procedure below applies only to the Hobourne-Eaton unit, as the latter type is serviced as an assembly only (Fig. C:39).

In most cases of wear or damage to the components of the oil pump, it will be more economical to obtain a complete new pump rather than to obtain new parts and repair the existing unit. The pump should be dismantled and inspected to determine its condition as follows:-

Remove the screw securing the cover to pump body and detach the cover. Note that the cover is also located by two dowels on the pump body. Withdraw the rotors and the pump drive shaft from the body.

Wash all parts in solvent and dry thoroughly. Use a brush to clean the inside of the pump housing. Ensure that all metal particles and dirt are removed.

Inspect the inside of the pump housing and the rotors for damage and signs of excessive wear. Inspect the inside face of the pump cover for scores, grooves or other signs of wear; if present, the cover must be replaced.

If the pump appears satisfactory, refit the rotors in

the pump body, ensuring that the chamfered edge of the outer rotor enters the pump body first.

Check the clearance between the lobes of the inner and outer rotors (Figs. C:40, or C:41). The wear limit is 0.006 in (0.152 mm).

Check the clearance between the outer rotor and the pump housing. The wear limit in this case is 0.010 in (0.254 mm).

Check the rotor end-float by placing a straight-edge across the face of the pump body, and measuring the clearance between the straight-edge and the end of the rotors. The clearance must not exceed 0.005 in (0.127 mm). If the end-float is excessive, but the other clearances are within the wear limits, the pump face can be carefully lapped on a flat surface, after removing the two locating dowels, to bring the end-float within the limit.

If the components are in satisfactory condition, re-assemble the pump. Lubricate the rotors and pump housing liberally with engine oil before fitting the pump cover. Finally, check the pump for freedom of action.

CAMSHAFT & CAM FOLLOWERS . . . . . . [11]

The engine/transmission unit must be removed from the car to enable removal of the camshaft and followers. In the case of the 1275 GT, which does not have detachable side covers on the cylinder block, the camshaft can be removed downwards and therefore the transmission unit must first be removed to enable their removal.

TRANSMISSION UNIT (MANUAL). . . . . . [12]

Removal (Fig. C:45)

With the engine/transmission unit removed from the car, remove the clutch cover, the flywheel and clutch assembly and the flywheel housing, following the relevant steps given under the appropriate headings previously. It should be noted that the engine oil must be drained from the power unit during removal.

If required, the crankshaft primary gear can be removed from the end of the crankshaft, together with its thrust washers.

Remove the bolts securing the radiator to the left-hand engine mounting bracket and detach the radiator assembly.

If required, remove the oil filter cartridge or filter bowl from the filter head.

Remove all the nuts, bolts and spring washers securing the engine to the transmission casing, then lift the engine to separate it from the transmission unit.

Remove the gaskets and oil way sealing ring from the joint faces, and the oil seal from the front main bearing cap.

Installation

Installation is basically a reversal of the removal procedure.

Ensure that the joint faces on both the crankcase and transmission casing are clean and free from old gasket material before fitting new gaskets on the transmission casing. Check that the oil feed O-ring is in good condition and correctly in place at the oil feed hole on the transmission casing flange.

Lubricate the new oil sealing strip before fitting it in position at the engine front main bearing.

Lower the engine onto the transmission unit and fit and tighten the securing bolts and nuts.

If a replacement transmission unit is being fitted, it will be necessary to check the idler gear end-float before finally assembling the flywheel housing to the unit. The primary gear assembly must be removed from the crankshaft for this operation.

a) Fit the existing thrust washer onto the longer spindle of idler gear shaft and assemble to gear to the transmission with this end into the transmission casing.

b) Using two thin washers of suitable inside diameter to fit over the idler gear shaft, interpose a piece of dental wax between the washers and assemble them onto the flywheel side of the idler gear (Fig. C:46).

c) Fit a new flywheel housing gasket onto the engine/transmission unit flange and assemble the flywheel housing to unit. Fit the housing securing nuts and bolts and tighten to their specified torques.

d) Now remove the flywheel housing and discard the gasket. The gasket must not be re-used when finally assembling the housing.

e) Carefully remove the two washers with the dental wax interposed and measure the total thickness of the assembly with a micrometer. From the measurement figure obtained, subtract 0.004 - 0.007 in (0.102 - 0.178 mm) to give the specified gear end-float.

f) Select a thrust washer of the required thickness from the range available. There are four sizes of thrust washer from 0.132 to 0.139 in (3.35 - 3.53 mm) in stages of 0.002 in (0.05 mm).

g) Assemble the selected thrust washer on the idler gear, refit the primary gear with its thrust washers and backing ring and fit the flywheel housing using a new gasket.

CRANKSHAFT, CONRODS & PISTONS . . . [13]

Removal

1. Remove the engine/transmission unit from the car, and separate the engine from the transmission unit as detailed previously.

2. Remove the cylinder head following the relevant steps given under the appropriate heading previously.

3. Invert the cylinder block so that it is resting on the cylinder head face.

4. For each piston and connecting rod in turn:-

a) Turn the crankshaft as necessary to bring the connecting rod to the bottom of its travel.

b) Check that the rod and big end bearing cap are suitably marked with their respective cylinder numbers.

c) On 1275 GT models, release the multi-sided nuts securing the big end cap (Fig. C:48). Tap the ends of the studs with the handle of a hammer, or similar, to release the bearing cap and detach the cap together with its bearing shell.

d) On all other models, release the locking plate tabs and unscrew the cap retaining bolts two or three turns (Fig. 47). Tap the bolts to release the big end bearing cap, then completely remove the bolts and locking plate and detach the cap together with its bearing shell.

e) Push the piston and connecting rod assembly up the cylinder bore and carefully withdraw it from the top of the block.

f) If required, remove the bearing shells from the cap and rod. Suitably identify the shells with their respective locations if they are to be re-used.

5. Remove the timing cover and the timing chain and gears as detailed previously.

6. Remove the generator/alternator adjusting link bracket.

7. Remove the three bolts securing the camshaft locating plate and lift off the plate.

8. Remove the retaining screws and detach the first adaptor plate from the front face of the cylinder block (Fig. C:49).

9. Withdraw the 'C' shaped thrust washer locating the crankshaft primary gear and slide the backing ring, primary gear and front thrust washer off the rear end of the crankshaft.

10. Check that the main bearing caps are suitably marked with their respective locations.

11. Release the cap retaining bolts and detach the three main bearing caps together with their bearing shells. The bottom halves of the crankshaft thrust washers will be removed with the centre main bearing cap (Fig. C:50).

12. Carefully lift the crankshaft out of the crankcase.

13. Remove the remaining halves of the thrust washers from each side of the centre main bearing.

14. Remove the upper bearing shells from their locations in the crankcase. Identify the bearing shells and thrust washers if they are to be re-used.

Inspection and Overhaul

NOTE: The components of the cylinder head assembly have already been dealt with under the heading 'CYLINDER HEAD'.

Cylinder Bores

Inspect the cylinder walls carefully for any signs of damage, i.e. scoring, scuffing or roughness. Examine the top of the bore at the limit of piston travel for evidence of a ridge or step, especially at right-angles to the crankshaft axis, indicating bore wear.

If the bores appear in reasonable condition they should be checked for taper and ovality with an accurate internal micrometer.

Pistons

Three different methods of retaining the piston pin are used depending on application, and each requires a different dismantling technique. In each case, ensure that the

cylinder number and the relationship of the piston to the connecting rod is suitably marked before dismantling as the big end offset may be positioned either at the front or at the rear of the assembly, depending on the location of the rod in the engine.

On 848 cc models the piston pin is clamped in the connecting rod small end by a clamp bolt (Fig. C:52). To remove the piston pin, hold the pin in a vice between two plugs to avoid damaging the piston, and unscrew the clamp bolt. Push out the piston pin and separate the piston from the connecting rod.

998 cc and 1098 cc models have fully-floating piston pins which are located in the piston by a circlip at each end (Fig. C:53). Mark the piston and pin before dismantling to ensure that the pin is refitted in the same side of the piston from which it was removed. Remove the circlips and press out the piston pin by hand. It may be necessary to expand the piston by immersing it in hot water to enable the pin to be removed.

On 1275 GT models, the piston pin is a press fit in the connecting rod small end, and only the interference fit of the pin in the small end retains it in position. The piston pin can sometimes be driven out using a suitable drift, but there is a real danger that the piston may be damaged or distorted during this operation. It is best to have the pin pressed out and refitted by an Authorised Dealer or Specialist who will have the proper tools to carry out this job. As before, the piston and pin should be suitably marked before dismantling.

The 848 cc, 998 cc and 1098 cc pistons have the piston pin bore offset in relation to the centre-line of the piston. When installed in the engine, the offset must be towards the camshaft side and therefore it is essential that the pistons are correctly fitted to their respective connecting rods. The word 'FRONT' or arrow head symbol on the piston crown must be towards the front of the engine, and the number stamped on the connecting rod and cap facing towards the camshaft side of the engine.

The 1275 GT pistons do not have an offset piston pin bore but the piston will normally still have the front side marked for ease of fitment.

Piston Rings

It is recommended that new piston rings be fitted as a matter of course when overhauling the engine.

Where new rings are being installed in a used cylinder, the glaze must first be removed from the cylinder wall. A proper Glaze Breaker tool should ideally be used for this purpose, but in its absence fine emery cloth can be used instead. In this latter case, ensure that all traces of abrasive are cleaned off the cylinder walls when the job is completed.

Before fitting the rings to the pistons, check the end-gap of each piston in its respective cylinder bore with the feeler gauges (Fig. C:55). Use an inverted piston to position the ring squarely in the bore. If the gap is outside the specified limits, try another ring set.

Also check the fit of each ring in its respective piston groove. The ring should seat easily in the groove and be able to rotate freely around the circumference of the groove without binding.

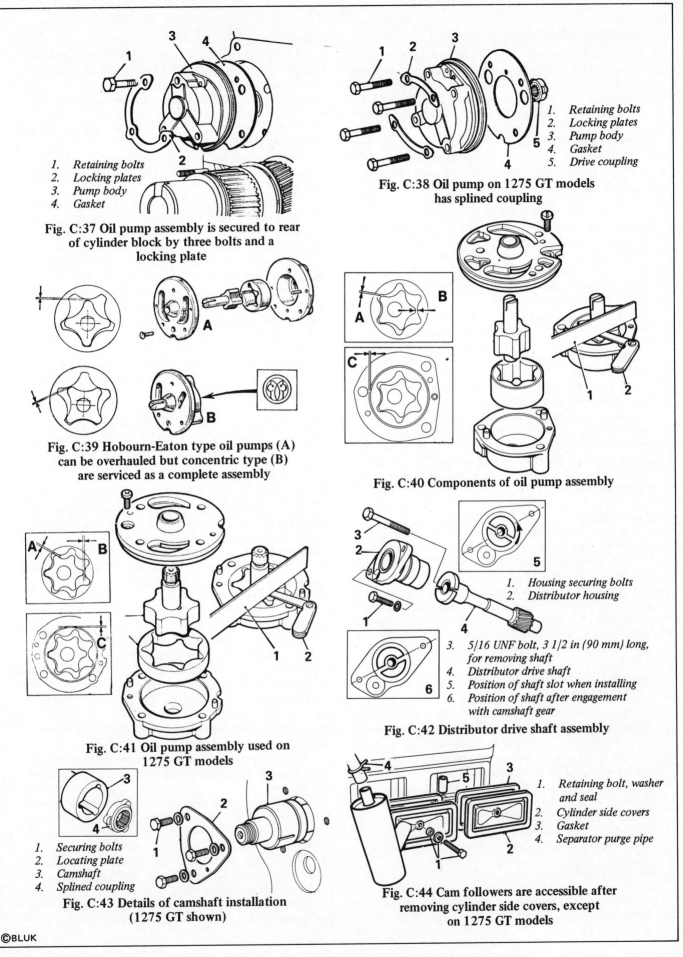

1. Retaining bolts
2. Locking plates
3. Pump body
4. Gasket

Fig. C:37 Oil pump assembly is secured to rear
of cylinder block by three bolts and a
locking plate

1. Retaining bolts
2. Locking plates
3. Pump body
4. Gasket
5. Drive coupling

Fig. C:38 Oil pump on 1275 GT models
has splined coupling

Fig. C:39 Hobourn-Eaton type oil pumps (A)
can be overhauled but concentric type (B)
are serviced as a complete assembly

Fig. C:40 Components of oil pump assembly

Fig. C:41 Oil pump assembly used on
1275 GT models

1. Housing securing bolts
2. Distributor housing
3. 5/16 UNF bolt, 3 1/2 in (90 mm) long,
   for removing shaft
4. Distributor drive shaft
5. Position of shaft slot when installing
6. Position of shaft after engagement
   with camshaft gear

Fig. C:42 Distributor drive shaft assembly

1. Securing bolts
2. Locating plate
3. Camshaft
4. Splined coupling

Fig. C:43 Details of camshaft installation
(1275 GT shown)

1. Retaining bolt, washer
   and seal
2. Cylinder side covers
3. Gasket
4. Separator purge pipe

Fig. C:44 Cam followers are accessible after
removing cylinder side covers, except
on 1275 GT models

©BLUK

Connecting Rods

In the 848 cc, 998 cc and 1098 cc engines, the connecting rod big end is split at 45°, but the big end bosses on alternate rods are offset to different sides of the assembly in relation to the rod centre line. The odd pair of rods have the offset to the rear and the even pair have it to the front (Fig. C:58). The connecting rod assemblies for No. 1 and No. 3 cylinders are identical and are interchangeable when new, as are those for the No. 2 and No. 4 cylinders. However, when refitting used parts it is essential that they should be fitted in their original positions.

These rods, once installed in the engine, must be located with the big end split angled upwards towards the camshaft side of the engine (Fig. C:47). The stamped number on the rod and cap, where present, should also face towards the camshaft. With the clamped-type rod, the small end clamp bolt should also be on the camshaft side of the assembly (Fig. C:52).

In the 1275 GT engine, the connecting rod bosses are also offset, but, as the big end is split horizontally, all the rods are similar and interchangeable. Where the rods are numbered, this is normally marked on the camshaft side of the assembly (Fig. C:48).

The connecting rods used in the 1098 cc engine differ from the others in that they have a bronze bush fitted at the small end, and this can be replaced if worn or damaged (Fig. C:54). All the others have a plain small end. The old bush must be pressed out and a new one pressed in, then the bush reamed to size. This job is best left to a Specialist who will have the proper equipment to carry out the work.

Crankshaft

Inspect each bearing journal for signs of scratches, grooves or other damage.

The diameter of each journal should be measured in at least four places with an accurate micrometer to determine taper, ovality or undersize. If wear is excessive or if any of the journal surfaces are severely marred, the crankshaft should be reground or replaced. If any journals will not clean up within the minimum specified regrind diameter, the crankshaft must be replaced.

Main & Big End Bearings, and Thrust Washers

The bearing surface of each bearing shell should be inspected carefully for signs of chips, pitting or excessive wear. The bearing base may be visible, but this does not necessarily mean that the bearing is excessively worn. It is not necessary to fit new bearing shells in this case unless the bearing clearance is outside the specified limits.

Check the clearance of bearings which appear to be satisfactory, as described below.

Inspect the thrust washer halves in a similar manner to the bearing shells and replace if worn or damaged.

Bearing Clearances

The procedure given below is for checking the main bearing clearances, but the big end bearings are checked in a similar manner.

1. Ensure that the crankshaft surface, bearing shells and bearing caps are prefectly clean and free from oil and dirt.
2. Fit the upper halves of the bearing shells into their locations in the crankcase, then carefully lower the crankshaft into place in the crankcase.
3. Fit the lower half of the shell into the cap of the bearing being measured.
4. Place a piece of Plastigage across the full width of the crankshaft journal and about 1/4 in (6 mm) off-centre (Fig. C:59).
5. Plastigage is a trade name for an accurately calibrated plastic filament and is available in three different diameters for the range between 0.001 and 0.009 in (0.025 - 0.23 mm). In most cases the small diameter Type PG1 (Green) pack for the range 0.001 - 0.003 in (0.025 - 0.075 mm) will suffice.
6. Install the main bearing cap and tighten the cap bolts to their normal specified torque of 63 lb ft (8.7 kg m). None of the remaining bearing caps must be fitted during this procedure. Each bearing must be measured individually.
7. Release the cap bolts and remove the bearing cap. Note that the crankshaft must not be moved while the Plastigage is in position.
8. Measure the width of the compressed plastic filament, using the scale provided on the Plastigage pack (Fig. C:61). The widest point will give the minimum clearance and the narrowest point the maximum clearance. The difference between the two readings will therefore give the taper on the journal.
9. To check the journal for ovality, clean all traces of Plastigage material from both the journal and bearing shell. Rotate the crankshaft a quarter of a turn and repeat the measuring procedure. The difference between the two readings will indicate the out-of-round of the journal.
10. When measurement is completed, clean all Plastigage material off both bearing shell and crankshaft journal. This is most important.

Installation

1. Install the crankshaft in the reverse order of removal, with special attention to the following points:-
a) Ensure all oilways in the crankshaft are clear. This can be done by blowing out the passages with an air line, but in some cases it may be necessary to probe the passages with a piece of wire.
b) If the original bearing shells are being re-used, ensure that they are refitted in their original locations.
c) Ensure that the locating tag on each bearing shell correctly engages the corresponding notch in the crankcase or bearing cap.
d) Fit the half thrust washers on each side of the main bearing and cap with the oil grooves facing away from the bearing housing (Fig. C:50). The tab on the lower washers must locate in the slot on the centre main bearing cap.
e) Ensure that all the bearing surfaces are perfectly clean, then lubricate the bearing surfaces with clean engine oil before assembly.
f) Ensure that the bearing caps are refitted in their correct positions, indicated by the identification marks made

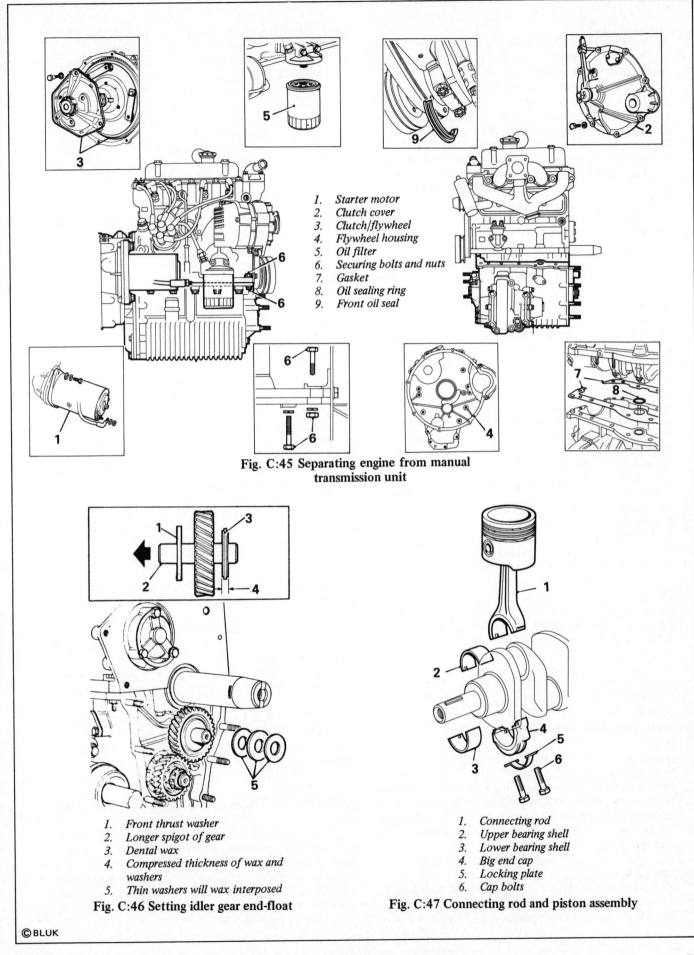

1. Starter motor
2. Clutch cover
3. Clutch/flywheel
4. Flywheel housing
5. Oil filter
6. Securing bolts and nuts
7. Gasket
8. Oil sealing ring
9. Front oil seal

Fig. C:45 Separating engine from manual transmission unit

1. Front thrust washer
2. Longer spigot of gear
3. Dental wax
4. Compressed thickness of wax and washers
5. Thin washers will wax interposed

Fig. C:46 Setting idler gear end-float

1. Connecting rod
2. Upper bearing shell
3. Lower bearing shell
4. Big end cap
5. Locking plate
6. Cap bolts

Fig. C:47 Connecting rod and piston assembly

previously.

g) Tighten the cap bolts evenly to their specified torque of 63 lb ft (8.7 kg m), then check that the crankshaft rotates freely and smoothly.

2. Check the crankshaft end-float using either a dial gauge or feeler gauges. In the former case, locate the dial gauge with the stylus in contact with the machined surface of the crankshaft throw, then lever the crankshaft fully forward and zero the dial gauge. Lever the crank in the opposite direction and note the gauge reading. If the end float exceeds the specified limits of 0.001 - 0.005 in (0.025 - 0.127 mm), rectify by selecting and fitting new thrust washers of the required thickness. If feeler gauges are being used, measure the clearance between the thrust washers and the crankshaft face with the crankshaft pushed fully in one direction.

3. If the pistons were separated from their connecting rods, they should now be reassembled, noting the following points:-

a) When fitting used parts it is essential that they be refitted in their original positions.

b) The cylinder number on the piston should match that on the connecting rod and cap.

c) The 'FRONT' or arrow head marking on the piston crown must be positioned to the front, and the number stamped on the connecting rod and cap must be to the left-hand side (camshaft side) of the assembly (Fig. C:53).

d) Check that the big end boss has the correct offset. The odd (1 and 3) pair of rods have the offset towards the rear of the engine, and the even (2 and 4) pair have it towards the front (Fig. C:58).

e) Apply a light coat of graphited oil to the piston pin and the bosses in the piston and connecting rod, then fit the piston pin. The pin should be a thumb push-fit at normal room temperature (20°C).

f) Tighten the small end clamp bolt, or secure the pin in the piston with the two retaining circlips, as appropriate. In the latter case ensure that both circlips seal correctly in their grooves.

g) On 1275 GT models the piston pin is an interference fit in the connecting rod small end and must be pressed into place. This operation is best left to an Authorised Dealer or Specialist who will have the proper equipment to carry out the job.

4. Assemble the piston rings on the piston, following the instructions supplied with the new rings. The rings must be fitted from the top of the piston. The rings will normally be marked 'TOP' on one face, and this side should face towards the piston crown (Fig. C:56). Service rings for use in worn bores normally have a stepped top ring to avoid the wear ridge at the top of the bore. It is most important that these rings be fitted with the stepped portion uppermost, otherwise breakage of the rings will result when the engine is run. Where possible, proper piston ring pliers should be used to expand the rings when fitting them as this will eliminate the possibility of ring breakage or damage to the piston.

5. For each piston and connecting rod assembly in turn:-

a) Lubricate the cylinder bore and piston rings liberally with clean engine oil.

b) Install the piston assembly in its correct respective bore with 'FRONT' or arrow head mark on the piston crown pointing towards the front of the block.

c) Position the piston rings so that their gaps are spaced out equally on the non-thrust side of the piston.

d) Compress the piston ring using a proper ring compressor tool, such as that shown in Fig. C:48. Do NOT attempt to fit the pistons by hand otherwise breakage of the rings may result. Carefully tap the piston into the cylinder bore, using the handle end of a hammer, until the piston crown is slightly below the top of the cylinder. Take great care to avoid the connecting rod hitting the crankshaft journal.

e) Fit the bearing shells dry in the connecting rod and caps, ensuring that the locating tag on each shell correctly engages the corresponding notch in the bearing housing.

f) Coat the crankshaft journal and bearings liberally with engine oil, then pull the connecting rod assembly down firmly onto the crankpin and fit the cap to the rod.

g) Check that the identification numbers on the cap and rod match, and are on the same side of the assembly (Fig. C:48, and C:53).

h) On 1275 GT models, ensure that the cap is correctly located, then fit the two multi-sided nuts and tighten to their specified torque of 33 lb ft (4.6 kg m).

i) On 850, 1000 and 1100 models, fit the big end cap bolts with a new locking plate and tighten to their specified torque of 37 lb ft (5.1 kg m). Tap over the locking plate tabs to secure (Fig. C:47).

j) Check that the connecting rod has sufficient end-float on the crank-pin.

6. Refit the adaptor plate to the front face of the cylinder block, using a new gasket, and tighten the securing screws (Fig. C:49).

7. Refit the camshaft locating plate, with the white metal side towards the camshaft journal, and secure with the three bolts.

8. Refit the generator/alternator adjusting link bracket on the cylinder block.

9. Reassemble the timing chain and gears, and the timing cover as detailed under the appropriate heading previously.

10. Refit the crankshaft primary gear assembly, and check and adjust the gear end-float, if necessary, as detailed previously.

11. Refit the cylinder head assembly, noting the points given under the heading 'CYLINDER HEAD' earlier in this section.

12. Finally, assemble the engine to the transmission casing and refit the power unit in the car. Refer to the appropriate headings previously for details of any special points of note.

AUTOMATIC TRANSMISSION MODELS. . [14]

The subsequent items in this section apply specifically to models fitted with automatic transmission. In most cases, in the interests of brevity and simplicity, only the variations in procedure from the equivalent operations for the manual transmissions models are given, and back-reference to the relevant previous headings should be made where indicated.

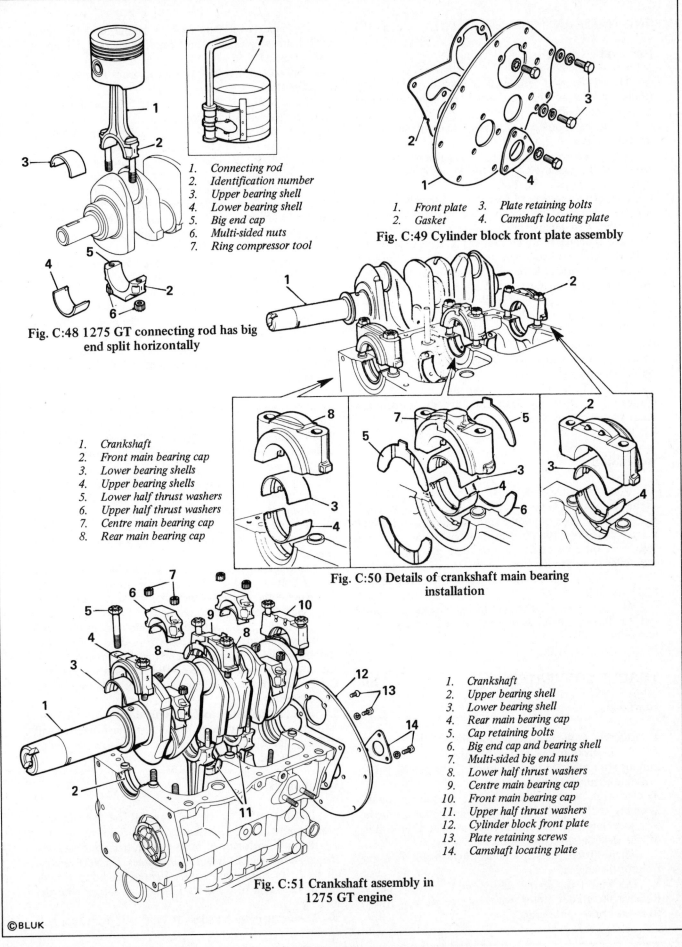

1. Connecting rod
2. Identification number
3. Upper bearing shell
4. Lower bearing shell
5. Big end cap
6. Multi-sided nuts
7. Ring compressor tool

Fig. C:48 1275 GT connecting rod has big end split horizontally

1. Front plate
2. Gasket
3. Plate retaining bolts
4. Camshaft locating plate

Fig. C:49 Cylinder block front plate assembly

1. Crankshaft
2. Front main bearing cap
3. Lower bearing shells
4. Upper bearing shells
5. Lower half thrust washers
6. Upper half thrust washers
7. Centre main bearing cap
8. Rear main bearing cap

Fig. C:50 Details of crankshaft main bearing installation

1. Crankshaft
2. Upper bearing shell
3. Lower bearing shell
4. Rear main bearing cap
5. Cap retaining bolts
6. Big end cap and bearing shell
7. Multi-sided big end nuts
8. Lower half thrust washers
9. Centre main bearing cap
10. Front main bearing cap
11. Upper half thrust washers
12. Cylinder block front plate
13. Plate retaining screws
14. Camshaft locating plate

Fig. C:51 Crankshaft assembly in 1275 GT engine

Engine

ENGINE/TRANSMISSION (AUTO) . . . . [15]

Removal

The engine and transmission unit is removed in a similar manner to that described previously for manual transmission models.

In this case, however, obviously no clutch slave cylinder will be fitted.

The kickdown linkage control rod must be disconnected from the carburettor throttle lever before the carburettor can be removed (Fig. C:62).

Instead of the manual gearchange assembly, the gear selector cable must be disconnected at the transmission. To do this, first remove the cover plate (or rubber sleeve on early models) from the bell-crank arm. Slacken the locknut at the selector cable fork and remove the fork, locknut, both rubber ferrules and the sleeve (where fitted) from the cable. Remove the cable front adjusting nut from the outer cable and pull the cable clear of the bracket or abutment on the transmission (Fig. C:60).

The drive shafts in this case have a universal-jointed flange at the inboard end and this locates on studs in the final drive unit flange. The flanges are secured by four self-locking nuts (Fig. C:62).

When lifting out the power unit, raise it only sufficiently at first to release the drive shafts from the studs on the driving flanges.

Installation

When installing the power unit, lower it into the engine compartment to a position where the drive shaft flanges can be engaged on the studs on the final drive unit flanges and screw the nuts on loosely. Tighten the nuts fully once the power unit is lowered into position.

After reconnecting the gear selector cable, it must be adjusted as detailed in the 'AUTOMATIC TRANSMISSION' section.

Also, after reconnecting the kickdown linkage control rod, the linkage setting should be checked and adjusted if necessary.

TORQUE CONVERTER . . . . [16]

Removal

1. Disconnect the earth strap from the battery.
2. It will make for easier access if the bonnet is first removed, after marking the fitted position of the hinges to facilitate alignment when refitting.
3. On later models which have a plastic air intake assembly at the right-hand wing valance, withdraw the intake assembly into the engine compartment after pulling off the flexible pipe from beneath the wing.
4. Where fitted, detach the ignition shield from the front of the engine.
5. Disconnect the starter cable from the starter motor. Remove the starter motor (with distance piece, if fitted) from the converter housing.

6. On models with the starter solenoid mounted on the right-hand wing valance, disconnect the wiring and remove the solenoid.
7. Disconnect the engine tie-rod from the rear of the cylinder block.
8. Remove the oil filter bowl and filter head assembly from the transmission front cover.
9. Remove the nuts securing the radiator upper support bracket to the thermostat housing, and the bolts securing it to the radiator cowl, and remove the bracket.
10. Jack up the front of the car and support on stands located under the front sub-frame side-members.
11. Remove the air cleaner assembly and disconnect the exhaust down-pipe at the manifold flange. From underneath the car, also detach the exhaust pipe clip from the transmission casing.
12. Support the power unit with a hydraulic jack positioned under the transmission casing.
13. Remove the two bolts and nuts securing the right-hand engine mounting to the sub-frame side member.
14. Now raise the right-hand end of the engine sufficiently with the jack to allow the converter cover retaining bolts and nuts and the clutch cover to be removed, but take great care not to let the cooling fan blades damage the radiator core.
15. Remove the cover retaining bolts and nuts, turn the converter cover slightly anti-clockwise and remove the cover complete with the engine mounting attached (Fig. C:63). Note that the engine earth strap is normally secured by one of the cover front retaining bolts.
16. Bend back the tab on the lock washer and unscrew the converter centre-bolt, while holding the converter from turning with a screwdriver inserted through the inspection hole in the converter housing.
17. Remove the centre-bolt and lock washer and lever out the keyed washer locating the converter to the crankshaft (Fig. C:65).
18. Bend back the locking tabs and remove three equally spaced bolts from the centre of the converter (Fig. C:64).
19. Rotate the converter until the slot in the end of the crankshaft is positioned horizontally.
20. Insert the plug of the special puller tool into the end of the crankshaft to protect the threads. Fit the puller tool onto the converter and screw in the centre-bolt until the converter is released from the crankshaft taper (Fig. C:66). The converter will have to be held as before to prevent it turning.
21. Remove the puller tool and refit the three bolts.
22. Lift off the converter. Note that the converter will still contain a quantity of oil and some may be spilled during removal.

Installation

Installation is a simple reversal of the removal procedure, with special attention to the following points:-
a) Remove each pair of bolts in turn from the centre of the converter and fit new locking plates. Do NOT remove all six bolts at the same time. Tighten the bolts to their specified torque of 20 lb ft (2.9 kg m) secure with the locking plate tabs.
b) Ensure that the crankshaft taper and converter hub

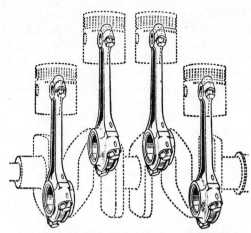

Fig. C:52 Clamp bolt secures piston pin in connecting rod small end on 848cc engine

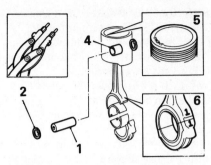

1. Piston pin   4. Small end bush
2. Circlip   5. Front marking on piston
3. Circlip pliers 6. Identification number on big end

Fig. C:53 Fully floating type piston pin is retained by circlips

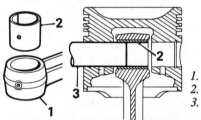

1. Connecting rod small end
2. Small end bush
3. Piston pin

Fig. C:54 Oil hole in small end bush must align with hole in rod, and split must be on cam-shaft side of assembly

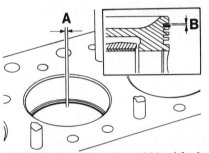

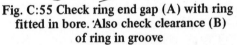

Fig. C:55 Check ring end gap (A) with ring fitted in bore. Also check clearance (B) of ring in groove

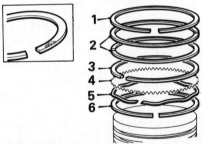

1. Chrome-plates compression ring   4. Expander ring
2. Tapered compression ring   5. Side spring
3. Top rail of oil control ring   6. Bottom rail of oil control ring

Fig. C:56 Details of piston ring installation

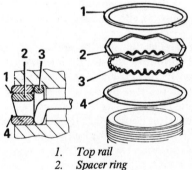

1. Top rail
2. Spacer ring
3. Expander ring
4. Bottom rail

Fig. C:57 Alternative type oil control ring

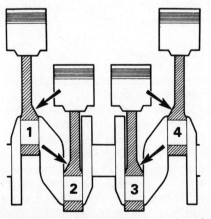

Fig. C:58 Connecting rods must be installed with big end bosses offset as shown

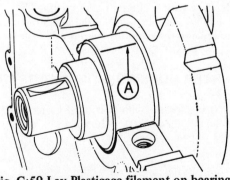

Fig. C:59 Lay Plastigage filament on bearing journal, about ¼ in (6 mm) off-centre

© BLUK

bore are perfectly clean and free from grease. They must be assembled dry. This is most important.

c) Refit the converter onto the output gear and align the offset slot in the converter with that in the end of the crankshaft. Refit the keyed washer.

d) Fit a new lock washer under the converter centre-bolt and tighten the bolt to 112 lb ft (15.5 kg m) while holding the converter to prevent it turning. Secure the bolt with the lock washer tab.

e) Use a new gasket when refitting the oil filter assembly to its mounting flange. Ensure that the gasket is correctly located in relation to the inlet and outlet ports on the flange and filter head.

f) When assembly is complete, check the engine oil level and top up if required.

CONVERTER HOUSING OIL SEAL . . . . . . [17]

The converter housing oil seal can be replaced with the power unit in position, once the torque converter has been removed.

Remove the old seal from the housing by hooking or levering it out of its location. Ensure that the bore in the housing is clean and undamaged.

It is important that the new seal be fitted to the correct depth in the housing in order that the drain hole behind the seal remains open.

Measure the depth of the housing from any convenient point on the front face to the undercut face (Fig. C:68). This measurement will be approximately 3/8 in (9.5 mm), but should it be more or less, the difference must be either added or subtracted from this figure.

For example, if the dimension of measurement obtained is 3/8 in, fit the seal flush with the front face of the housing. If the measurement is less than 3/8 in, fit the seal proud of the face by the difference of the measurement obtained.

The converter housing face is not machined, therefore the initial measurement position and that used when fitting a new seal must always be taken from the same position on the housing.

Lubricate the new seal liberally with clean engine oil then press it into position in the housing to the depth determined previously. Ideally the same tool as is recommended for replacing the Flywheel Housing Oil Seal should be used with a different adaptor ring (Fig. C:67), but it should be possible to install the seal by merely pressing or tapping on the outer diameter if care is used.

CONVERTER HOUSING & OUTPUT GEAR [18]

The engine/transmission unit must be removed from the car to enable the converter housing to be removed.

Removal

1. Remove the torque converter as detailed previously.
2. Remove the securing bolts and detach the low pressure valve, together with its gasket from the lower face of the converter housing (Fig. C:69).

3. Remove the self-locking nut from the transmission input shaft, previously covered by the low pressure valve. It will be necessary to hold the crankshaft to prevent it turning while the nut is removed, and a tool which fits over the output gear splines, similar to that shown in the illustration, will be required.

4. Disconnect the selector linkage bell crank lever from the transverse rod on the transmission. Remove the lever pivot bolt (or nut on early models) and detach the bell crank lever from the converter housing. On early models, also unscrew the pivot stud from the housing.

5. Fit tape or foil over the splines of the converter output gear to protect the converter housing oil seal as the housing is removed. This will be unnecessary if the seal is to be renewed anyway. A proper protector sleeve is available as a special tool, but the makeshift solution above will do the same job if a bit of care is used.

6. Remove the nuts and bolts securing the converter housing to the engine and transmission unit (Fig. C:70). Partially withdraw the housing, then disconnect the converter oil feed pipe from the housing.

7. The converter housing can then be fully withdrawn and the housing gasket removed. The needle bearing of the idler gear shaft and the transmission input gear bearing will come away with the converter housing.

8. Withdraw the 'C' shaped thrust washer locating the converter output gear on the crankshaft, and slide off the backing ring, output gear and front thrust washer (Fig. C:71).

Inspection & Overhaul — Converter Housing

If required, the idler gear shaft needle bearing in the converter housing can be renewed in a similar manner to that described for the idler gear bearing in the flywheel housing on manual transmission models previously.

The transmission input gear bearing can be renewed, if necessary, by removing the circlip and pressing the bearing from the housing. Install the new bearing and secure with the circlip.

Also check that the converter housing bush has not come loose in its housing.

If worn or damaged, the output gear oil seal in the converter housing can be renewed as detailed under the appropriate heading previously.

Installation

1. Ensure that the mating faces of the converter housing, cylinder block and transmission casing are clean and free from old gasket material.

2. If the idler gear or idler gear thrust washers have been changed, it will be necessary to check the idler gear end-float and adjust if necessary, as detailed under the 'TRANSMISSION UNIT' heading later in this section.

3. If the converter output gear or thrust washers have been changed, the gear end-float should be checked and adjusted in a similar manner to that described for the crankshaft primary gear on manual models previously.

4. Fit the protector sleeve or tape over the converter output gear splines to protect the converter housing oil seal.

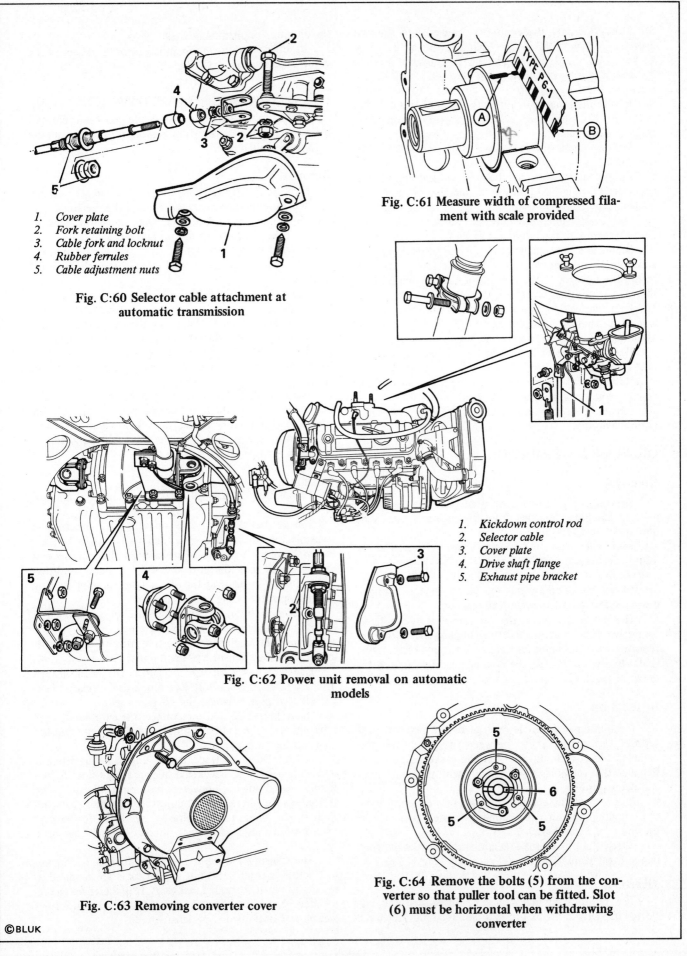

1. Cover plate
2. Fork retaining bolt
3. Cable fork and locknut
4. Rubber ferrules
5. Cable adjustment nuts

Fig. C:60 Selector cable attachment at
automatic transmission

Fig. C:61 Measure width of compressed filament with scale provided

1. Kickdown control rod
2. Selector cable
3. Cover plate
4. Drive shaft flange
5. Exhaust pipe bracket

Fig. C:62 Power unit removal on automatic
models

Fig. C:63 Removing converter cover

Fig. C:64 Remove the bolts (5) from the converter so that puller tool can be fitted. Slot
(6) must be horizontal when withdrawing
converter

©BLUK

5. Two pilot bars, made up and screwed into the two bottom tapped holes in the cylinder, similar to those shown in Fig. C:32, will help locate the converter housing in position during installation and take the weight off the converter output gear oil seal.

6. Ensure the transmission input gear shims and the idler gear thrust washer are correctly in position on their respective gear shafts.

7. Position a new housing gasket on the engine/transmission face.

8. Lubricate the converter housing oil seal and fit the converter housing into position, connecting the converter oil feed pipe to the housing. Ensure that the oil feed pipe and the nylon pipe assembly at the valve block are aligned, then push the housing fully home.

9. Secure the housing in position with the retaining nuts and bolts. Note that those with the UNC (coarse) threads secure the housing to the transmission casing, while those threaded UNF (fine) screw into the cylinder block.

10. Refit the washer and self-locking nut to the transmission input shaft and tighten to 70 lb ft (9.7 kg m) while again holding the converter output gear from turning.

11. Refit the selector linkage bell crank lever and reconnect it to the transverse rod.

12. Refit the low pressure valve to the lower face of the converter housing, using a new gasket.

13. Finally, refit the torque converter noting the points given previously.

OIL PUMP (AUTOMATIC). . . . . [19]

Removal

The oil pump is easily removed once the converter housing has been detached from the engine transmission unit as detailed previously.

Lever the main oil feed pipe from between the oil pump and the transmission casing (Fig. C:72).

Using a suitable size of Allen key, remove the socket-headed screws securing the oil pump to the cylinder block, and withdraw the pump and gasket.

The pump is driven from the camshaft by a splined 'star-drive' type coupling and this coupling may either be removed with the pump or remain in the end of the camshaft. In the latter case, the coupling can be easily withdrawn if required.

Installation

Installation is a simple reversal of the removal procedure. Use a new gasket between the pump and the cylinder block face. Ensure that the gasket is correctly fitted so that the holes align correctly with the pump inlet and delivery ports.

Ensure that the splined shaft engages correctly with the coupling, and that the coupling registers correctly in the end of the camshaft.

Check that the oil seals on and in the oil feed pipe are in good condition, and renew if necessary (Fig. C:72).

Overhaul

The pump assembly should be dismantled and inspected in a similar manner to that described previously for the oil pump on manual models.

In this case the pump inner rotor is keyed to the pump drive shaft (Fig. C:73).

TRANSMISSION UNIT (AUTOMATIC). . . . [20]

Once the engine/transmission unit has been removed from the car, the transmission is easily separated from the engine as detailed below.

Removal

Remove the torque converter and converter housing, following the relevant steps given under the previous headings. It should be noted that the engine oil must be drained from the power unit during removal.

If required, the converter output gear can be removed from the end of the crankshaft, together with its thrust washers.

Disconnect the external oil feed pipe from the adaptor on the transmission casing and the connection on the cylinder block (Fig. C:74). Lever the main oil feed pipe from the oil pump and the transmission case (Fig. C:72).

Remove the bolts securing the radiator to the left-hand engine mounting bracket and detach the radiator assembly.

Remove all the nuts, bolts and spring washers securing the engine to the transmission casing, then lift the engine to separate it from the transmission unit.

Remove the gaskets from the joint faces, and the oil seal from the front main bearing cap.

Installation

Installation is basically a reversal of the removal procedure.

Ensure that the joint faces on both the crankcase and transmission housing are clean and free from old gasket material before fitting new gaskets on the transmission casing. Check that the oil feed O-ring is in good condition and correctly in place at the oil feed pick-up pipe hole on the transmission casing flange.

Lubricate the new oil sealing strip before fitting it in position at the engine front main bearing.

Lower the engine onto the transmission unit and fit and tighten the securing bolts and nuts.

Check that the oil seals on and in the main oil feed pipe are in good condition, and renew as necessary. Refit the oil feed pipe between the oil pump and the transmission case (Fig. C:72). Also reconnect the external oil feed pipe between the cylinder block and the adaptor on the transmission casing (Fig. C:74).

If a replacement transmission unit is being fitted, it will be necessary to check the idler gear end-float before finally assembling the converter housing to the unit. The procedure for checking and adjusting the idler gear end-float is the same as that already described for manual transmission models and back-reference should be made for details.

The transmission input gear is pre-loaded, by the use of a selective shim pack, but special tools are required to set the pre-load for individual gears. It is therefore recommended that this operation be left to an Authorised Dealer or Transmission Specialist.

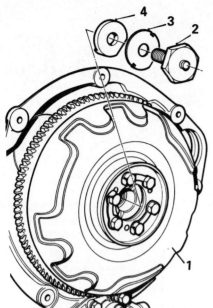

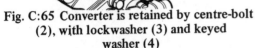

Fig. C:65 Converter is retained by centre-bolt (2), with lockwasher (3) and keyed washer (4)

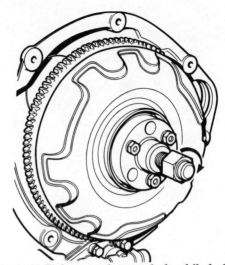

Fig. C:66 Tighten tool centre bolt while holding converter to prevent it turning

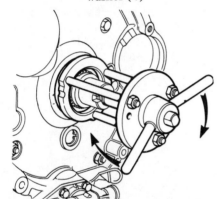

Fig. C:67 Installing converter housing oil seal

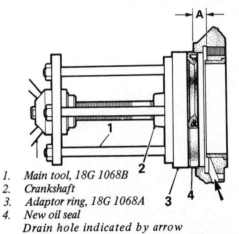

1. Main tool, 18G 1068B
2. Crankshaft
3. Adaptor ring, 18G 1068A
4. New oil seal
   Drain hole indicated by arrow

Fig. C:68 Measure depth 'A' of converter housing bore to determine fitted position of new oil seal

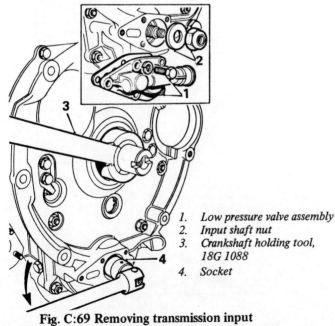

1. Low pressure valve assembly
2. Input shaft nut
3. Crankshaft holding tool, 18G 1088
4. Socket

Fig. C:69 Removing transmission input shaft nut

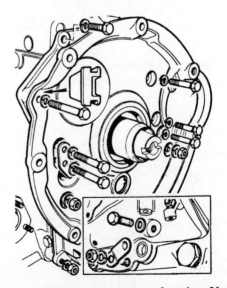

Fig. C:70 Removing converter housing. Note protector sleeve fitted over gear splines to protect housing oil seal

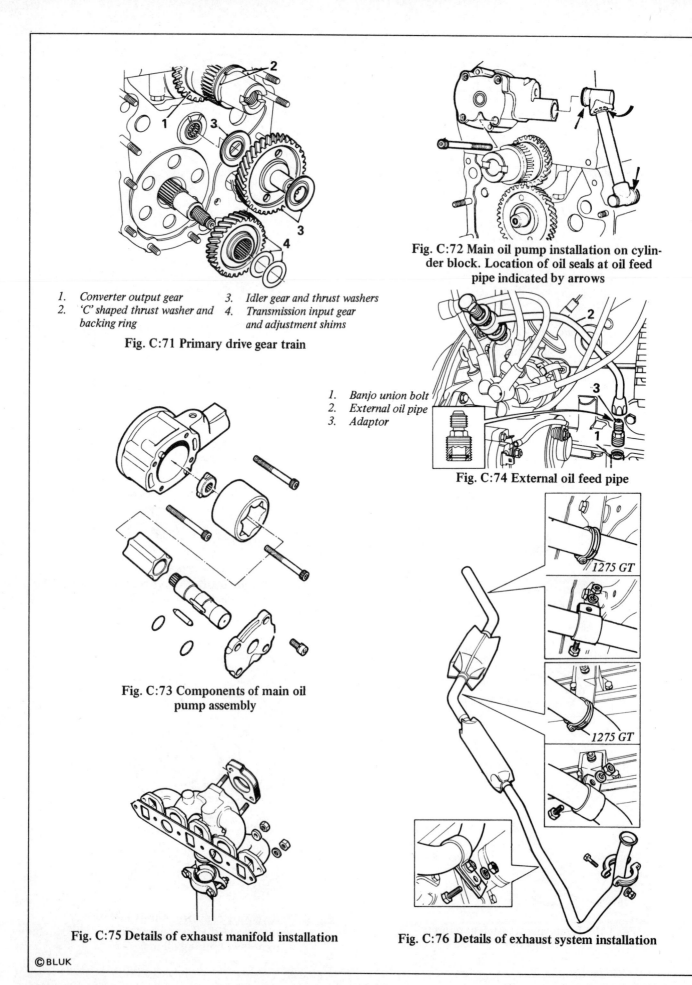

1. Converter output gear
2. 'C' shaped thrust washer and backing ring
3. Idler gear and thrust washers
4. Transmission input gear and adjustment shims

Fig. C:71 Primary drive gear train

Fig. C:72 Main oil pump installation on cylinder block. Location of oil seals at oil feed pipe indicated by arrows

1. Banjo union bolt
2. External oil pipe
3. Adaptor

Fig. C:74 External oil feed pipe

1275 GT

1275 GT

Fig. C:73 Components of main oil pump assembly

Fig. C:75 Details of exhaust manifold installation

Fig. C:76 Details of exhaust system installation

Engine

Technical Data

GENERAL DATA

848 cc ENGINE

Capacity . . . . .848 cc (51.7 cu in)
Bore . . . . .2.478 in (62.94 mm)
Stroke. . . . . .2.687 in (68.26 mm)
Compression ratio . . . . 8.3:1 (8.9:1, auto 1965 to 74)

PISTONS

Clearance of skirt in cylinder
    Top . . . . .0.0026 - 0.0036 in (0.066 - 0.081 mm)
    Bottom . . . . .0.0006 - 0.0016 in (0.015 - 0.030 mm)
Number of rings . . . . 4 (3 compression, 1 oil control)
Width of ring grooves:
    Top, second and third . . . . .0.0715 - 0.0725 in (1.805 - 1.843 mm)
    Oil control . . . . .0.1265 - 0.1275 in (3.213 - 3.238 mm)
Piston pin bore . . . . .0.6245 - 0.6247 in (15.867 - 15.872 mm)
Oversizes available . . . . + 0.010; + 0.020; + 0.030; + 0.040 in
                                         (0.254; 0.508; 0.762; 1.016 mm)

PISTON RINGS

Compression rings:
    Fitted gap . . . . 0.007 - 0.012 in (0.178 - 0.305 mm)
    Ring to groove clearance . . . . .0.0015 - 0.0035 in (0.038 - 0.089 mm)
Oil control ring
    Fitted gap . . . . 0.007 - 0.012 in (0.178 - 0.305 mm)
    Ring to groove clearance . . . . .0.0015 - 0.0035 in (0.038 - 0.089 mm)

CRANKSHAFT

Journal diameter . . . . 1.7505 - 1.751 in (44.46 - 44.47 mm)
Minimum regrind diam. . . . . .1.7105 in (43.45 mm)
Bearing clearance . . . . 0.001 - 0.0027 in (0.025 - 0.068 mm)
Crankshaft end-float . . . . 0.001 - 0.005 in (0.025 - 0.127 mm)
Big end bearings
    Crankpin journal diameter . . . . .1.6254 - 1.6259 in (41.28 - 41.29 mm)
    Minimum regrind diameter . . . . .1.5854 in (40.27 mm)
    Bearing clearance . . . . 0.001 - 0.0025 in (0.025 - 0.064 mm)

CAMSHAFT

Camshaft end-float . . . . 0.003 - 0.007 in (0.076 - 0.178 mm)

VALVES

Inlet valve:
    Stem to guide clearance . . . . .0.0015 - 0.0025 in (0.038 - 0.064 mm)
    Seat angle . . . . .45°
Exhaust valve:
    Stem to guide clearance . . . . 0.002 - 0.003 in (0.051 - 0.076 mm)
    Seat angle . . . . .45°

VALVE TIMING

Rocker timing clearance . . . . 0.019 in (0.48 mm)
Inlet valve
    Opens . . . . 5° BTDC
    Closes . . . . 45° ABDC
Exhaust valve
    Opens . . . . 40° BBDC
    Closes . . . . 10° ATDC

VALVE CLEARANCES

Inlet & exhaust valves (cold) . . . . .0.012 in (0.305 mm)

LUBRICATION SYSTEM

Sump capacity (engine/trans. unit inc. filler)
   with manual geabrox, refill . . . . .8½ pints (4.83 litres)
   with auto. trans., refill . . . . .9 pints (5 litres)
   total . . . . .13 pints (7.38 litres)
System pressure
   running . . . . 60 lb/sq in (4.22 kg/cm^2)
   idling . . . . 15 lb/sq in (1.05 kg/cm^2)
Relief valve opening pressure . . . . 60 lb/sq in (4.22 kg/cm^2)
Oil pump:
   Type. Hobourn - Eaton rotor type or Concentric
   Inner to outer rotor clearance . . . . .0.006 in (0.152 mm) max.
   Outer rotor to housing clearance . . . . .0.010 in (0.254 mm) max.
   Rotor end-float. . . . . .0.005 in (0.127 mm) max.

The following information gives only the points of difference from the 848 cc engine
and should be used in conjunction with the preceding specifications.

GENERAL DATA   **998 cc ENGINE**

Capacity . . . . .998 cc (60.96 cu in)
Bore . . . . .2.543 in (64.588 mm)
Stroke. . . . . 3.000 in (76.2 mm)
Compression ratio
   HC . . . . 8.3:1 (8.9:1, auto 1965 to 74)
   LC 7.6:1

PISTONS

Clearance of skirt in cylinder:
   Top . . . . .0.0022 - 0.0033 in (0.060 - 0.085 mm)
   Bottom . . . . .0.0004 - 0.0014 in (0.010 - 0.026 mm)
Width of ring grooves:
   Top, second & third. . . . . .0.0645 - 0.0655 in (1.638 - 1.663 mm)

PISTON RINGS

Compression rings:
   Ring to groove clearance. 0.002 - 0.004 in (0.051 - 0.102 mm)

The following information gives only the points of difference from the 848 cc engine
and should be used in conjunction with the specification for the 848 cc models given previously.

GENERAL DATA   **1098 cc ENGINE**

Capacity . . . . 1098 cc (67 cu in)
Bore . . . . .2.543 in (64.58 mm)
Stroke. . . . . .3.296 in (83.72 mm)
Compression ratio 8.5:1

PISTONS

Clearance of skirt in cylinder:
   Top . . . . 0.0021 - 0.0033 in (0.05 - 0.08 mm)
   Bottom . . . . .0.0005 - 0.0015 in (0.013 - 0.040 mm)
Width of ring grooves:
   Top, second & third. .0.0645 - 0.0655 in (1.638 - 1.663 mm)

PISTON RINGS

Compression rings:
    Ring to groove clearance . . . . 0.002 - 0.004 in (0.051 - 0.102 mm)
Oil control
    Fitted gap
        Rails . . . . 0.012 - 0.028 in (0.305 - 0.711 mm)
        Side springs . . . . .0.10 - 0.15 in (2.54 - 3.81 mm)

VALVES
Inlet valve & Exhaust vlave
    Stem to guide clearance .0.0015 - 0.0025 in (0.040 - 0.080 mm)

VALVE TIMING
Rocker timing clearance . . . . .0.021 in (0.533 mm)
Inlet valve
    Opens . . . . 5° BTDC
    Closes . . . . 45° ABDC
Exhaust valve
    Opens . . . . 51° BBDC
    Closes . . . . 21° ATDC

The following information gives only the point of difference from the 848 cc engine
and should be used in conjuction with the specifications for the 848 cc models given previously.

GENERAL DATA   1275 cc ENGINE

Capacity . . . . .1274.86 cc (77.8 cu in)
Bore . . . . 2.78 in (70.61 mm)
Stroke . . . . 3.2 in (81.28 mm)
Compression ratio
    HC 8.8:1
    LC 8.0:1

PISTONS
Clearance of skirt in cylinder:
    Top . . . . .0.0029 - 0.0045 in (0.070 - 0.114 mm)
    Bottom . . . . .0.0012 - 0.0022 in (0.031 - 0.056 mm)
Width of ring grooves:
    Top, second and third . . . . .0.0484 - 0.0494 in (1.230 - 1.250 mm)
    Oil control . . . . .0.1578 - 1.1588 in (4.001 - 4.003 mm)

PISTON RINGS
Compression rings:
    Fitted gap
        Top ring . . . . 0.011 - 0.016 in (0.28 - 0.41 mm)
        Second and third . . . . 0.008 - 0.013 in (0.20 - 0.33 mm)
Oil control ring:
    Fitted gap: Rails & side springs . . . . 0.010 - 0.040 in (0.254 - 1.02 mm)

CRANKSHAFT
Main bearings:
    Journal diameter . . . . 2.0012 - 2.0017 in (50.83 - 50.84 mm)
    Minimum regrind diam. . . . . .1.9605 in (49.78 mm)
Big end bearings:
    Crankpin journal diameter. . . . . 1.7497 - 1.750 in (44.44 - 44.46 mm)
    Minimum regrind diam. . . . . .1.7102 in (43.44 mm)

VALVE TIMING
Rocker timing clearance . . . . .0.021 in (0.533 mm)
Inlet valve
    Opens . . . . 5° BTDC
    Closes . . . . 45° ABDC
Exhaust valve
    Opens . . . . 51° BBDC
    Closes . . . . 21° ATDC

ENGINE

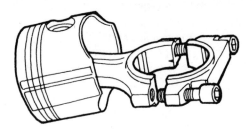

Trouble Shooter

FAULT	CAUSE	CURE
Noisy tappet (with correct clearance)	1. Wear in rocker pad face and/or rocker sleeve and shift (OHV). 2. Worn cam follower (OHC).	1. Reface pad surface, replace rockers or shaft (OHV). 2. Fit new followers (OHC).
Lack of compression	1. Faulty valve seat, excessive wear in stem or guide. 2. Faulty head gasket. 3. Worn pistons, rings and bores.	1. Recut seat and valve, fit new guide and valve. 2. Fit new gasket or reface head. 3. Either fit new rings, pistons and rings and rebore. If engine badly worn then recon. engine.
Smoke from exhaust. Lack of power	1. As above. 2. Blocked crankcase breather.	1. As above. 2. Check breathing apparatus as above.
Piston slap	1. As above (except blocked breather).	1. As above
Big-end knock	1. Wear between big-end shell and crankcase. Wrong torque on bolts.	1. Depending on wear, fit new shells, regrind crankshaft and check torque.
Mains rumble	1. Wear between main bearing shells and crankshaft.	1. As above.
Cam follower tap	1. Camshaft worn or follower dished.	1. Examine and replace followers or camshaft. Or both.
Knocking when clutch depressed. Movement at crank pulley	1. Excessive crankshaft end-float. Wear between crank and thrust washer.	1. Fit new thrust washers and recheck clearance.
Clattering from front of engine	1. Worn or slack timing chain, worn chain tensioner.	1. Fit new chain and tensioner. Adjust chain where necessary.
Small-end or gudgeon pin knock	1. Excessive wear between gudgeon pin and con-rod.	1. Fit new bush to con-rod.
Lack of oil pressure	1. Excessive wear in crankshaft journals. 2. Faulty oil pump. 3. Blocked oil pick-up strainer. 4. Faulty pressure-relief valve. 5. Blocked oil filter. 6. Lack of Oil.	1. Overhaul engine. 2. Fit new pump. 3. Clean pick-up. 4. Fit new relief valve. 5. Fit new filter. 6. Install fresh oil.
Oil leaks	1. Sump gaskets or packings. 2. Front and rear crankshaft oil seal. 3. Rocker or camshaft gasket. 4. Oil filter.	1. Fit new gaskets. 2. Fit new seals. 3. Fit new gasket. 4. Check filter seal.
Lack of power (engine in good condition)	1. Faulty ignition timing. Faulty sparking plugs, points or condenser. Wrong valve clearance.	1. Tune engine.

Engine Electrics

DISTRIBUTOR. . . . .[1]

Distributor lubrication and replacement of the contact breaker points has already been covered in the 'TUNE-UP' section previously, and reference should be made for details, if required.

Removal

Where fitted, remove the distributor shield from the bonnet lock platform. On Clubman and 1275 GT models, release the three clips and remove the ignition shield from the three brackets on the front of the engine.

Disconnect the HT leads from the spark plugs and the ignition coil. If necessary, label the spark plug leads with their respective cylinder numbers to ensure correct fitment on reassembly. Remove the distributor cap from the distributor body.

Disconnect the distributor low tension lead from the terminal blade on the distributor body (25D4 distributor) or from the 'Lucar' connector (45D4 type). Disconnect the vacuum pipe from the vacuum control unit on the distributor.

Remove the two bolts securing the distributor clamp plate to the pedestal on the cylinder block and withdraw the distributor, complete with its clamp plate.

Installation

Install the distributor in the reverse order of removing, paying special attention to the following points:-
a) When offering up the distributor to the engine, position it with the vacuum control unit pointing upwards towards the No. 3 spark plug, as shown in Fig. D:1.
b) Rotate the distributor shaft until the lugs on the driving dog engage in the slots in the distributor gear. The slots in the gear and the lugs on the dog are offset and can only engage each other in one position.
c) Turn the distributor body until the clamp plate holes are aligned with those in the pedestal, then fit the two securing bolts.
d) When installation is completed, check the ignition timing and reset if necessary, as detailed in the TUNE-UP section previously.

Overhaul

In most cases of wear or damage to the main components of the distributor (distributor shaft, cam assembly, advance mechanism, bearings etc.) it will probably be more economical and convenient to exchange the complete distributor, rather than attempt to overhaul or repair it. This will be particularly applicable if the unit has seen a long period of use.

The components of the distributor assembly are shown in Fig. D:2 & D:3.

DYNAMO. . . . .[2]

Removal & Installation

Dynamo removal is a straight-forward operation and is merely a matter of disconnecting the two leads from the rear of the unit and removing the mounting bolts. The unit can then be lifted away from the engine.

When installing the dynamo, set the drive belt tension so that a free-play of approximately ½ in (13 mm) exists at the midway point along the longest belt run.

If a replacement unit has been fitted, it should be 'polarised' before reconnecting the leads to the two terminals. To do this, connect a short lead between the two terminals on the dynamo and connect another longer lead to one of the terminals. At the starter solenoid, touch the other end of the long lead to the large battery feed terminal (opposite terminal to starter lead attachment) several times. The dynamo will now be correctly polarised to suit the electrical system. Remove the temporary leads and connect up the two dynamo leads to the large and small terminal respectively on the rear of the unit.

Brushes

Most faults associated with the dynamo are normally due either to the brushes or the rear bearing. In the latter case, excessive wear at the rear bearing bush allows the armature shaft to run eccentric and touch the field coils, in which case the complete unit is best exchanged. This condition is easily identified as excessive side movement at the rear end of the shaft when the drive pulley is moved

C

side-to-side.

To examine the brushes, unscrew the two through-bolts at the rear end bracket and withdraw the end bracket from the dynamo yoke.

Check the condition and length of the two carbon brushes in the end bracket, and the condition of the surface on the commutator. If the brushes are worn to or are approaching their minimum length of ¼ in (6 mm), they should be renewed.

To renew the brushes, detach the old brush leads from the holders on the end bracket by removing the screw and lock washer. Note the positions of the terminal tags before disconnecting the leads. Ensure that the replacement brushes are of the correct type and length. Secure the new brushes in position on the end bracket.

Inspect the contact surface on the commutator for signs of wear, burning or blackening of the segments. The latter indicates a short circuit. An open circuit will cause burned spots between the segments. Ideally the commutator surface should be smooth with a dark grey colour. If backened or dirty, it can be cleaned up with a petrol-moistened cloth. Slight imperfections can be removed with fine glass paper - not emery cloth. Use the glass paper over the whole surface of the commutator.

If the commutator is grooved, scored, pitted or badly worn, it must be skimmed down or replaced.

Fit each brush into its holder in turn and check for freedom of movement. If a brush sticks, it can usually be freed by cleaning both the brush and the holder with a petrol-moistened cloth, or by lightly polishing the sides of the brush with a smooth file.

Locate the brush springs on the side of each brush to hold them in the raised position. Check that the fibre thrust washer is in position on the end of the armature shaft, then refit the commutator end bracket. Ensure that the locating pip on the end bracket correctly engages the notch in the dynamo yoke. Fit the two through-bolts and tighten securely.

Release the brushes onto the commutator by inserting a thin screwdriver through the ventilation hole in the end bracket adjacent to the brush holders and gently levering up the spring end on to the top of the brush.

Before refitting the dynamo on the car, add one or two drops of light oil to the rear bearing through the hole in the centre of the end bracket. Do not over-lubricate the bearing otherwise oil may be thrown onto the brush gear in use.

Overhaul (Fig. D:5)

If any repair work, other than replacing the brushes, is necessary it will probably be more economical and convenient to have the dynamo repaired by an electrical specialist, or to exchange it for a replacement unit.

If the unit is being exchanged, it will be necessary to remove the drive pulley as this will not normally be supplied with the new unit. After removing the pulley nut, the pulley can be levered off the keyed shaft, but care should be taken to avoid damaging the rim of the pulley.

ALTERNATOR OVERHAUL............[3]

Two different types of Lucas alternator are used on Mini models; the 11AC alternator and the later 16 ACR unit, and these can be identified from the illustrations in Figs. D:6 & D:8.

The 11AC type was used on early models which had positive earth electrical system, but this was superseded by the 16 ACR type coincident with the adoption of negative earth in approximately October 1969. They differ mainly in that the later type has an integral voltage regulator incorporated in the rear end of the unit, whereas the 11AC type has a separate control unit. The 16 ACR type also has the slip-rings mounted behind the rear rotor shaft bearing outside the slip ring end bracket.

It should be noted that the 16 ACR unit cannot be used on the earlier models with positive earth, as this type of alternator can only be used with a negative earth system.

Most faults allied to the alternator charging system are due either to worn or damaged brushes, or a defective regulator. Replacement of both the brushes and the regulator unit is detailed under the appropriate headings below. If anything more involved, such as the rectifier diodes, slip rings, bearings, etc., is at fault, it is recommended that the alternator be given to an Electrical Specialist for repair, or an exchange unit obtained. In most cases this will be found to be the most economical and convenient solution rather than attempt to obtain replacement parts and repair it.

It should be noted that the battery should ALWAYS be disconnected before starting work on the charging system to avoid the possibility of damage to the semi-conductor devices in the alternator.

ALTERNATOR ....[4]

(11AC Type)

The 11AC alternator charging circuit includes an alternator control unit, a field isolating relay and a warning light control unit (Fig. D:7). The electronic control unit is a Lucas 4TR type and is mounted remotely from the alternator. The voltage output is adjustable by means of a potentiometer adjuster at the rear of the control unit, but it is not recommended that this be attempted without proper equipment and knowledge.

The Lucas 6RA field isolating relay acts to de-energise the alternator field windings when the engine is stationary by disconnecting the supply from the rotor field immediately the ignition is switched off. If the contacts inside the relay fail to close when the ignition is switched on, the alternator will not generate.

The warning light control unit is a thermally operated relay and is electrically connected to the centre point of one pair on diodes in the alternator. It enables a warning light to be used to indicate that the alternator is charging when the engine is running at normal speed. It should be noted that the 3AW control unit is externally similar to

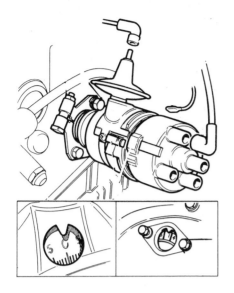

Fig. D:1 Distributor installation (45D4 type shown)

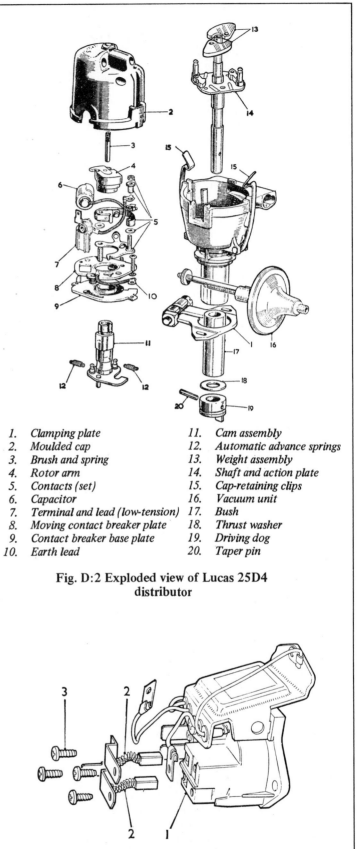

1.	Distributor cap		
2.	Brush and spring		
3.	Rotor arm		
4.	Capacitor		
5.	Earth lead		
6.	Base plate		
7.	Felt pad		
8.	Spacer		
9.	Steel washer		
10.	Low tension lead		
11.	Thrust washer		
12.	Drive dog		
13.	Retaining pin		
14.	Screws vacuum unit		
15.	Vacuum control unit		
16.	Advance weights		
17.	Cam spindle assembly		
18.	Screws - base plate		
19.	LT lead connector		
20.	Contact set		
21.	Screw - contact set		

1.   Clamping plate   11.   Cam assembly
2.   Moulded cap   12.   Automatic advance springs
3.   Brush and spring   13.   Weight assembly
4.   Rotor arm   14.   Shaft and action plate
5.   Contacts (set)   15.   Cap-retaining clips
6.   Capacitor   16.   Vacuum unit
7.   Terminal and lead (low-tension)   17.   Bush
8.   Moving contact breaker plate   18.   Thrust washer
9.   Contact breaker base plate   19.   Driving dog
10. Earth lead   20.   Taper pin

Fig. D:2 Exploded view of Lucas 25D4 distributor

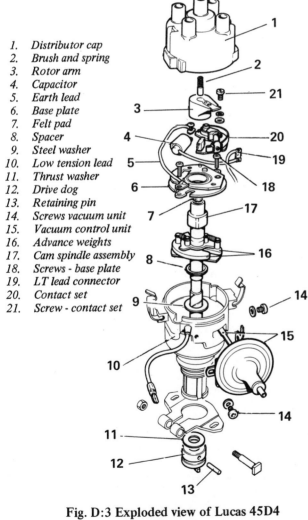

Fig. D:3 Exploded view of Lucas 45D4 distributor

1.   Brush box moulding
2.   Brush and spring assemblies
3.   Retaining screws

Fig. D:4 Details of brush installation - 16ACR with 8TR regulator

the FL5 type indicator flasher unit, and thus is identified by a distinctive green label applied to the aluminium case of the unit. These two types of unit cannot and must not be interchanged.

Removal & Installation

Removal and installation of the alternator is a straight-forward operation, similar to that described for the dynamo previously. However, in this case it is most im important that the battery must be disconnected before starting work on the alternator as the alternator main feed cable is live at all times. Do not reconnect the battery until installation is complete and all leads have been properly reconnected.

It should be noted that 'polarisation' of the alternator is not necessary and in fact, if carried out, will probably cause damage to some of the semi-conductor devices in the charging circuit.

Brushes

Remove the nuts, washers and insulating pieces from the output terminal (B) at the rear of the alternator. Remove the two brush box retaining screws and withdraw the brush box assembly from the rear end bracket. Take care not to lose the two washers fitted between the brush box moulding and the end bracket as these must be refitted in their original locations on reassembly.

To remove the brushes from the brush box, close up the retaining tongue at the base of each field terminal blade and withdraw the brush, spring and terminal assembly from the brush box.

Check the brushes for wear. The brush length when new is 5/8 in (16 mm). If worn to, or approaching the wear limit of 5/16 in (8 mm) the brush assemblies should be renewed. New brush assemblies are supplied complete with their spring and 'Lucar' field terminal blade.

It should be noted that the brush which bears on the inner slip ring is always connected to the positive side of the electrical system, since the lower linear speed of the inner slip ring results in reduced mechanical wear and helps to offset the higher rate of electrical wear peculiar to the positive connected brush.

If the original brushes assemblies are to be re-used, clean them with a cloth moistened in petrol or white spirit, then dry thoroughly.

Check the brushes for freedom of movement in their holders. If necessary lightly polish the brush sides on a smooth file, then clean off and refit.

To reassemble the brushes to their holders, push each brush complete with its spring and terminal blade into its holder until the tongue on the terminal blade registers in the brush box. To ensure the terminal blades are properly retained, the tongue should be levered up with a small screwdriver to make an angle of about 30° with the terminal blade.

Before refitting the brush box assembly, inspect the slip rings for any signs of damage or contamination. The surface of the rings should be smooth and free from oil or other matter. The easiest way of removing surface dirt

from the slip rings is to press a petrol-moistened cloth through the hole in the end bracket and hold it in contact with the slip ring surface while rotating the pulley.

If more serious contamination or damage is evident on the ring surface, the alternator must be partially dismantled to gain access. In this case the drive pulley and fan must first be removed to allow the three through-bolts to be unscrewed. The alignment of the end brackets and stator should be marked so that they may be reassembled in the correct angular relation to each other. The drive end bracket and rotor can then be separated from the stator and slip ring end bracket to allow inspection of the slip rings.

The surface of the slip rings can be cleaned using very fine glass paper but on no account must emery cloth or similar abrasive be used. If badly scored, pitted or burned, the complete rotor assembly must be renewed.

When inspection is completed, refit the brush box assembly to the slip ring end bracket and secure with the two retaining screws. Assemble the insulating pieces, washers and nuts on the output terminal.

Overhaul

If any repair work, other than replacing the brushes, is necessary it will probably be more economical and convenient to have the alternator repaired by an electrical specialist, or to exchange it for a replacement unit.

16 ACR Type

In the 16 ACR alternator charging circuit, all the electrical components of the charging system are incorporated in the alternator. These include the control unit (voltage regulator) and the rectifier pack, which are mounted on the rear of the alternator under the black plastic cover.

Several modifications have been made to the internal components of the 16 ACR alternator since its introduction. These mainly affect the voltage control unit which may be an 8TR, 11TR or 14TR on later models, but the termination is also different on later units, as improvements to the internal wiring have resulted in the elimination of the 'battery sensing' wire and the separate earth wire used on previous units. The alternator now earths through the unit casing.

These later units have a single connector block with two leads to it, whereas earlier alternators have two connector blocks. Details of the wiring conversion necessary when fitting a later unit as a replacement for the earlier type are given under the appropriate heading below.

It should be noted that the 16 ACR alternator is suitable only for fitment to vehicles having a negative earth electrical system.

Removal & Installation

Removal and installation is carried out in a similar manner to that described for the 11AC alternator previously.

Where a replacement unit with European termination is being fitted in place of an earlier type, the alternator

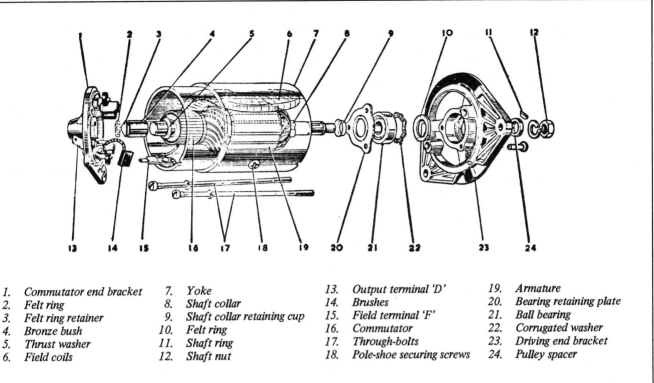

1.	Commutator end bracket	7.	Yoke
2.	Felt ring	8.	Shaft collar
3.	Felt ring retainer	9.	Shaft collar retaining cup
4.	Bronze bush	10.	Felt ring
5.	Thrust washer	11.	Shaft ring
6.	Field coils	12.	Shaft nut

13.	Output terminal 'D'	19.	Armature
14.	Brushes	20.	Bearing retaining plate
15.	Field terminal 'F'	21.	Ball bearing
16.	Commutator	22.	Corrugated washer
17.	Through-bolts	23.	Driving end bracket
18.	Pole-shoe securing screws	24.	Pulley spacer

Fig. D:5 Exploded view of Lucas C40 dynamo

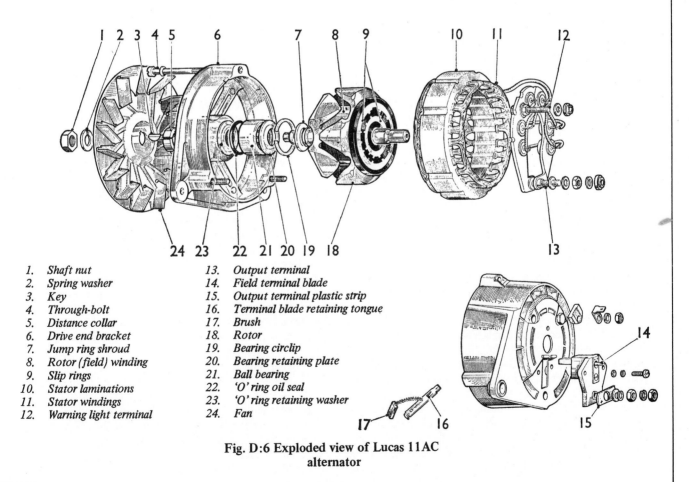

1.	Shaft nut	13.	Output terminal
2.	Spring washer	14.	Field terminal blade
3.	Key	15.	Output terminal plastic strip
4.	Through-bolt	16.	Terminal blade retaining tongue
5.	Distance collar	17.	Brush
6.	Drive end bracket	18.	Rotor
7.	Jump ring shroud	19.	Bearing circlip
8.	Rotor (field) winding	20.	Bearing retaining plate
9.	Slip rings	21.	Ball bearing
10.	Stator laminations	22.	'O' ring oil seal
11.	Stator windings	23.	'O' ring retaining washer
12.	Warning light terminal	24.	Fan

Fig. D:6 Exploded view of Lucas 11AC
alternator

Engine Electrics

wiring will have to be modified to suit and reference should be made to the heading below for details.

Conversion to European Termination

Later alternators have only one connector block at the rear instead of the two used on earlier units. This is due to improvements in the internal wiring which have resulted in the elimination of the 'battery sensing' wire (B+) and the separate earth wire (−) used on previous units. The connector block incorporates only two leads; one is the alternator main feed wire (+) and the other is the connection to the charge warning indicator light (IND).

Earlier units have a two-way connector and an L-shaped three-way connector. These connector blocks can only be fitted one way round. The two-way connector block incorporates connections for the alternator main output lead (+) and the unit earth lead (−). The three-way connector block incorporates connections for the battery sensing lead (B+) and the charge warning light lead (IND) and a short link lead between the 'IND' connection and the third position in the connector block.

When fitting a later unit in place of an early type one, the alternator wiring must be converted to suit the new connections. The use of the proper Lucas Plug Conversion Kit 54960402 is recommended.

First, disconnect the battery. Cut off all the leads from the existing plugs after noting, or preferably labelling them with, their respective locations. Solder on the two new Lucar connectors supplied with the kit to the alternator main feed wire (+) and the charge warning light wire (IND). The large Lucar connector goes on the main feed wire, and the small connector on the 'IND' lead. Push first the small Lucar connector into its location in the European termination plug, then the large main lead connector into the adjacent slot in the plug, and snap on the plug cover. Connect the plug to the alternator and secure with the clip.

Discard the link wire and tape back separately the other leads from the original alternator. Finally, reconnect the battery.

Voltage Regulator

Remove the black plastic cover from the rear of the alternator. This is secured by two retaining screws with either cross heads or hexagon heads. In the latter case a small box spanner or socket will be required to release them.

Identify the type of regulator fitted. The early 8TR type has two short mounting screws, one securing it along with the earth lead to the end bracket and the other securing it to the top of the brush box assembly (Fig. D: 9). The 11TR type is secured by a single longer screw to the top of the brush box moulding only, and in this case a spacer is fitted between the brush box and the regulator flange. The earth lead is secured by one of the brush box mounting screws. Both of these units have four connecting leads. The later 14TR type regulator is similar to the 11TR type but has only two leads, one an earth lead se-cured by one of the brush box mounting screws. The regulator field connection in this case is by a flat connecting link between the regulator mounting screw and the adjacent brush assembly. Again an insulating spacer is fitted at the mounting screw.

Carefully note the respective positions of the leads before disconnecting them. Disconnect the wiring connectors from the top of the brush box, and from the brush box securing screw, where applicable. Remove the screw (or screws - 8TR) securing the regulator and withdraw the unit. With the 14TR type it may be necessary to slacken the field link retaining screw to allow the field link to be moved aside. Where fitted, retain the small plastic spacer fitted between the regulator and brush box at the retaining screw.

Position the new regulator on the brush box moulding and secure it in position. On 11TR and 14TR units, ensure that the plastic spacer is correctly fitted, and on the 14TR unit also the connecting link. Reconnect the regulator leads to the positions noted previously. Refit the rear cover.

Brushes

The slip ring brushes are located in the brush box at the rear of the alternator and can be easily replaced if worn or damaged. First remove the alternator rear cover as described above for removing the regulator.

Remove the four screws securing the two brush retaining plates and withdraw the brush assemblies from the brush box moulding (Fig. D:4). Note the respective positions of the leads secured by brush plate screws before disconnecting them. With the 14TR type regulator, it may be necessary to slacken the regulator mounting screw to allow the field connecting link to be moved aside.

Fit the new brushes assemblies into the brush box and secure the retaining plates in position with the securing screws. Ensure that the various terminals are located as before at the screws. Refit the end cover.

Alternatively, the complete brush box assembly, together with the regulator unit can be removed from the slip ring end bracket. This will allow inspection of the slip rings and the brush holders.

Where a surge protection diode is fitted, first remove the screw securing the diode to the slip ring end bracket. The diode is then removed with the brush box assembly.

Disconnect the brush box lead (and regulator lead, where applicable) from the rectifier pack. Note the terminal to which the lead was connected for reassembly. Remove the screws securing the brush box and regulator to the slip ring end bracket and lift off the complete assembly. Note that the regulator earth lead is also secured by one of these screws.

Inspect the brushes for wear. With the brushes in the free position, measure the amount by which they protrude beyond the brush box moulding. The brush length when new is ½ in (13 mm). If the amount protruding is worn to or approaching the wear limit of ¼ in (6 mm), the brush assemblies should be renewed.

Remove the old brush assemblies from the brush box and fit the new ones as detailed above.

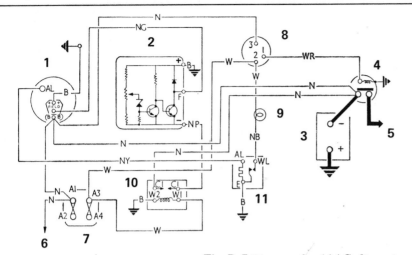

1. Alternator
2. 4TR control unit
3. 12-volt battery
4. Starter solenoid
5. Starter motor
6. Lighting switch
7. Fuse unit; 1-2, 35-amp.; 3-4, 35-amp.
8. Ignition/starter switch
9. Ignition warning lamp
10. Alternator field isolating relay
11. Alternator charge indicator unit 3AW

Fig. D:7 Diagram for 11AC alternator charging circuit

1. End cover
2. Voltage regulator
3. Brush holder
4. Rectifier earthing link
5. Slip ring end bracket
6. Stator
7. O-ring
8. Rectifier pack
9. Connecting lead
10. Surge protection diode
11. Brush assemblies
12. Key
13. Front bearing assembly
14. Drive pulley and fan
15. Distance piece
16. Drive end bracket
17. Distance piece
18. Rotor
19. Rear bearing
20. Slip rings

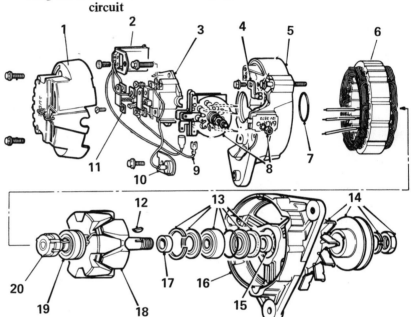

Fig. D:8 Exploded view of Lucas 16ACR alternator. (Late type with single wiring plug termination shown)

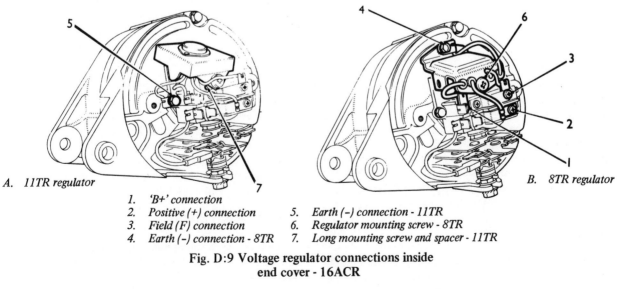

A. 11TR regulator

B. 8TR regulator

1. 'B+' connection
2. Positive (+) connection
3. Field (F) connection
4. Earth (–) connection - 8TR
5. Earth (–) connection - 11TR
6. Regulator mounting screw - 8TR
7. Long mounting screw and spacer - 11TR

Fig. D:9 Voltage regulator connections inside end cover - 16ACR

Engine Electrics

Check the new brushes for freedom of movement in their holders. Clean any brush which is stiff with a petrol-moistened cloth, or by lightly polishing the brush sides on a smooth file if necessary.

Inspect the surface of the slip rings on the end of the rotor. If there is any evidence of roughness or burning this can usually be cleaned off with very fine glass paper, but on no account must emery cloth or similar abrasive be used. If the surface is badly scored, pitted or burned, the slip ring assembly on the rotor must be renewed.

Before refitting the brush box, clean off any dirt which may have collected around the slip ring end bracket or the apertures in the plastic end cover.

Check that the brushes are correctly positioned in their holders, then locate the brush box assembly on the slip ring end bracket and secure with the retaining screws. Ensure that the regulator earth lead is also secured by one of the screws. Where applicable, refit the surge protection diode in position on the end bracket. Reconnect the brush box lead (and regulator lead, where applicable) to the rectifier pack. Finally, refit the end cover.

Overhaul

If any repair work, other than replacing the brushes or regulator unit is necessary it will probably be more economical and convenient to have the alternator repaired by an electrical specialist, or to exchange it for a replacement unit.

STARTER MOTOR . . . . [5]

Removal & Installation

First, disconnect the battery. Remove the nut from the terminal on the end of the starter motor and disconnect the starter cable. Remove the two bolts (lower one first) retaining the starter motor to the engine and withdraw the starter motor from its location.

Install the starter motor in the reverse order of removing.

The starter motor may be either a Lucas M35G or a M35J type, the latter being a later fitment. Although externally similar, apart from the brush cover band on the M35G type, they differ mainly in two respects. The M35G type has a peripheral contact commutator on which the brushes bear from the side, whereas the M35J has a face-type commutator where the brushes bear on the end face. In the M35J unit, the field windings are earthed to the starter yoke but the brush box assembly and the commutator end plate brushes are fully insulated. The end terminal post is connected directly to the end plate brushes. The M35G field windings are insulated from the yoke and incorporate the field terminal post, but the end plate brushes are earthed directly to the end plate.

Brushes - M35G Starter

A good indication of the brush condition can be obtained by inspecting the brushes through the apertures in the starter body, after sliding away the cover band. If the brushes are damaged or worn so that they no longer make good contact on the commutator, they should be renewed as a set.

The brushes can be further inspected by lifting the brush springs, using a piece of hooked wire, and withdrawing them from their holders on the commutator end plate.

If the brushes are to be replaced, remove the nuts, washers and insulation bush from the field terminal post at the end plate. Unscrew the two through-bolts and withdraw the end plate from the starter body.

Inspect the contact surface on the outside of the commutator for any signs of wear, burning or other damage. If the surface is blackened or dirty, it should be wiped clean with a petrol-moistened cloth. Slight imperfections can be removed with fine glass paper, but emery cloth or similar abrasive must not be used. If the commutator is grooved, scored or badly worn, it should be skimmed or replaced.

To renew the earthed brushes on the commutator end plate, unsolder the flexible lead from the terminal eyelet adjacent to the brush holder. Open the eyelet, then insert the replacement brush lead, squeeze the eyelet closed and resolder the connection.

To renew the insulated brushes on the field coils, cut the existing brush leads approximately ¼ in (6 mm) from the field coil connection. Clean the ends of the copper leads still attached to the field coils and solder the new brush leads to them. Note that the insulated brushes have longer leads then the earthed brushes, and also have a braided covering.

Check the new brushes for freedom of movement in their respective holders. Ease them if necessary by cleaning both the brushes and holders with a petrol-moistened cloth, or by polishing the sides of the brushes lightly with a fine file.

Check that the insulator band is fitted between the starter body and the end of the field coils, and that the insulating bush for the field terminal post is also fitted to the commutator end plate. Also check that the thrust washer is in place in the end of the armature shaft.

Pass the field brushes out through the apertures in the starter body. Fit the earthed brushes in their respective holders in the end plate and locate the brush springs on the side of each brush to hold them in the raised position. Assemble the end plate to the starter body, ensuring that the locating dowel on the plate correctly engages the notch in the yoke. Fit the through-bolts and tighten securely. Assemble the insulation bush, washers and nuts on the field terminal post.

Lift the brush springs and fit the field brushes into their respective holders. Press the brushes down into the commutator, then lift the brush springs into position on top of the brushes. Refit the brush cover band over the brush apertures and tighten the clamp screw to secure.

Brushes - M35J Starter

In this case the commutator end plate must be removed to allow inspection of the brushes as inspection apertures are not provided.

Remove the two retaining screws and withdraw the commutator end plate from the starter yoke. Withdraw the two field brushes from the brush box on the end plate and separate the end plate from the yoke.

Inspect the brushes for wear or damage. Brushes which are worn to, or are approaching the wear limit of 3/8 in (10 mm) must be renewed as a set.

Inspect the contact surface on the end of the commutator for any signs of scoring, burning or other damage. If the surface is grooved or badly scored, the commutator should be skimmed or replaced. If the surface is merely blackened or dirty it can be cleaned with a petrol-moistened cloth, or fine glass paper, but emery cloth or similar abrasive must not be used for this purpose.

If the brushes on the commutator end plate are to be renewed, these are supplied attached to a new terminal post. Withdraw both brushes from their holders, then remove the nuts, washers and insulation sleeve from the terminal post and withdraw the terminal post and remove the insulation piece. Install the new brushes and terminal post in the reverse order of removing. Ensure that the insulation piece and sleeve are correctly located. Retain the longer brush lead under the clip on the end plate.

If the field winding brushes are to be renewed, these are supplied attached to a common lead. Cut the old brush leads approximately ¼ in (6 mm) from their joint on the field windings. Clean the leads still attached to the joint and solder the common lead of the new brushes to them. Do not attempt to solder directly to the field winding strip as this may be made of aluminium.

Check the brushes for freedom of movement in their respective holders. Any brushes which are stiff should be cleaned with a petrol-moistened cloth, or eased by lightly polishing the sides of the brush with a fine file.

Install the two commutator end brushes and the two filed winding brushes in their respective holders on the brush box. Check that the thrust washer is in position on the end of the armature shaft, then assemble the commutator end plate to the starter yoke. Secure the end plate with the two retaining screws.

Drive Pinion

If difficulty is experienced with the starter motor pinion not meshing correctly with the flywheel ring gear, it may be that the drive assembly requires cleaning. The pinion and barrel assembly should move freely on the screwed sleeve. If there is dirt or other foreign matter on the sleeve it should be washed off with paraffin. Do not use grease or oil on the drive assembly as this would attract dirt.

To replace the drive pinion assembly, compress the main drive spring using a suitable clamping device (e.g. Bendix Spring Compressor Tool) and remove the jump ring from its groove at the end of the armature shaft. Release the clamping device and remove the spring cup, drive spring, thrust washer and drive pinion assembly from the shaft. It may be necessary to depress the pinion assembly and turn it slightly to disengage it from the shaft splines.

It should be noted that, if the screwed sleeve is worn or damaged, it is essential that it is renewed together with the barrel and pinion.

Fit the new pinion assembly on the armature shaft, with the pinion teeth towards the starter body. Assemble the thrust washer, drive spring and spring seat on the shaft, compress the drive spring and fit the jump ring. Ensure that the ring is correctly seated in the shaft groove once the spring is released.

Technical Data

DISTRIBUTOR

Make/type	Lucas DM2 (early 848 cc only), 25D4 or 45D4 (43D4 on certain export models with air injection emission control equipment)
Contact points gap	0.014 - 0.016 in (0.35 - 0.40 mm)
Dwell angle:	
DM2 & 25D4	$60^0 \pm 3^0$
43D4 & 45D4	$51^0 \pm 5^0$
Condenser capacity	0.18 - 0.24 mfd
Rotor rotation	Anti-clockwise
Ignition timing	See 'Tune-Up' data

IGNITION COIL

Make/type	Lucas LA12
Certain export models (Canada & Sweden)	A.C. Delco, Lucas 11 C 12, Lucas 16 C 6 or Lucas A12 (Low voltage type with 1.4 ohm ballast resistor)

DYNAMO

Make/type . . . . Lucas C40
Maximum output . . . . 22 amps
Cut-in speed . . . . 1450 rpm at 13.5 volts
Control box . . . . Lucas RB 106/2
Regulating voltage . . . . 12.7 - 13.3 volts

ALTERNATOR - EARLY TYPE

Make/type . . . . Lucas 11AC
Polarity . . . . Positive earth
Maximum output . . . . 43 amps
Brush length
   new . . . . 0.63 in (16 mm)
    wear limit . . . . 0.31 in (8 mm)
Control unit . . . . Lucas 4TR
Field isolating relay . . . . Lucas 6RA
Warning light control unit . . . . Lucas 3RA

ALTERNATOR – LATER TYPE

Make/type . . . . Lucas 16 ACR
Polarity . . . . Negative earth
Nominal output . . . . 34 amps at 6,000 rpm (2,800 rpm - engine)
Nominal system voltage . . . . 14.2 volts at 20% nominal output
Brush length (above holder)
   New . . . . 0.5 in (13 mm)
    Wear limit . . . . 0.25 in (6 mm)
Voltage regulator . . . . Lucas 8TR, 11TR or 14TR Integral

STARTER MOTOR

Make/type . . . . Lucas M35G or M35J, inertia type
Commutator min. diam. (M35G) . . . . 1.34 in (34 mm)
Commutator min. thickness (M35J) . . . . 0.08 in (2.03 mm)
Armature end-float
   M35G . . . . 0.004 - 0.012 in (0.1 - 0.3 mm)
   M35J . . . . 0.010 in (0.25 mm)
Min. brush length (M35J) . . . . 0.31 in (8 mm)

SYSTEM POLARITY

Early models . . . . Positive earth
Later models (Oct '69 on) . . . . Negative earth

Cooling

RADIATOR . . . . [1]

Removal (Fig. E:1)

1. Easier access to the radiator will be provided if the bonnet is first removed. In this case, mark the fitted position of the hinges to facilitate alignment on installation.
2. Drain the cooling system by removing the cylinder block drain plug and/or disconnecting the bottom hose at the radiator.
3. Disconnect the top and bottom hose from the radiator, if not already done. Also pull off the overflow pipe. On models with the one-piece radiator cowling, the bottom hose must be completely removed.
4. Remove the two nuts securing the radiator upper support bracket to the cylinder head, and the two bolts securing the bracket to the radiator cowl, and remove the bracket.
5. On Clubman and 1275 GT models, remove the long through-bolt securing the radiator lower support bracket to the engine mounting (see insert on illustration).
6. On models with the two-piece cowling, remove the six screws securing the radiator to the cowling and lift out the top half of the cowling. Bend back the bottom hose to the outside of the lower cowling and lift out the radiator.
7. On models with the one-piece cowling, remove the four screws securing the radiator to the cowling and lift out the radiator and cowling.

Installation

Install the radiator in the reverse order of removing. Finally, refill the cooling system and check for water leaks.

THERMOSTAT. [2]

Replacement (Fig. E:2)

The thermostat is located under the water outlet elbow at the radiator end of the cylinder head and is easily replaced.

Drain the cooling system sufficiently to bring the coolant level below that of the water outlet housing.

Disconnect the radiator top hose from the water outlet elbow. Remove the two bolts securing the radiator upper support bracket to the radiator cowling. Remove the nuts securing the water outlet elbow to the cylinder head, and lift off the radiator support bracket.

Remove the water outlet elbow together with its gasket and lift the thermostat from its location in the cylinder head.

Clean all old gasket material from the mating faces on the outlet elbow and the cylinder head before installing the new thermostat. Also ensure the thermostat seating in the head is clean.

Install the thermostat with the coil spring side positioned downwards into the head recess. The radiator side of the thermostat is normally marked on the top flange. It is important that the thermostat be correctly positioned in the engine, otherwise overheating will result.

Position a new gasket on the cylinder head face and locate the water outlet elbow over the thermostat. Fit the radiator support bracket in position and secure the bracket and outlet elbow with the three nuts and spring washers. Attach the bracket to the radiator cowling with the two bolts.

Reconnect the radiator top hose and top up the system. Run the engine up to normal operating temperature and check for leaks. Recheck the coolant level once the engine has cooled down.

Testing

Inspect the thermostat for obvious faults. If the valve is stuck in the open position the thermostat is defective and must be renewed.

To test the operation of the thermostat, suspend it fully submerged along with a suitable thermometer in a container of water. Both the thermostat and the thermometer should be suspended in such a way that they do not touch the sides of the container.

Heat the water gradually and observe the action of the thermostat valve. Note the temperature at which the valve opens. The nominal temperature at which the thermostat opens is normally stamped on the base of the thermostat bulb.

If the thermostat does not function correctly, it must be replaced with a new unit.

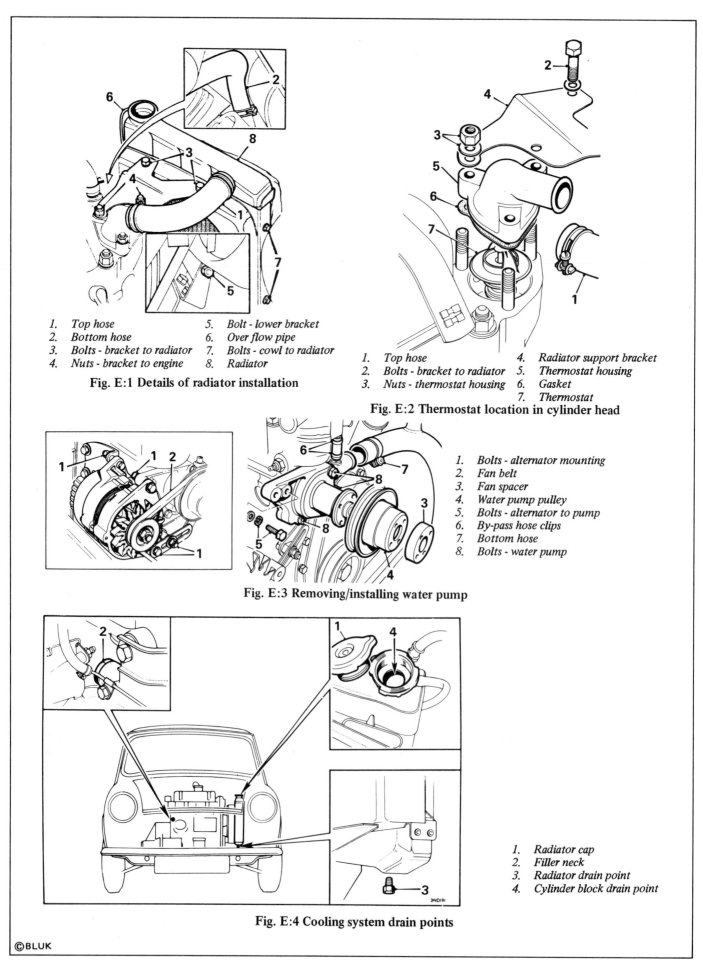

1. Top hose
2. Bottom hose
3. Bolts - bracket to radiator
4. Nuts - bracket to engine
5. Bolt - lower bracket
6. Over flow pipe
7. Bolts - cowl to radiator
8. Radiator

Fig. E:1 Details of radiator installation

1. Top hose
2. Bolts - bracket to radiator
3. Nuts - thermostat housing
4. Radiator support bracket
5. Thermostat housing
6. Gasket
7. Thermostat

Fig. E:2 Thermostat location in cylinder head

1. Bolts - alternator mounting
2. Fan belt
3. Fan spacer
4. Water pump pulley
5. Bolts - alternator to pump
6. By-pass hose clips
7. Bottom hose
8. Bolts - water pump

Fig. E:3 Removing/installing water pump

1. Radiator cap
2. Filler neck
3. Radiator drain point
4. Cylinder block drain point

Fig. E:4 Cooling system drain points

WATER PUMP . . . . [3]

Removal (Fig. E:3)

1. Drain the cooling system and remove the radiator as described above.
2. Slacken the alternator mounting bolts, press the alternator towards the engine and detach the fan belt from the pulleys.
3. Remove the four retaining bolts and detach the cooling fan, spacer and drive pulley from the water pump hub.
4. Remove the two alternator pivot bolts and swing the alternator outwards away from the mounting flange on the water pump.
5. Slacken the clips on the small by-pass hose between the water pump and the underside of the cylinder head, and disconnect the hose.
6. Disconnect the radiator bottom hose from the pump inlet.
7. Remove the four bolts securing the water pump to the cylinder block face and detach the pump together with its gasket.

Installation

8. Clean all old gasket material from the mating face on the cylinder block (and pump, if original is to be refitted).
9. Position a new gasket on the cylinder block face, using grease to retain it in position.
10. Locate the water pump on the engine and secure with the four retaining bolts.
11. Reconnect the by-pass hose and radiator bottom hose to the pump.
12. Assemble the drive pulley, spacer and cooling fan to the pump hub, then fit the fan belt and adjust the tension so that a total free movement of approximately ½ in (13 mm) is present at the midway point on its longest run.
13. Finally, install the radiator and refill the cooling system.
14. When installation is complete, run the engine up to normal operating temperature and check for leaks.

Technical Data

System type . . . . Pressurised, thermo-syphon, pump and fan assisted

System capacity:
 with heater . . . . .6¼ pints (3.55 litres)
 without heater . . . . 5¼ pints (3.0 litres)
Anti-freeze . . . . .To BS 3151 or BS 3152

Solution	Amount of anti-freeze			Commences freezing		Frozen solid	
%	Pt	U.S. pt	Litres	°C	°F	°C	°F
25	1½	1.8	0.85	−13	9	−26	−15
33⅓	2	2.5	1.2	−19	−2	−36	−33
50	3¼	3.75	1.8	−36	−33	−48	−53

Pressure cap:
 Up to 1974 . . . . 13 lb/sq in (0.91 kg/cm^2)
 1974 on (to ECE15) . . . . 15 lb/sq in (1.05 kg/cm^2)
Thermostat:
 Standard . . . . .82°C (180°F)
 Cold climate . . . . .88°C (188°F)
 Hot climates . . . . 74°C or 77°C (165°F or 170°F)
 1976 on . . . . .88°C (188°F)
Fan belt tension . . . . ½ in (13 mm) deflection on longest run

COOLING
Trouble Shooter

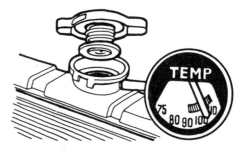

FAULT	CAUSE	CURE
Loss of coolant	1. Damaged radiator 2. Leak at heater connection or plug 3. Damaged cylinder head gasket 4. Cracked cylinder block. 5. Cracked cylinder head. 6. Loose cylinder head bolts	1. Repair or replace radiator. 2. Repair or replace. 3. Replace gasket. Check engine oil and refill as necessary. 4. Replace cylinder block. Check engine oil in crankcase for mixing with water. 5. Replace cylinder head. 6. Tighten cylinder head bolts.
Poor circulation	1. Restriction in system 2. Insufficient coolant 3. Inoperative water pump 4. Loose fan belt 5. Inoperative thermostat	1. Check hoses for crimping. Clear the system of rust and sludge. 2. Replenish. 3. Replace water pump. 4. Adjust for belt. 5. Replace thermostat.
Corrosion	1. Excessive impurity in water 2. Infrequent flushing and draining of system	1. Use soft, clean water. 2. Flush thoroughly at least twice a year.
Overheating	1. Inoperative thermostat 2. Radiator fin choked with mud, leaves etc. 3. Incorrect ignition and valve timing 4. Dirty oil and sludge in engine 5. Inoperative water pump 6. Loose fan belt 7. Restricted radiator 8. Inaccurate temperature gauge 9. Impurity in water	1. Replace thermostat. 2. Clean out air passage. 3. Tune engine. 4. Change engine oil and filter. 5. Replace (or check-electrical). 6. Adjust tension. 7. Flush radiator. 8. Replace temperature gauge. 9. Use soft, clean water.
Overcooling	1. Inoperative thermostat 2. Inaccurate temperature gauge	1. Replace thermostat. 2. Replace temperature gauge.

Fuel System

ELECTRIC FUEL PUMP . . . .[1]

(PD Type)

It is just possible that somewhere one of the very early 848 cc models is still running about with the original SU PD type fuel pump so a few words about this version have been included.

Due to its construction, little servicing can be carried out on the PD pump and this is limited to cleaning the filter and the contact points. If the pump fails, it must be replaced. The procedure for cleaning the pump filter is included in the TUNE-UP section, as is an illustration of the pump installation.

It should be noted that a peculiarity of the PD pump is that when the ignition is switched on the pump will continue to tick even when the engine is not running and the float chamber of the carburettor is full of petrol.

Contact Points

The pump is best removed from its location on the rear sub-frame to inspect the points. Take off the top cover and clean the contact points by drawing a piece of clean paper or card between them. Care should be taken to avoid overstressing the contact blades while doing this. Check that both pairs of contact points make good contact and that the gap between the end of the upper contact blade and its top face is not less than 0.015 in (0.4 mm). No adjustment is provided for the contact points. Also, the contact breaker mechanism is not serviced separately.

SP & AUF 201 Type

Later Mini models, up to the adoption of negative earth electrical system in October 1969, all used either the SU SP or AUF 201 type fuel pump. The two types of pump are of similar construction differing only in respect of the pump body which incorporates the inlet and outlet nozzles, filter and fuel valves. The AUF 201 pump is fitted to later models and can be identified by the two plastic nozzles retained by a clamp plate on the end of the pump body.

The three main sources of trouble with these types of pumps are the contact breaker points, fuel valve and diaphragm. Another common fault is air leakage into the fuel lines, particularly on the inlet side of the pump, causing a constant 'ticking' of the pump without proper fuel delivery when the ignition is switched on.

The pump is best removed from its location at the rear sub-frame for inspection, and this is a straight-forward operation. However, when refitting the pump, ensure that the outlet is located at the top. The outlet must be vertically above the inlet port with the outlet nozzles horizontal.

Overhaul (Fig. F:1)

Contact Points

First remove the end cover and inspect the contact points. The end cover is normally sealed with tape and a rubber band around the joint and these must be removed. Next remove the nut, Lucar connector and star washer from the end terminal screw and take off the bakelite end cover. The points can then be inspected after slackening the screw securing the spring blade and withdrawing the blade which is slotted at its fixed end. The blade retaining screw also secures the long coil lead and need not be completely removed at this time.

Examine the two sets of contact points for signs of burning or pitting, if either is evident the brass rocker assembly and spring blade must be removed and renewed. Replacement of the rocker assembly will be covered in due course.

Now for inspection of the diaphragm which is located between the coil housing and the pump body. Note or mark the relative positions of the housing and body to ensure correct reassembly. Best to note or mark the position of the earth screw hole in the housing in relation to the pump body. Remove the six securing screws and separate the pump body from the coil housing and diaphragm. The neoprene diaphragm can now be examined after carefully peeling back the plastic protective sheet. If either the diaphragm or plastic sheet show signs of damage or deterioration, the diaphragm assembly must be renewed. The diaphragm and central spindle are serviced only as a unit and no attempt should be made to separate them.

MECHANICAL FUEL PUMP . . . . [2]

With the change to negative earth electrical system in October 1969, the electrical type fuel pump was replaced by a mechanical one, mounted on the engine at the rear and driven by an eccentric on the camshaft. Most models will be fitted with the 700 series type pump which has a detachable domed cover for access to the fuel filter screen. However, some later models are fitted with the 800 series type which is a sealed unit and in this case no maintainance or overhaul is possible.

The mechanical pump installation is shown in Fig. F: 5, but removal is a difficult task while the engine is installed in the car and it will be necessary to remove the surrounding components to gain access to the unit. On some models it is difficult even to find enough room to remove the top cover to allow the filter screen to be cleaned. When refitting the pump, always ensure that the total thickness of the pump insulating block with its two gaskets remains unaltered (Fig. F:7).

The main sources of trouble with the mechanical type pump are the fuel valves and the diaphragm, but as stated above these can be serviced only on the 700 series pump.

CARBURETTOR . . . . [3]

Most Mini models are fitted with an SU type HS4 carburettor, the exceptions being early 850/1000 models with manual transmission up to 1974. These latter cars are equipped with an HS2 carburettor. Although both types are of similar design they differ mainly in respect of the position of the float chamber and the throttle lever assembly which are on opposite sides for the two types.

Idle Adjustment

The procedure for adjusting the carburettor slow running is fully described in the TUNE-UP section previously, and reference should be made for details.

Removal and Installation

Unscrew the wing nut or wing nuts on the air cleaner lid and lift the air cleaner assembly off the carburettor air intake duct. On some models it may be necessary to first disconnect the engine breather hose and/or the connector pipe from the air temperature control valve flange.

Disconnect the fuel feed hose from the float chamber, the engine breather hose from the carburettor adaptor (where applicable) and the distributor vacuum advance pipe (Fig. F:8).

Disconnect the throttle return spring from the throttle lever and its abutment bracket, then disconnect the throttle cable. On models with automatic transmission it will also be necessary to disconnect the fork end of the kick-down control rod from the throttle lever. Disconnect the choke cable.

Remove the two nuts and spring washers securing the carburettor to the inlet manifold studs and lift off the carburettor assembly complete with the cable abutment plate.

If required, the air intake duct can now be detached from the carburettor intake.

Installation is a simple reversal of the removal procedure. Use new gaskets between the manifold face, abutment plate and carburettor flange if they have been damaged during removal.

When reconnecting the choke cable, allow approximately 1/16 in (2 mm) free movement before the cable starts to pull on the fast idle cam lever. The throttle pedal should also have approximately 1/8 in (3 mm) of free movement before the throttle starts to open.

When installation is complete, check the idle and mixture settings as described in the TUNE-UP section previously.

On automatic models, check the adjustment of the kick-down control linkage as described in the AUTOMATIC TRANSMISSION section.

Cleaning the Float Chamber

On some models it may first be necessary to remove the air cleaner to gain access to the float chamber.

Disconnect the fuel feed pipe from the float chamber lid. Mark the relative positions of the float chamber lid and body to ensure correct alignment on reassembly. Remove the three screws securing the lid to the float chamber body and detach the lid assembly, together with its gasket (Fig. F:9). Retain the part number tag fitted to one of the retaining screws.

Clean any sediment from the float chamber - this can best be done by soaking up the fuel in the chamber with a suitable absorbent lint-free cloth, then blowing any remaining sediment out of the chamber with an air-line.

If required, the fuel float can be removed and the fuel needle withdrawn from its housing to check its condition. Hold the float hinge pin at its serrated end when withdrawing it. Examine the fuel needle for wear i.e. small ridges or grooves on the seat end of the needle. Also check that the spring-loaded plunger on the opposite end operates freely, (later type needles only). Renew the needle valve and seating if worn. The seating is a screw fit in the float chamber lid.

Reassemble the components in the reverse order of removing. The fuel needle is inserted, coned-end first, into its seating.

On early models which have a brass or nylon float with a metal float lever, the float level setting should be checked as follows:

With the float chamber lid held upside-down, insert a drill or gauge rod of suitable diameter between the hinged lever and the machined lip of the float chamber lid (Fig. F:10). The end of the lever should just rest on the rod when the needle is on its seating. Use a 5/16 in (8 mm) rod for the brass float, and and 1/8 in (3 mm) rod with the nylon float.

If adjustment is necessary, this should be carried out at the point where the end of the lever meets the shank. Do NOT bend the shank, which must be perfectly flat and at right-angles to the needle when on its seating.

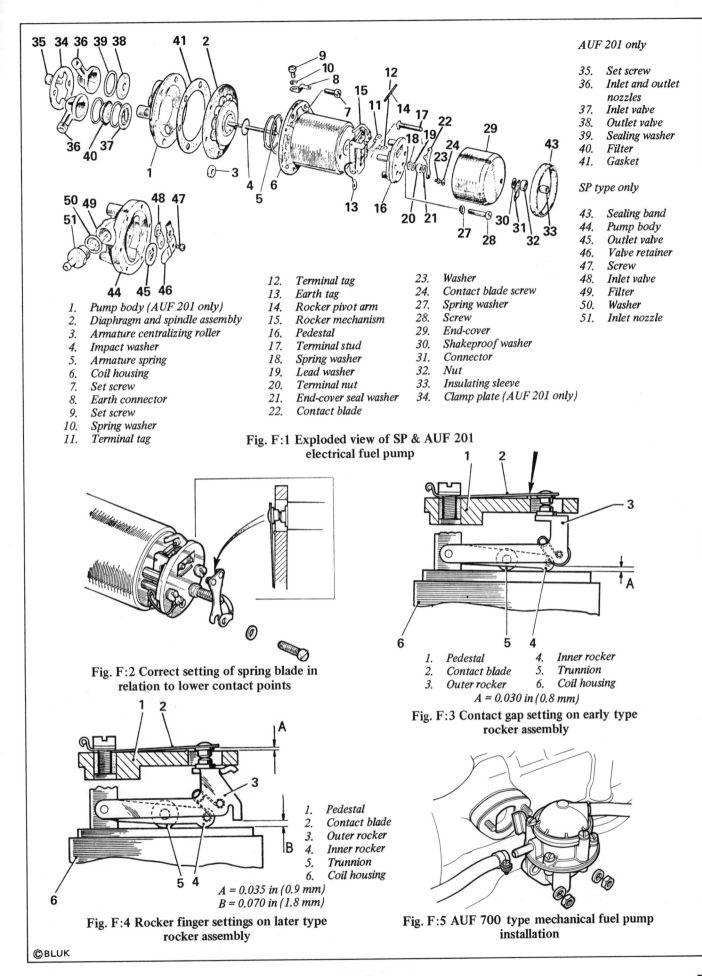

35. Set screw
34. Clamp plate (AUF 201 only)

AUF 201 only

35. Set screw
36. Inlet and outlet
    nozzles
37. Inlet valve
38. Outlet valve
39. Sealing washer
40. Filter
41. Gasket

SP type only

43. Sealing band
44. Pump body
45. Outlet valve
46. Valve retainer
47. Screw
48. Inlet valve
49. Filter
50. Washer
51. Inlet nozzle

1. Pump body (AUF 201 only)
2. Diaphragm and spindle assembly
3. Armature centralizing roller
4. Impact washer
5. Armature spring
6. Coil housing
7. Set screw
8. Earth connector
9. Set screw
10. Spring washer
11. Terminal tag

12. Terminal tag
13. Earth tag
14. Rocker pivot arm
15. Rocker mechanism
16. Pedestal
17. Terminal stud
18. Spring washer
19. Lead washer
20. Terminal nut
21. End-cover seal washer
22. Contact blade

23. Washer
24. Contact blade screw
27. Spring washer
28. Screw
29. End-cover
30. Shakeproof washer
31. Connector
32. Nut
33. Insulating sleeve
34. Clamp plate (AUF 201 only)

Fig. F:1 Exploded view of SP & AUF 201 electrical fuel pump

Fig. F:2 Correct setting of spring blade in relation to lower contact points

1. Pedestal
2. Contact blade
3. Outer rocker
4. Inner rocker
5. Trunnion
6. Coil housing

A = 0.030 in (0.8 mm)

Fig. F:3 Contact gap setting on early type rocker assembly

1. Pedestal
2. Contact blade
3. Outer rocker
4. Inner rocker
5. Trunnion
6. Coil housing

A = 0.035 in (0.9 mm)
B = 0.070 in (1.8 mm)

Fig. F:4 Rocker finger settings on later type rocker assembly

Fig. F:5 AUF 700 type mechanical fuel pump installation

©BLUK

Centring the Jet (Fig. F:18)

If the piston does not fall freely on the carburettor bridge with a distinct metal click when the jet adjusting nut is screwed to its uppermost position, the carburettor jet must be centralised as follows:

It should be noted that this procedure applied only to early type carburettors, as later carburettors have a spring-loaded needle which is self-centring (Fig. F:12).

Remove the air cleaner assembly to allow access. Support the plastic moulded base of the jet, then remove the screw retaining the jet pick-up link and link bracket to the jet head (Fig. F:11). Unscrew the sleeve nut from the base of the float chamber and disconnect the jet flexible feed tube. Withdraw the jet assembly from the bottom of the carburettor. Unscrew the jet adjusting nut, remove the locking spring and refit the nut without the spring. Screw the nut up as far as possible. Now slacken the jet bearing locking nut until the jet bearing can be turned with the fingers. Refit the jet assembly in the jet bearing and hold it in the uppermost position with a finger.

Remove the damper piston from the top of the suction chamber and, using a pencil or similar instrument, apply gentle pressure to the top of the piston rod to push the piston down onto the bridge. Tighten the jet locking nut while holding the jet against the jet bearing. Ensure that the jet is in its correct angular position during this operation.

With the jet still in the fully raised position, lift the piston with the lifting pin then release it and check that it falls freely onto the carburettor bridge with a soft metallic click. Lower the jet with the adjusting nut and repeat the check. An identical sound should be heard with the jet raised or lowered. If a sharper click is heard with the jet in the lowered position, repeat the centring procedure.

If difficulty is encountered in correctly centring the jet, this can often be achieved by raising the piston and allowing it to fall onto the jet bridge. The slight impact should locate the jet in its central position in relation to the piston needle.

When the centring procedure is successfully completed, remove the jet assembly and refit the adjusting nut with its locking spring. Screw the nut up as far as possible, then turn it down two complete turns (12 flats) to provide the initial setting.

Refit the jet in the bearing and reconnect the flexible feed tube to the float chamber. Ensure that the end of the tube projects a minimum of 3/16 in (5 mm) beyond the sealing gland before fitting the tube. Tighten the sleeve nut only until the gland is compressed as over-tightening can cause leakage.

Support the jet head and reconnect the pick-up link and link bracket with the securing screw.

Top up the piston damper with light oil, as necessary, to bring the oil level approximately 1/2 in (13 mm) above the top of the hollow piston rod. Refit the air cleaner assembly.

Finally, check the idle and mixture settings and adjust if necessary as described in the TUNE-UP section previously.

Cleaning the Piston and Suction Chamber

A sticking piston will inhibit acceleration and smooth running and can be ascertained by removing the piston damper from the top of the suction chamber and raising the piston with the lifting pin, or a finger inserted into the carburettor intake. The piston should move up quite freely when raised, and fall back smartly when released.

If sticking does occur, the whole assembly should be removed and cleaned as described below:

Remove the air cleaner assembly. Mark the position of the suction chamber in relation to the carburettor body to ensure correct alignment on reassembly. Thoroughly clean the outside of the suction chamber and the adjacent surface on the carburettor body.

Remove the damper from the top of the suction chamber. Remove the three securing screws and lift off the suction chamber. Remove the piston spring. Carefully lift the piston assembly out of the carburettor body and empty the oil from the hollow in the end of the piston rod.

Carefully clean all fuel deposits, etc., from the inside of the suction chamber and the two diameters of the piston, using petrol, or preferably methylated spirit, then wipe the components dry. Do NOT use abrasives to clean these items.

The operation of the suction chamber and piston can be checked as follows if required: Plug the transfer holes in the bottom of the piston with rubber plugs or Plasticene (Fig. F:14). Insert the piston fully into the suction chamber and refit the damper assembly. Secure a large flat washer to one of the suction chamber fixing holes with a screw and nut so that it overlaps the bore.

With the assembly held upside-down, hold the piston and check the time taken for the suction chamber to fall the full extent of its travel. This should take five to seven seconds. If this time is exceeded, check both the piston and the suction chamber for cleanliness and mechanical damage. If the suction chamber has been dropped at any time this may have damaged the bore and be the cause. Renew the piston and suction chamber assembly if the time taken cannot be brought within these specified limits.

Lubricate the piston rod lightly with a drop of light oil - one of the non-oil lubricants such as WD 40 may be used for this purpose. Reassemble the components in the reverse order of removing, not forgetting the piston spring. Ensure that the assembly marks made previously are correctly aligned, then tighten the securing screws evenly.

Finally, fill the piston damper with light oil until the level is approximately ½ in (13 mm) above the top of the hollow piston rod, then refit the piston damper.

THROTTLE CABLE . . . . [4]

Replacement (Fig. F:15)

Detach the throttle return spring from the throttle lever and its abutment bracket. Slacken the clamp nut to release the cable at the throttle lever then withdraw the

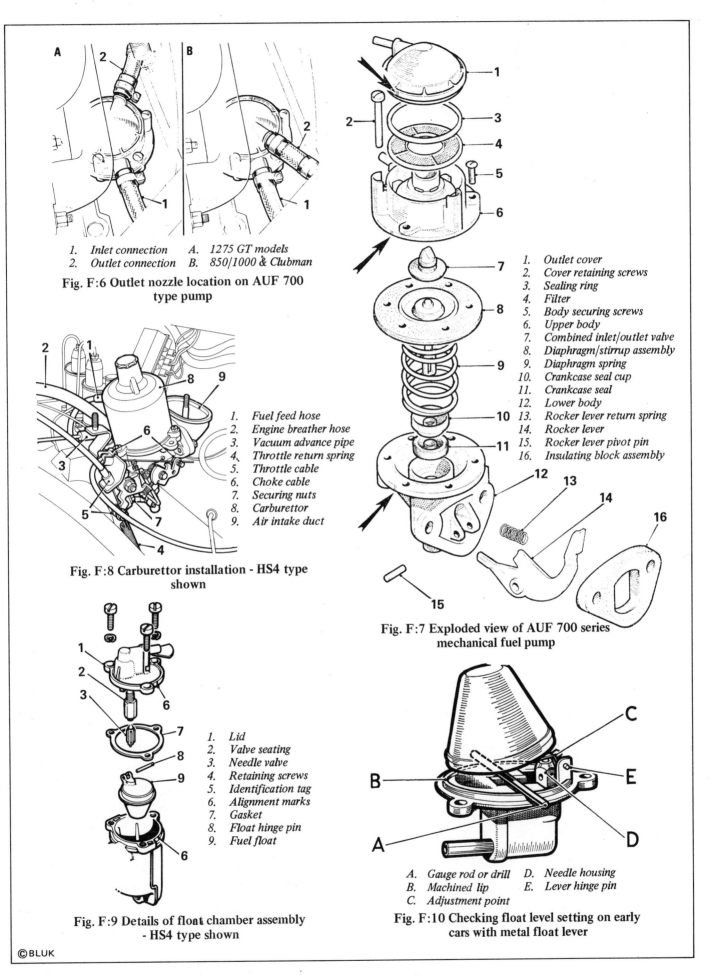

A. 1275 GT models
B. 850/1000 & Clubman

1. Inlet connection
2. Outlet connection

Fig. F:6 Outlet nozzle location on AUF 700 type pump

1. Fuel feed hose
2. Engine breather hose
3. Vacuum advance pipe
4. Throttle return spring
5. Throttle cable
6. Choke cable
7. Securing nuts
8. Carburettor
9. Air intake duct

Fig. F:8 Carburettor installation - HS4 type shown

1. Outlet cover
2. Cover retaining screws
3. Sealing ring
4. Filter
5. Body securing screws
6. Upper body
7. Combined inlet/outlet valve
8. Diaphragm/stirrup assembly
9. Diaphragm spring
10. Crankcase seal cup
11. Crankcase seal
12. Lower body
13. Rocker lever return spring
14. Rocker lever
15. Rocker lever pivot pin
16. Insulating block assembly

Fig. F:7 Exploded view of AUF 700 series mechanical fuel pump

1. Lid
2. Valve seating
3. Needle valve
4. Retaining screws
5. Identification tag
6. Alignment marks
7. Gasket
8. Float hinge pin
9. Fuel float

Fig. F:9 Details of float chamber assembly - HS4 type shown

A. Gauge rod or drill
B. Machined lip
C. Adjustment point
D. Needle housing
E. Lever hinge pin

Fig. F:10 Checking float level setting on early cars with metal float lever

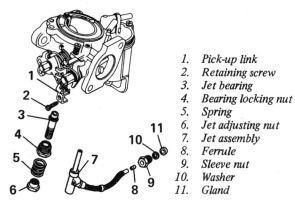

1. Pick-up link
2. Retaining screw
3. Jet bearing
4. Bearing locking nut
5. Spring
6. Jet adjusting nut
7. Jet assembly
8. Ferrule
9. Sleeve nut
10. Washer
11. Gland

Fig. F:11 Details of jet assembly

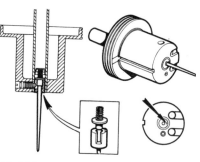

Fig. F:12 Needle assembly to piston on later models with spring - loaded needle

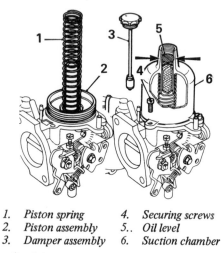

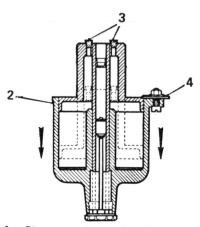

1. Piston assembly
2. Suction chamber
3. Plugs
4. Washer

Fig. F:14 Checking operation of suction chamber and piston

1. Piston spring
2. Piston assembly
3. Damper assembly
4. Securing screws
5. Oil level
6. Suction chamber

Fig. F:13 Piston and suction chamber assembly

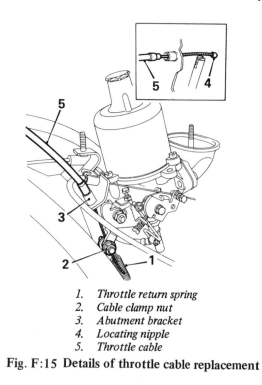

1. Throttle return spring
2. Cable clamp nut
3. Abutment bracket
4. Locating nipple
5. Throttle cable

Fig. F:15 Details of throttle cable replacement

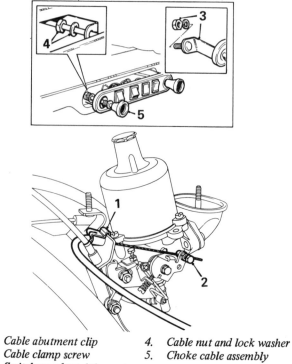

1. Cable abutment clip
2. Cable clamp screw
3. Switch panel retaining nuts
4. Cable nut and lock washer
5. Choke cable assembly

Fig. F:16 Details of choke cable replacement

Fuel System

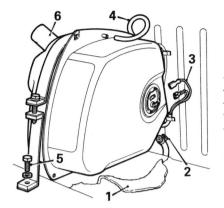

Fig. F:17 Details of fuel tank installation -
Saloon models

1. Under felt
2. Fuel supply hose
3. Gauge unit leads
4. Breather pipe
5. Strap bolt
6. Filler neck

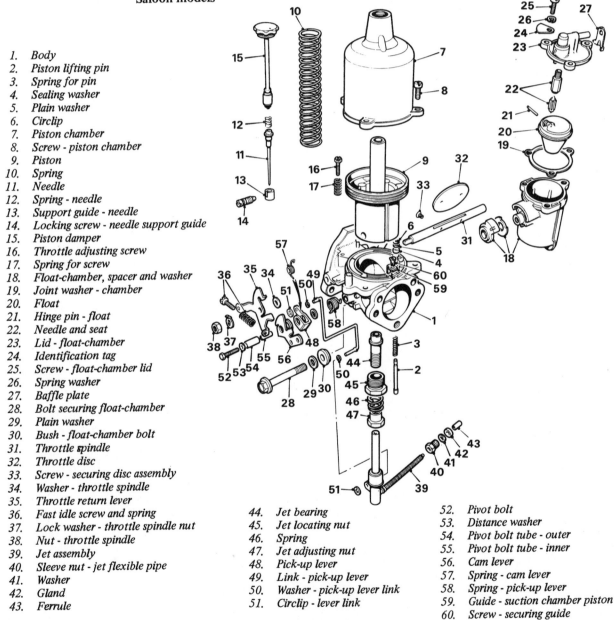

1. Body
2. Piston lifting pin
3. Spring for pin
4. Sealing washer
5. Plain washer
6. Circlip
7. Piston chamber
8. Screw - piston chamber
9. Piston
10. Spring
11. Needle
12. Spring - needle
13. Support guide - needle
14. Locking screw - needle support guide
15. Piston damper
16. Throttle adjusting screw
17. Spring for screw
18. Float-chamber, spacer and washer
19. Joint washer - chamber
20. Float
21. Hinge pin - float
22. Needle and seat
23. Lid - float-chamber
24. Identification tag
25. Screw - float-chamber lid
26. Spring washer
27. Baffle plate
28. Bolt securing float-chamber
29. Plain washer
30. Bush - float-chamber bolt
31. Throttle spindle
32. Throttle disc
33. Screw - securing disc assembly
34. Washer - throttle spindle
35. Throttle return lever
36. Fast idle screw and spring
37. Lock washer - throttle spindle nut
38. Nut - throttle spindle
39. Jet assembly
40. Sleeve nut - jet flexible pipe
41. Washer
42. Gland
43. Ferrule
44. Jet bearing
45. Jet locating nut
46. Spring
47. Jet adjusting nut
48. Pick-up lever
49. Link - pick-up lever
50. Washer - pick-up lever link
51. Circlip - lever link
52. Pivot bolt
53. Distance washer
54. Pivot bolt tube - outer
55. Pivot bolt tube - inner
56. Cam lever
57. Spring - cam lever
58. Spring - pick-up lever
59. Guide - suction chamber piston
60. Screw - securing guide

Fig. F:18 Exploded view of HS4 type carburettor

Fuel System

cable from the abutment-bracket.

At the throttle pedal, release the nipple end from the slot in the top of the pedal lever and push the cable through the bulkhead into the engine compartment. Remove the rubber clip securing the cable to the heater hose and withdraw the cable assembly.

Fit the new cable in the reverse sequence. Ensure that the throttle pedal has approximately 1/8 in (4 mm) free movement before if begins to open the throttle.

CHOKE CABLE . . . . [5]

Replacement (Fig. F:16)

Remove the air cleaner assembly to allow access. Detach the clip securing the choke cable to the abutment bracket, then slacken the clamp screw at the cable trunnion and disconnect the cable from the carburettor.

Working inside the car, remove the screws securing the heater assembly under the parcel shelf and lower the heater to gain access to the rear side of the switch panel. Disconnect the lead from the heater switch. Remove the nuts securing the switch panel and pull the panel forward from the dash. Remove the locking nut and washer securing the choke outer cable to the switch panel. Pull the complete cable assembly through the bulkhead grommet and withdraw it from the switch panel.

Install the new cable in the reverse order of above. Ensure that the cable has 1/16 in (2 mm) free movement before it starts to pull on the fast idle cam lever.

FUEL TANK. . . . . [6]

Removal & Installation - Saloon (Fig. F:17)

As a safety precaution, first disconnect the battery.

Empty all possible fuel from the tank. This is best done either by syphoning or pumping it out.

Remove the floor covering from the luggage compartment and lift out the spare wheel. Where underfelt is fitted in the luggage compartment, fold it back from around the fuel tank.

Disconnect the fuel supply hose from the bottom of the tank. Disconnect the leads from the tank gauge unit and the breather pipe from its connection at the top of the tank (where fitted).

Remove the bolt securing the tank retaining straps and withdraw the tank, releasing the filler neck from the grommet in the rear wing panel. Remove the tank from the luggage compartment.

If a new tank is being fitted, the tank gauge unit should be transferred to the new tank. Unscrew the unit locking ring and withdraw the gauge unit, together with its sealing ring from the tank. Use a new sealing ring when installing the gauge unit in the new tank.

The tank is installed in the reverse order of removing.

Removal & Installation - Estate

As a safety precaution, first disconnect the battery. Remove the drain plug from the fuel tank and drain out the fuel into a suitable container. Unscrew and disconnect the fuel supply pipe from the tank. Release the pipe from the retaining clips. Remove the filler cap. Disconnect the leads from the tank gauge unit.

Remove the tank securing screws, noting the plastic spacers, and lower the fuel tank out of its location.

If a new tank is being fitted, the tank gauge unit should be transferred to the new tank. Remove the screws securing the gauge unit and withdraw the unit, together with its gaskets from the tank. Use a new gasket when installing the gauge unit in the new tank.

Install the tank in the reverse sequence of removing.

Technical Data

CARBURETTOR - 850

	1959-72 (Manual)	1965-69 (Automatic)	72-74 (Manual)	74-76 (Manual) (ECE 15)	1976 on (Manual) (ECE 15)
Type.	SU Type HS2	SU Type HS4	SU Type HS2	SU Type HS4	SU Type HS4
Piston spring.	Red	Red	Red	Red	Red
Jet size	0.090 in (3 mm)	0.090 in	0.090 in	0.090 in	0.090 in
Idle speed	500 rpm	650 rpm	800 rpm	800 rpm	750 rpm
Fast idle	900 rpm	1050 rpm	1100-1200 rpm	1100-1200 rpm	1200 rpm
EGA reading, at idle.	—	—	3.5-4.5% Co	3.5-4.5% Co	3% Co

CARBURETTOR - 1000/CLUBMAN 1000

	1967-72 (Manual)	1972-74 (Manual)	1967-74 (Automatic)	74-76 (Man & Auto) (ECE 15)	1976 on (Man & Auto) (ECE 15)
Type	SU Type HS2	SU Type HS2	SU Type HS4	SU Type HS4	SU Type HS4
Piston spring	Red	Red	Red	Red	Red
Jet size	0.090 in (3 mm)	0.090 in	0.090 in	0.090 in	0.090 in
Idle speed	500 rpm	800 rpm	650 rpm	750 rpm	750 rpm
Fast idle	900 rpm	1100 rpm	1050 rpm	1100-1200 rpm	1300 rpm (1200 rpm, Auto)
EGA reading, at idle	—	3.5-4.5% Co	—	3.5-4.5% Co	3% Co

CARBURETTOR - CLUBMAN 1100

	1974-76 (Manual) (ECE 15)	1976-78 (Manual) ECE 15)
Type	SU Type HS4	SU Type HS4
Piston spring	Red	Red
Jet size	0.090 in (3 mm)	0.090 in
Idle speed	750 rpm	750 rpm
Fast idle	1100-1200 rpm	1200 rpm
EGA reading, at idle	3-4.5% Co	3% Co

CARBURETTOR - 1275 GT

	1969-72 (Manual)	1972-76 (Manual) (ECE 15)	1976-77 (Manual) (ECE 15)	1978 (Manual) (ECE 15)
Type	SU Type HS4	SU Type HS4	SU Type HS4	SU Type HS4
Piston spring	Red	Red	Red	Red
Jet size	0.090 in (3 mm)	0.090 in	0.090 in	0.090 in
Idle speed	650 rpm	750 rpm	850 rpm	750 rpm
Fast idle	1050 rpm	1100-1200 rpm	1300 rpm	1100 rpm
EGA reading, at idle	—	3-4.5% Co	3% Co	3% Co

FUEL TANK

Capacity:
Saloon*	5½ galls (25 litres)
Van & Pick-up	6 galls (27.3 litres)
1275 GT	
up to 1974	5½ galls (25 litres)
1974 on	7½ galls (34 litres)

* Some Clubman 1100 Saloon models have 7½ galls (34 litres) capacity

FUEL
Trouble Shooter

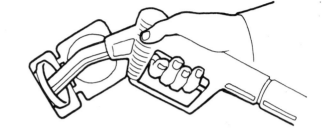

FAULT	CAUSE	CURE
Flooding	1. Improper seating or damaged float needle valve or seat 2. Incorrect float level 3. Fuel pump has excessive pressure	1. Check and replace parts as necessary. 2. Adjust float level. 3. Check fuel pump.
Excessive fuel consumption	1. Engine out of tune 2. Float level too high 3. Loose plug or jet 4. Defective gasket 5. Fuel leaks at pipes or connections 6. Choke valve operates improperly 7. Obstructed air bleed	1. Tune engine. 2. Adjust float level. 3. Tighten plug or jet. 4. Replace gaskets. 5. Trace leak and rectify. 6. Check choke valve. 7. Check and clear.
Stalling	1. Main jet obstructed 2. Incorrect throttle opening 3. Slow-running adjustment incorrect 4. Slow-running fuel jet blocked 5. Incorrect float level	1. Clean main jet. 2. Adjust throttle. 3. Adjust slow-running. 4. Clean jet. 5. Adjust float level.
Poor acceleration	1. Defective accelerator pump (if fitted) 2. Float level too low 3. Incorrect throttle opening 4. Defective accelerator linkage 5. Blocked pump jet	1. Overhaul pump. 2. Adjust float level. 3. Adjust throttle. 4. Adjust accelerator linkage. 5. Clean pump jet.
Spitting	1. Lean mixture 2. Dirty carburettor 3. Clogged fuel pipes 4. Manifold draws secondary air	1. Clean and adjust carburettor. 2. Clean carburettor. 3. Clean or replace pipes. 4. Tighten or replace gasket.
Insufficient fuel supply	1. Clogged carburettor 2. Clogged fuel pipe 3. Dirty fuel 4. Air in fuel system 5. Defective fuel pump 6. Clogged fuel filter	1. Dismantle and clean carburettor. 2. Clean fuel pipe. 3. Clean fuel tank. 4. Check connections and tighten. 5. Repair or replace fuel pump. 6. Clean or replace filter.
Loss of fuel delivery	1. Pump faulty (electric) 2. Slotted body screws loose 3. Diaphragm cracked 4. Loose fuel pipe connections 5. Defective valves 6. Cracked fuel pipes	1. Replace pump. 2. Tighten body screws. 3. Overhaul fuel pump. 4. Tighten fuel pipe connections. 5. Replace valves. 6. Replace fuel pipes.
Noisy pump	1. Loose pump mounting 2. Worn or defective rocker arm (if manual) 3. Broken rocker arm spring (if manual)	1. Tighten mounting bolts. 2. Replace rocker arm. 3. Replace spring.

Emission Control

GENERAL DESCRIPTION. . . . . [1]

Some export models are fitted with emission control devices to meet the Emission Control Regulations of the countries in which they are marketed. In Europe, the Control Regulations are met at present by recalibration of the carburettor jets, the idle mixture strengths and the ignition systems. For the North American market, however, with its more stringent U.S.A. and Canadian Federal requirements, an additional air injection system is used to extend the combustion process into the engine's exhaust system by the injection of air into the exhaust ports. This sustains and supports the combustion process beyond the combustion chambers in order to reduce the hydrocarbon (HC) and carbon monoxide (CO) content of the exhaust gases.

The efficient operation of the emission control system depends on the engine being correctly tuned, and for this reason the tuning specifications for engines with emission control systems must be strictly adhered to at all times. These are given in 'Technical Data' at the end of this section.

Proper test equipment is necessary to carry out a satisfactory check of the emission control systems. This is particularly applicable in countries where the systems must be checked in accordance with the local regulations and a certificate issued after the check. In this case, all adjustments and settings on the systems should be entrusted to an Authorised Dealer or Specialist.

MAINTENANCE ITEMS. . . . . [2]

Air Pump Drive Belt

It is important that the air pump drive belt be correctly tensioned to ensure efficient operation of the air injection system. When the belt is correctly adjusted, a total deflection of ½ in (13 mm) should be possible under normal finger pressure at the midway point of the belt run between the two pulleys.

If adjustment is necessary, slacken the pump securing bolts and the adjusting link bolt and move the pump to the required position to achieve the correct tension (Fig. G:3). Avoid over-tightening the belt. Recheck the tension after tightening the adjusting link and pump mounting bolts.

The condition of the pump drive belt should also be checked periodically and the belt replaced if nicked, cut, excessively worn or otherwise damaged.

To replace the belt, proceed as for adjusting but press the pump fully in towards the engine and detach the belt from the air pump and water pump pulleys. Feed the belt between the tips of the fan blades and the radiator cowling at the top as the blades are rotated, then pull the belt out from between the fan and radiator. It may be necessary to detach the radiator top mounting bracket and top hose and pull the radiator away from the engine to obtain sufficient clearance for the old belt to be removed and the new one fitted. Adjust the tension of the new belt as described above.

It should be noted that the tension of a new belt should be checked after approximately 100 miles (160 km) use.

Gulp Valve

To check the operation of the gulp valve, first disconnect the air supply hose at the air pump. Connect a 'T' adaptor and vacuum gauge to the gulp valve hose, as shown in Fig. G:4. Start the engine and run it at idle speed; the engine must remain at idle during this test. Seal the open end of the 'T' adaptor with the finger and check that the vacuum gauge reads zero for approximately 15 seconds. If a vacuum reading is obtained, the gulp valve must be renewed.

Repeat the test, but open the throttle rapidly; the gauge should register a vacuum reading. Remove the finger from the 'T' piece to release the vacuum. Repeat this test several times. If a vacuum is not registered, renew the gulp valve.

When the test is completed remove the gauge and 'T' adaptor and reconnect the air supply hose. Tighten the hose clips securely.

Diverter Valve

The air diverter valve which controls the air supply to the injection manifold is actuated by the operation of the carburettor choke mechanism and may be either cable-operated, or vacuum operated on early models. In either case the general condition of the diverter valve should be checked before attempting to check its operation. Also ensure that the air silencer is in place.

To check the operation of the cable-operated type valve, first pull out the choke control knob sufficiently to obtain a clearance of 0.010 - 0.015 in (0.25 - 0.38 mm) between the jet housing and the adjusting nut at the carburettor. Check the clearance between the operating lever and the valve stem at the diverter valve. This should be 0.0015 - 0.003 in (0.04 - 0.08 mm). If necessary, slacken the trunnion at the operating cable and adjust the position of the operating lever to obtain the correct setting. Retighten the trunnion.

Disconnect the air supply hose from the exhaust check valve. Start the engine and run it at idle speed. Air pressure should be felt at the air supply hose end. Pull out the choke control knob and check that the air supply is now completely cut off. If air pressure is still felt at the hose end, the diverter valve is defective and must be renewed.

The checking operation is similar for the vacuum operated type diverter valve, but obviously the cable adjustment procedure given above will not apply in this case.

Exhaust Check Valve

The exhaust check valve can be easily tested once removed from its location in the pump supply line. When disconnecting the valve from the air manifold, hold the manifold union to prevent it twisting while unscrewing the valve.

Using the mouth, blow into the valve from each end in turn. Air should only pass through the valve from the air supply end (hose connection end). If air passes through from the threaded (air manifold) end, the valve is defective and must be renewed.

Air Temperature Control Valve

The air temperature control valve is incorporated in the air intake to the air cleaner and its operation can be checked by depressing the valve flap, then releasing it The valve should return easily to its original position. The valve seat should also be inspected for any signs of damage or deterioration.

When the engine is cold, the valve should be in the closed position, so that only hot air from around the exhaust manifold is drawn into the cleaner intake.

Fuel Line Filter

An in-line fuel filter is incorporated in the fuel supply line at the carburettor, and should be renewed as an assembly at the recommended intervals. Ensure that the new filter is fitted with the flow arrow pointing towards the carburettor. On some types of filter the filter inlet con connection may be marked 'IN' instead, and the inlet hose should be connected to this side.

Absorption Canister

The absorption canister for the Fuel Evaporative Loss Control system must be renewed at the recommended intervals to ensure proper and efficient operation of the system.

The canister is easily replaced in the following way: After disconnecting the hoses, remove the retaining screw and open the bracket sufficiently to withdraw the canister. Ensure that the hoses are properly and securely reconnected to the canister.

At the same time, disconnect the purge hose from the rocker cover elbow and examine the restrictor orifice for any signs of dirt or deposits. Clean, if necessary, using a length of soft wire. Reconnect the purge hose.

Carburettor Throttle Damper

Where a throttle damper is fitted at the carburettor, its setting should be checked and adjusted if necessary. The air cleaner and air temperature control valve assembly must first be removed to allow access. The engine idle speed must also be correctly set before carrying out this check.

Insert a 0.080 in (2.03 mm) feeler gauge between the lever pad and the damper plunger and depress the lever The idle adjusting screw should contact and the damper plunger should be fully depressed. If not, the damper lever should be adjusted as follows.

Slacken the lever clamp. Insert the feeler gauge between the lever pad and the damper plunger. Depress the lever and hold the plunger at the bottom of its stroke. Ensure the throttle is closed and that a clearance exists between the lever clamp and the carburettor body. Retighten the clamp nut and check the action of the throttle linkage. Finally, refit the air cleaner and temperature control valve.

Carburettor Tuning

The use of an Exhaust Gas Analyser (Co meter) is essential to check the carburettor mixture setting and, as it is unlikely that the normal ownerdriver will possess such expensive equipment, it is therefore advised that the checking and adjustment of the carburettor settings be left to an Authorised Dealer or Specialist.

On models fitted with Emission Control equipment, additional maintenance items must be carried out at specified intervals to ensure that the systems operate at their correct level of efficiency (see Technical Data).

The efficient operation of the systems is also dependent on the general state of tune of the engine and great care must be taken to ensure that the engine and its associated components (valve clearances, ignition and spark plug settings, carburettor setting etc.) are in good condition and/or correctly adjusted in accordance with the specifications given in 'Technical Data'.

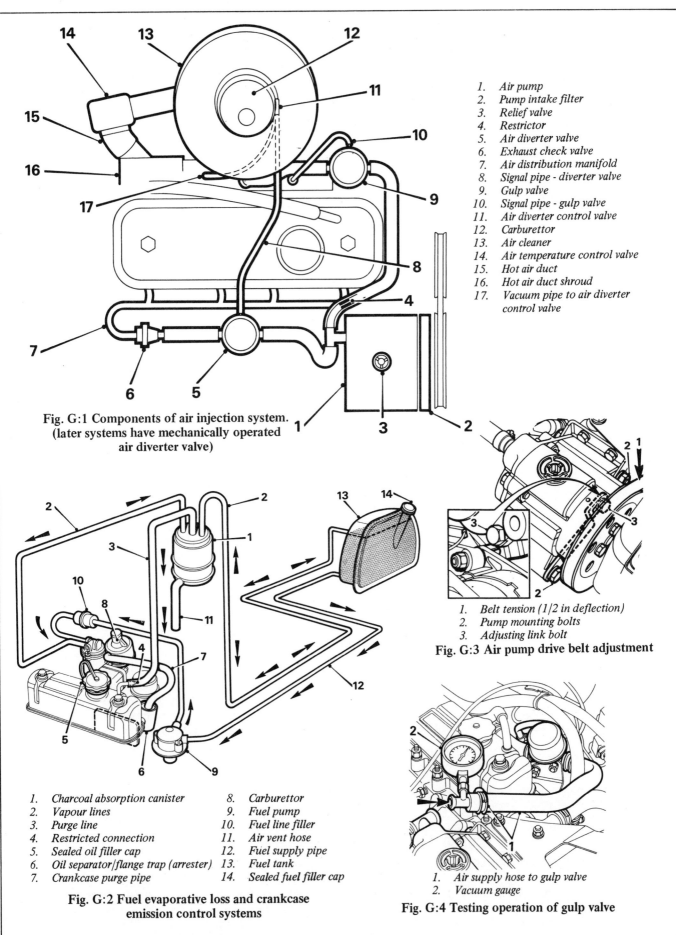

Fig. G:1 Components of air injection system.
(later systems have mechanically operated
air diverter valve)

1. Air pump
2. Pump intake filter
3. Relief valve
4. Restrictor
5. Air diverter valve
6. Exhaust check valve
7. Air distribution manifold
8. Signal pipe - diverter valve
9. Gulp valve
10. Signal pipe - gulp valve
11. Air diverter control valve
12. Carburettor
13. Air cleaner
14. Air temperature control valve
15. Hot air duct
16. Hot air duct shroud
17. Vacuum pipe to air diverter
    control valve

1. Belt tension (1/2 in deflection)
2. Pump mounting bolts
3. Adjusting link bolt

Fig. G:3 Air pump drive belt adjustment

1. Charcoal absorption canister	8. Carburettor
2. Vapour lines	9. Fuel pump
3. Purge line	10. Fuel line filler
4. Restricted connection	11. Air vent hose
5. Sealed oil filler cap	12. Fuel supply pipe
6. Oil separator/flange trap (arrester)	13. Fuel tank
7. Crankcase purge pipe	14. Sealed fuel filler cap

Fig. G:2 Fuel evaporative loss and crankcase
emission control systems

1. Air supply hose to gulp valve
2. Vacuum gauge

Fig. G:4 Testing operation of gulp valve

Technical Data

MINI 1000 (CANADA) - 1970 to 75

Engine type	99H
Capacity	998 cc
Compression ratio	8,9:1

Idling speed
to 1973	800 rpm
1973 on	850 rpm
Fast idle speed	1200 - 1300 rpm

Ignition timing:
Static (to 1972)	1° BTDC
Stroboscopic (to 1972)	(vacuum disconnected) 9° BTDC at 1000 rpm
Static (1972)	2° BTDC
Stroboscopic (1972)	(vacuum disconnected) 9° BTDC at 1000 rpm
Static (1973 on)	6° BTDC
Stroboscopic (1973 on)	(vacuum disconnected) 8° BTDC at 1500 rpm
Exhaust emission level at idle speed	4.5% Co (maximum)

MINI 1000 (CANADA) - 1975 to 77

Engine type	99H 834 V
Capacity	998 cc
Compression ratio	8,3:1
Idling speed	850 ± 100 rpm
Fast idle speed	1250 ± 100 rpm
Ignition timing: Stroboscopic	8° BTDC at 1500 rpm
Fuel octane rating	91 minimum
Exhaust emission level at idle speed	5% ± ½% Co with AIS disconnected

MINI 1000 (CANADA) - 1977 to 78

Engine type	99H
Capacity	998 cc
Compression ratio	8.3:1
Idling speed	850 ± 100 rpm
Fast idle speed	1250 ± 100 rpm
Ignition timing: Stroboscopic	8° BTDC at 1500 rpm
Fuel octane rating	91 minimum
Exhaust emission level at idle speed	5% ± ½% CO with AIS disconnected

MINI 1000 (SWEDEN) - 1977 to 78

Engine type	99H
Capacity	998 cc
Compression ratio	8.3:1
Idling speed	850 ± 100 rpm
Fast idle speed	1250 ± 100 rpm
Ignition timing: Stroboscopic	8° BTDC at 1500 rpm
Fuel octane rating	91 minimum
Exhaust emission level at idle speed	5% ± 1% Co with AIS disconnected

SERVICE SCHEDULE FOR EMISSION CONTROL VEHICLES
EVERY 3,000 MILES (5,000 KM) OR 3 MONTHS

- Check air pump drive belt tension and condition.
- Check exhaust system for leaks and security.
- Check fuel system for leaks.

EVERY 12,000 MILES (20,000 KM) OR 12 MONTHS
As for 3,000 mile check above, plus the following additional items

- Check air injection system hoses and pipes for condition and security.
- Check operation of gulp valve, exhaust check valve and air diverter valve.
- Check crankcase breather system and evaporative loss system hoses, pipes and restrictor for condition, security and blockage.
- Renew evaporative loss system absorption canister.
- Check operation of carburettor air intake temperature control system.
- Renew fuel line filter.
- Check condition of fuel filler cap seal

Clutch & Transmission

CLUTCH ASSEMBLY. . . . . [1]

Removal

1. Disconnect the earth strap from the battery.
2. Remove the bonnet, after first marking the fitted position of the hinges to facilitate alignment when refitting.
3. Where fitted, detach the ignition shield from the front of the engine.
4. On models where the ignition coil mounting bracket is attached to one of the cylinder head studs, remove the cylinder head nut retaining the coil bracket and move the coil and bracket to one side out of the way.
5. On later models which have a plastic air intake assembly at the righthand front wing valance, withdraw the intake assembly into the engine compartment after pulling off the flexible pipe from beneath the wing.
6. Where the horn is mounted on the bonnet locking platform, disconnect and remove the horn, where necessary.
7. Disconnect the starter cable from the starter motor. Remove the starter motor from the flywheel housing.
8. Where the ignition or starter solenoid is mounted on the flywheel housing, disconnect the wiring and remove the coil or solenoid.
9. On models with the starter solenoid mounted on right-hand wing valance disconnect the wiring and remove the solenoid.
10. Disconnect the return spring from between the clutch operating lever and the slave cylinder.
11. Remove the nuts securing the radiator upper support bracket to the thermostat housing, and the bolts securing it to the radiator cowl, and remove the bracket.
12. Jack up the front of the car and support on stands located under the front sub-frame side-members.
13. Remove the air cleaner assembly and disconnect the exhaust down-pipe at the manifold flange. From underneath the car, also detach the exhaust pipe clip from the transmission casing.
14. Support the power unit with a hydraulic jack positioned under the transmission casing.

15. Remove the two bolts and nuts securing the right-hand engine mounting to the sub-frame side-member.
16. Now raise the power unit sufficiently with the jack to allow the clutch cover retaining bolts and the clutch cover to be removed, but take great care not to let the cooling fan blades damage the radiator core.
17. Remove the cover retaining bolts and detach the clutch cover. Note that the engine earth strap is normally secured by one of the cover front retaining bolts.
18. On very early models (pre September 1964), with the coil spring type clutch remove the three nuts securing the clutch thrust plate to the pressure spring housing and detach the thrust plate (Fig. H:2).
19. On models with the diaphragm spring clutch, slacken the three dowel bolts (driving pins) retaining the diaphragm spring cover. Slacken the bolts evenly to release the spring pressure, then remove the bolts and detach the diaphragm cover (Fig. H:3).
20. Turn the crankshaft until the 1/4 timing mark on the outside edge of the flywheel is at TDC position. The slot in the crankshaft and flywheel should now be horizontal. It is essential that the crankshaft be correctly positioned before attempting to remove the flywheel as the 'C' shaped washer which locates the crankshaft primary gear will then be positioned with its open side downwards and thus be unable to drop out. If this precaution is not observed, the 'C' washer may fall out of position and cause severe damage and/or possibly make it impossible to remove the flywheel.
21. Knock back the lock washer tab securing the flywheel retaining bolt. Hold the flywheel to prevent it turning and remove the retaining bolt (1½ in AF). Remove the keyed washer locating the flywheel to the crankshaft.
22. Withdraw the flywheel off the crankshaft taper using a suitable puller. First locate the thrust button of the puller set into the end of the crankshaft to protect the internal threads (Fig. H:4). Screw the three adaptor screws into the threaded holes provided in the flywheel. Fit the plate of the puller tool over the screws and secure with the three nuts. Tighten the nuts evenly so that the plate remains parallel with the flywheel. Screw in the tool centre-bolt until it contacts the thrust button then tighten

further while holding the flywheel to prevent it turning. Once the flywheel is freed, the puller can be removed.

NOTE: The adaptor screws for use on the diaphragm clutch are different from those for the coil spring clutch and must not be interchanged.

23. On models with the diaphragm spring clutch, remove the flywheel, clutch disc and pressure plate as individual items from the flywheel housing (Fig. H:5).

24. On early models with the coil spring type clutch, the clutch and flywheel are removed as an assembly. If required, they can be separated as described under the appropriate heading later.

NOTE: Very early models have lubricated bushes at the crankshaft primary gear and in this case an additional oil seal fitted to the flywheel. As the flywheel is pulled from the shaft, oil from the annulus behind the seal may spill down the face of the flywheel onto the clutch disc and be wrongly interpreted as oil which has leaked past the seal during normal running. The flywheel should be maintained in a vertical position during removal to avoid this oil contaminating the clutch disc linings.

Installation

Installation is a simple reversal of the removal procedure, with special attention to the following points:

a) Ensure that the crankshaft taper and flywheel hub bore are perfectly clean and free from grease. They must be assembled dry. This is most important.

b) Lightly smear the splines of the crankshaft primary gear with molybdenum disulphide grease.

c) Ensure that the crankshaft is correctly positioned, with the open side of the primary gear 'C' washer facing downwards.

d) On very early engines where a flywheel oil seal is fitted, lubricate the oil seal lips before installing the flywheel. Some of these early engines also have a rubber plug fitted into the gear end of the crankshaft as an added precaution against oil leaking past the normal brass taper plug. An improved brass plug was used later and the rubber plug disconnected.

e) On the diaphragm spring clutch, the clutch pressure plate and diaphragm cover are stamped with a balance mark 'A' which must be aligned with the 1/4 timing mark on the flywheel (Figs. H:5 and H:6).

f) To assemble the diaphragm spring clutch, first fit the pressure plate into the flywheel housing with the 'A' mark to the top, then fit the clutch disc with the hub facing inwards. Centralise the pressure plate onto the clutch disc then fit the flywheel onto the crankshaft taper so that the 1/4 timing mark aligns with the 'A' mark on the pressure plate (Fig. H:5). Temporarily fit the three dowel bolts (driving pins) lightly into the pressure plate to align the assembly and pull it together. Once the flywheel retaining bolt has been fitted and tightened, the dowel bolts can be removed and the diaphragm cover installed with its balance mark 'A' aligned with the 1/4 timing mark (Fig. H:6). Fit and pregressively tighten the three dowel bolts ensuring that they pass squarely through each pair of driving straps. Incorrect assembly can cause 'clutch judder'. Tighten the dowel bolts to 16 lb ft (2.2 kgm).

g) When fitting the flywheel retaining bolt, first align the offset slot in the end of the crankshaft and flywheel, then refit the keyed washer. Fit a new lock washer under the flywheel bolt and tighten the bolt to 115 lb ft (15.5 kg.m), while holding the flywheel to prevent it turning. Secure the bolt with the lock washer tab.

h) When assembly is complete, check the clutch stop setting and adjust if necessary as detailed in the 'ROUTINE MAINTENANCE' section previously.

Dismantling & Reassembly (Coil Spring Type Clutch)

Once the flywheel and clutch assembly has been removed from the engine, it can be dismantled as follows: Three screws (Service Tool 18G 304 M) will be required to hold the pressure springs compressed while removing the driving pins (Fig. H:7).

Mark the driving pins so that they can be refitted in their original positions. Also note the balance mark 'A' and the clutch spring cover (Fig. H:6).

Insert the three special screws through the holes in the spring cover and screw them into the threaded holes provided in the flywheel. Screw the nuts down against the cover with the fingers, then tighten them one turn at a time until the load is released from the driving pins. Unscrew and remove the three driving pins. Unscrew the three nuts gradually to release the spring cover, then lift off the cover and the springs. The pressure plate will then be released from the flywheel and the individual items can be separated.

When reassembling the components, the balance mark 'A' on the pressure plate and spring cover must be aligned with the 1/4 mark on the flywheel (Fig. H:6). Place the clutch disc on the pressure plate with its longer boss towards the plate. Special Tool 18G 571 will be required to centralise the clutch disc with the flywheel hub. Locate the coil springs, spring housing on the flywheel, then fit the special screws and tighten the nuts evenly to compress the pressure springs. Fit the driving pins in their original locations, ensuring that they pass squarely through each pair of driving straps, and tighten them to 16 lb ft (2.2 kgm). Release the nuts and remove the special screws.

THROW-OUT STOP ADJUSTMENT . . . . [2]

This adjustment will normally only be necessary if the stop has been removed from the clutch end cover during overhaul.

Slacken the locknut and screw the plunger stop away from the housing to the limit of its travel (Fig. H:9). Get a second person to fully depress the clutch pedal, then screw the plunger stop up against the housing. Release the pedal and screw the stop in a further one flat of the stop which is approximately 0.007 - 0.10 in (0.20 - 0.25 mm). Hold the plunger stop and tighten the locknut.

Now pull the clutch release lever outwards away from the stop bolt on the clutch cover and measure the gap between the lever and the stop with a feeler gauge. This should be 0.020 in (0.5 mm). Adjust if necessary by slack-

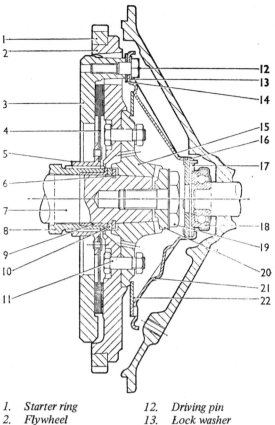

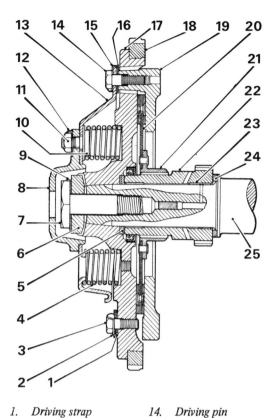

1.	Starter ring	12.	Driving pin
2.	Flywheel	13.	Lock washer
3.	Pressure plate	14.	Driving strap
4.	Driven plate	15.	Flywheel hub
5.	Driven plate hub	16.	Thrust plate
6.	Circlip	17.	Plate retaining spring
7.	Crankshaft	18.	Thrust bearing
8.	Crankshaft primary gear	19.	Flywheel screw
9.	Primary gear bearing	20.	Keyed washer
10.	Thrust washer	21.	Cover
11.	Flywheel	22.	Tab

Fig. H:1 Sectional view of flywheel and diaphragm spring clutch assembly

1.	Driving strap	14.	Driving pin
2.	Lock washer	15.	Lock washer
3.	Driving pin	16.	Driving strap
4.	Pressure spring	17.	Flywheel
5.	Circlip	18.	Starter ring
6.	Key plate	19.	Pressure plate
7.	Flywheel screw	20.	Driven plate
8.	Thrust plate	21.	Driven plate hub
9.	Locking washer	22.	Crankshaft primary
10.	Pressure spring guides		gear
11.	Guide nut	23.	Primary gear bearing
12.	Lock washer	24.	Thrust washer
13.	Pressure spring housing	25.	Crankshaft

Fig. H:2 Section through early coil spring type clutch

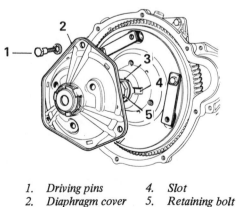

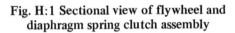

1.	Driving pins	4.	Slot
2.	Diaphragm cover	5.	Retaining bolt
3.	Lock washer		

Fig. H:3 Removing clutch diaphragm cover from flywheel

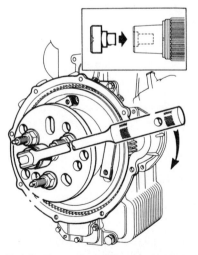

Fig. H:4 Puller tool will be required to draw flywheel off crankshaft taper

Clutch & Transmission

ening the stop bolt locknut and screwing the bolt in or out as necessary to obtain the correct clearance. Tighten the locknut and recheck the gap.

SLAVE CYLINDER . . . . [3]

Removal & Installation

If a new slave cylinder is to be fitted, have the replacement cylinder at hand for immediate fitment to minimise fluid loss. Otherwise, either the hose end must be plugged, or the hydraulic system drained to prevent fluid being spilled. To drain the system, attach a bleed tube to the bleed valve on the slave cylinder, open the valve and pump the clutch pedal until all the fluid is drained out.

To remove the slave cylinder, first disconnect the release lever return spring from the lever and the tag at the bleed valve (Fig. H:10). Slacken the hose connection at the cylinder. Remove the two bolts securing the cylinder to the flywheel housing and pull the cylinder off the push rod. Unscrew the unit from the hose connection.

Install the slave cylinder in the reverse order of removing. Screw the cylinder fully onto the hose before attaching it to the flywheel housing. The connection should be fully tightened once the unit is secured in place. When installation is completed, bleed the clutch hydraulic system as detailed later in this section.

Seal Replacement

A cylinder overhaul kit containing all the necessary seals, etc., should be obtained before starting work on the cylinder.

Detach the dust cover from the end of the cylinder, extract the retaining circlip and remove the piston, cup seal, cup filler and coil spring from the cylinder bore (Fig. H:11).

Clean all the components with methylated spirits and inspect carefully. Check the cylinder bore for any signs of scores, ridges or corrosion pits. If the bore is in good condition, a new seal can be fitted, otherwise the complete unit must be renewed.

Lubricate all the internal components with clean brake fluid. Insert the return spring, small end outermost, into the bore, then fit the cup filler, new seal and piston. The cup seal is fitted with the hollow side towards the bottom of the bore. Secure the components in position with the circlip. Smear rubber lubricant around the sealing areas on the dust cover, then fit the cover onto the end of the cylinder.

MASTER CYLINDER. . . . . [4]

Removal & Installation

Drain the clutch hydraulic system as described for clutch slave cylinder removal.

Where applicable, disconnect the heater air intake flexible tube from the heater and from the wheel arch.

From inside the car, remove the split pin and withdraw the clevis pin securing the master cylinder push rod to the clutch pedal (Fig. H:12).

Disconnect the hydraulic pipe union from the master cylinder. Remove the two nuts and spring washers securing the master cylinder to the bulkhead and lift off the master cylinder.

Installation is a simple reversal of the removal procedure. When installation is completed, bleed the clutch hydraulic system as detailed later in this section.

Seal Replacement

As with the slave cylinder, a cylinder overhaul kit should be obtained before starting work on the unit.

Remove the filler cap from the fluid reservoir and drain out any remaining fluid. Detach the rubber boot from the end of the cylinder and slide it down the push rod. Extract the retaining circlip from the cylinder bore and remove the internal components, as shown in Fig. H:13, from the cylinder. Remove the secondary cup from the piston.

Clean all the internal components with methylated spirits and inspect carefully. Check the master cylinder bore for any signs of scoring, ridging or corrosion pits. If the bore is damaged in any way, the complete unit must be renewed. Also check that the inlet and outlet ports are free from obstruction.

Lubricate all the internal components with clean hydraulic fluid. Carefully assemble the secondary cup to the piston. The flat face of the seal must abut the end flange of the piston.

Fit the spring retainer into the small diameter end of the piston, and insert the spring into the bore, large diameter first. Fit the main cup seal and the cup washer over the spring retainer. The main cup must be fitted carefully, lip edge first. Insert the piston assembly, then refit the push rod assembly and secure with the circlip. Refit the rubber boot on the end of the cylinder.

BLEEDING THE CLUTCH. . . . . [5]

If any components of the clutch hydraulic system have been disconnected, or if any air is present in the system - indicated by a 'soft' pedal - the system should be bled as follows:

Fill or top up the master cylinder reservoir as necessary. Clean the area around the bleed valve on the slave cylinder and remove the rubber dust cap from the valve, where fitted. Fit one end of a bleed tube to the bleed valve and submerge the other end in a small quantity of hydraulic fluid in a clean jar.

Open the bleed valve three-quarters of a turn and slowly depress the clutch pedal. Close the bleed valve just before the pedal reaches the bottom position and allow the pedal to return unassisted. Repeat this procedure until the fluid emerging from the bleed tube is completely free from air bubbles. Do not allow the reservoir to become less than half full during this operation.

When bleeding is successfully completed, remove the

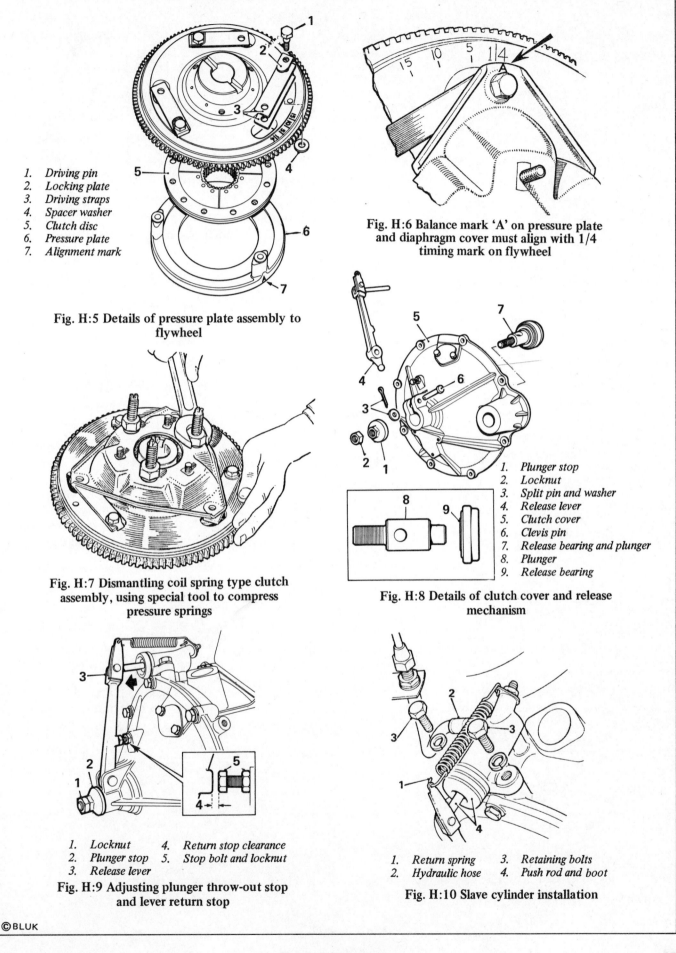

1. Driving pin
2. Locking plate
3. Driving straps
4. Spacer washer
5. Clutch disc
6. Pressure plate
7. Alignment mark

Fig. H:5 Details of pressure plate assembly to flywheel

Fig. H:6 Balance mark 'A' on pressure plate and diaphragm cover must align with 1/4 timing mark on flywheel

Fig. H:7 Dismantling coil spring type clutch assembly, using special tool to compress pressure springs

1. Plunger stop
2. Locknut
3. Split pin and washer
4. Release lever
5. Clutch cover
6. Clevis pin
7. Release bearing and plunger
8. Plunger
9. Release bearing

Fig. H:8 Details of clutch cover and release mechanism

1. Locknut   4. Return stop clearance
2. Plunger stop 5. Stop bolt and locknut
3. Release lever

Fig. H:9 Adjusting plunger throw-out stop and lever return stop

1. Return spring   3. Retaining bolts
2. Hydraulic hose   4. Push rod and boot

Fig. H:10 Slave cylinder installation

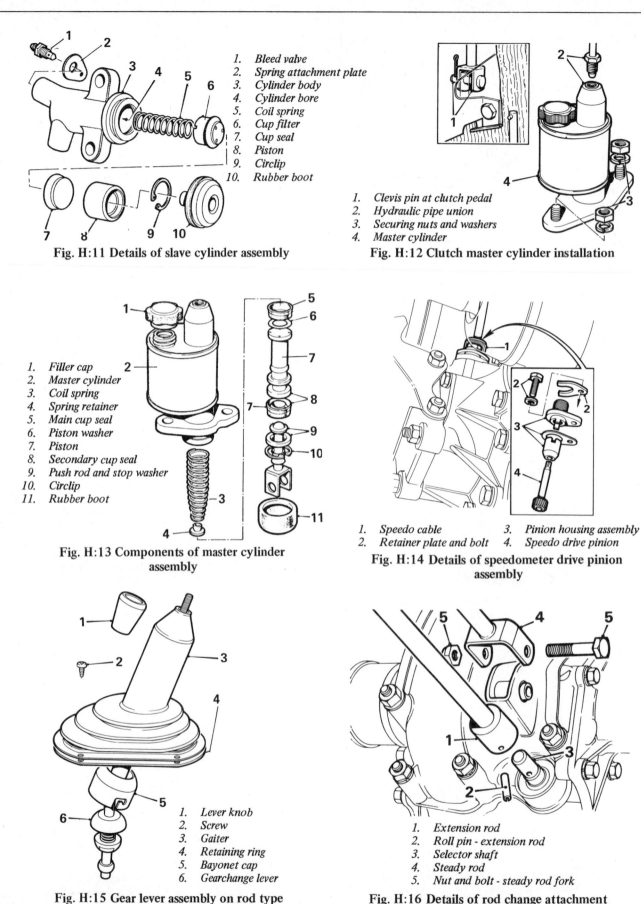

1. Bleed valve
2. Spring attachment plate
3. Cylinder body
4. Cylinder bore
5. Coil spring
6. Cup filter
7. Cup seal
8. Piston
9. Circlip
10. Rubber boot

Fig. H:11 Details of slave cylinder assembly

1. Clevis pin at clutch pedal
2. Hydraulic pipe union
3. Securing nuts and washers
4. Master cylinder

Fig. H:12 Clutch master cylinder installation

1. Filler cap
2. Master cylinder
3. Coil spring
4. Spring retainer
5. Main cup seal
6. Piston washer
7. Piston
8. Secondary cup seal
9. Push rod and stop washer
10. Circlip
11. Rubber boot

Fig. H:13 Components of master cylinder assembly

1. Speedo cable
2. Retainer plate and bolt
3. Pinion housing assembly
4. Speedo drive pinion

Fig. H:14 Details of speedometer drive pinion assembly

1. Lever knob
2. Screw
3. Gaiter
4. Retaining ring
5. Bayonet cap
6. Gearchange lever

Fig. H:15 Gear lever assembly on rod type remote control gearchange

1. Extension rod
2. Roll pin - extension rod
3. Selector shaft
4. Steady rod
5. Nut and bolt - steady rod fork

Fig. H:16 Details of rod change attachment at transmission

Clutch & Transmission

bleed tube. Check the bleed valve is properly closed without over-tightening it, then refit the rubber dust cap on the valve. Finally, top up the master cylinder reservoir with fresh hydraulic fluid as required and refit the filler cap.

TRANSMISSION UNIT ....[6]

Removal & Installation

The transmission assembly must be removed as a unit with the engine, then separated. Full details of the respective operations are given under the appropriate headings in the ENGINE section.

Overhaul

Because of the number of special tools required to successfuly strip and rebuild the gearbox, it is recommended that any work of this nature be left to a specialist. As an alternative, it would probably be more economical and convenient to exchange the gearbox for a reconditioned or rebuilt unit if defective.

Technical Data

CLUTCH

Type.	Borg & Beck, diaphragm type (coil spring type on early 848 cc models, prior to Sept. '64)
Clutch plate diameter.	7.13 in (180.9 mm)
Master cylinder diam..	0.75 in (19.05 mm)
Slave cylinder diam..	0.88 in (22.2 mm)
Clutch release lever clearance.	0.020 in (0.5 mm)
Early models without shouldered throw-out stop.	0.060 in (1.5 mm)

GEARBOX

	Early 848 cc/998 cc models (prior to Aug/Sept. '68)	Later 848 cc/998 cc * & 850/1000/1100 inc Clubman	1275 GT —
Type.	Synchromesh 2nd, 3rd, 4th	All synchromesh	All synchromesh
Gear ratios:			
1st gear	.3.627	.3.52	.3.30
2nd gear . . . . :	.2.172	.2.21	.2.07
3rd gear	.1.412	.1.43	.1.35
4th gear	.1.000	.1.00	.1.00
Reverse	.3.627	.3.54	.3.35
Final drive ratio	.3.765	.3.444 (998 cc models) . . . . 3.765 (848 cc models, & 998 cc van and pick-up up to 1974-ECE 15)	3.647:1 (Early models) 3.444:1 (Jan. '71 on)

* 848 cc from Eng. No 8AM - WE - H - 101
998 cc from Eng. No 99H - 159 - H - 101 (Saloon)
99H - 251 - H - 101 (Estate)

FINAL DRIVE

Ratio	3.444:1 (18/62) 3.647:1 (17/62) 3.765:1 (17/64)

CLUTCH
Trouble Shooter

FAULT	CAUSE	CURE
Clutch slips	1. Clutch facing worn. 2. Clutch facing contaminated. 3. Warped clutch cover or pressure plate. 4. Incorrect adjustment (if adjustable).	1. Replace clutch assy. 2. Replace clutch assy. 3. Replace clutch assy. 4. Adjust clutch.
Clutch drags	1. Faulty clutch hydraulics (if hydraulic). 2. Faulty clutch adjustment (if adjustable). 3. Clutch disc warped. 4. Clutch hub splines worn or rusty. 5. Diaphragm worn or mal-adjusted.	1. Overhaul or replace clutch hydraulics. 2. Adjust clutch. 3. Replace clutch disc. 4. Replace or lubricate clutch. 5. Replace pressure plate.
Clutch chatter	1. Faulty pressure plate. 2. Faulty clutch disc. 3. Loose or worn engine mounting.	1. Replace pressure plate. 2. Replace clutch disc. 3. Replace mounting.
Clutch noise	1. Insufficient grease on bearing sleeve. 2. Clutch installed incorrectly.	1. Lubricate. 2. Check installation.
Clutch noise (pedal down)	1. Faulty release bearing.	1. Replace bearing.
Clutch noise (pedal on the way up)	1. Damaged or worn pilot bearing.	1. Fit new bearing.
Clutch grabs	1. Contaminated clutch lining. 2. Clutch worn or loose rivets. 3. Clutch splines worn or rusted. 4. Warped flywheel or pressure plate. 5. Loose mountings on engine or power unit	1. Replace clutch. 2. Replace clutch. 3. Clean or replace. 4. Repair or replace. 5. Tighten or replace.

Automatic Transmission

Because of the specialised tools and knowledge required to service the automatic transmission, it is recommended that any adjustments or overhaul procedures, other than those described in this section be entrusted to an Authorised Dealer or Transmission Specialist.

ADJUSTMENTS........................[1]

Selector Linkage Transverse Rod (Fig. I:1)

NOTE: This adjustment applies only to early models fitted with the original forged-type bell-crank lever. Later transmissions with the pressed-type bell-crank have a fixed transverse rod bracket and the rod length cannot be adjusted (Fig. I:2).

With the handbrake fully applied, start the engine. Move the selector lever to the R position and check that reverse is engaged. Move the lever slowly backwards towards the N position and check that reverse is disengaged just before or as soon as the lever drops into the N position on the quadrant. Repeat for the 1st gear position. If adjustment is necessary, proceed as described below.

At the bell-crank lever on the transmission unit, pull back the rubber boot, extract the split pin and remove the clevis pin from the transverse rod fork.

NOTE: Do NOT start the engine while the transverse rod is disconnected.

Check that the clevis fork is screwed tightly onto the transverse rod. Also ensure that the rod is pushed fully into the transmission case. Swivel the bell-crank lever clear of the clevis fork and refit the clevis pin.

Check the dimension 'A' between the clevis pin centre line and the flat machined face of the transmission case - NOT the oil seal retainer. This should be 25/32 in (20 mm). If not, slacken the locknut and turn the clevis fork until the correct setting is obtained. Retighten the locknut, ensuring that the clevis fork is correctly aligned with the bell-crank lever.

Reconnect the fork to the bell-crank lever and secure the clevis pin with a new split pin. Pull the rubber boot back into position over the fork.

Selector Cable (Figs. I:1 and I:2)

Pull back the rubber sleeve or detach the cover plate from the bell-crank lever on the transmission unit. On models with the original forged type bell-crank lever extract the split pin and remove the clevis pin securing the selector cable fork to the bell-crank lever (Fig. I:1). On units fitted with the later pressed-type bell-crank lever, the cable fork is secured to the lever by a nut and bolt instead of a clevis pin (Fig. I:2).

Select 'N' in the transmission by moving the bell-crank lever to pull the transverse rod fully out, the push rod back TWO detent, or ONE detent on early transmissions with seven selector positions instead of six.

Move the selector lever to the 'N' position on the quadrant, then check that the hole in the selector cable fork aligns with the bore in the bell-crank lever, and the clevis pin or bolt can easily be inserted. If not, slacken the selector cable adjusting nuts and adjust the position of the cable threaded sleeve relative to its abutment until this condition is obtained.

Ensure that the clevis fork is correctly aligned with the bell-crank lever before reconnecting.

If required, further adjustment can be obtained by screwing the cable clevis fork along the threaded end of the inner cable.

When adjustment is complete, check the linkage setting as described above for the transverse rod. Also check that the start inhibitor switch adjustment is still correct.

Check that all adjusting and locknuts are correctly tightened and clevis pins are secured with split pins. Where a rubber boot is fitted, it should be packed with Duckhams Laminol Grease, or equivalent, before refitting. Refit the metal guard over the bell-crank lever, where applicable.

The operation of the transmission in each selector position should be finally checked by carrying out a road test.

Start-Inhibitor Switch (Figs. I:4 and I:5)

The start-inhibitor switch is located at the rear of the selector lever housing. Some switches also incorporate the reverse light switch and these have four terminals - two for the ignition/starter circuit and two for the reverse light. Other switches have only two terminals and the reverse light switch in this case is a separate unit which is screwed into the reverse check plunger bore in the front of the transmission casing.

When the start-inhibitor switch is functioning correctly, the starter will operate only when the selector lever is in the 'N' position. If the starter will not operate in the N position, or if it operates in any other selector positions, then the switch requires adjustment. The reverse light switch (where incorporated) should also operate only when the selector lever is in R.

Before attempting to adjust the switch, check the adjustment of the selector cable and the transverse rod as described above.

To adjust the switch, place the selector lever in N and disconnect the electrical connection from the switch. Slacken the switch locknut (arrowed on illustration). Connect a small battery and test lamp across the 2 and 4 terminals (red/white wiring connections) on the switch.

Unscrew the switch almost out of the housing, then screw it in again until the test lamp just illuminates and mark the position of the switch. Continue screwing in the switch noting the number of turns required, until the lamp just goes out. Remove the test lamp and battery and unscrew the switch from the housing half the number of turns counted.

Tighten the switch locknut and reconnect the electrical leads to their respective terminals. The ignition/starter circuit leads can be fitted either way round to the 2 and 4 terminals, and the reverse light leads (where fitted) to the 1 and 3 terminals.

Check that the switch functions as described above. If the switch still does not operate correctly, check the switch wiring and connections before renewing the switch.

Idling Speed

Correct idle speed adjustment is essential to avoid stalling in traffic or an excessive thump on engagement of gear from 'N'. A high idling will cause excessive 'creep'.

With the engine at normal operating temperature and the selector in the 'N' position, set the idle speed to 750 rpm, or 650 rpm for models prior to 1974, using an accurate electric tachometer. It is normal for the idle speed to drop 50 - 100 rev/min when a gear is selected.

Governor Control Rod (Kick-Down) (Fig. I:6)

Prior to attempting to adjust the governor control rod, check that the throttle cable operates freely without sticking and is correctly adjusted. When the accelerator is fully depressed, it should open the throttle completely.

Disconnect the governor control rod and return spring from the carburettor throttle lever. Insert a 1/4 in (6.4 mm) diameter drill or gauge rod through the hole in the intermediate bell-crank lever and locate it in the corresponding hole in the transmission casing (Fig. I:9).

Check that the hole in the control rod fork aligns with the bore in the throttle lever, and that the fulcrum pin is an easy sliding fit through both. If not, slacken the locknut on the lower end of the control rod and turn the rod until the correct length is obtained. Ensure that the rod fork is correctly aligned with the throttle lever after tightening the locknut.

Reconnect the control rod and return spring at the carburettor, then remove the checking rod. Check that full throttle opening has not been restricted. This is very important.

Road test the car and check the transmission kickdown shift speeds.

If the shift speeds are low, the rod should be screwed into the swivel joint housing to effectively shorten the rod. If the speeds are high, the rod should be lengthened slightly. After adjusting, recheck the shift switch on road test.

TORQUE CONVERTER.................[2]

The removal and installation of the torque converter is covered in the ENGINE section previously. The converter is serviced only as a unit, and no attempt should be made to dismantle or repair it.

SELECTOR LEVER MECHANISM ....[3]

Removal (Fig. I:8)

Pull back the rubber sleeve (early models) or remove the cover plate (later models) from the bell-crank lever on the transmission unit. On models with the original forged-type bell-crank lever, extract the split pin and remove the clevis pin securing the selector cable fork to the bell-crank arm. On units fitted with later pressed-type bell-crank lever, the cable fork is secured to the lever by a nut and bolt instead of a clevis pin.

Slacken the locknut at the selector cable fork and remove fork, locknut, both rubber ferrules and the sleeve (where fitted) from the cable. Remove cable front adjusting nut from the outer cable and pull the cable clear of the bracket or abutment on the transmission.

Remove the screw securing the cable retaining clip to the floor panel, and pull the cable clear of the transmission unit.

Disconnect the wiring from the start-inhibitor switch at the rear of the selector lever housing, working from under the car. Note the respective position of the leads.

From inside the car, pull back the front floor covering. Remove the four nuts securing the selector mechanism mounting plate to the floor panel and remove the selector mechanism, with the cable attached, from the car. Note that a joint washer is fitted between the mounting plate and the floor panel.

On early models the selector housing is secured directly to the floor by four bolts and in this case the assembly is removed by carefully pulling the cables through the rubber dust excluder.

Installation

Installation is a reverse of the removal procedure, with special attention to the following points:-
a) If seizure of the bell-crank lever has occured on models fitted with the original forged-type bell-crank lever due to over-tightening of the pivot pin nut, replace the

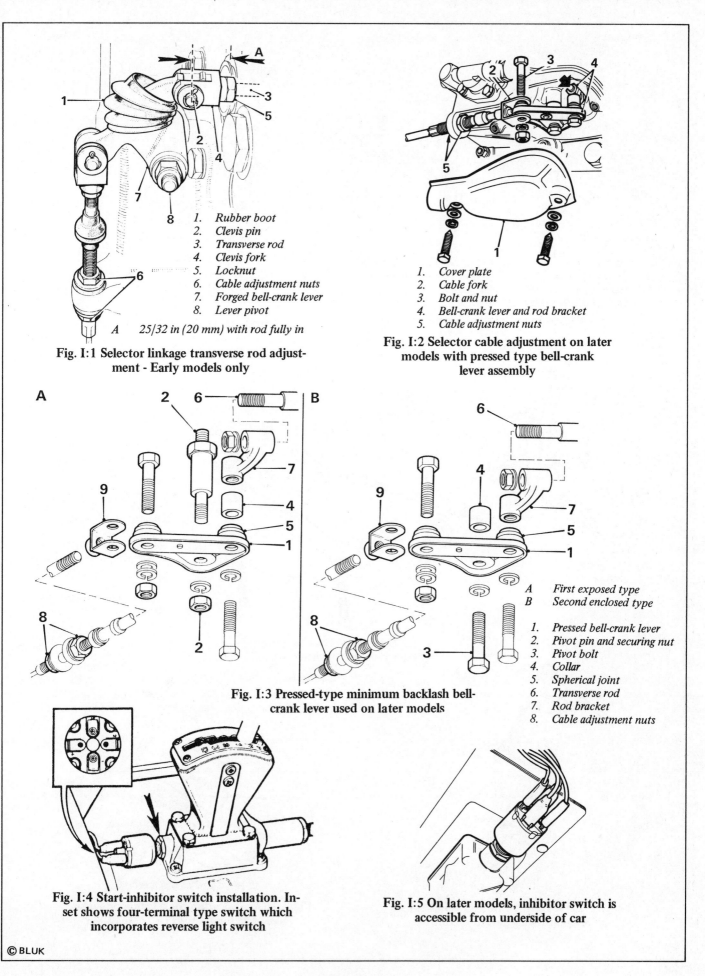

1. Rubber boot
2. Clevis pin
3. Transverse rod
4. Clevis fork
5. Locknut
6. Cable adjustment nuts
7. Forged bell-crank lever
8. Lever pivot

A   25/32 in (20 mm) with rod fully in

Fig. I:1 Selector linkage transverse rod adjustment - Early models only

1. Cover plate
2. Cable fork
3. Bolt and nut
4. Bell-crank lever and rod bracket
5. Cable adjustment nuts

Fig. I:2 Selector cable adjustment on later models with pressed type bell-crank lever assembly

A   First exposed type
B   Second enclosed type

1. Pressed bell-crank lever
2. Pivot pin and securing nut
3. Pivot bolt
4. Collar
5. Spherical joint
6. Transverse rod
7. Rod bracket
8. Cable adjustment nuts

Fig. I:3 Pressed-type minimum backlash bell-crank lever used on later models

Fig. I:4 Start-inhibitor switch installation. Inset shows four-terminal type switch which incorporates reverse light switch

Fig. I:5 On later models, inhibitor switch is accessible from underside of car

Automatic

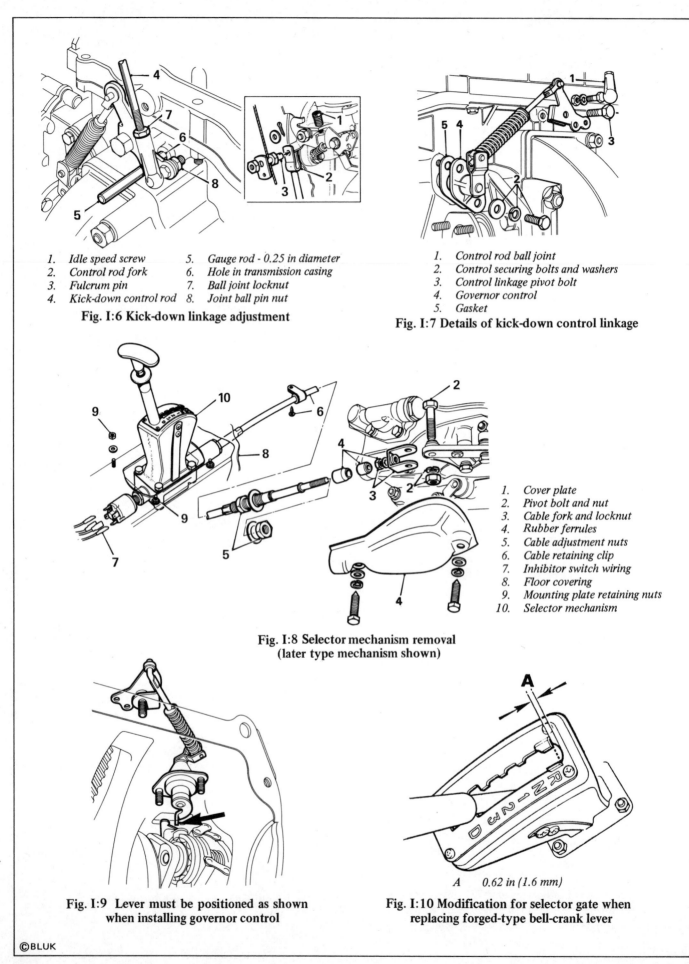

1. Idle speed screw
2. Control rod fork
3. Fulcrum pin
4. Kick-down control rod
5. Gauge rod - 0.25 in diameter
6. Hole in transmission casing
7. Ball joint locknut
8. Joint ball pin nut

Fig. I:6 Kick-down linkage adjustment

1. Control rod ball joint
2. Control securing bolts and washers
3. Control linkage pivot bolt
4. Governor control
5. Gasket

Fig. I:7 Details of kick-down control linkage

1. Cover plate
2. Pivot bolt and nut
3. Cable fork and locknut
4. Rubber ferrules
5. Cable adjustment nuts
6. Cable retaining clip
7. Inhibitor switch wiring
8. Floor covering
9. Mounting plate retaining nuts
10. Selector mechanism

**Fig. I:8 Selector mechanism removal
(later type mechanism shown)**

**Fig. I:9 Lever must be positioned as shown
when installing governor control**

A   0.62 in (1.6 mm)

**Fig. I:10 Modification for selector gate when
replacing forged-type bell-crank lever**

©BLUK

pivot pin and distance tube with a modified pivot pin having a shoulder.

b) If backlash is excessive on the original forged-type bell-crank lever, replace with the later pressed-type minimum backlash bell-crank lever assembly. Remove the bell-crank lever and its pivot pin, then the front cover and the transverse rod. Fit modified type of pivot pin and clevis, non-adjustable transverse rod and pressed-type bell-crank lever. Refit the front cover.

c) If pressed-type bell-crank lever assembly has been fitted in place of the original forged-type lever, reverse position of the selector lever indicator gate should be modified to ensure that the selector valve detent is fully engaged when the selector lever is moved into reverse position. Unscrew the handle from the gear selector lever, then remove four screws securing the indicator gate to the quadrant. File a radius 1/16 in (1.6 mm) deep in the end of the gate as shown in Fig. I:10. Refit the gate and lever handle.

d) If slip or loss of drive occurs in reverse gear after a replacement transmission with pressed-type minimum backlash bell-crank lever has been fitted, check whether the indicator gate has been modified as described above. If not, and adjusting the selector cable as described under 'Adjustments' heading fails to remedy the fault, then the gate modification should be carried out.

e) When installation of the selector housing and cable is complete, adjust the cable, transverse rod (where applicable) and start-inhibitor switch as detailed under 'Adjustments' heading previously.

Dismantling

1. Slacken start-inhibitor switch locknut and unscrew the switch from the rear end of the housing.
2. Release the reverse return spring from the underside of the housing. Remove four bolts securing the quadrant to the housing and lift off the quadrant and lever assembly. Lift off the mounting plate and joint washer (where fitted).
3. Unscrew the outer cable securing nut from the front of the housing and withdraw the cable and lever plunger from the housing. Slacken the inner cable locknut and screw the plunger off the cable end.

Reassembly

Reassemble the components in the reverse order of dismantling, with special attention to the following points:-

a) Lubricate all parts with grease prior to reassembly.
b) When reassembling the quadrant and lever assembly to the housing, ensure that the gear lever engages correctly with the lever plunger. The slot in the plunger is relieved on one side only and this side must be positioned upwards so that it engages with the lever.

Technical Data

AUTOMATIC TRANSMISSION

Type	Automatic Products AP4, 4 forward speed automatic with manual over-ride

Gear Ratios:

1st	2.690:1
2nd	1.845:1
3rd	1.460:1
4th	1.000:1
Reverse	2.690:1
Final drive	3.270:1
Speedometer gear ratio	7/17

TORQUE CONVERTER

Type	3 Element
Ratio	2:1, Maximum
Converter output gear ratio	1.15:1
Converter output gear end-float	0.0035-0.0065 in (0.089-0.164 mm)

Front Suspension

SWIVEL HUB ASSEMBLY...............[1]

Removal
(Drum Brake Models)

1. With the car still on its wheels, remove the split pin and slacken the hub nut on the end of the drive shaft. Also slacken the road wheel nuts.
2. Jack up the front of the car and support on stands, then remove the road wheel.
3. If the driving flange is required to be removed from the drive shaft, release the brake shoe adjustment and withdraw the brake drum. Remove the hub nut together with its thrust washer, then pull the driving flange off the drive shaft splines, using a suitable hub puller. Note the distance ring fitted between the driving flange and the hub bearing - this ring must be fitted with the chamfered side towards the driving flange (Fig. J:4).
4. If required, the brake shoes can also be removed from the backing plate at this time.
5. Slacken the flexible brake hose at the brake backplate. The hose will be detached later. Ideally the brake hose should be sealed by clamping it with a proper brake hose clamp, otherwise the hose end must be plugged to minimise fluid loss.
6. Remove the ball pin nut and disconnect the track rod end from the steering arm, using a suitable joint separator tool.
7. Similarly, separate the upper and lower swivel joints from their respective suspension arms.
8. Press or lever down on the lower suspension arm and tie rod to disengage the lower swivel joint from the arm, then pull the swivel hub down to disengage the upper swivel joint.
NOTE: It will aid removal if the rebound rubber under the upper suspension arm is removed and a solid wedge of roughly the same thickness fitted in its place (Fig. J:8). However, this must be done at the outset, while the car is still standing on its wheels.
9. If the driving flange was removed previously, pull the swivel hub outwards to release it from the drive shaft.
10. If the driving flange is still in place in the hub, remove the hub nut and thrust washer and tap the end of the drive shaft to drive it inwards out of the flange and hub. This should be done with a soft-headed mallet to avoid damaging the drive shaft threads.

11. Disconnect the brake hose by rotating the backplate assembly to release the hose connection threads from the wheel cylinder. Plug or cap the hose end to prevent loss of fluid. The hose is reconnected in the same manner on reassembly.

Installation

The swivel hub is refitted in the reverse order of removing, with special attention to the following points:
a) Ensure that the plastic water shield on the drive shaft is positioned ¼ in (6 mm) from the shouldered edge of the shaft (Fig. J:4).
b) Reconnect the brake hose to the backplate before fitting the hub assembly over the drive shaft. Rotate the backplate to screw the hose connection into the wheel cylinder union. Do not forget to fully tighten the hose connection once the swivel hub assembly has been fitted.
c) If the driving flange was removed, ensure that it locates correctly in the spacer ring between the hub bearings before tapping it fully into position on the drive shaft splines.
d) Tighten the swivel joint ball pin nuts to 38 lb ft (5.3 kgm) and the track rod ball pin nut to 22 lb ft (3.0 kgm).
e) Adjust the brake shoes and bleed the hydraulic system as detailed in the BRAKES section.
f) Once the car is lowered back into its wheels, tighten the drive shaft nut to 60 lb ft (8.3 kgm) and secure with a new split pin. Align the nut to the next split-pin hole, if necessary.

Swivel Hub Assembly
Removal (Disc Brake Models)

1. With the car still on its wheels, remove the split pin and slacken the hub nut on the end of the drive shaft. Also slacken the road wheel nuts.
2. Jack up the front of the car and support on stands, then remove the road wheel.
3. Remove the two securing bolts and detach the brake caliper from the swivel hub. Support the caliper from a suitable point on the suspension to avoid straining the brake hose.
4. Remove the hub nut together with its split tapered collar, then withdraw the driving flange and brake disc assembly from the drive shaft, using a suitable hub puller.

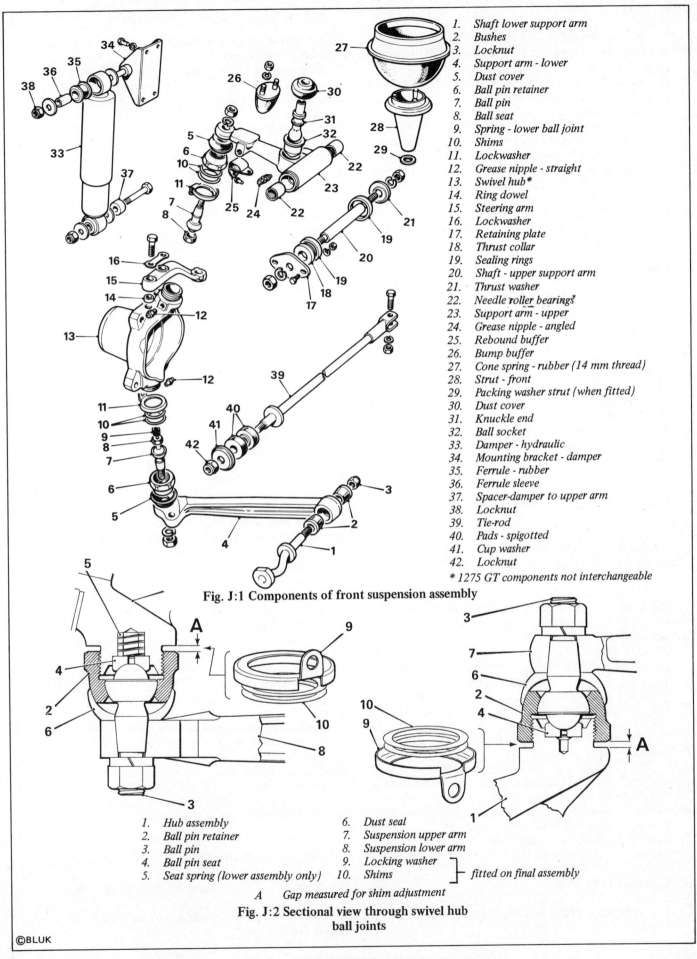

Fig. J:1 Components of front suspension assembly

1. Shaft lower support arm
2. Bushes
3. Locknut
4. Support arm - lower
5. Dust cover
6. Ball pin retainer
7. Ball pin
8. Ball seat
9. Spring - lower ball joint
10. Shims
11. Lockwasher
12. Grease nipple - straight
13. Swivel hub*
14. Ring dowel
15. Steering arm
16. Lockwasher
17. Retaining plate
18. Thrust collar
19. Sealing rings
20. Shaft - upper support arm
21. Thrust washer
22. Needle roller bearings
23. Support arm - upper
24. Grease nipple - angled
25. Rebound buffer
26. Bump buffer
27. Cone spring - rubber (14 mm thread)
28. Strut - front
29. Packing washer strut (when fitted)
30. Dust cover
31. Knuckle end
32. Ball socket
33. Damper - hydraulic
34. Mounting bracket - damper
35. Ferrule - rubber
36. Ferrule sleeve
37. Spacer-damper to upper arm
38. Locknut
39. Tie-rod
40. Pads - spigotted
41. Cup washer
42. Locknut

* 1275 GT components not interchangeable

1. Hub assembly
2. Ball pin retainer
3. Ball pin
4. Ball pin seat
5. Seat spring (lower assembly only)
6. Dust seal
7. Suspension upper arm
8. Suspension lower arm
9. Locking washer   ⎤
10. Shims   ⎦ fitted on final assembly

A   Gap measured for shim adjustment

Fig. J:2 Sectional view through swivel hub
ball joints

©BLUK

Front Suspension   107

5. Remove the ball pin nut and disconnect the track rod end from the steering arm, using a suitable joint separator tool.

6. Similarly, separate the upper and lower swivel joints from their respective suspension arms.

7. Press or lever down on the lower suspension arm and tie rod to disengage the lower swivel joint from the arm, then pull the swivel hub down to disengage the upper swivel joint. It will facilitate removal if the rebound rubber under the upper suspension arm is removed and a solid wedge of roughly the same thickness fitted in its place (Fig. J:8). However, this must be done at the outset, while the car is still standing on its wheels.

8. Pull the swivel hub assembly outwards to release it from the drive shaft.

Installation

Installation is basically a reversal of the removal procedure, but special attention should be paid to the following points:

a) Ensure that the plastic water shield on the drive shaft is located ¼ in (6 mm) from the shouldered edge of the shaft (Fig. J:5).

b) Tighten the swivel hub ball pin nuts to 38 lb ft (5.3 kgm) and the track rod ball pin nut to 22 lb ft (3.0 kgm).

c) Once the car is lowered back onto its wheels, tighten the drive shaft nut to 150 lb ft (20.7 kgm) and secure with a new split-pin. Align the nut to the next split-pin hole, if necessary.

SWIVEL HUB BALL JOINTS. . . . . [2]

The swivel hub upper and lower ball joints are incorporated in the swivel hub assembly and each comprises mainly of a hardened steel ball pin, ball pin seat and pin retainer. Wear in these joints is normally due to lack of regular lubrication and it is very important that these joints be greased frequently to keep them adequately lubricated and prevent the ingress of dirt and water. A grease nipple for this purpose is provided at each joint.

Only dismantling will show the extent of wear of the components. If the main components mentioned above are in good condition, it may be possible to re-shim the joint, but if wear is present, all the components of the joint should be renewed. These are normally available either as complete joint assembly, or as a kit of four. All the new components in the kit should be used when reassembling.

The swivel joints can be overhauled without completely removing the swivel hub assembly from the car, but this operation is made for easier if the assembly is removed and the work carried out under the more ideal conditions of a workshop. In the former case, the joint ball pins must be separated from the suspension arms and the track rod disconnected from the steering arm.

Overhaul (Fig. J:2)

1. Remove the swivel hub assembly from the car, as detailed previously.

2. Secure the swivel hub assembly in a vice with the appropriate ball joint uppermost.

3. Remove the rubber dust cover from the ball pin. Knock back the lockwasher tabs and unscrew the ball pin retainer from the joint. A special socket or key will be required to unscrew the retainer, but these are available from most motor accessory shops.

4. Remove the retainer, together with the ball pin, then extract the ball pin seat from the recess in the housing. In the case of the lower swivel joint, a small spring is fitted below the ball seat and this should also be removed.

5. Unscrew the grease nipple and lift off the retainer lockwasher, together with the adjustment shims.

6. Thoroughly clean all the components of the joint assembly, then examine them carefully. If the contact surfaces on either the ball pin, seat or retainer show any signs of wear, ridging, scoring or corrosion, all the components of the joint assembly should be renewed.

7. To determine the thickness of shim pack required, assemble the ball pin without the shims or lockwasher. In the case of the lower joint, also leave out the coil spring. Tighten the retainer until there is no free movement between the ball pin and its seating, but the pin is still free to swivel. Now measure the gap, 'A' in illustration, between the lower edge of the retainer and the hub with feeler gauges. The thickness of a new lockwasher is 0.035 in (0.90 mm) and this figure should be deducted from the gap measured to obtain the thickness of shim pack required. When correctly adjusted, the ball pin must have no nip to 0.003 in (0.08 mm) end-float. Add a further 0.002 in shim, if necessary. Shims available are as follows, and these are normally supplied in the ball joint kit: 0.002/003/005/010/020 in (0.05/08/13/51 mm).

8. Great care should be taken during this adjustment procedure, as it is imperative that the ball joint should be able to rotate freely in all planes after adjustment has taken place.

9. When the shim pack has been selected, assemble a new lockwasher on the housing and secure lightly in position with the grease nipple. Position the shim pack on top of the lockwasher.

10. Pack the joint with grease then assemble the ball seat, ball pin and retainer to the housing. In the case of the lower joint, remember to fit the coil spring under the ball seat. Press down lightly on the ball pin to hold the seat correctly in position in its recess while tightening the retainer.

11. Tighten the retainer to its specified torque of 75 lb ft (10.3 kgm), then secure by tapping the lock washer against three flats of the retainer - one adjacent to the brake backplate/disc. Fully tighten the grease nipple.

12. Finally, refit the swivel hub assembly on the car. Do not forget to fit the rubber dust cover at each of the joint ball pins before connecting them to the suspension arms.

FRONT HUB BEARINGS. . . . . [3]

Replacement (Drum Brake Models) (Fig. J:4)

1. Remove the swivel hub assembly from the car as previously detailed.

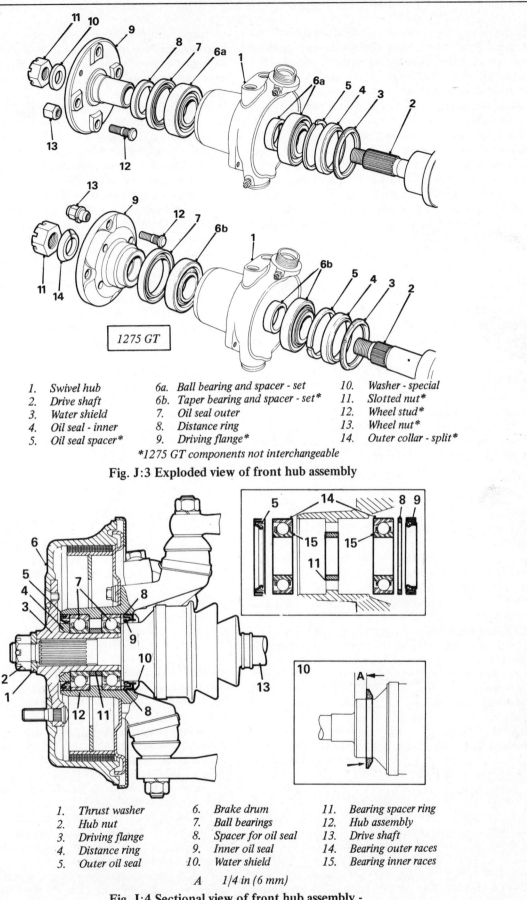

1. Swivel hub
2. Drive shaft
3. Water shield
4. Oil seal - inner
5. Oil seal spacer*
6a. Ball bearing and spacer - set
6b. Taper bearing and spacer - set*
7. Oil seal outer
8. Distance ring
9. Driving flange*
10. Washer - special
11. Slotted nut*
12. Wheel stud*
13. Wheel nut*
14. Outer collar - split*

*1275 GT components not interchangeable

Fig. J:3 Exploded view of front hub assembly

1. Thrust washer
2. Hub nut
3. Driving flange
4. Distance ring
5. Outer oil seal
6. Brake drum
7. Ball bearings
8. Spacer for oil seal
9. Inner oil seal
10. Water shield
11. Bearing spacer ring
12. Hub assembly
13. Drive shaft
14. Bearing outer races
15. Bearing inner races

A   1/4 in (6 mm)

**Fig. J:4 Sectional view of front hub assembly -
drum brake models**

© BLUK

Front Suspension

2. If the driving flange is still in position in the hub, the brake drum should be removed and the flange tapped out of the hub assembly from the inboard side, using a suitable mandrel.

NOTE: The distance ring fitted between the driving flange and the outer bearing must be fitted with the chamfered side towards the driving flange.

The brake shoes should also be removed to avoid the possibility of contamination by grease during the subsequent operations.

3. Extract the outer oil seal from the outboard end of the hub bore. Similarly, remove the inner oil seal together with its spacer ring from the opposite end of the bore. Discard the oil seals. Also remove the plastic water shield from the drive shaft.

4. Drift out the inner race of each bearing and remove the spacer ring fitted between the bearings. Drive out the bearing outer races from the hub bore, but take great care to avoid damaging the bore.

5. Clean all old grease, etc., from the hub bore.

6. Pack the new bearings with suitable high-melting point grease, then install them in the hub with the spacer ring between them. The bearings must be fitted with the sides marked 'THRUST' facing inwards towards each other. Tap the bearings squarely into position, bearing only on the outer race.

7. Lubricate the new oil seals before fitting them. The seals must be installed with the sealing lips facing inwards. Note that the inner seal also has a lip on its outer face. The seals can normally be installed by pressing them into position by hand, or by tapping gently on their outer edge.

8. Fit the water shield on the drive shaft so that it is positioned ¼ in (6 mm) from the shouldered edge (see illustration). Fill the sealing face of the water shield with grease.

9. Assemble the swivel hub on the car as detailed previously. When refitting the driving flange, ensure that it locates correctly in the bearing spacer before tapping it fully into position. The distance ring must be positioned on the driving flange, with its chamfered side towards the flange, before installing. It should be noted that the brake backplate must be fitted before the driving flange is installed.

10. Once the car is lowered back onto its wheels, tighten the drive shaft nut to 60 lb ft (8.3 kg m) and secure with a new split-pin. Align the nut to the next split pin hole, if necessary.

Front Hub Bearings - Disc Brake Models

Replacement (Fig. J:5)

1. Remove the swivel hub assembly from the car as detailed previously. This should include withdrawing the driving flange and brake disc assembly.

2. Extract the outer oil seal from the outboard end of the hub bore. Similarly, remove the inner oil seal, together with its spacer ring from the opposite end of the bore. Discard the oil seals. Also remove the plastic water shield from the drive shaft.

3. Remove the bearing inner races, together with the

bearing spacer ring, from the hub bore. The inner bearing race may be left on the drive shaft when the swivel hub assembly is removed. Drive out the bearing outer races from the hub bore, but take great care to avoid damaging the bore.

4. Clean all old grease, etc., from the hub bore.

5. Tap the outer races of the new bearings into position in the hub bore, bearing only on their outer edge. Ensure that the races are correctly seated. Pack inner race and roller assemblies with high-melting point grease then install them in the hub with the spacer ring between them.

6. Lubricate the new oil seals before fitting them. The seals must be installed with the sealing lips facing inwards. Note that the inner seal also has a lip on its outer face. The seals can normally be installed by pressing them into position by hand, or by tapping gently on their outer edge. Pack the space between each seal and its adjacent bearing with grease, but do not fill the space between the bearings.

7. Fit the water shield on the drive shaft so that is is positioned ¼ in (6 mm) from the shouldered edge (see illustration). Fill the sealing face of the water shield with grease.

8. Assemble the swivel hub on the car as detailed previously. When fitting the driving flange and brake disc assembly, ensure that the split tapered collar is correctly fitted under the drive shaft nut.

9. Once the car is lowered back onto its wheels, tighten the drive shaft nut to 150 lb ft (20.7 kg m) and secure with a new split-pin. Align the nut to the next split-pin hole, if necessary.

SHOCK ABSORBERS. . . . . [4]

Telescopic shock absorbers are fitted only to models with 'dry' suspension. The front shock absorber installation is shown in Fig. J:6. and is mainly self-explanatory.

Ensure that a large washer is fitted on each side of the mounting bush, and the spacer is fitted adjacent to the suspension arm at the lower mounting. Use new self-locking nuts if the existing ones are worn.

LOWER SUSPENSION ARMS . . . . [5]

Removal & Installation (Fig. J:7)

Before jacking up the car, fit a packing piece between the upper suspension arm and the rebound rubber; this will take the strain off the swivel hub lower joint and make it easier to disconnect the lower arm.

Jack up the front of the car and support on stands, then remove the road wheel.

Remove the retaining nut and separate the swivel hub ball joint from the lower suspension arm, using a suitable joint separator tool. Remove the through-bolt and nut securing the tie-rod to the lower arm.

At the lower arm pivot shaft, remove the nut and washer from the rear end of the shaft, then tap the shaft forwards to release the arm. Remove the arm mounting brushes.

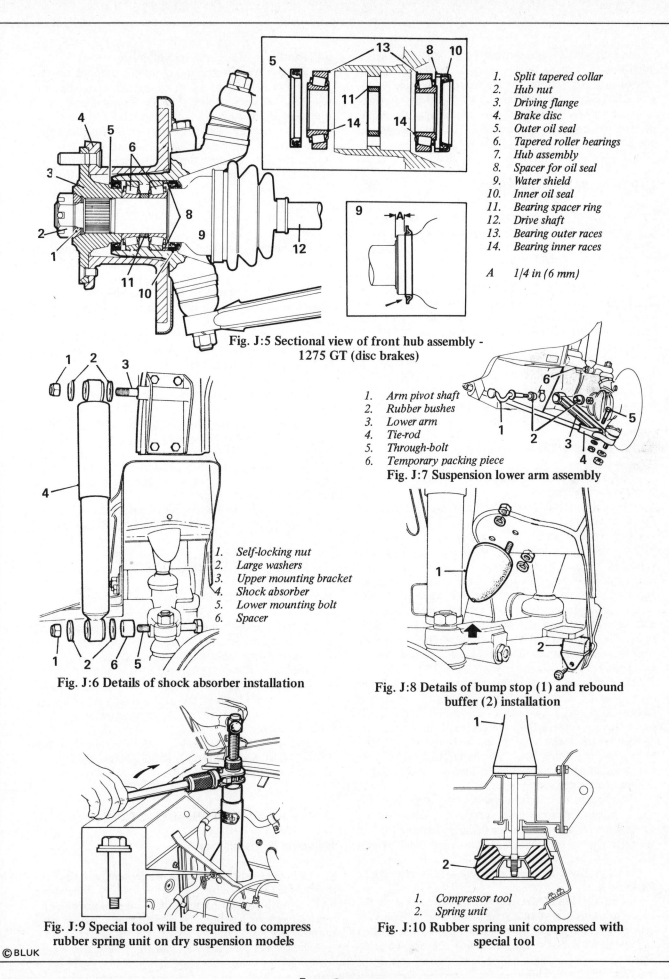

1. Split tapered collar
2. Hub nut
3. Driving flange
4. Brake disc
5. Outer oil seal
6. Tapered roller bearings
7. Hub assembly
8. Spacer for oil seal
9. Water shield
10. Inner oil seal
11. Bearing spacer ring
12. Drive shaft
13. Bearing outer races
14. Bearing inner races

A   1/4 in (6 mm)

**Fig. J:5 Sectional view of front hub assembly -
1275 GT (disc brakes)**

1. Arm pivot shaft
2. Rubber bushes
3. Lower arm
4. Tie-rod
5. Through-bolt
6. Temporary packing piece

Fig. J:7 Suspension lower arm assembly

1. Self-locking nut
2. Large washers
3. Upper mounting bracket
4. Shock absorber
5. Lower mounting bolt
6. Spacer

Fig. J:6 Details of shock absorber installation

**Fig. J:8 Details of bump stop (1) and rebound
buffer (2) installation**

1. Compressor tool
2. Spring unit

**Fig. J:9 Special tool will be required to compress
rubber spring unit on dry suspension models**

**Fig. J:10 Rubber spring unit compressed with
special tool**

© BLUK

Installation is a simple reversal of the above procedure. Ensure that the flat on the head on the pivot shaft locates correctly with the tab at the mounting hole.

The pivot shaft nut should not be fully tightened until the suspension is supporting the weight of the car, to prevent pre-tensioning of the rubber bushes. Tighten the pivot shaft nut to 33 lb ft (4.5 kg m).

UPPER SUSPENSION ARMS. . . . . [6]

Removal of the upper suspension arm is only normally required to allow replacement of the suspension spring unit. It is unusual that removal be occasioned by the need to renew the arm pivot bearings, which are of the needle roller type.

On models with Hydrolastic suspension, the Hydrolastic system on the appropriate side of the car must be depressurised once the arm has been refitted. Full details of these operations are included in the REAR SUSPENSION section.

On models with 'dry' suspension, a special compressor tool will be required to compress the rubber cone spring unit before the arm can be removed. This tool is shown in Fig. J:9, and is generally available for hire from most good accessory and tool hire shops.

Removal (Fig. J:11)

Jack up the front of the car and support on stands, then remove the road wheel.

On models with Hydrolastic suspension, depressurise the Hydrolastic system .

On models with 'dry' suspension, compress the rubber cone spring unit. The access hole in the engine bulkhead crossmember is covered by a cover plate which must first be moved aside by slackening one of the securing bolts and removing the other one. These bolts also secure the sub-frame tower to the crossmember. Refit the bolt and tighten both after moving the plate to one side. Insert the threaded (14 mm) spindle of the compressor tool through the access hole and locate the body of the tool over the two sub-frame bolts (Fig. J:9). Screw the spindle nine complete turns into the spring unit. Using the ratchet handle of the tool, tighten the centre nut until it makes contact with the body of the tool. Hold the centre screw to prevent further rotation and then turn the ratchet handle clockwise to compress the spring sufficiently to allow the spring strut to be extracted from between the upper suspension arm and the spring unit (Fig. J:10). Do not over-compress the spring.

Disconnect the hydraulic shock absorber from the upper suspension arm, where applicable. Compress the shock absorber to clear it from the arm. Remove the ball pin retaining nut and disconnect the swivel hub ball joint from the upper suspension arm, using a suitable joint separator tool. Support the swivel hub to prevent straining the brake hose.

Lever the spring strut ball end from its seat in the upper suspension arm and extract the strut assembly. It may be necessary to remove the rebound rubber located under the suspension arm to enable the arm to drop

sufficiently for the strut to be withdrawn.

Remove the nut and spring washer from the rear end of the arm pivot shaft. Remove the two screws securing the thrust collar retaining plate to the sub-frame at the front end of the shaft. Lever the pivot shaft forward, twist the suspension arm outwards and pull it from the pivot shaft. Remove the rear thrust washer and seals from the suspension arm. Remove the arm assembly from the front of the sub-frame. Remove the front thrust collar from the pivot shaft.

Installation

Installation is basically a reversal of the removal procedure, but special attention should be paid to the following points:-
a) When fitting the shaft thrust washers, they must be located with their lubrication grooves towards the suspension arm.
b) Grease the arm pivot shaft before installing it.
c) Apply suitable grease, such as Dextragrease Super G.P., to the strut cup in the suspension arm.
d) Once the spring strut has been installed, ensure that the dust cover at the ball end locates correctly around the nylon cup.
e) Tighten the upper arm pivot shaft nuts to 53 lb ft (7.3 kg m), and the swivel hub ball pin nut to 38 lb ft (5.3 kg m).
f) After releasing the compression on the rubber cone spring, check that the strut is correctly located at the suspension arm and spring unit.
g) On Hydrolastic models, repressurise the Hydrolastic system as detailed in the REAR SUSPENSION section.

RUBBER CONE SPRING UNITS. . . . . [7]

Removal & Installation

A rubber cone spring unit is used on models with 'dry' suspension, and is located in the sub-frame tower. The upper suspension arm must first be removed as detailed before the spring unit can be removed.

Turn the ratchet on the spring compressor tool anti-clockwise, while holding the centre screw, to release the spring compression. Unscrew the tool centre spindle from inside the sub-frame tower.

The spring unit is installed in the reverse order of removing. Ensure that the spring unit locates correctly in the sub-frame tower.

HYDROLASTIC DISPLACER UNITS . . . . . . [8]

Removal & Installation

On models with Hydrolastic suspension, a Hydrolastic displacer unit is used in place of the rubber cone spring unit. As with the spring unit above, the suspension arm must be removed before the displacer unit can be withdrawn.

Disconnect the displacer hose from the union on the

Front Suspension

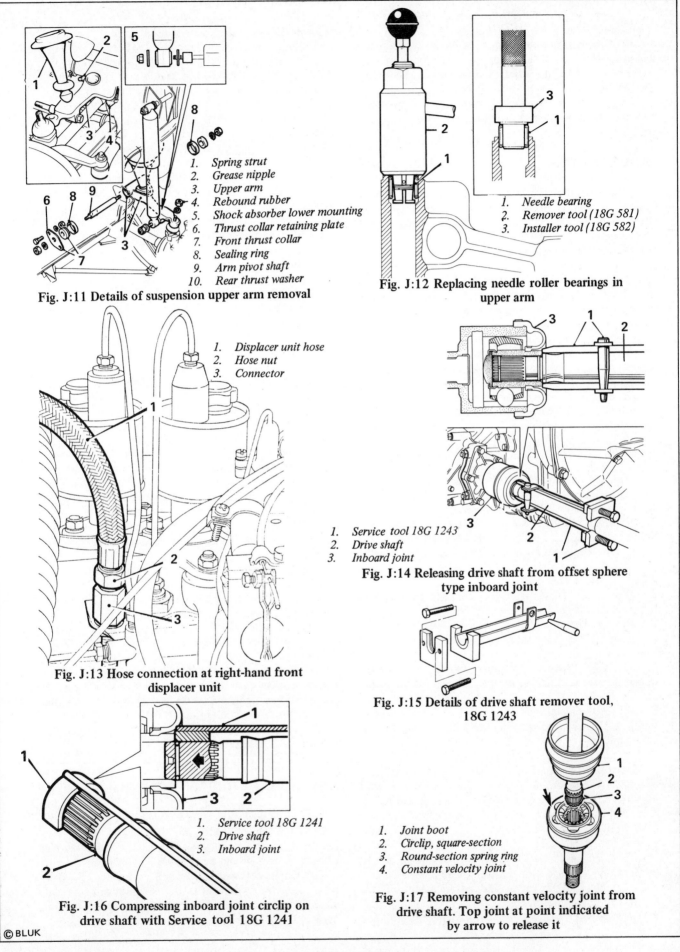

1. Spring strut
2. Grease nipple
3. Upper arm
4. Rebound rubber
5. Shock absorber lower mounting
6. Thrust collar retaining plate
7. Front thrust collar
8. Sealing ring
9. Arm pivot shaft
10. Rear thrust washer

Fig. J:11 Details of suspension upper arm removal

1. Needle bearing
2. Remover tool (18G 581)
3. Installer tool (18G 582)

Fig. J:12 Replacing needle roller bearings in upper arm

1. Displacer unit hose
2. Hose nut
3. Connector

Fig. J:13 Hose connection at right-hand front displacer unit

1. Service tool 18G 1243
2. Drive shaft
3. Inboard joint

Fig. J:14 Releasing drive shaft from offset sphere type inboard joint

Fig. J:15 Details of drive shaft remover tool, 18G 1243

1. Service tool 18G 1241
2. Drive shaft
3. Inboard joint

Fig. J:16 Compressing inboard joint circlip on drive shaft with Service tool 18G 1241

1. Joint boot
2. Circlip, square-section
3. Round-section spring ring
4. Constant velocity joint

Fig. J:17 Removing constant velocity joint from drive shaft. Top joint at point indicated by arrow to release it

© BLUK

engine compartment bulkhead (Fig. J:13).

Push the displacer unit upwards and remove the two screws to release the displacer bracket from inside the sub-frame tower. Turn the displacer unit anti-clockwise and withdraw it from the sub-frame tower.

When refitting the displacer unit, rotate it clockwise to lock it into the registers on the locating plate.

DRIVE SHAFTS. . . . . [9]

Three different types of drive shaft are used, and the removal technique varies dependent on the type fitted. Early manual models have drive shafts which have a rubber coupling with 'U' bolts at the inboard end and a sliding joint connecting the inner flange to the main member of the shaft. Later models have an offset sphere type joint at the inboard end and the drive shaft is splined into the inner member of the joint. The joint assembly itself is a splined fit in the final drive unit stub shaft.

On models with automatic transmission, the drive shaft is similar to the early manual one, but a Hardy Spicer flanged universal joint is fitted at the inboard end. *NOTE: In each case the drive shaft can be removed as an assembly with the swivel hub if required. In this case the procedure given for swivel hub removal should be followed, then the drive shaft disconnected at its inboard end.*

Removal

1. With the car still on its wheels, remove the split pin and slacken the hub nut on the end of the drive shaft. Also slacken the wheel nuts.
2. It will facilitate disconnection of the swivel hub upper ball joint later if the rebound rubber at the upper suspension arm is removed and a solid wedge of roughly the same thickness fitted in its place. This should be done before the car is jacked up.
3. Jack up the front of the car, and support on stands, then remove the road wheel.
4. Remove the retaining nut and disconnect the track rod from the steering arm, using a suitable joint separator tool.
5. Similarly, disconnect the upper swivel joint from the upper suspension arm. Refit the ball pin retaining nut loosely.
6. On early manual models, disconnect the inner end of the drive shaft by removing the 'U' bolts securing the rubber coupling.
7. On automatic models, remove the four bolts securing the universal joint flange to the final drive unit.
8. On later manual models with the offset sphere type inboard joint, a special tool (18G 1243), as shown in Fig. J:15, will be required to release the inner end of the drive shaft from the joint. Assemble the tool to the drive shaft, press it hard against the inboard joint and fit the tapered pin, as shown in Fig. J:14. Insert the 'U' shaped part of the tool into the groove on the shaft, then tighten the two bolts evenly until the drive shaft is released from the inboard joint. Remove the tool.
9. Remove the nut from the swivel hub upper joint and separate the joint from the suspension arm. Support the swivel hub to avoid straining the brake hose.
10. On models with the offset sphere type inboard joint, hold the inboard joint boot in position and at the same time withdraw the drive shaft from the joint. Push the shaft inwards and over the top of the final drive unit.
11. On the other models, prise off the larger retaining clip at the sliding joint rubber seal, turn back the seal and slide the joint flange off the drive shaft splines.
12. Remove the hub nut from the outer end of the drive shaft and carefully tap the drive shaft out of the driving flange. This should be done with a soft-headed mallet to avoid damaging the drive shaft threads.
13. Withdraw the drive shaft out of the swivel hub assembly, and then outwards away from under the car.

Installation

Install the drive shaft assembly in the reverse order of removing, with special attention to the following points:-
a) Ensure that the plastic water shield on the drive shaft is positioned ¼ in (6 mm) from the shouldered edge of the shaft. Figs. J:4 and J:5 refer.
b) On models with disc front brakes, when inserting the drive shaft into the swivel hub, ensure that the shaft locates correctly in the spacer ring between the hub bearings as it is pushed through.
c) On drive shafts with the sliding joint, after assembling the joint flange to the drive shaft, secure the joint seal with a new retaining clip or iron wire.
d) On models with the offset sphere type inboard joint, push the drive shaft smartly into the inboard joint to lock the shaft into the joint. It may be necessary to compress the circlip in the end of the shaft to enable it to enter the joint. The special tool for compressing the circlip is shown in Fig. J:16, but this can also be done using two small screwdrivers.
e) With the rubber coupling type inboard joint, new-locking nuts should be used on the 'U' bolts. Tighten the nuts equally until approximately 1/16 in (1.6 mm) of thread protrudes beyond the nuts.
f) Tighten the swivel hub ball pin nut to 38 lb ft (5.3 kg m), and the track rod ball pin nut to 22 lb ft (3.0 kg m).
g) Once the car is lowered back onto its wheels, tighten the drive shaft nut and secure with a new split pin. The nut should be tightened to 60 lb ft (8.3 kg m) on models with drum front brakes, and 150 lb ft (20.7 kg m) on models with disc front brakes. Align the nut to the next split pin hole, if necessary.

DRIVE SHAFT RUBBER COUPLINGS. . . . [10]

Early manual models have a rubber coupling with 'U' bolts at the inboard end of the drive shafts. These coupling are prone to deterioration through age and contamination by oil and should be renewed if they show any signs of movement between the two 'X' members. If left too long, excessive movement in the coupling will eventually allow it to contact the transmission casing, causing damage to both the casing and the joint 'U' bolts.

Replacement

1. Jack up the front of the car and support on stands, then remove the road wheel.
2. Disconnect the upper and lower swivel joint from their respective suspension arms, using a suitable joint separator tool.
3. Remove the 'U' bolts and nuts securing the rubber coupling to the drive shaft and final drive unit flanges.
4. Press or lever down on the lower suspension arm and tie rod to disengage the lower swivel joint from the arm, then pull the swivel hub down to disengage the upper swivel joint.
5. Pull the swivel hub assembly outwards sufficiently to allow the rubber coupling to be removed.
6. Support the swivel hub assembly until it is refitted, to avoid straining the brake hose.
7. Before fitting the new coupling, check that the 'U' bolts will fit easily in their respective locations in the drive flanges. It may be necessary to squeeze the threaded ends together in the jaws of a vice to close them up slightly until they are in alignment. Use new self-locking nuts at the 'U' bolts.
8. Fit the coupling to the final drive flange first, then re-fit the swivel hub assembly to the suspension arms, at the same time engaging the drive shaft flange with the coupling. Tighten the 'U' bolt nuts equally until approximately 1/16 in (1.6 mm) of thread protrudes beyond the nuts.
9. Tighten the swivel hub joint nuts to 33 lb ft (4.6 kg m).

CONSTANT VELOCITY JOINTS. . . . . [11]

A constant velocity joint is incorporated at the hub end of the drive shaft and is enclosed by a rubber boot. Most cases of wear or damage to the C/V joint are caused by damage to the boot, thus allowing dirt and water into the joint. The boot should be examined periodically for any signs of tears or grease leakage, indicating damage, and renew if necessary.

Wear in the C/V joint is normally indicated by 'knock-on-lock'. That is, a clicking sound from the front wheel in question when the steering is on lock.

Joint Replacement

The C/V joint is easily replaced once the drive shaft has been removed from the car. The new joint is supplied as a complete assembly with the stub shaft.

Prise off the clips securing the joint boot and pull the boot back from the joint. It is recommended that only a new boot be used on reassembly.

If the old boot is to be re-used, it should be examined very carefully for any signs of tears or other damage.

The drive shaft is retained in position in the C/V joint by a round section spring ring, located in the end of the shaft, which expands into the chamfered end of the joint inner race bore. To remove the drive shaft, this ring must be contracted into the groove. This is done by holding the shaft vertically, as shown in Fig. J:17, and giving the outer edge of the joint a sharp tap with a soft-faced mallet. This should contract the spring ring so that the joint can be drawn off the shaft. It should not be necessary to use heavy blows for this operation.

If not pre-lubricated, pack the new C/V joint with 1 oz (30 cc) of Duckhams Bentone Grease Q5795. A satchet of grease is normally supplied with a new boot kit.

Remove the spring ring from the end of the drive shaft, and fit a new spring ring in the groove. Start the drive shaft splines into the bore of the joint inner member. Compress the spring ring using one or two small screwdrivers, then tap the end of the shaft to drive it fully into place. Make sure that the shaft is fully engaged in the joint, with the outer circlip against the inner race.

Fit the rubber boot and secure with new retaining clips. Ensure that the ends of the boot engage correctly in the locating grooves in the joint housing and drive shaft. The retaining clips must be fitted with the tab folded back away from the direction of forward rotation of the shaft.

Boot Replacement

The joint rubber boot should be replaced if perished, worn or otherwise damaged. Before fitting the new boot, the C/V joint should be removed from the drive shaft for inspection. If there is any sign of wear, road dirt or corrosion in the joint, it is recommended that a new joint assembly be fitted. The joint should be dismantled only if there is reason to believe that it is still serviceable.

1. Remove the old boot and C/V joint from the drive shaft as detailed above.
2. If the joint is to be dismantled, wash it thoroughly first with petrol and dry it off.
3. Mark the relative positions of the joint inner and outer members and the ball cage with paint to ensure correct alignment on reassembly. This is most important if the joint is to be re-used.
4. Tilt the joint inner race, as shown in 'A' Fig. J:18, until one ball is released. It may be necessary to ease each ball out with a pointed tool.
5. Swivel the cage upwards, as shown in 'B', and turn it until two opposite elongated windows coincide with two lands of the joint housing. One land will drop into a window, allowing the cage and inner race assembly to be lifted out.
6. Swivel the inner race at right-angles to the cage and turn it until two of the lands between the inner race tracks are opposite elongated windows in the cage ('C' in illustration refers). One land will drop into a window, allowing the inner race to be extracted from the cage.
7. Clean all the components and examine carefully for any signs of wear, damage or corrosion pits. Discard the joint if any of these conditions are present.
8. If the joint is in serviceable condition, reassemble it in the reverse order of dismantling. It is important that the components be assembled in their original relative positions as marked prior to dismantling. The components should go together easily and no force should be required.
9. After assembling, check that the inner race articulates freely with the cage in the joint housing, but take care not to release the balls.
10. Pack the joint with 1 oz (30 cc) of Duckhams Bentone Grease Q5795. A satchet of grease is normally

supplied with a new boot kit.

11. Assemble the C/V joint and new boot to the drive shaft as detailed previously for Joint Replacement.

INNER UNIVERSAL JOINTS . . . . [12]

A universal joint is fitted at the inner end of the drive shaft on models with automatic transmission. The joint is similar to the type normally used on prop shafts, and the overhaul procedure is also similar.

If wear has taken place in the joint bearings, a service kit containing a new journal spider, bearings, etc., is available.

Overhaul

1. Remove the retaining circlip from each of the joint bearings with a pair of long nosed pliers and prise them out with a screwdriver. If a circlip cannot be removed easily, tap the end of the bearing race to relieve the pressure on the clip.
2. Hold the joint in one hand and support the underside of the yoke on the top of a vice. Tap the radius of the yoke lightly with a copper mallet until the bearing race emerges from the yoke ('A', Fig. J:19).
3. Turn the joint over and grip the bearing race in the vice. Tap the underside of the yoke until the bearing race is extracted ('B' in illustration).
4. Repeat this operation on the opposite bearing.
5. Support the two exposed bearing trunnions on the top of the vice, with wood or soft metal packings between the vice and the bearing trunnions. Tap the top lug of the flange yoke, as in Item 2 above, to extract the two remaining bearing races.
6. Withdraw the journal spider from the drive shaft yoke (Fig. J:20).
7. Check that the bearing apertures in the yoke journals are clean and undamaged.
8. Smear the inside of the new bearing races to hold the needle rollers in position. Also fill the bottom of each race to a depth of 1/8 in (3 mm) with grease.
9. Tap one of the new bearing races into position in the yoke journal. Insert the spider into the yoke and engage it into the bearing race. Repeat this operation on the opposite side of the yoke, holding the spider into the race as it is drifted into position to retain the needle rollers in position.
10. Engage the other joint journal over the spider and repeat the operation above.
11. Fit the bearing circlips, ensuring that they are firmly located in their grooves.
12. Finally, tap each of the yoke journals lightly with a wooden mallet to relieve the pressure of the bearing races on the ends of the journals, then check that the joint articulates freely without binding.

DRIVE SHAFT INBOARD JOINTS . . . . [13]

The offset sphere type joint is used on later manual models and is a splined fit onto the final drive unit stub shaft. The joint is retained by a circlip on the splined shaft which expands to lock the shaft in the joint.

Joint Replacement

The drive shaft must first be withdrawn out of the inboard joint, as detailed for 'DRIVE SHAFT - Removal' previously.

A special service tool (18G 1240) is required to lever the joint assembly out of the final drive unit, but it should be possible to make up a suitable tool to do the job. The special tool is shown in Fig. J:21 for reference.

Insert the tool between the joint and the final drive unit end cover, with its relieved side against the joint. Drift it into position until the block is adjacent to the end cover bolt (Fig. J:22). Give the tool a sharp blow on its outside face to release the joint.

Withdraw the joint assembly from the final drive unit and remove the oil flinger from the joint.

Check the condition of the nylon oil flinger and fit a replacement if it has been damaged in any way.

Insert the new inboard joint into the final drive unit and push it in until the joint is securely engaged over the retaining circlip on the splined shaft.

Refit the drive shaft, following the relevant steps given under the appropriate heading previously.

Boot Replacement

The joint rubber boot should be replaced if perished, worn or otherwise damaged. Before fitting the new boot, the inboard joint should be inspected for any signs of wear, road dirt or corrosion in the joint. If any of these conditions are present, it is recommended that a new joint assembly be fitted. The joint should be dismantled only if there is reason to believe that it is still serviceable.

To replace the boot, the drive shaft must first be withdrawn out of the inboard joint, as detailed for 'DRIVE SHAFT - Removal' previously.

Remove the outer retaining ring securing the boot to the joint housing. Turn back the boot and remove the inner retaining ring securing the small diameter of the boot to the joint inner member. Remove the rubber boot from the inboard joint.

Inspect the internal components of the joint assembly. If necessary, the joint can be dismantled for cleaning and further inspection as detailed below.

Fit a new 'endless' type retaining clip to the inner neck of the rubber boot, with the chamfered end of the ring towards the inside of the boot (see inset, Fig. J:23). Fold back the boot and fit the smaller diameter over the inner member of the inboard joint. The use of a special mandrel and sleeve (18G 1251) is recommended for this operation to facilitate fitment of the boot (Fig. J:23). In this case, the mandrel must be lubricated with a liquid detergent or rubber lubricant to ease fitting.

If necessary, pack the joint with 50 cc of Shell S7274 Tivella 'A' grease. This is normally supplied in a satchel with the new boot kit.

Turn the boot back and locate it on the outside of the joint housing. Secure the boot with a new retaining clip as shown in Fig. J:23. This clip must be fitted with the tab folded back away from the direction of forward rotation of the joint.

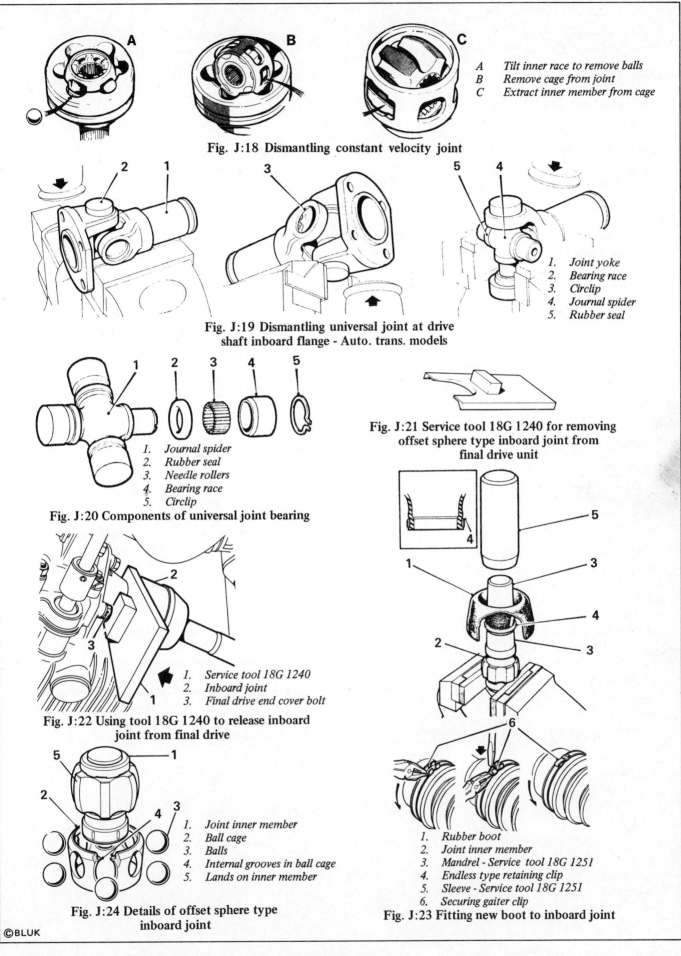

A   Tilt inner race to remove balls
B   Remove cage from joint
C   Extract inner member from cage

Fig. J:18 Dismantling constant velocity joint

Fig. J:19 Dismantling universal joint at drive
shaft inboard flange - Auto. trans. models

1.   Joint yoke
2.   Bearing race
3.   Circlip
4.   Journal spider
5.   Rubber seal

1.   Journal spider
2.   Rubber seal
3.   Needle rollers
4.   Bearing race
5.   Circlip

Fig. J:20 Components of universal joint bearing

Fig. J:21 Service tool 18G 1240 for removing
offset sphere type inboard joint from
final drive unit

1.   Service tool 18G 1240
2.   Inboard joint
3.   Final drive end cover bolt

Fig. J:22 Using tool 18G 1240 to release inboard
joint from final drive

1.   Joint inner member
2.   Ball cage
3.   Balls
4.   Internal grooves in ball cage
5.   Lands on inner member

Fig. J:24 Details of offset sphere type
inboard joint

1.   Rubber boot
2.   Joint inner member
3.   Mandrel - Service tool 18G 1251
4.   Endless type retaining clip
5.   Sleeve - Service tool 18G 1251
6.   Securing gaiter clip

Fig. J:23 Fitting new boot to inboard joint

©BLUK

Front Suspension

Finally, refit the drive shaft following the relevant steps given under the appropriate heading previously.

Joint Overhaul

1. Remove the inboard joint from the final drive unit housing as detailed previously for 'Joint Replacement'.
2. Remove the rubber boot from the joint.
3. Withdraw the joint inner member and ball cage assembly from the joint housing.
4. Push the balls out of the ball cage by inserting a screwdriver between the joint inner member and each ball in turn.
5. Rotate the ball cage until the grooves inside the cage coincide with the lands on the joint inner member, then withdraw the cage from the inner member.

6. Clean all the components of the joint and examine carefully for any signs of wear, damage or corrosion pits. Discard the joint if any of these conditions are present.
7. If the joint is in serviceable condition, reassemble the inner member, ball cage and balls in the reverse order of dismantling. Ensure that the long tapered end of the ball cage faces towards the drive shaft end of the inner member.
8. Fit the inner member assembly into the joint housing.
9. Pack the joint with 50 cc of Shell S7274 Tivella 'A' grease. A satchet of grease is normally supplied with a new boot kit.
10. Fit the rubber boot to the joint as detailed above. Fig. J:23 refers.
11. Finally, refit the inboard joint to the final drive housing and refit the drive shaft as detailed previously.

Technical Data

SUSPENSION

Type - Saloons . . . ."Dry" suspension; Rubber cone springs with hydraulic telescopic shock absorbers, or "Wet" suspension; Hydrolastic displacers (see 'Technical Data' at end of REAR SUSPENSION for details of model fitment and dates)

DRIVE SHAFTS

Type . . . . Hardy Spicer, solid shaft with outboard constant velocity joint
Constant velocity joint . . . . Hardy Spicer, hemispherical bell-joint
Inner coupling:
  Early models .Flexible rubber coupling with 'U' bolts, sliding joint
  Later models . . . . .Off-set sphere joint
  Auto. trans. models . . . . .Flanged coupling with Hardy Spicer needle roller bearing universal joint, sliding joint.

TYRE INFLATION PRESSURES

	Front	Rear
5.20-10 Crossply -		
Normal conditions	24 lb/sq in (1.7 kg/cm^2)	22 lb/sq in (1.5 kg/cm^2)
Fully laden	24 lb/sq in (1.7 kg/cm^2)	24 lb/sq in (1.7 kg/cm^2)
145-10 Radial ply -		
All conditions	28 lb/sq in (2.0 kg/cm^2)	26 lb/sq in (1.8 kg/cm^2)
145/70 SR-12 Radial ply -		
All conditions	28 lb/sq in (2.0 kg/cm^2)	28 lb/sq in (2.0 kg/cm^2)
155/65 SF-310 'Denovo' -		
All conditions	26 lb/sq in (1.8 kg/cm^2)	24 lb/sq in (1.7 kg/cm^2)

Rear Suspension

REAR HUB BEARINGS. . . . .[1]

It should be noted that 1275 GT models have a slightly different rear hub assembly in that they are fitted with taper roller bearings instead of the ball bearings used on the other models. This necessitates a slightly different overhaul procedure and details are included in the procedure below.

Replacement (Fig. K:2)

1. Jack up the rear of the car and support on stands. Remove the road wheel.
2. Release the handbrake. Slacken off the brake shoe adjustment; then remove the two retaining screws and withdraw the brake drum.
3. Prise the dust cap from the centre of the rear hub. Extract the split pin, unscrew the hub nut and remove the special thrust washer from the stub axle. Note that the nut at the left-hand hub assembly has a left-hand thread, as opposed to the normal right-hand thread at the right-hand hub.
4. On 1275 GT models, withdraw the hub assembly from the stub axle. The bearings will normally come away with the hub. Remove the bearing inner race and roller assembly from the outer end of the hub bore. Also remove the spacer ring fitted between the bearings. Extract the oil seal from the inboard end of the hub bore and withdraw the inner bearing inner race and roller assembly. Drive out the bearing outer races from the hub bore.
5. On other models, a hub puller will probably be required to withdraw the hub assembly from the stub axle. Drift out the inner race of each of two bearings and remove the spacer ring fitted between the bearings. The oil seal at the inboard end of the hub will be driven out with the inner bearing. Drive out the bearing inner races from the hub bore.
6. Clean all old grease, etc., from the hub bore.
7. Pack the new bearings with suitable high-melting point grease.
8. On 1275 GT models, tap the outer races of the new bearings into position in the hub bore, bearing only on their outer edge. Ensure that the races are correctly seated. Install the bearing inner race and roller assemblies in the hub with the spacer ring between them. Lubricate the new oil seal and install it at the inner end of the hub bore with the sealing lip away from the bearing.
9. On other models, install the new bearings in the hub with the spacer ring between them. Tap the bearings squarely into position, bearing only on the outer race. Lubricate the new oil seal and install it at the inner end of the hub bore with the sealing lip facing towards the inner bearing.
10. The oil seal can normally be installed by pressing it into position by hand, or by tapping gently on its outer edge.
11. Assemble the hub on the stub axle and fit the thrust washer and hub nut. The thrust washer must be fitted with its chamfered bore towards the bearing.
12. Tighten the hub nut to 60 lb ft (8.3 kg m), not forgetting that a left-hand thread is used at the left-hand hub. Align the nut to the next split pin hole, if necessary, then secure the nut with a new split pin.
13. Refit the dust cap to the hub, but do not fill the cap with grease.
14. Refit the brake drum and adjust the brake shoes, then fit the road wheel and lower the car onto its wheels.

SHOCK ABSORBERS. . . . .[2]

Telescopic hydraulic shock absorbers are fitted only to models with 'dry' suspension.

On saloon models, the petrol tank must be removed to gain access to the top mounting at the shock absorber. Details of the tank removal are included in the FUEL SYSTEM section.

To replace the shock absorber, first jack up the rear of the car on the appropriate side and support on stands. Remove the road wheel.

Working from inside the luggage compartment, remove the buffer from the damper top mounting stud, when fitted. Hold the damper mounting stud and unscrew the self-locking nut securing the top mounting. Remove the upper cupped washer and the spigotted rubber mounting bush.

At the radius arm, remove the self-locking nut and large washer securing the damper lower mounting to the arm. Compress the damper, then rotate it rearwards to the horizontal and remove it from the mounting stud on the radius arm.

Remove the rubber bush and lower cupped washer (where fitted) from the top of the damper.

If a new shock absorber is being fitted, it should first be bled as detailed in the FRONT SUSPENSION section to expel any entrapped air.

Install the damper in the reverse order of removing. Ensure that the rubber bushes and cupped washers are correctly located at the top mounting, and that a large washer is fitted at either side of the lower mounting bush. When raising the radius arm to reconnect the shock absorber top mounting, ensure that the spring unit strut is correctly engaged at both the spring unit and the radius arm.

RUBBER CONE SPRING UNITS . . . . [3]

Removal & Installation (Fig. K:3)

A rubber cone spring unit is used on models with 'dry' suspension, and is located in the sidemember of the rear sub-frame.

First remove the shock absorber as detailed above. Lower the radius arm and pull or lever the trumpet-shaped connecting strut from the spring unit and the ball seat in the radius arm.

Release the rubber cone spring unit from its location on the sub-frame.

If required, the ball foot or end can be removed from the strut to fit a replacement. The ball foot is merely a push fit in the end of the strut. The nylon seat in the radius arm can also be replaced after levering it out of its location.

Refit the spring unit in the reverse order of removing. Apply suitable grease, such as Detragrease Super G.P., to the strut ball foot and nylon cup before installing the strut. Ensure that the dust cover at the ball end locates correctly around the nylon cup.

As the radius arm is raised to refit the shock absorber, ensure that the strut is correctly engaged at both the spring unit and the radius arm.

HYDROLASTIC DISPLACER UNITS . . . . . . [4]

Removal and Installation

On models with Hydrolastic suspension, a Hydrolastic displacer unit is used in place of the rubber cone spring unit mentioned above.

Jack up the rear of the car and support on stands, then remove the road wheel. Remove the retaining clip and disconnect the lower end of the suspension helper spring from the spigot on the radius arm. It may be necessary to raise the radius arm to allow the spring to be detached.

Depressurise the Hydrolastic system as detailed under the 'HYDROLASTIC SYSPENSION' heading later in this section. Disconnect the displacer unit hose from the valve assembly on the rear member of the sub-frame (Fig. K:-11).

Depress the radius arm sufficiently to allow the displacer unit strut to be extracted from the displacer unit, then pull the tube-shaped strut rearwards to disengage its ball end from the seat in the radius arm. Turn the displacer unit anti-clockwise to release it from its locating plate on the sub-frame, then withdraw the displacer unit (Fig. K:4).

The ball foot is a simple push-fit in the end of the connecting strut and can be removed to fit a replacement. The nylon seat in the radius arm can also be levered out if a replacement is to be fitted.

When refitting the displacer unit, turn it clockwise to lock it in position on the locating plate lugs. Lubricate the strut ball end and the nylon cup in the radius arm with a suitable grease, such as Dextragrease Super G.P., before installing the strut. Ensure the rubber dust cover at the ball end locates correctly around the lip of the nylon cup.

When installation is completed, evacuate and repressurise the Hydrolastic system as detailed later in this section. Ensure that the strut remains correctly engaged at both the displacer unit and the radius arm.

The radius arms pivot on a bronze bush at the outer end of the pivot shaft and a needle roller bearing at the inner end. These are one of the main points of wear at the rear suspension, and this is invariably due to lack of regular lubrication. A grease nipple is provided at the outer end of each pivot shaft and it is very important that these be greased frequently to keep the bearings adequately lubricated and prevent the ingress of dirt and water.

The bearings can be checked for wear once the wheel is jacked up clear of the ground. Grasp the wheel at the front and rear edge and rock the whole suspension assembly in and out. Wear will be indicated by movement of the arm casting in relation to the sub-frame at its outer pivot point. The bronze bush at the outer pivot point is more susceptible to wear than the needle bearing at the inner end.

RADIUS ARMS . . . . [5]

It should be noted that different radius arms are used on 'wet' and 'dry' suspension models. The Hydrolastic arm is most easily identified by the bump stop platform on the top side of the arm and the unthreaded spigot opposite the stub axle for the helper spring attachment. The 'dry' arm has a threaded spigot for mounting the lower end of the shock absorber and no bump stop is fitted. The brake pipe attachment bracket is on the top of the 'dry' arm, and on the bottom on Hydrolastic models. The strut foot housing is also in a different position, being set further forward on the arm on hydrolastic models, but this will be less obvious.

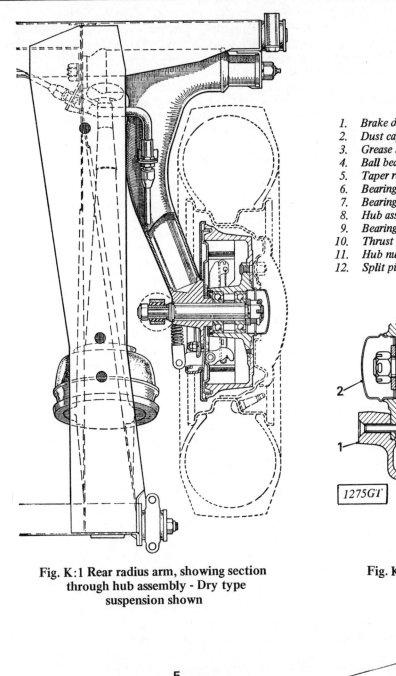

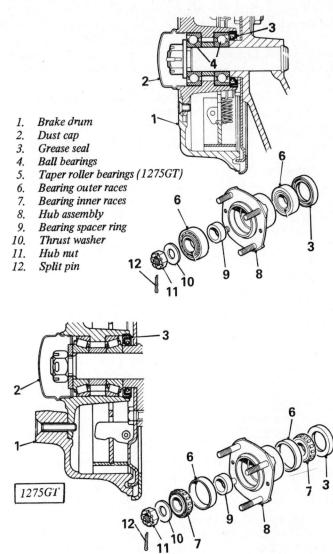

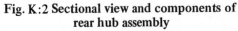

1. Brake drum
2. Dust cap
3. Grease seal
4. Ball bearings
5. Taper roller bearings (1275GT)
6. Bearing outer races
7. Bearing inner races
8. Hub assembly
9. Bearing spacer ring
10. Thrust washer
11. Hub nut
12. Split pin

1275GT

Fig. K:1 Rear radius arm, showing section
through hub assembly - Dry type
suspension shown

Fig. K:2 Sectional view and components of
rear hub assembly

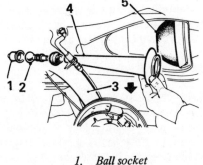

1. Ball socket
2. Knuckle end
3. Radius arm
4. Spring strut
5. Spring unit

Fig. K:3 Removing rubber cone spring unit

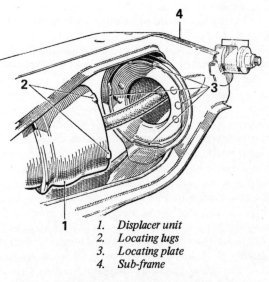

1. Displacer unit
2. Locating lugs
3. Locating plate
4. Sub-frame

Fig. K:4 Hydrolastic displacer unit is located
by bayonet fitting on sub-frame

Removal (Fig. K:6)

1. Jack up the rear of the car and support on stands beneath the sub-frame side members. Remove the road wheel.

2. On 'dry' suspension models, support the radius arm and remove the shock absorber as detailed previously.

3. On Hydrolastic models, depressurise the Hydrolastic system as detailed under the appropriate heading in this section. Support the radius arm and detach the helper spring from its mounting spigot on the radius arm.

4. Remove the clevis pin and disconnect the handbrake cable from the lever at the brake backplate. Also detach the cable from the abutment bracket at the backplate.

5. At the handbrake cable sector on the underside of the radius arm, lever back the flange at the sector corners where it retains the cable and release the cable from the sector.

6. Disconnect the brake pipe from the brake hose, then release the brake hose from the abutment bracket on the radius arm. Plug the hose and pipe ends to prevent loss of fluid and the ingress of dirt. Ideally, the brake hose should be sealed using a brake hose clamp.

7. Remove the support from under the radius arm and depress the arm sufficiently to allow the connecting strut to be extracted from the spring unit or displacer. Pull the strut rearwards to disengage its ball end from the seat in the radius arm.

8. Remove the nut and spring washer securing the inner end of the arm pivot shaft to the sub-frame.

9. Remove the end finisher panel from the sill panel, where fitted. Remove the nut and spring washer securing the outer end of the pivot shaft to the support bracket. Remove the four bolts securing the support bracket to the sub-frame and detach the bracket.

10. Withdraw the radius arm assembly from the sub-frame. Retain the thrust washers and rubber seals fitted at either end of the arm pivot shaft.

Installation

Installation is basically a reversal of the removal procedure, but special attention should be paid to the following points:-

a) Invariably, the reason for removing the radius arm is to renew the pivot shaft and bearings and in this case ensure that both the pivot shaft and bearings are liberally lubricated with grease before installing the shaft in the arm.

b) Assemble the thrust washers on the ends of the pivot shaft with the lubrication grooves towards the radius arm. The large washer is fitted at the inner end of the shaft, and the small washer at the outer end. Fit the rubber sealing ring over the thrust washer and the spigot at each end of the arm. Ensure that neither the thrust washers or sealing rings are displaced during installation of the arm.

c) Tighten the pivot shaft nuts to 53 lb ft (7.3 kg m).

d) Lubricate the strut ball end and the nylon cup in the radius arm with a suitable grease, such as Detragrease Super G.P., before installing the strut. Ensure that the rubber dust cover at the ball end is located correctly around the lip of the nylon cup.

e) When raising the radius arm to reconnect the shock absorber or helper spring, ensure that the strut is correctly engaged at both the spring or displacer unit and the radius arm seat.

f) Bleed the brake hydraulic system as detailed in the BRAKES section.

g) On Hydrolastic models, repressurise the Hydrolastic system as detailed later in this section.

Pivot Shaft Bearings

As mentioned previously, the radius arm pivot shaft runs in a bronze bush at its outer end and a needle roller bearing at its inner end. These bearings are a press fit in the radius arm and require special tools to remove and install them. The bronze bush must be fitted first and line-reamed to size before installing the needle bearing. A lubrication tube is fitted between the two bearings and must be installed with its small diameter towards the bush.

Because of the work involved and the need for special tools, it is recommended that this job be left to a Specialist Machine Shop who will have the necessary equipment and knowledge to carry out the work successfully.

The pivot shaft and bearings are normally supplied as a complete kit containing all the parts necessary for overhaul.

SUB-FRAME MOUNTINGS . . . . [6]

Front Mounting Replacement

Replacement of the sub-frame front mounting involves removal of the radius arm to gain access to the support pin nut at the sub-frame front member (Fig. K:7) Once the radius arm is removed, remove the locknut and washer from the inner end of the support pin. This will normally be hidden under caked mud and dirt which will have to be scraped away. Remove the two bolts securing the mounting trunnion block to the body, then lever the sub-frame downwards away from the body and extract the trunnion assembly. Withdraw the support pin from the trunnion and remove the bushes.

Assemble the trunnion with new bushes and refit it in the reverse order of removing. Note that the step in the trunnion block and the short bolt are at the top.

Rear Mounting Replacement

Replacement of the rear mounting is quite straight forward after jacking up the car and removing the road wheel. The mounting trunnion block is secured to the mounting pin on the sub-frame by a self-locking nut and washer and to the body by two bolts and nuts, or merely two bolts on Estate, Van and Pick-up models (Fig. K:8). Lever the sub-frame away from the body and detach the trunnion assembly. Extract the bushes and fit new ones.

Assemble the trunnion to the sub-frame and body in the reverse order of removing. Note that the step on the trunnion and the short screw are at the front.

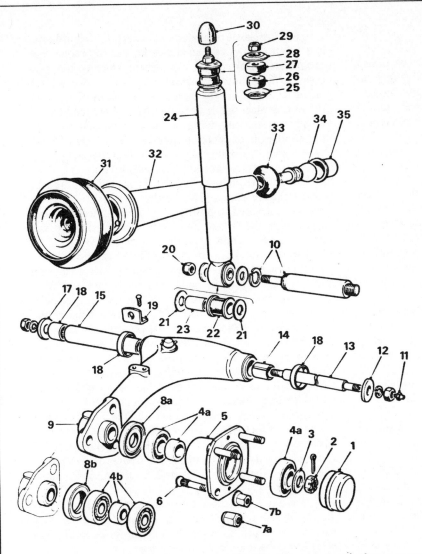

1. Grease retaining cap
2. Nut - stub shaft (L.H. Thd. L.H. shaft)
3. Washer - special
4a Ball bearing and spacer - set
4b Taper bearing and spacer - set (1275GT)
5. Rear hub
6. Wheel stud
7a Wheel nut
7b Wheel nut (1275GT)
8a Oil seal
8b Oil seal (1275GT)
9. Radius arm
10. Stub shaft and circlip (L.H. Thd. L.H. shaft)
11. Lubricating nipple
12. Thrust washer
13. Pivot shaft
14. Bush - bearing
15. Lubricating tube
16. Needle roller bearing
17. Thrust washer
18. Sealing rings
19. Hose bracket
20. Locknut - damper to pin
21. Washers - special
22. Ferrule - rubber
23. Ferrule sleeve
24. Damper - hydraulic
25. Retaining washer (Armstrong damper only)
26. Mounting rubber - plain
27. Mounting rubber - spigotted
28. Retaining washer
29. Locknut
30. Buffer - damper
31. Cone spring - rubber
32. Strut - rear
33. Dust cover
34. Knuckle end
35. Ball socket

Fig. K:5 Components of rear suspension
assembly

1. Shaft outer nut & washer
2. Shaft retaining bracket
3. Thrust washer - small
4. Bronze bush
5. Rubber sealing ring
6. Brake pipe connection
7. Radius arm
8. Strut knuckle joint
9. Lubrication tube
10. Needle roller bearing
11. Rubber sealing ring
12. Thrust washer - large
13. Shaft inner nut and washer
14. Arm pivot shaft
15. Grease nipple
16. Shock absorber
17. Handbrake cable attachment

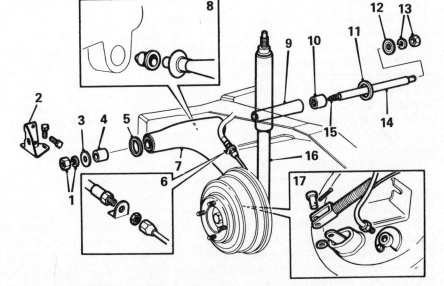

Fig. K:6 Details of radius arm removal (Dry
suspension shown)

Rear Suspension

SUB-FRAME. . . . . [7]

Replacement of the rear sub-frame is occasioned more often by corrosion damage than accident damage, as this appears to be the Achilles Heel on these models. Repair, in terms of 'plating' the affected areas, should only be regarded as a temporary measure as replacement of the sub-frame is the only real answer.

Removal

1. Disconnect the battery leads and remove the battery. The non-earth lead (positive or negative, dependent on the age of the car) to the front of the car will have to be released from the luggage compartment to allow it to clear the sub-frame when it is removed. This is best accomplished either by cutting the terminal off the end of the battery lead and fitting a new screw-clamp type one on reassembly, or by making the hole in the luggage compartment floor big enough to allow the existing terminal to be pushed through. If the floor panel is pulled back carefully to minimise the amount of tearing, it can be easily pushed back on reassembly and the tear sealed with a suitable body sealer.

2. On Hydrolastic models, the Hydrolastic suspension system on both sides of the car should be depressurised before the car is jacked up. However, remember that the ride height of the car will drop as the system pressure is released and it may then be difficult to get a jack underneath the rear.

3. Jack up the rear of the car to a suitable working height, bearing in mind that sufficient clearance should be left to lower the sub-frame. Support the rear end of the car securely on stands at the jacking points at the rear ends of the sill panels. Remove both road wheels.

4. Detach the complete exhaust system and remove it from under the car.

5. At each rear brake assembly, remove the clevis pin and disconnect the handbrake cable from the lever at the backplate. Also detach the cable from the abutment bracket at the backplate. At the handbrake cable sector on the underside of the radius arm, lever back the flange at the sector corners where it retains the cable and release the cable from the sector. Pull the cable through the sub-frame towards the centre of the car and detach it from the guide plate at the centre of the sub-frame.

6. Disconnect the main brake pipe from the brake pressure regulating valve on the sub-frame. Fit a suitable plug in the valve and cap the pipe end to prevent loss of fluid and the ingress of dirt (and stop brake fluid dripping onto you!).

7. Support each radius arm in turn and remove the shock absorber ('dry' suspension) or disconnect the helper spring from the radius arm (Hydrolastic suspension). On 'dry' suspension models, leave the fuel tank in its removed position as access to the sub-frame rear near-side mounting bolts will be required later on.

8. On models with the fuel pump mounted on the rear sub-frame, disconnect the fuel pipes and detach the pump, together with its mounting bracket from the sub-frame. Plug the fuel pipe from the tank to prevent loss of fuel.

9. On Hydrolastic models, disconnect the Hydrolastic pipes from the valve assemblies at the sub-frame rear crossmember. Take great care when releasing the pipe unions as these pipes are easily crushed if excessive force is used. If the pipes are corroded, the unions may break off and new pipes will have to be fitted on reassembly.

10. Support the sub-frame on wooden blocks, or something similar, at the brake drums and the sub-frame front crossmember. A wooden plank about 36 inches long, bearing on the sub-frame sidemembers will also do.

11. Where fitted, remove the end finishers from the rear ends of the sill panels. The finisher is merely a piece of trim and is secured in position by screws - these will probably shear off when unscrewed. On reassembly the finishers can be left off as on the later models.

12. The four sub-frame mounting blocks can now be unbolted from the body. The mountings are located at each corner of the sub-frame and a fair bit of poking with a screwdriver may be required to uncover the securing bolts from the accumulated road dirt. The two bolts at the front mountings go forward into tapped holes in the cross-panel on the body, whereas the rear mountings are secured by bolts and nuts through the floor panel on saloon models, or merely bolts into tapped holes on Estate, Van and Pick-up models (Figs. K:7 and K:8). On saloon models the rear mounting bolts are accessible from inside the luggage compartment, but the fuel tank will have to be displaced to gain access to the near-side bolts. These rear mounting bolts can be sheared off if seized, or at worst drilled out from inside the boot, but if the front ones shear they must be drilled out and the hole retapped to size.

13. Carefully lower the sub-frame assembly out of position, or lift the rear of the car up to clear the sub-frame. It may be necessary to lever the mountings clear of their body locations to release the sub-frame.

Installation

Installation is mainly a reversal of the removal procedure, noting the various points mentioned during removal.

If the either of the Hydrolastic pipes is corroded or was damaged during sub-frame removal, it should be replaced as detailed later in this section, before the sub-frame is installed.

When installation is completed, bleed the braking system as detailed in the BRAKES section.

On Hydrolastic models, evacuate and repressurise the Hydrolastic suspension system as detailed later in this section.

Replacement

If a new sub-frame is being fitted, all the components should be transferred from the old unit. This should be done systematically, and it is recommended that the sequence of removing the parts from the existing sub-frame be noted down to facilitate their reassembly to the new unit. A few points of note when building up the new sub-frame assembly are given below:-

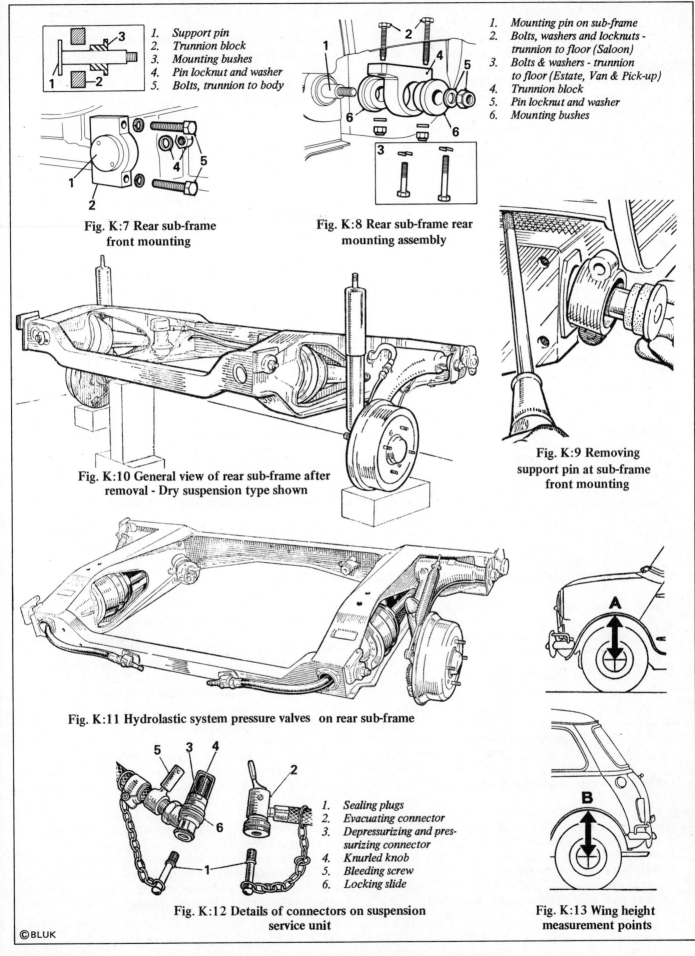

1. Support pin
2. Trunnion block
3. Mounting bushes
4. Pin locknut and washer
5. Bolts, trunnion to body

Fig. K:7 Rear sub-frame front mounting

1. Mounting pin on sub-frame
2. Bolts, washers and locknuts - trunnion to floor (Saloon)
3. Bolts & washers - trunnion to floor (Estate, Van & Pick-up)
4. Trunnion block
5. Pin locknut and washer
6. Mounting bushes

Fig. K:8 Rear sub-frame rear mounting assembly

Fig. K:9 Removing support pin at sub-frame front mounting

Fig. K:10 General view of rear sub-frame after removal - Dry suspension type shown

Fig. K:11 Hydrolastic system pressure valves on rear sub-frame

1. Sealing plugs
2. Evacuating connector
3. Depressurizing and pressurizing connector
4. Knurled knob
5. Bleeding screw
6. Locking slide

Fig. K:12 Details of connectors on suspension service unit

Fig. K:13 Wing height measurement points

© BLUK

Rear Suspension

a) Renew any brake pipes or hoses which appear in any way defective. When fitting a new brake pipe, use the old pipe as a template for bending the new pipe.

b) Mark the locations of all clips, brackets, etc., on the new sub-frame with paint, using the old sub-frame for reference.

c) Check that the hole for the radius arm pivot shaft in the new sub-frame has sufficient clearance for the shaft to fit in easily. It may be necessary to relieve the hole with a round file.

d) Check that the threads in the bolt holes for the pivot shaft support bracket are clear and not clogged with paint by screwing in the bolts prior to assembling them properly.

e) Change over the parts of one radius arm assembly first so that the position and location of the components can be compared.

f) If the radius arm pivot shaft bearings are worn, they should be renewed before assembling the radius arm assembly to the new sub-frame.

g) On models with Hydrolastic suspension, do not forget to change over the radius arm bump stops from the sub-frame front crossmember. Each is secured by a nut and bolt.

h) On models with Hydrolastic suspension, it may be necessary to saw up old sub-frame in order to release the Hydrolastic valve connector assemblies from the sub-frame rear crossmember, if the retaining nuts are seized. It should then be possible to slacken off nuts with the assemblies secure in a vice. A spark plug socket spanner fits these nuts.

i) When changing over the Hydrolastic displacer unit, ensure that the plastic sleeves at the hose apertures are also changed over. These are secured by three cross-head screws.

HYDROLASTIC SUSPENSION . . . . [8]

NOTE: On models with Hydrolastic suspension, an auxiliary coil spring is located between the rear end of each of the rear radius arms and the body to limit the arm movement on rebound.

Depressurising & Repressurising the System

Before any major work can be carried out on the suspension or its components, the Hydrolastic system must be depressurised. For this operation a special piece of equipment, namely a Hydrolastic Suspension Service unit, is required. Such units are generally available for hire, together with suitable suspension fluid, from most tool hire shops.

In most cases, instructions for operating the unit are supplied with it and are normally printed on the top of the unit. These instructions should be read through carefully before attempting to use the unit, and followed accurately throughout the operation.

The unit consists basically of a vacuum pump, a pressure pump and a fluid reservoir. Before using the unit,

check the fluid level in the pressure/vacuum tank and top up with fluid if necessary. The vacuum and pressure valves are normally identified by colour; YELLOW for vacuum, and BLACK for pressure (Fig. K:12).

The Hydrolastic system pressure valves are located at the rear of the car on the sub-frame crossmember (Fig. K:11).

Remember that the ride height of the car will drop as the Hydrolastic system is depressurised, so be careful when working at the rear of the car.

It should be noted that, with the Hydrolastic system in the depressurised state, the suspension arms will contact the bump rubbers at both front and rear, but the car can still be driven with complete safety at speeds up to 30 mph (50 kph) over metalled roads.

When any part of the Hydrolastic system has been disconnected, or after fitting new displacer units or interconnecting pipes, it is essential that the air is evacuated from the system and a partial vacuum created before the system is pressurised. Once evacuated, the system should be pressurised with the car resting on all four wheels in an unladen condition and with a maximum of 4 galls (18.2 litres) of petrol in the tank.

If a new displacer unit has been fitted, pressurise the system initially to 400 psi (28 kg/sq.cm), or 350 psi (24.5 kg/sq.cm) on early models - see Technical Data for details of specific models application. The system should be left in this over-pressurised condition for about 30 minutes to allow the vehicle to settle, then the pressure reduced to its normal specified setting.

Checking/Adjusting the System Pressure

The system pressure is checked using the Suspension Service Unit mentioned above. The car must be resting on all four wheels with a load as described above for pressurising.

The pressure tank on the unit should be pumped up to the system specified working pressure before opening the connector valve, which will already have been connected to the system pressure valve. If a different pressure reading is now indicated, the system pressure should be adjusted by operating the pressure pump to raise the pressure, or opening the pressure valve on the unit to lower the pressure, until the specified figure is obtained.

Checking the Vehicle Ride Height

The car ride height is governed by the Hydrolastic system pressure and should be checked with the car resting on level ground and a load condition as described above for pressurising the system.

Measure the height from the axle centre-line to the underside of the wing opening at both the front and rear of the car and compare with the specified trim heights given in Technical Data at the end of this section (Fig. K:13). If the dimensions are outside the specified limits, the system pressures should be checked and adjusted if necessary to obtain the correct ride height.

The system pressures can be adjusted slightly from the specified figures to obtain the specified trim heights, but large variations will indicate wear or damage to the suspension components or body shell.

HYDROLASTIC PIPES. . . . . [9]

The Hydrolastic system interconnecting pipes are made from Bundy tubing, and therefore, like the brake pipes, are susceptible to corrosion damage after a period of time. The worst areas for corrosion appear to be the points at which the pipes pass between the sub-frames and the vehicle floor pan, and particular attention should be paid here for any signs of fluid leakage. This is usually easily spotted as the suspension fluid is bright green in colour.

The pipes may also suffer physical damage from the impact of stones, etc., due to their open location on the underside of the car. Damage may also be caused to the pipes when attempting to disconnect them, particularly at the rear, as the pipe unions are especially susceptible to corrosion.

Replacement of the interconnecting pipes is reasonably straight-forward but is time consuming in that it involves dropping the rear edge of the front sub-frame and the front edge of the rear sub-frame to allow the old pipe to be removed and the new pipe to be installed. The procedure for dropping the front sub-frame is similar to that described for removing the steering unit.

Needless to say, the Hydrolastic system must be depressurised and repressurised, as described previously, in the course of the work.

Ensure that the pipe unions are tightened securely, as even a slight leakage will prevent the system from retaining its correct pressure.

Technical Data

SUSPENSION

Type. . . . . "Dry" suspension; Rubber cone springs with hydraulic telescopic shock absorbers, or "Wet" suspension; Hydrolastic displacers

SUSPENSION ALIGNMENT

Rear wheel toe-setting . . . . .1/8 in (3.18 mm) toe-in
Rear wheel camber . . . . .1° positive, + 1.5° max/− 0.5° min

HYDROLASTIC SUSPENSION

Hydrolastic fluid. . . . . BMC Part No. 97H 2801
Fluid capacity. . . . . 4 Imp Pts (2.27 litres) approx.
System pressure (unladen)
  Mini Clubman & 1275 GT. . . . . .292 psi (20.6 kg/cm^2)
  All others
    Early models . . . . .263 psi (18.5 kg/cm^2)
    Later models*. . . . . .282 psi (19.7 kg/cm^2)

NOTE: later cars were fitted with modified displacer units those helper springs and rear suspension struts, and their components are not interchangeable individually with those fitted to earlier cars.

SUSPENSION TRIM HEIGHT

Mini Clubman & 1275 GT (front & rear) . . . . .13.5 ± 0.375 in (343 - 9.5 mm)
All others - Early models
  Front . . . . 13.0 ± 0.25 in (330 ± 6.35 mm)
  Rear . . . . 13.5 ± 0.25 in (343 ± 6.35 mm)
Later models
  Front . . . . 12.625 ± 0.25 in (320.7 ± 6.35 mm)
  Rear . . . . 13.14 ± 0.25 in (333.4 ± 6.35 mm)

NOTE: Trim height is measured from wheel centre line to underside of wing opening, with car in unladen condition and a maximum of 4 Imp Galls (18.2 litres) of petrol in tank. Adjust system pressure to obtain specified height.

Steering

FRONT WHEEL ALIGNMENT . . . . [1]

The toe setting of the front wheels is the amount by which the wheels point in or out at the front, in relation to the vehicle centre-line, and is normally given as a dimensional difference measured at the wheel rims; it may also be given as an angular measurement. When the wheels point inwards they are said to have toe-in or negative toe, and toe-out or positive toe when they point outwards.

The front wheels in this case should have a toe setting of 1/16 in (1.6 mm) toe-out with the car in an unladen condition, and the track rods should be of equal length.

Specialist equipment, preferably that of the optical measuring type, is necessary to accurately check the wheel alignment. It is therefore recommended that this operation be entrusted to an Authorised Dealer or other specialist such as a Tyre Centre who will have the necessary equipment.

Adjustment of the toe setting is achieved by altering the effective length of the track rods. This involves slackening the track rod end locknut and the steering rack gaiter clip at each track rod, and turning one or both track rods until the correct setting is obtained. However, it is important that the steering rack be set and maintained in the central, straight-ahead position and both front wheels have the same dimensional setting in relation to the vehicle centre-line. Both track rods should also be exactly the same length after adjustment. When retightening the gaiter clips, ensure that the gaiters are not under stress from twist.

A modified steering rack, giving a smaller turning circle, is used on later models (Mk II models, onwards - October 1967 approximately) and with this unit the rack can be set in the straight-ahead position by inserting a locator pin into a hole in the unit housing (Fig. L:3). Access to the hole is gained from inside the car, on the opposite side to the steering column. Remove the grommet adjacent to the 'U' bolt nuts in the floor panel and unscrew the plastic plug. On late models, a suitable size of Allen key will be required to unscrew the plug. Insert a ¼ in (6 mm) diameter dowel or drill shank into the hole in the rack housing and traverse the rack slightly until the pin fully engages with the rack to lock it in the central position. Do not forget to remove the pin and refit

the plug afterwards.

It should be noted that this hole must not be used for topping up the rack with lubricant.

With this later type of rack it is vitally important that correct wheel alignment is maintained, as an incorrect setting could result in excess articulation of the drive shaft constant velocity joints, and subsequent fouling of the suspension tie-rods by the front wheels when on full lock. The clearance between the front wheels and the tie-rods should be checked with the vehicle resting on its wheels. Turn the steering onto each lock in turn. The clearance should be not less than 3/4 in (20 mm), or ¼ in (6.4 mm) with the suspension at full rebound. Correct adjustment of each track rod will be indicated by the clearance figure being approximately the same on each side of the vehicle.

TRACK ROD ENDS. . . . . [2]

Replacement

Wear in the track rod end ball joints cannot be compensated for by adjustment, and thus renewal of the complete track rod end is necessary. It is recommended that the track rod ends on both sides of the vehicle be replaced at the same time.

Jack up the front of the car and support on stands. Remove the road wheel.

Slacken the locknut adjacent to the track rod end. Extract the split-pin (when fitted) and remove the castellated or self-locking nut securing the track rod ball stud to the steering arm. Disconnect the ball stud from the steering arm, using a suitable ball joint separator (Fig. L:2). Do not knock out the ball stud as this is liable to damage the steering arm or rack. If a proper tool is not available it may be possible to shock the ball stud free by striking both sides of the steering arm simultaneously using two hammers. In this case, take great care to avoid distorting the arm.

Unscrew the track rod end, noting the number of turns required to free it from the track rod. Apply a smear of grease to the track rod threads and screw on the new track rod end, using the same number of turns as was required to remove the old end. Connect the joint stud to

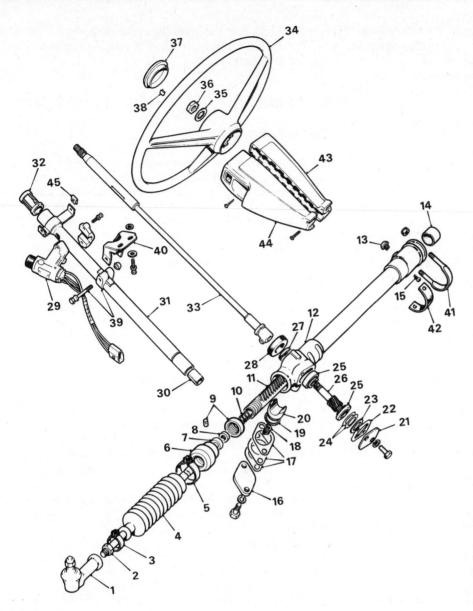

1. Ball joint
2. Locking nut
3. Clip - small
4. Rack housing seal (bellows)
5. Clip - large (or soft iron wire)
6. Ball housing
7. Tie-rod
8. Ball seat
9. Locknut and grooved pin
10. Thrust spring
11. Rack
12. Rack housing
13. Plug - rack centring
14. Rack bearing
15. Retaining screw - bearing
16. Cover plate - damper
17. Shims
18. Thrust spring
19. 'O' ring seal
20. Rack support yoke
21. End cover - pinion
22. Joint washer
23. Shim - standard
24. Shims
25. Pinion bearings
26. Pinion
27. Pinion seal
28. Sealing washer - pinion to floor
29. Ignition switch and setting lock with shear bolts
30. Lower bush - left
31. Steering column - outer
32. Upper bush
33. Steering column - inner
34. Steering wheel
35. Locking washer
36. Nut - wheel to column
37. Hub cover

38. Retaining clip
39. Column clip and shear bolt
40. Clamp plate - column to parcel shelf
41. 'U' bolt
42. Anti-friction strip - 'U' bolt
43. Cowl - L.H.
44. Cowl - R.H.
45. Spring nut

Fig. L:1 Exploded view of steering assembly

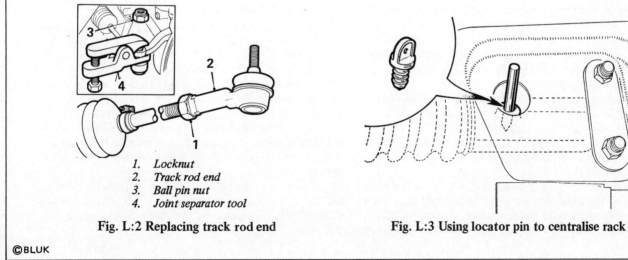

1. Locknut
2. Track rod end
3. Ball pin nut
4. Joint separator tool

Fig. L:2 Replacing track rod end

Fig. L:3 Using locator pin to centralise rack

©BLUK

Steering

E

the steering arm and fit and tighten the securing nut. Where a castellated nut is used, secure it with a new split pin. Tighten the locknut at the track rod end.

Repeat for the track rod at the other side of the car, then refit the road wheels and lower the car to the ground.

Finally, have the front wheel toe setting checked as detailed previously.

STEERING UNIT GAITERS . . . . [3]

Replacement

It is important that no tears exist in the rubber gaiters which protect the steering rack as this would allow the lubricant to escape and dirt to enter the unit with obvious and expensive consequences. If damaged, the gaiter can easily be renewed as follows:

Remove the track rod end and locknut from the track rod, as detailed previously, noting the number of turns required to unscrew the track rod end.

Slacken the small and large clip securing the gaiter to the track rod and the steering gear housing respectively (Fig. L:4). In some cases, a wire retaining clip may be used to secure the gaiter to the rack housing.

Place a drip tray under the steering gear to catch the oil which will be released when the gaiter is removed. Detach the gaiter from the rack housing and slide it down and off the track rod. Allow the oil to drain from the steering rack. It is important to drain out as much oil as possible to prevent overfilling when refilling the steering gear.

Discard the old securing clips along with the damaged gaiter. Use the new clips supplied with the gaiter kit when reassembling.

Apply a light smear of grease to the inside surface of the new gaiter where it will contact the track rod and the rack housing. Position the securing clips on the gaiter and slide the gaiter up the track rod and into position at the rack housing.

With the rack centralised, inject 1/3 pint (0.2 litres) of SAE 90 EP gear oil into the rack housing at the new gaiter. Slide the gaiter into position on the rack housing and secure with the retaining clips.

Ensure that the gaiter is located correctly on the housing, and that its smaller end engages correctly in the groove in the track rod. Also ensure that the gaiter is not twisted or strained before tightening the retaining clips. Turn the rack slowly from lock to lock to distribute the oil through the housing.

It should be noted that, while the car is jacked up with the front wheels clear of the ground, the rack must not be moved forcefully from lock to lock, otherwise the rack gaiters may be ruptured or displaced by the hydraulic pressure in the unit, or damage may occur to the internal components of the assembly.

Assemble the locknut and track rod end to the track rod, using the same number of turns required to remove it. Reconnect the track rod to the steering arm and secure with the retaining nut. Tighten the rod end locknut, then

refit the road wheel and lower the car to the ground.

Finally, have the front wheel toe-setting checked as detailed previously.

STEERING UNIT . . . . [4]

Removal (Fig. L:5)

1. Remove the front floor covering from inside the car.
2. Remove the through-bolt securing the steering column upper support bracket at the parcel shelf. Mark the position of the clamp on the column outer tube to facilitate alignment on reassembly. On later models a shear-bolt is used at the upper support bracket and a saw cut will have to be made in the bolt to enable it to be removed using a screwdriver. The right-hand cowl will first have to be removed from the column to gain access to the bolt.
3. Remove the pinch bolt securing the lower end of the steering column to the steering unit pinion shaft, then pull the column assembly upwards to disengage it from the pinion shaft.
4. Still inside the car, remove the four self-locking nuts securing the rack 'U' bolts to the toe-board.
5. Inside the engine compartment, remove the air cleaner assembly from the carburettor. Also disconnect the exhaust pipe from the exhaust manifold.
6. Disconnect the engine steady rod from the cylinder block and move the rod out of the way. On later models, note that the engine earth strap is also secured by the steady rod bolt.
7. Remove the two bolts securing the sub-frame towers to the body crossmember at the engine compartment bulkhead.
8. Jack up the front of the car and support on stands positioned under the edge of the floor panel at the front jacking points. Use wooden blocks between the stands and the floor panel. Remove both front wheels.
9. On models with 'dry' suspension, disconnect the shock absorbers from the mounting pins on the suspension upper arms.
10. Disconnect both track rod ends from their respective steering arms, using a suitable joint separator tool.
11. Disconnect the exhaust pipe from the support bracket on the final drive unit housing.
12. On models with remote-control gearchange, detach the gearchange extension housing rear mounting from the floor panel. On later models with the single-rod type remote change, remove the through-bolt securing the gearchange housing to its mounting bracket and free the housing from the bracket. It may be necessary to lever the housing over to enable the through-bolt to be removed.
13. Support the sub-frame with a jack and wooden batten positioned across the car so that it locates on the underside of the sub-frame at the lower suspension arm pivot points.
14. Slacken, but do not remove, the centre-bolts securing the sub-frame front mountings to the body. These are accessible through the apertures in the front panel below the bumper.

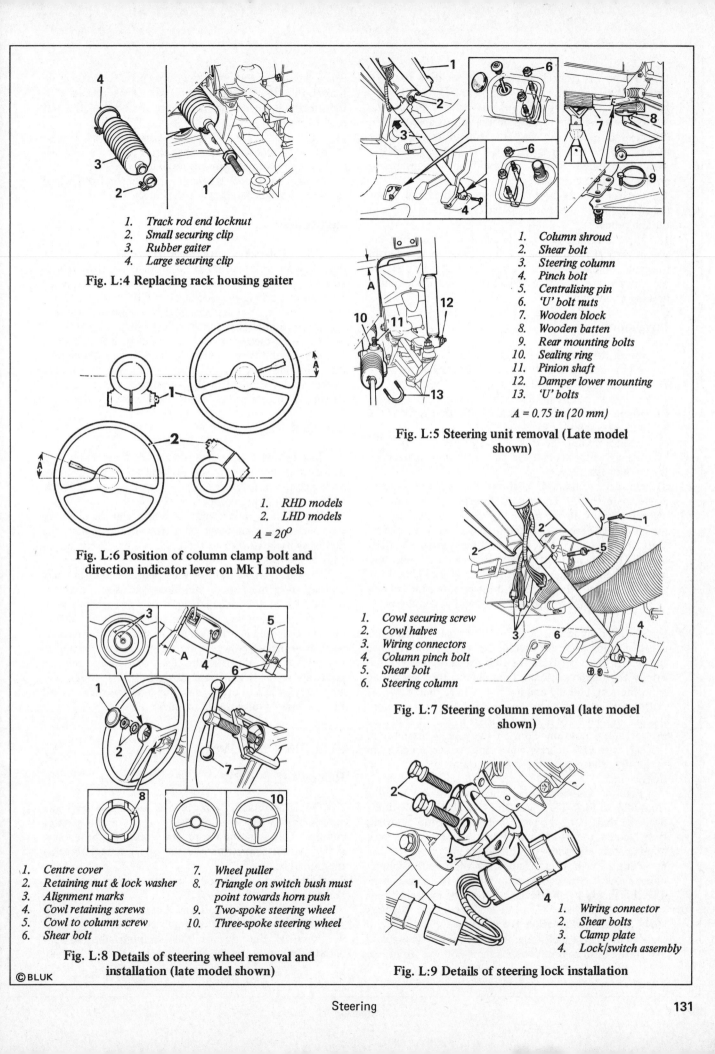

1. Track rod end locknut
2. Small securing clip
3. Rubber gaiter
4. Large securing clip

Fig. L:4 Replacing rack housing gaiter

1. Column shroud
2. Shear bolt
3. Steering column
4. Pinch bolt
5. Centralising pin
6. 'U' bolt nuts
7. Wooden block
8. Wooden batten
9. Rear mounting bolts
10. Sealing ring
11. Pinion shaft
12. Damper lower mounting
13. 'U' bolts

A = 0.75 in (20 mm)

Fig. L:5 Steering unit removal (Late model shown)

1. RHD models
2. LHD models

A = 20°

Fig. L:6 Position of column clamp bolt and direction indicator lever on Mk I models

1. Cowl securing screw
2. Cowl halves
3. Wiring connectors
4. Column pinch bolt
5. Shear bolt
6. Steering column

Fig. L:7 Steering column removal (late model shown)

1. Centre cover
2. Retaining nut & lock washer
3. Alignment marks
4. Cowl retaining screws
5. Cowl to column screw
6. Shear bolt
7. Wheel puller
8. Triangle on switch bush must point towards horn push
9. Two-spoke steering wheel
10. Three-spoke steering wheel

Fig. L:8 Details of steering wheel removal and installation (late model shown)

1. Wiring connector
2. Shear bolts
3. Clamp plate
4. Lock/switch assembly

Fig. L:9 Details of steering lock installation

15. Remove the four bolts and nuts securing the sub-frame rear mountings.

16. Release the jack under the sub-frame and allow the rear of the sub-frame to drop until a gap of about 3/4 in (20 mm) is present between the top of the sub-frame turrets and the valance aperture ('A' in illustration). Use a wedge if required, to force the sub-frame downwards to obtain sufficient clearance.

17. Extract the 'U' bolts and plastic anti-friction strips (when fitted) from between the steering unit housing and the sub-frame.

18. Move the rack downwards and turn it to bring the pinion vertical to clear the aperture. Carefully manoeuvre the unit out from between the sub-frame and the body on the driver's side. Note the sealing ring fitted at the pinion housing on the unit.

Installation

Install the steering unit in the reverse order of removing, but pay special attention to the following points:-

a)   Ensure that the sealing ring is in position at the pinion housing before installing the steering unit.

b)   Where fitted, use new plastic anti-friction strips at the 'U' bolts, if required.

c)   When installing the rack, initially tighten the rack 'U' bolts only lightly so that the pinion can be aligned with the column assembly.

d)   On Mk I models, position the steering column assembly in the car and engage the split portion of the column clamp with the marked spline on the steering unit pinion shaft. Push the assembly down onto the pinion shaft until the pinch bolt can be easily inserted. On RHD models, the clamp must be positioned with the bolt axis below the column and parallel to the rack axis (Fig. L:6). On LHD models, the bolt axis must be above the column at an angle of 16° to the rack housing. Tighten the pinch bolt.

e)   On later models, set the steering gear in the straight-ahead position with the locator pin (Fig. L:3). Remove the rubber grommet from the floor panel on the opposite side to the steering column, then remove the plastic plug from the rack housing and insert a ¼ in (6 mm) dowel or drill shank into the hole. Traverse the rack slowly until the pin engages fully in the rack shaft to lock the steering in the central position. Position the column assembly in the car, with the steering wheel spokes positioned symmetrically, and engage the column clamp on the pinion shaft splines.

Remove the centralising pin and turn the steering from lock to lock. Now push the column assembly down onto the shaft until the pinch bolt can be easily inserted, then tighten the pinch bolt. Refit the plug in the rack housing and the grommet in the floor panel.

f)   With the rack 'U' bolts still slack, offer up the column upper support clip to the clamp plate at the parcel shelf. The clip should be able to engage the clamp plate without any sideways strain to align the two. Should any sideways strain be necessary, slacken the screws securing the clamp plate to the parcel shelf, align the clip into the clamp plate and fit the through-bolt. Where a shear-bolt was fitted, use a new shear-bolt. Retighten the clamp plate to parcel shelf screws, then tighten the column clip bolt. On models with the shear-bolt, tighten the bolt until the head of the bolt shears off.

g)   Tighten the rack 'U' bolts progressively a half-turn at a time until secure. Ensure that the thread on each 'U' bolt protrudes equally through each nut.

h)   When installation is completed, have the front wheel toe setting checked as detailed previously.

Adjustment

Two adjustments of the steering gear are possible; the rack support yoke clearance adjustment, and the pinion bearing pre-load adjustment. Both these adjustments are effected by varying the thickness of a shim pack under a cover plate. The steering gear must be removed from the car to carry out either of these adjustments.

Accurate measurement is essential to ensure correct adjustment of the unit, and it is therefore recommended that this be left to a specialist or other suitably experienced personnel as the adjustment can have great bearing on the life and efficiency (and safety) of the unit.

Overhaul

In most cases of wear or damage to the steering unit, it will probably be more economical and convenient to exchange the complete assembly for a new or reconditioned unit rather than attempt to repair it.

The most common points of wear are at the rack support bush, the gear teeth on the rack and pinion, the pinion shaft bearings and the track rod ball joints at the ends of the rack.

Wear at the rack bush, at the opposite end of the rack housing from the pinion, will allow excessive movement of the rack at that end. Damaged or worn gear teeth on the rack or pinion will make the steering noisy or stiff in use. Excessive side movement at the pinion shaft indicates worn bearings. If either of the track rods fails to stay in any set position, this is a sure sign that the rack end ball joints are worn. If the track rods are difficult to move or are noisy when moved, this indicates damage caused through lack of lubricant in the rack.

STEERING COLUMN. . . . .[5]

Removal (Fig. L:7)

1.   On later models, remove the securing screws and detach the two halves of the cowl from the steering column. This is necessary to gain access to the column switch wiring connectors and the upper support bracket through-bolt.

2.   Disconnect the column switch wiring connectors below the parcel shelf.

3.   Remove the pinch-bolt securing the lower end of the steering column to the steering unit pinion shaft.

4.   Remove the through-bolt securing the steering column to the upper support bracket at the parcel shelf.

Mark the position of the clamp on the column tube to facilitate alignment on reassembly. On later models, a shear bolt is used at the upper support bracket and a saw cut will have to be made in the bolt to enable it to be removed using a screwdriver.

5. Set the front road wheels in the striaght-ahead position, then pull the column assembly upwards to disengage it from the pinion shaft.

Installation

Installation is basically a reversal of the removal procedure. Details of the procedure for aligning the steering column with the steering unit pinion shaft, and aligning the column with its upper support bracket are given in 'STEERING UNIT - Installation' previously. It may be necessary to slacken the rack 'U' bolts to enable the pinion shaft to align with the column.

On early models, check that the direction indicator lever is positioned as shown in Fig. L:6, with the indicator cancelling stud exactly midway between the two cancelling lugs of the indicator switch. If not, adjust the stud to obtain this condition. The combined measurement of the column and the stud should be 1.176 - 1.195 in (29.87 - 30.35 mm). Ensure that the longitudinal head of the stud is parellel to the column before tightening the locknut.

On later models, ensure that the outer column is positioned to give a clearance of about 1/16 in (2 mm) between the steering wheel hub and the boss of the indicator switch. There should also be a clearance of about 1/8 in (3 mm) between the wheel hub and the cowl. If necessary, slacken the column upper clamp bolt and move the outer column as necessary to obtain this clearance.

STEERING COLUMN LOCK . . . . [6]

Replacement (Fig. L:9)

Access to the steering column lock/ignition switch is gained by removing the two halves of the shroud from around the steering column.

The lock assembly is secured to the steering by a clamp plate and two shear bolts which must be removed by dot punching and drilling out. It may be possible to remove the bolts by tapping them round with a centre-punch then unscrewing them.

The switch wiring is connected to the wiring loom by means of a push-fit multi-connector under the parcel shelf.

Position the new lock housing on the steering column and centralise it over the slot in the outer column. Fit the clamp plate and secure with the two shear bolts, but tighten them only finger-tight at this stage. Connect the multi-plug connector and check that the steering lock and ignition switch operate correctly. If satisfactory, tighten the shear bolts until their heads break off.

Technical Data

STEERING UNIT

Type.	.Rack and pinion
Turns of wheel, lock to lock:	
Clubman & 1275 GT	2.7
Other models	.2.33
Lubricant.	SAE 90 EP Gear oil
Capacity	1/3 Imp pt (0.2 litres)

TURNING CIRCLE (KERB TO KERB)

Mk I (848 cc):	
Saloon.	31 ft 7 in (9.63 m)
Estate, Van & Pick-up	32 ft 9 in (9.89 m)
Moke	31 ft (9.4 m)
Mk II on, Clubman & 1275 GT:	
Saloon.	28 ft 6 in (8.55 m)
Estate, Van & Pick-up	29 ft (8.84 m)

FRONT WHEEL ALIGNMENT (UNLADEN)

Front wheel toe setting.	1/16 in (1.6 mm) toe-out, or $0^0 15'$ included angle
Lock angles	$21^0 30' \pm 1^0 30'$ at inner wheel for 20^0 at outer wheel
King pin (swivel hub) inclination	$.9^0 30'$
Castor angle	$.3^0 \pm 1^0$ positive
Camber angle	$.2^0 \pm 1^0$ positive

STEERING

Trouble Shooter

FAULT	CAUSE	CURE
Steering feels stiff	1. Low tyre pressures 2. Incorrect wheel alignment 3. Stiff track rod ends 4. Steering box/rack needs adjustment	1. Correct tyre pressures. 2. Correct wheel alignment. 3. Check and replace if necessary. 4. Adjust if necessary.
Steering wheel shake	1. Wheels and tyres need balancing 2. Tyre pressures incorrect 3. Incorrect wheel alignment 4. Wheel hub nut loose 5. Wheel bearings damaged 6. Front suspension distorted 7. Steering box/rack needs adjustment 8. Shock absorbers faulty	1. Balance as necessary. 2. Correct. 3. Correct alignment. 4. Adjust wheel bearings. 5. Replace wheel bearings. 6. Check, repair or replace. 7. Adjust as necessary. 8. Check and rectify.
Steering pulls to one side	1. Uneven tyre pressure 2. Wheel alignment incorrect 3. Wheel bearings worn or damaged 4. Brakes improperly adjusted 5. Shock absorbers faulty 6. Suspension distorted 7. Steering box/rack worn	1. Correct. 2. Correct. 3. Replace and adjust. 4. Adjust brakes. 5. Check and rectify. 6. Check and rectify. 7. Adjust or replace.
Wheel tramp	1. Over-inflated tyres 2. Unbalanced tyre and wheel 3. Defective shock absorber 4. Defective tyre	1. Correct pressure. 2. Check and balance if necessary. 3. Check and rectify. 4. Repair or replace.
Abnormal tyre wear	1. Incorrect tyre pressure 2. Incorrect wheel alignment 3. Excessive wheel bearing play 4. Improper driving	1. Check pressures. 2. Check wheel alignment. 3. Adjust wheel bearings. 4. Avoid sharp turning at high speeds, rapid starting and braking, etc.
Tyre noises	1. Improper tyre inflation 2. Incorrect wheel alignment	1. Correct tyre pressures. 2. Correct wheel alignment.

Brakes

HYDRAULIC SYSTEM OVERHAUL.......[1]

Any components of the braking system which show signs of fluid leakage should be overhauled or replaced immediately. Only units which appear satisfactory after careful examination of the components should be reassembled using new seals. Any unit which has damaged bores or pistons must be discarded and replaced by a new unit. If in any doubt, replace the unit - your safety could depend on it!

When overhauling any components of the hydraulic system, this must be carried out under conditions of scrupulous cleanliness. This cannot be over-emphasised. Clean all dirt and grease from the exterior of components before removal or dismantling.

Wash all components in methylated spirit or clean brake fluid only. Do not use any mineral-based oils, such as petrol, paraffin or carbon tetrachloride. All internal passages should be blown out with compressed air.

Inspect the piston and cylinder bore surfaces carefully for any signs of scores, ridges or corrosion pits. The unit must be discarded if any of these conditions are present.

Only new seals should be used when reassembling. These are generally available in the form of a repair kit containing all the necessary parts required for overhaul of a particular unit.

All seals, even when new, should be inspected carefully before fitting. Discard any seal which does not appear perfect, no matter how minute the blemish may appear to be.

BRAKE ADJUSTMENT.................[2]

The procedure for adjusting the drum brakes and the handbrake is included in the ROUTINE MAINTENANCE section at the beginning of the manual, and reference should be made for details.

The disc front brakes fitted to 1275 GT models are self-compensating and thus do not require periodic adjustment.

FRONT BRAKE SHOES.................[3]

Some early Mk I models are fitted with leading and trailing shoe type front brakes, instead of the twin leading shoe type used on subsequent models (Fig. M:6). These early type front brakes are similar to the rear brakes described later in this section and reference should be made for details of brake shoe replacement. The procedure below applies specifically to the twin-leading shoe type brakes.

Replacement

1. With the front of the car jacked up and safely supported on stands, remove the road wheels.
2. Slacken off the brake shoes adjusters. Remove the two brake drum securing screws and withdraw the brake drum.
3. Where shoe steady spring are fitted at the wheel cylinder end of the brake shoes, release the springs from the wheel cylinder pistons. These may be omitted on some models.
4. Lever the leading edges of the brakes shoes away from the wheel cylinders, and the trailing edges away from the brake shoe adjusters and remove both brake shoes together with their return springs (Fig. M:2).
5. Fit an elastic band or suitable clamp over the wheel cylinders to retain their pistons in position.
6. Clean out the brake drum and backplate using a soft brush. Check for any signs of oil, grease or brake fluid contamination. If any of these are present, the cause must be established and dealt with before fitting new brake shoes. Grease or oil can be cleaned off with petrol or paraffin; brake fluid should be removed using methylated spirits.

7. Check that the brake shoe adjusters turn freely in the backplate. Apply a small amount of suitable grease to the adjuster spindles, the support points on the tips of the neck brake shoes, and sparingly to the brake shoe support pads on the backplate.

8. Remove the elastic band or clamp from each wheel cylinder. Assemble the return springs to the new brake shoes, ensuring that they are engaged in the correct holes in the shoe webs (Fig. M:1). Also ensure that the shoes are correctly positioned.

9. Lever the shoes into position in the adjusters and the wheel cylinders, then fit the shoe steady springs, where applicable.

10. When correctly located, the shoes should be positioned with the toe (end at which the greatest portion of web platform is exposed) engaged in the wheel cylinder piston.

11. Check that both shoes are correctly seated, and that the brake adjusters are in the fully released position, then install the brake drum.

12 Finally, adjust the brake shoes as detailed in the ROUTINE MAINTENANCE section.

FRONT WHEEL CYLINDERS . . . . [4]

Replacement (Fig. M:3)

1. Remove the brake shoes from the backplate as detailed previously.

2. Disconnect the bridging pipe from the appropriate wheel cylinder and plug the pipe end to prevent loss of fluid and the ingress of dirt. Ideally, the brake hose should be clamped with a proper brake pipe clamp to minimise fluid loss.

3. If removing the front wheel cylinder, slacken the brake hose at the wheel cylinder. If removing the rear cylinder, unscrew the bleed valve from the wheel cylinder.

4. Remove the two bolts securing the wheel cylinder to the backplate and detach the cylinder together with its gasket. In the case of the front wheel cylinder, pull the cylinder through the backplate and unscrew the cylinder from the brake hose. Plug the hose end to prevent loss of fluid.

5. Install the new wheel cylinder in the reverse order of removing. Screw the front cylinder onto the brake hose before securing the cylinder to the backplate.

6. Refit the brake shoes, then bleed the braking system as detailed later in this section.

Seal Renewal

The cylinder piston seals can be replaced without removing the wheel cylinder from the backplate, but great care must be taken to ensure that all dirt, etc., is cleaned away from the exterior of the cylinder and the surrounding area on the backplate before dismantling.

With the brake shoes removed as detailed previously, ease the rubber dust cover off the end of the cylinder and withdraw the piston assembly from the cylinder bore (Fig. M:4). Remove the dust cover and rubber seal from the piston.

Clean and inspect the components as described in 'HYDRAULIC SYSTEM OVERHAUL' at the beginning of this section.

If the piston and cylinder bore are in good condition, lubricate the piston with clean brake fluid and fit the new seal to the piston. The flat face on the seal must face towards the slotted outer end of the piston. Lubricate the cylinder bore with brake fluid and insert the piston, seal end first, into the bore. Take great care to avoid damaging the seal lip during this operation. Fit the new dust cover to the end of the cylinder and the piston.

Refit the brake shoes, then bleed the braking system as detailed later under the appropriate heading.

FRONT BRAKE PADS . . . . [5]

1275 GT models are fitted with disc front brakes, and the brake pads are replaced as follows:-

Replacement

1. With the front of the car jacked up and safely supported on stands, remove the road wheels.

2. Straighten the legs of the pad retaining pins, depress the pad anti-rattle springs and withdraw the two pins from the caliper (Fig. M:7). Remove the anti-rattle springs.

3. Withdraw the brake pads and anti-squeal shims from the caliper, using long-nosed pliers, if necessary.

4. Clean all dust, dirt, etc., from the caliper recess and inspect the piston dust covers for any signs of damage. Also examine the brake disc for any signs of damage or excessive wear. Wear on one side may indicate that one of the caliper pistons is seized, in which case, the caliper should be overhauled.

5. Rotate the brake disc by hand and remove all scale and rust from around the edge of the disc with a scraper. Also scrape any rust or deposits from the pad locating surfaces in the caliper.

6. Press each of the caliper pistons back into their cylinder using a tyre lever or other flat piece of metal. Lever against the hub of the brake disc during this operation, not the outside edge of the disc. The fluid level in the master cylinder reservoir will rise when the pistons are pressed back, and it may be necessary to syphon off excess fluid to prevent it overflowing. Alternatively, fluid can be drained off by opening the caliper bleed nipple while the piston is being pressed back.

7. Check that the cut-away portion on each piston is position upwards, then fit the new brake pads and shims in the caliper. Ensure that both the pads and shims are correctly positioned, and that the pads are free to move easily in the caliper recess.

8. Fit the pad anti-rattle springs, press them down and insert the new retaining pins from the outboard side of the caliper. Splay the legs of the pins to secure them in position.

9. Depress the brake pedal several time to bring the pads into their correct working clearance with the disc.

10. Finally, when the operation has been completed at both front brakes, lower the car back onto its wheels and

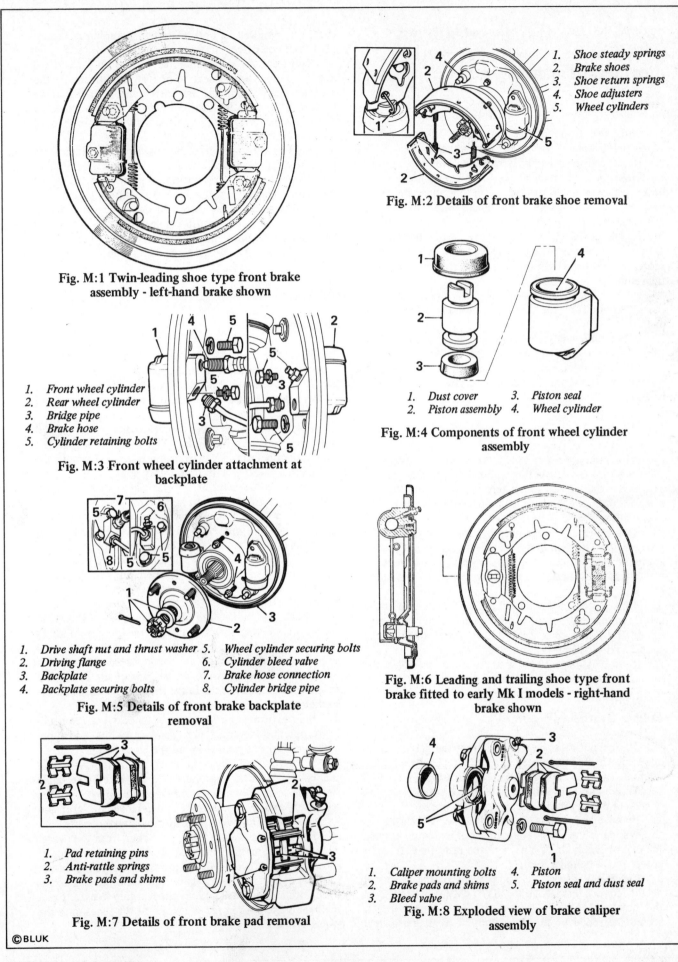

Fig. M:1 Twin-leading shoe type front brake assembly - left-hand brake shown

1. Shoe steady springs
2. Brake shoes
3. Shoe return springs
4. Shoe adjusters
5. Wheel cylinders

Fig. M:2 Details of front brake shoe removal

1. Front wheel cylinder
2. Rear wheel cylinder
3. Bridge pipe
4. Brake hose
5. Cylinder retaining bolts

Fig. M:3 Front wheel cylinder attachment at backplate

1. Dust cover
2. Piston assembly
3. Piston seal
4. Wheel cylinder

Fig. M:4 Components of front wheel cylinder assembly

1. Drive shaft nut and thrust washer
2. Driving flange
3. Backplate
4. Backplate securing bolts
5. Wheel cylinder securing bolts
6. Cylinder bleed valve
7. Brake hose connection
8. Cylinder bridge pipe

Fig. M:5 Details of front brake backplate removal

Fig. M:6 Leading and trailing shoe type front brake fitted to early Mk I models - right-hand brake shown

1. Pad retaining pins
2. Anti-rattle springs
3. Brake pads and shims

Fig. M:7 Details of front brake pad removal

1. Caliper mounting bolts
2. Brake pads and shims
3. Bleed valve
4. Piston
5. Piston seal and dust seal

Fig. M:8 Exploded view of brake caliper assembly

© BLUK

check the fluid level in the master cylinder reservoir.

DISC BRAKE CALIPERS............[6]

Removal

1. With the front of the car jacked up and safely supported on stands, remove the road wheel.
2. If the caliper is being removed for overhaul, remove the brake pads as detailed previously, then depress the brake pedal to move the caliper pistons outwards from their wheel cylinders and thus facilitate removal of the pistons later.
3. If the caliper is to be removed from the car, as opposed to merely being moved to one side to allow access to another component, slacken the brake hose at the caliper.
4. Remove the two bolts securing the brake caliper to the swivel hub and slide the caliper assembly off the brake disc.
5. If the caliper is to be removed, unscrew the caliper from the brake hose and cap the hose end to prevent loss of fluid. Otherwise, merely suspend the caliper from a suitable point on the suspension to avoid straining the brake hose.

Installation

Installation is a simple reversal of the removal procedure, with special attention to the following points:
a) If the caliper was completely removed from the car, screw it onto the brake hose before attaching it to the swivel hub.
b) Ensure that the brake hose is positioned so that it is not twisted and will not foul the body or suspension components during steering and suspension movement.
c) Tighten the caliper mounting bolts to 38 lb ft (5.3 kg m).
d) If disconnected, finally tighten the brake hose at the caliper connection once the caliper is bolted in position.
e) If the brake pads were removed, refit them in the caliper as detailed previously.
f) If the braking system was broken in to, bleed the brakes as detailed later in this section.

Caliper Overhaul (Fig. M:8)

The caliper must be removed from the brake disc to allow overhaul, but it need not be completely removed from the car. The brake hose can remain attached.
1. Thoroughly clean the outside of the caliper, especially around the pad recess and the cylinder bores.
2. Remove the pistons, one at a time, from their respective cylinder bores. Extract the dust seal and retainer from the top of the cylinder bore, and the piston seal from its groove in the cylinder bore.
3. Clean and inspect the components of the caliper as detailed under 'HYDRAULIC SYSTEM OVERHAUL' at the beginning of this section. If the cylinder bore is scored, corroded or showning signs of wear, the caliper

should be renewed. If only the pistons are damaged, new pistons can be fitted.
4. Lubricate the cylinder bores with clean brake fluid and fit a new piston seal to the groove in one of the cylinder bores. Lubricate the piston and insert it, crown first, into the bore with the cut-away at the top. Press the piston into the bore until approximately 0.32 in (8 mm) remains protruding.
5. Fit a new dust seal into the retainer ring and lubricate the lips with clean brake fluid. Fit the seal and retainer over the piston and press them into position at the top of the cylinder bore. Press the piston fully into the bore.
6. Assemble the other piston to the caliper in a similar manner. If the caliper is still connected to the car, it may be necessary to open the caliper bleed valve to enable the second piston to be pressed home in its bore.

REAR BRAKE SHOES.............[7]

Replacement

1. With the rear of the car jacked up and safely supported on stands, remove the road wheels.
2. Release the handbrake and slacken off the rear shoe adjuster. Remove the two brake drum securing screws and withdraw the brake drum.
3. Release the brake shoes from the adjuster wedges and then from the wheel cylinder (Fig. M:10). Disengage the handbrake operating lever from the shoes and remove the brake shoes together with their return springs.
4. Fit an elastic band or suitable clamp over the wheel cylinder to retain the pistons in position.
5. Clean out the brake drum and backplate using a soft brush. Check for any signs of oil, grease or brake fluid contamination. If any of these are present, the cause must be established and dealt with before fitting new brake shoes. Grease or oil can be cleaned off with petrol or paraffin; brake fluid should be removed using methylated spirits.
6. Check that brake shoe adjuster spindle turns freely in the backplate, and that the adjuster wedges are free to slide in the adjuster body. Apply a small amount of suitable grease to the adjuster spindle threads, the adjuster wedges, the support points on the tips of the new brake shoes, and sparingly to the brake shoe support pads on the backplate.
7. Before fitting the brake shoes, check that the handbrake operating lever is free to pivot on its link, and apply a small amount of grease around the pivot point.
8. If required, the link and lever can be removed from the backplate after disconnecting the handbrake cable from the lever. Disengage the rubber dust boot from the backplate and from the lever and remove the lever and link assembly. The assembly is not to be taken apart.
9. Remove the elastic band or clamp from the wheel cylinder. Position the new brake shoes on the backplate as shown in Fig. M:10, and fit the lower return spring. Ensure that the connecting wire between the spring coils is downwards otherwise it will rub on the rear hub in use. Locate the handbrake lever in the shoes and fit the shoes onto the wheel cylinder.

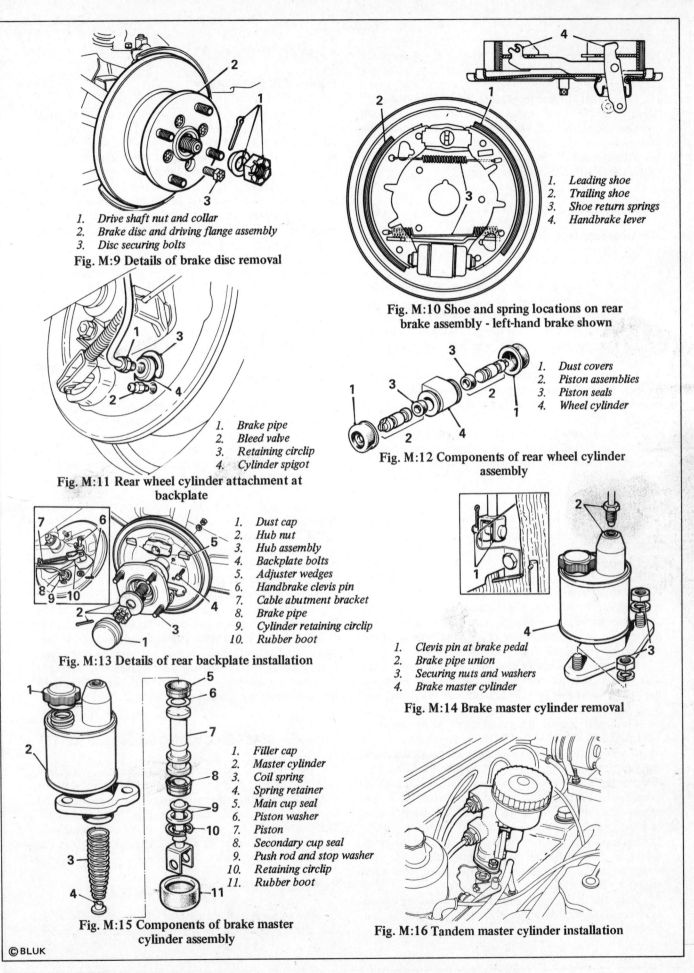

1. Drive shaft nut and collar
2. Brake disc and driving flange assembly
3. Disc securing bolts

Fig. M:9 Details of brake disc removal

1. Leading shoe
2. Trailing shoe
3. Shoe return springs
4. Handbrake lever

Fig. M:10 Shoe and spring locations on rear brake assembly - left-hand brake shown

1. Brake pipe
2. Bleed valve
3. Retaining circlip
4. Cylinder spigot

Fig. M:11 Rear wheel cylinder attachment at backplate

1. Dust covers
2. Piston assemblies
3. Piston seals
4. Wheel cylinder

Fig. M:12 Components of rear wheel cylinder assembly

1. Dust cap
2. Hub nut
3. Hub assembly
4. Backplate bolts
5. Adjuster wedges
6. Handbrake clevis pin
7. Cable abutment bracket
8. Brake pipe
9. Cylinder retaining circlip
10. Rubber boot

Fig. M:13 Details of rear backplate installation

1. Clevis pin at brake pedal
2. Brake pipe union
3. Securing nuts and washers
4. Brake master cylinder

Fig. M:14 Brake master cylinder removal

1. Filler cap
2. Master cylinder
3. Coil spring
4. Spring retainer
5. Main cup seal
6. Piston washer
7. Piston
8. Secondary cup seal
9. Push rod and stop washer
10. Retaining circlip
11. Rubber boot

Fig. M:15 Components of brake master cylinder assembly

Fig. M:16 Tandem master cylinder installation

© BLUK

Brakes

139

10. Fit the upper return spring between the appropriate holes in the shoe webs and lift the shoes into position on the adjuster wedges.

11. Check that the handbrake link and lever are correctly engaged in the shoe webs, and that the mechanism operates the shoes in the correct manner then install the brake drum.

12. Finally, adjust the brake shoes as detailed in the ROUTINE MAINTENANCE section.

REAR WHEEL CYLINDERS . . . . [8]

Replacement (Fig. M:11)

1. Remove the brake shoes from the backplate as detailed above.

2. Unscrew the brake pipe union from the rear of the wheel cylinder and pull the pipe outwards slightly so that it clears the cylinder spigot. Plug the pipe end to prevent loss of brake fluid. Ideally the system should be sealed off by clamping the flexible brake hose with a proper brake hose clamp.

3. Unscrew the bleed valve from the wheel cylinder. Extract the retaining circlip from the cylinder spigot protruding through the backplate and withdraw the wheel cylinder together with it gasket.

4. Install the new wheel cylinder in the reverse order of removing. It will facilitate reconnecting the brake pipe, if threads are started into the cylinder connection before the cylinder circlip is fitted. Use a new circlip to secure the wheel cylinder, and position the circlip as shown in the illustration.

5. Refit the brake shoes, then bleed the braking sytem as detailed later in this section.

Seal Renewal

As with the front brakes, the cylinder piston seals can be replaced without removing the wheel cylinder from the backplate, but again great care must be taken to ensure that all dirt, etc., is cleaned away from the exterior of the cylinder before dismantling.

With the brake shoes removed, remove the rubber dust covers from the ends of the cylinder and withdraw the piston assemblies (Fig. M:12). Remove the rubber seal from each piston.

Clean and inspect the components as described in 'HYDRAULIC SYSTEM OVERHAUL' previously.

If the pistons and cylinder bore are in good condition, lubricate the pistons with clean brake fluid and fit a new seal to each piston. The flat face of the seat must face towards the slotted outer end of the piston. Fit a new rubber dust cover at the slotted end of the pistons. Lubricate the cylinder bore with brake fluid and insert the pistons, seal end first, into the bore. Take care to avoid damaging the seal lips as they are installed. Fit the dust covers to the ends of the cylinders, ensuring that they engage correctly in their respective grooves.

Refit the brake shoes, then bleed the braking system as detailed under the appropriate heading later in this section.

MASTER CYLINDER. . . . . [9]

Removal & Installation

First drain the brake fluid out of the master cylinder reservoir. To do this, attach a bleed tube to the bleed valve on the nearest front brake, open the bleed valve and operate the brake pedal until the master cylinder reservoir is empty. Retighten the bleed valve.

Where applicable, disconnect the heater air intake flexible tube from the heater and from the wheel arch.

From inside the car, remove the split pin and withdraw the clevis pin securing the master cylinder push rod to the brake pedal (Fig. M:14).

Disconnect the hydraulic pipe union from the master cylinder. Remove the two nuts and spring washers securing the master cylinder to the bulkhead and lift off the master cylinder.

Installation is a simple reversal of the removal procedure. When installation is completed, bleed the braking system as detailed later in this section.

Seal Replacement

Remove the filler cap and drain out any remaining fluid from the reservoir. Detach the rubber boot from the end of the cylinder and slide it down the push rod. Extract the retaining circlip from the cylinder bore and remove the internal components, as shown in Fig. M:15, from the cylinder. Remove the secondary cup from the piston.

Clean and inspect the components of the master cylinder as described in 'HYDRAULIC SYSTEM OVERHAUL. at the beginning of this section.

If the piston and bore are in good condition, lubricate the piston with clean brake fluid and assemble the secondary cup to the piston. The flat face of the seal must abut the end flange of the piston.

Fit the spring retainer into the small diameter end of the piston spring and insert the spring into the bore, large diameter first. Fit the main cup seal and the cup washer over the spring retainer. The main cup must be fitted carefully, lip edge first. Insert the piston assembly, then refit the push rod assembly and secure with the circlip. Refit the rubber boot on the end of the cylinder.

TANDEM MASTER CYLINDER . . . . [10]

Two types of tandem master cylinder are used; one with an inbuilt pressure differential warning actuator (P.D.W.A.) and the other without. The two types can be identified from the illustraions in Figs. M:16 and M:17. The master cylinder with the actuator has a wiring connector to the nylon brake failure switch in the side of the cylinder.

Removal & Installation

The removal and installation procedure is similar to that already described for the single-line master cylinder.

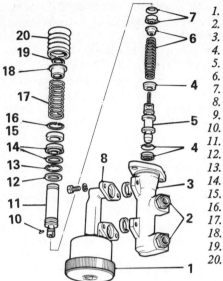

1. Filler cap
2. Connection adaptors
3. Cylinder body
4. Secondary piston seals and washer
5. Secondary piston
6. Coil spring and pin retainer
7. Primary piston seal and washer
8. Fluid reservoir
9. Sealing rings
10. Roll pin
11. Primary piston
12. Stop washer
13. Inner circlip
14. Secondary seal and washer
15. Nylon guide bearing
16. Piston retaining circlip
17. Return spring
18. Spring retainer
19. Spirolex ring
20. Rubber boot

Fig. M:17 Components of Tandem master
cylinder assembly

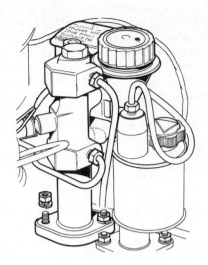

Fig. M:18 Tandem master cylinder with inbuilt P.D.W.A.

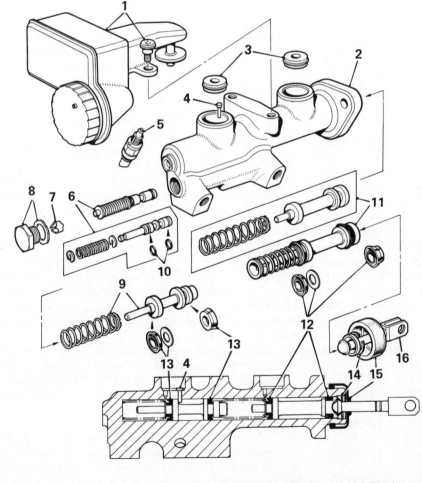

1. Fluid reservoir
2. Master cylinder
3. Sealing rings
4. Secondary piston stop pin
5. Brake failure switch
6. Pressure differential piston assembly
7. Distance piece
8. End plug and washer
9. Secondary piston assembly
10. Piston seals
11. Primary piston assembly
12. Primary piston seals and washer
13. Secondary piston seals and washer
14. Retaining circlip
15. Sealing boot
16. Push rod and stop washer

Fig. M:19 Exploded view of Tandem master
cylinder with inbuilt pressure differential
warning actuator

However, the fluid must be drained out of both sides of the master cylinder reservoir and this will entail repeating the draining procedure at the other front brake.

On the master cylinder without the inbuilt actuator it is unnecessary to disconnect the cylinder push rod from the brake pedal as the cylinder can be lifted off without the push rod.

In the case of the other type of cylinder, the wiring connector is a simple push fit at the failure warning switch.

Installation is a simple reversal of the removal procedure. When installation is completed, bleed both circuits of the split braking system as detailed under the appropriate heading later in this section.

PRESSURE REGULATING VALVE . . . . . . [11]

A pressure regulating valve is incorporated in the hydraulic line to the rear brakes to limit the pressure applied to them and thus prevent the rear wheels locking under normal conditions when heavy brake applications are made.

The valve is mounted on the front crossmember of the rear sub-frame and is easily removed if required (Fig. M:20). Merely disconnect the three hydraulic pipes and remove the nut or bolt securing the valve to the mounting bracket on the sub-frame.

The valve body contains a piston and spring which can be removed once the end cap is unscrewed (Fig. M:21). If the piston and valve bore are in good condition, the valve can be reassembled after fitting new seals to the piston. Also use a new sealing washer at the end cap.

INERTIA VALVE. . . . . [12]

On models with a split braking system, an inertia valve is fitted in the fluid line to the rear brakes in place of the pressure regulating valve described previously. The inertia valve is similarly located on the rear sub-frame and is secured in position by two bolts. The angle at which the assembly is mounted is important as this allows the steel ball inside the unit to hold the valve in the open position under normal conditions so that fluid may pass to the rear brakes. Under heavy braking the ball moves away from the valve which is then closed by a light spring and further pressure to the rear brakes is cut off.

When refitting the valve on the sub-frame, ensure that the 'FRONT' marking on the valve body is correctly positioned (Fig. M:22).

The valve assembly is incorporated in the unit end cap which can be unscrewed to allow the steel ball to be removed. If the unit body is in good condition a new valve and end plug assembly can be fitted, using a new copper washer. Tighten the end plug to 45 lb ft (6.2 kg m).

PRESSURE WARNING (PDWA) . . . . [13]

On models with a split braking system, a Pressure Differential Warning Actuator is incorporated in the system to warn of brake failure in either of the braking circuits.

On some models the PDWA is incorporated in the master cylinder, but where a separate unit is used this replaces the three-way brake pipe connector at the right-hand side of the engine compartment.

The unit incorporates a shuttle valve piston assembly which, when moved from the central position by a pressure differential in the two braking circuits, presses upwards on the warning switch plunger and thus activates the brake failure warning light.

Resetting

The brake failure warning light on the instrument panel should be checked periodically by pressing the test-push when the light should glow. If not, this indicates that the warning light bulb is blown.

When the brake pedal is pressed hard, the light should go out and stay out when the pedal is released. If the light does not go out the pressure in the system in unbalanced or the PDWA unit or its electrical switch are faulty. The switch can be checked by unscrewing it from the PDWA unit and depressing the switch plunger; the warning light should then illuminate.

If after bleeding the braking system, the warning light stays on, it may be necessary to centralise the shuttle valve piston assembly in the PDWA unit by opening one of the bleed valves and gently depressing the brake pedal until the warning light goes out. If this does not work at the first bleed valve, repeat this procedure for one of the bleed valves in the other braking circuit.

Overhaul

If required, the PDWA unit can be dismantled for inspection after removal by unscrewing the end plug from the unit body (Fig. M:23). Also unscrew the nylon switch, then withdraw the piston assembly.

If the piston and cylinder bore are in good condition, fit two new seals to the piston and reassemble the unit. Use a new copper washer when fitting the end plug.

SERVO UNIT. . . . . [14]

A vacuum servo unit is incorporated in the braking system as standard only on early 1275 GT models (prior to 1974). The servo unit is a Lockheed Type 6 and is mounted on the right-hand side of the engine compartment.

The only routine maintenance necessary is periodic cleaning of the filter element at the servo air intake, and this is fully detailed in the ROUTINE MAINTENANCE section.

Testing

With the engine stopped, depress the brake pedal several times to evacuate the vacuum in the system. Depress the pedal, hold it in this position and start the engine. If the servo is operating correctly, the pedal will tend to fall away under foot pressure, and less pressure will be required to hold the pedal in the applied position. If no difference is felt, the system is not functioning.

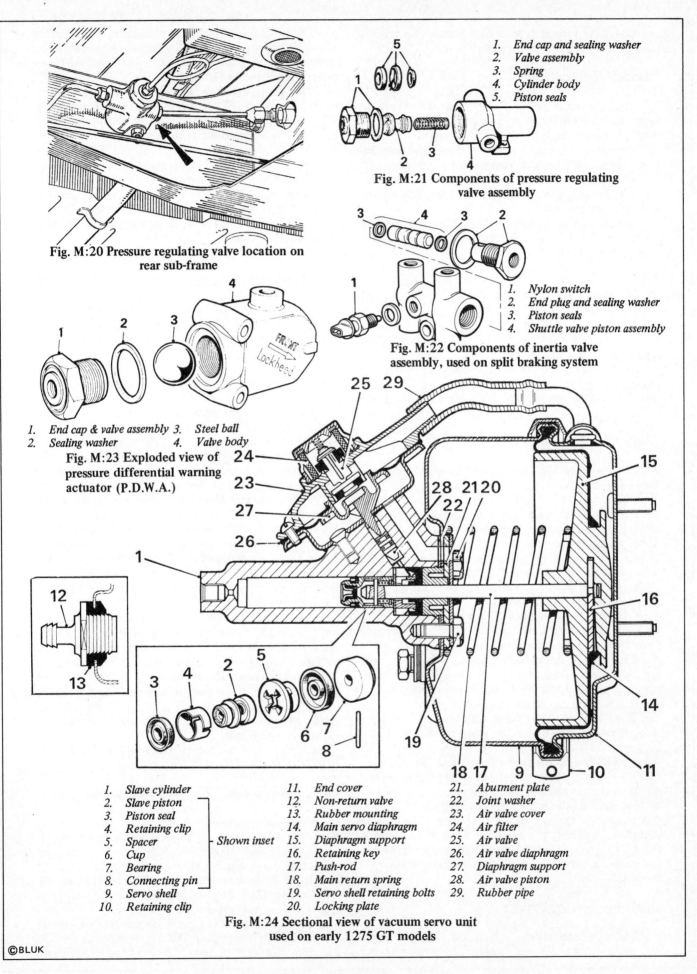

Fig. M:20 Pressure regulating valve location on rear sub-frame

Fig. M:21 Components of pressure regulating valve assembly

1. End cap and sealing washer
2. Valve assembly
3. Spring
4. Cylinder body
5. Piston seals

Fig. M:22 Components of inertia valve assembly, used on split braking system

1. Nylon switch
2. End plug and sealing washer
3. Piston seals
4. Shuttle valve piston assembly

1. End cap & valve assembly 3. Steel ball
2. Sealing washer   4. Valve body

Fig. M:23 Exploded view of pressure differential warning actuator (P.D.W.A.)

Shown inset

1. Slave cylinder
2. Slave piston
3. Piston seal
4. Retaining clip
5. Spacer
6. Cup
7. Bearing
8. Connecting pin
9. Servo shell
10. Retaining clip
11. End cover
12. Non-return valve
13. Rubber mounting
14. Main servo diaphragm
15. Diaphragm support
16. Retaining key
17. Push-rod
18. Main return spring
19. Servo shell retaining bolts
20. Locking plate
21. Abutment plate
22. Joint washer
23. Air valve cover
24. Air filter
25. Air valve
26. Air valve diaphragm
27. Diaphragm support
28. Air valve piston
29. Rubber pipe

Fig. M:24 Sectional view of vacuum servo unit used on early 1275 GT models

Brakes

Check the vacuum hose and connections for leaks or blockage before replacing the servo unit.

Removal & Installation

From beneath the right-hand front wing, pull the heater air hose off the intake unit, and then withdraw the intake unit from inside the engine compartment.

Disconnect the vacuum hose from the servo unit. Remove the securing bracket from the end of the servo unit, disconnect the brake pipes and plug the holes. Remove the nuts securing the servo unit to its mounting bracket and withdraw the unit.

Installation is a simple reversal of the removal procedure. Finally, bleed the braking system as detailed later in this section.

BLEEDING THE BRAKES . . . . [15]

The fluid level in the master cylinder reservoir must be maintained at a reasonable level throughout the bleeding operation as, if the level is allowed to drop excessively, air may be drawn into the system through the master cylinder. Use only fresh brake fluid for topping up. Never re-use fluid which has already been passed through the system.

Single Line Braking System

1. Remove the filler cap from the master cylinder reservoir and top up the fluid level as required.
2. Attach one end of a bleed tube to the bleed valve at the left-hand front brake and immerse the free end in a small quantity of hydraulic fluid in glass jar.
3. Open the bleed valve about three-quarters of a turn. Depress the brake pedal rapidly through its full travel and then allow it to return to the fully released position. Hydraulic fluid should have been pumped into the jar; if not, open the bleed valve further.
4. Continue depressing and releasing the pedal, pausing for a few seconds after each stroke, until the fluid coming from the bleed tube is completely free from air bubbles.
5. Finally, with the pedal held down to the floor, close the bleed valve. Take care not to over-tighten the valve; tighten it only sufficiently to seal. Remove the bleed tube and refit the dust cap on the bleed valve.
6. Bleed the right-hand front brake next in the same way, then the rear brakes, finishing at the rear brake nearest to the master cylinder (Fig. M:26).
7. Finally, top up the fluid reservoir and refit the filler cap, after checking that the vent hole in the cap is clear.
8. If even after bleeding, the brake pedal is still 'spongy' or goes right down to the floor, this indicates that air is still present in the system, and the bleeding operation should be repeated. If subsequent attempts at bleeding still fail to produce a satisfactory result, the system should be checked for leaks, as air is obviously being drawn into the system.

Dual Line Braking System

The dual line braking system may be split either diagonally or front to rear. However, in either case, the bleeding procedure is similar to that already described for the single line system, only the sequence of bleeding being different. The bleeding sequences for the various dual line systems are shown in Fig. M:26.

The pressure failure warning switch should be removed from the PDWA unit before commencing bleeding. When bleeding is completed it may be necessary to reset the PDWA as detailed under the appropriate heading previously.

On models which have a master cylinder with an inbuilt PDWA, if a new master cylinder has been fitted it may have a plastic spacer fitted between the pressure failure warning switch and the master cylinder body. The system should be bled with the spacer in position, then the spacer discarded.

HANDBRAKE . . . . [16]

Late models have a two-cable handbrake linkage which incorporates a separate front and rear cable, as opposed to the twin front-to-rear cable system used previously.

Cable Replacement - Twin Cable System

With this system, either of the two cables can be re-replaced separately without disturbing the other one.

With the handbrake lever fully released, screw the cable adjustment nuts off the front end of the cable at the lever trunnion. Remove the cable guide plate (fairlead) located in the centre of the floor between the front seats.

Jack up the rear of the car and support on stands. Remove the appropriate rear wheel. Draw the cable through the floor pan from underneath the car and release it from the guide channel on the sub-frame front crossmember. Lever back the corners of the flange at the sector on the rear radius arm and release the cable from the sector. Draw the cable through the aperture in the sub-frame towards the outside.

Remove the split pin and clevis pin securing the rear end of the cable to the handbrake lever at the brake backplate. Release the cable from the abutment bracket at the backplate and remove it from the car.

Install the new cable in the reverse order of removing the old one. Nip the corners of the sector flange to hold the cable in position. Also ensure that the guide channel, sector pivot and operating lever clevis pin are adequately lubricated with grease.

Finally, adjust the handbrake cable as detailed in the ROUTINE MAINTENANCE section previously.

Cable Replacement - Front to Rear Cable System

With this system, the front cable must first be removed before the rear cable assembly can be detached.

With the handbrake lever fully released, screw the cable adjustment nut off the front end of the cable and detach the cable from the handbrake lever (Fig. M:28). Detach the cable guideplate, together with its sealing pad, from the floor pan between the front seats.

Jack up the car and support on stands, then remove the appropriate rear wheel. Pull the front cable through the floor pan and disconnect it from the compensator

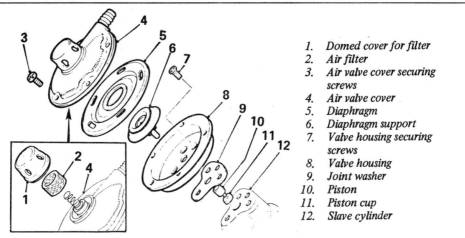

1. Domed cover for filter
2. Air filter
3. Air valve cover securing screws
4. Air valve cover
5. Diaphragm
6. Diaphragm support
7. Valve housing securing screws
8. Valve housing
9. Joint washer
10. Piston
11. Piston cup
12. Slave cylinder

Fig. M:25 Details of servo unit air valve assembly

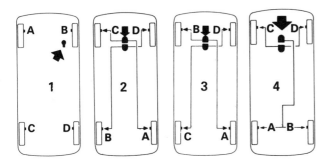

1. Single line braking system
2. Diagonal split system with separate PDWA
3. Diagonal split system with master cylinder with inbuilt PDWA
4. Front and rear split system with inbuilt PDWA

NOTE: Type 3 on LHD models is bled 'C', 'D', 'A', 'B'

Fig. M:26 Braking system bleeding sequence

Fig. M:27 Bleed valve at rear backplate

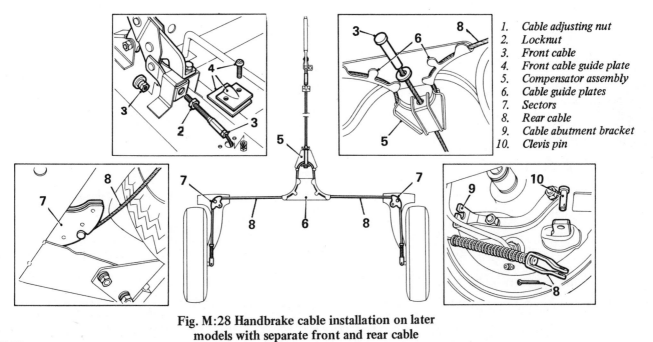

1. Cable adjusting nut
2. Locknut
3. Front cable
4. Front cable guide plate
5. Compensator assembly
6. Cable guide plates
7. Sectors
8. Rear cable
9. Cable abutment bracket
10. Clevis pin

Fig. M:28 Handbrake cable installation on later models with separate front and rear cable

assembly on the rear cable.

At each brake backplate, remove the split pin and clevis pin securing the rear end of the cable to the handbrake operating lever. Also release the cable from the abutment brackets at the backplates.

At the rear radius arms, lever back the flange at the sector corners where it retains the cable and release the cable from the sectors. Pull the cable through the aperture in the sub-frame towards the centre of the car. Lever back the retaining tags at the sub-frame guide plate and remove the rear cable complete with the compensator assembly.

Install the new cable in the reverse order of removing the old one. Nip the corners of the sector flange to hold the new cable in position. Ensure that the cable run is adequately lubricated with grease at the guide channel, sector pivots and operating lever clevis pins.

Finally, adjust the handbrake cable as detailed in the ROUTINE MAINTENANCE section previously.

Technical Data

MK I & II, 850/1000, CLUBMAN & CLUBMAN 1100

FRONT BRAKES

Type	Lockheed, drum, twin-leading shoe, manual adjustment
Drum diameter	7.0 in (178 mm)

REAR BRAKES

Type	Lockheed, drum, leading and trailing shoes, manual adjustment
Drum diameter	7.0 in (178 mm)

HYDRAULIC SYSTEM

Type	Single line with pressure regulating valve in circuit to rear brakes. Dual line, diagonally split or split front to rear, with pressure differential warning actuator (P.D.W.A.)
Brake fluid	Brake fluid conforming to specification SAE J1703C, with minimum boiling point of $260^{o}C$ ($500^{o}F$)

1275 GT

FRONT BRAKES - MODELS UP TO 1974

Type	Lockheed, disc, fixed caliper, twin opposed pistons
Disc diameter	7.5 in (190.5 mm)
Minimum pad thickness	1/16 in (1.6 mm)

FRONT BRAKES (MODELS TO ECE 15 REGS, 1974 ON)

Type	Lockheed, disc, fixed caliper, twin opposed pistons
Disc diameter	8.4 in (213.4 mm)

REAR BRAKES

Type	Lockheed, drum, leading and trailing shoe, manual adjustment
Drum diameter	7.0 in (177.8 mm)
Wheel cylinder bore diam.:	
Models up to 1974	0.75 in (19.05 mm)
Models to ECE 15 Regs	0.70 in (12.7 mm)

BRAKE SERVO UNIT

Application	Models up to 1974
Type	Lockheed, Type 6

BRAKES
Trouble Shooter

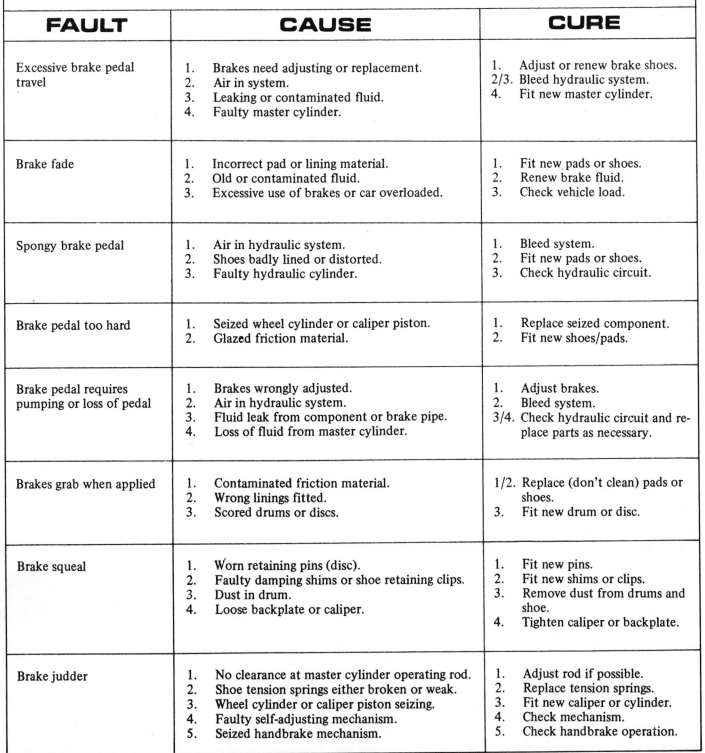

FAULT	CAUSE	CURE
Excessive brake pedal travel	1. Brakes need adjusting or replacement. 2. Air in system. 3. Leaking or contaminated fluid. 4. Faulty master cylinder.	1. Adjust or renew brake shoes. 2/3. Bleed hydraulic system. 4. Fit new master cylinder.
Brake fade	1. Incorrect pad or lining material. 2. Old or contaminated fluid. 3. Excessive use of brakes or car overloaded.	1. Fit new pads or shoes. 2. Renew brake fluid. 3. Check vehicle load.
Spongy brake pedal	1. Air in hydraulic system. 2. Shoes badly lined or distorted. 3. Faulty hydraulic cylinder.	1. Bleed system. 2. Fit new pads or shoes. 3. Check hydraulic circuit.
Brake pedal too hard	1. Seized wheel cylinder or caliper piston. 2. Glazed friction material.	1. Replace seized component. 2. Fit new shoes/pads.
Brake pedal requires pumping or loss of pedal	1. Brakes wrongly adjusted. 2. Air in hydraulic system. 3. Fluid leak from component or brake pipe. 4. Loss of fluid from master cylinder.	1. Adjust brakes. 2. Bleed system. 3/4. Check hydraulic circuit and replace parts as necessary.
Brakes grab when applied	1. Contaminated friction material. 2. Wrong linings fitted. 3. Scored drums or discs.	1/2. Replace (don't clean) pads or shoes. 3. Fit new drum or disc.
Brake squeal	1. Worn retaining pins (disc). 2. Faulty damping shims or shoe retaining clips. 3. Dust in drum. 4. Loose backplate or caliper.	1. Fit new pins. 2. Fit new shims or clips. 3. Remove dust from drums and shoe. 4. Tighten caliper or backplate.
Brake judder	1. No clearance at master cylinder operating rod. 2. Shoe tension springs either broken or weak. 3. Wheel cylinder or caliper piston seizing. 4. Faulty self-adjusting mechanism. 5. Seized handbrake mechanism.	1. Adjust rod if possible. 2. Replace tension springs. 3. Fit new caliper or cylinder. 4. Check mechanism. 5. Check handbrake operation.

Cont'd over

FAULT	CAUSE	CURE
Brake pull to one side only	1. Contaminated friction material on one side (grease, oil or brake fluid). 2. Loose backplate. 3. Seized cylinder. 4. Faulty suspension or steering.	1. Replace shoes/pads all round. 2. Tighten backplate. 3. Replace seized cylinder. 4. Check suspension and steering.
Handbrake ineffective	1. Worn rear shoes or pads. 2. Brakes require adjusting. 3. Faulty handbrake linkage. 4. Cable or rod requires adjustment.	1. Fit new pads/shoes. 2. Adjust brakes. 3. Check linkage and operating mechanism. 4. Adjust cable or rod.
Servo (where fitted) late in operation	1. Blocked filter. 2. Bad vacuum sealing or restricted air inlet.	1. Clean or replace filter. 2. Tighten vacuum hose connections and check hoses.
Loss of servo action when braking heavily	1. Air leak in servo - vacuum low.	1. Either overhaul servo or replace.
Loss of fluid (Servo only)	1. Seal failure. 2. Scored servo bores. 3. Damaged or corroded fluid pipes.	1/2. Replace or overhaul servo. 3. Inspect and fit new pipes.

Brakes

General Electrics

WIPER MOTOR . . . .[1]

Removal (Fig. N:1)

1. Disconnect the battery earth lead as a safety precaution.
2. Disconnect the wiring connector from the wiper motor. This is a simple push-fit. Also release the earth wire from the valance, where applicable.
3. Remove the wiper arms from the drive spindles.
4. Unscrew the sleeve nut securing the rack outer tubing to the motor gearbox.
5. Remove the screws securing the motor retaining strap and release the strap from the mounting bracket.
6. Withdraw the motor assembly, pulling the cable rack from its outer tubing.
7. If required, the wiper wheelboxes can now be removed as follows:
8. Remove the sound insulation material from the bulkhead.
9. Unscrew the retaining nut at each wiper spindle and remove the spacer (Fig. N:2).
10. Slacken the nuts clamping the wheelboxes to the rack outer tubing and release the Bundy tubing from the wheelboxes. The wheelboxes can then be removed.

Installation

Installation is a simple reversal of the removal procedure, but special attention should be paid to the following points:
a) Leave the tubing clamp nuts at the wheelboxes slack until after the cable rack has been inserted and the motor secured.
b) Ensure the cable rack is adequately lubricated before installing it in the outer tubing.
c) Ensure that the cable rack engages correctly with the wheelbox gear teeth.
d) After tightening the wheelbox clamp nuts, check the action of the wheelboxes before refitting the wiper arms.
e) When refitting the wiper arms, switch on the motor and stop it at the end of its stroke. Position the arms to give maximum wipe area and park position at the end of the stroke.

Brush Replacement (Fig. N:3)

1. Note the alignment marks on the motor yoke and gearbox casing for reassembly.
2. Unscrew the two through-bolts and withdraw the yoke and armature from the gearbox. Keep the yoke and armature clear of metallic particles which will be attracted to the pole pieces by their magnetic effect.
3. Note the respective positions of the wiring connectors at the limit switch and disconnect the brush wiring.
4. Remove the screws securing the brush gear assembly to the gearbox casing and detach the brush gear.
5. If required, the brushes can be withdrawn from their insulating plate.
6. If the main brushes (diametrically opposite) are worn down to 0.20 in (5 mm), or if the narrow section of the third brush is worn to the full width of the brush, the brushes must be renewed. If the brush springs are not satisfactory, the complete brush gear assembly should be replaced.
7. Assemble the brushes to the insulating plate and refit the plate on the gearbox casing.
8. Refit the yoke and armature, ensuring that the alignment marks are adjacent.
9. Reconnect the brush leads to the limit switch, ensuring that they are refitted in their original positions.
10. Test the motor before refitting it on the car.

IGNITION/STARTER SWITCH . . . .[2]

Replacement (Fig N:4)
(Column Mounted)

1. Remove the two screws retaining the right-hand half of the cowl to the steering column and detach the right-hand cowl.
2. Disconnect the ignition/starter switch wiring multi-connector plug.
3. Remove the single screw securing the switch to the rear of the steering column lock and withdraw the switch from the lock.
4. Fit the new switch in the reverse order of above.

STEERING COLUMN SWITCH . . . .[3]

On late models, the combined steering column switch incorporates the direction indicators, headlamp dip/flash and horn on the right-hand side of the column, and the windscreen wipe/wash switch on the opposite side. The switches are incorporated on a single mounting plate but the individual switch on either side can be replaced separately if required.

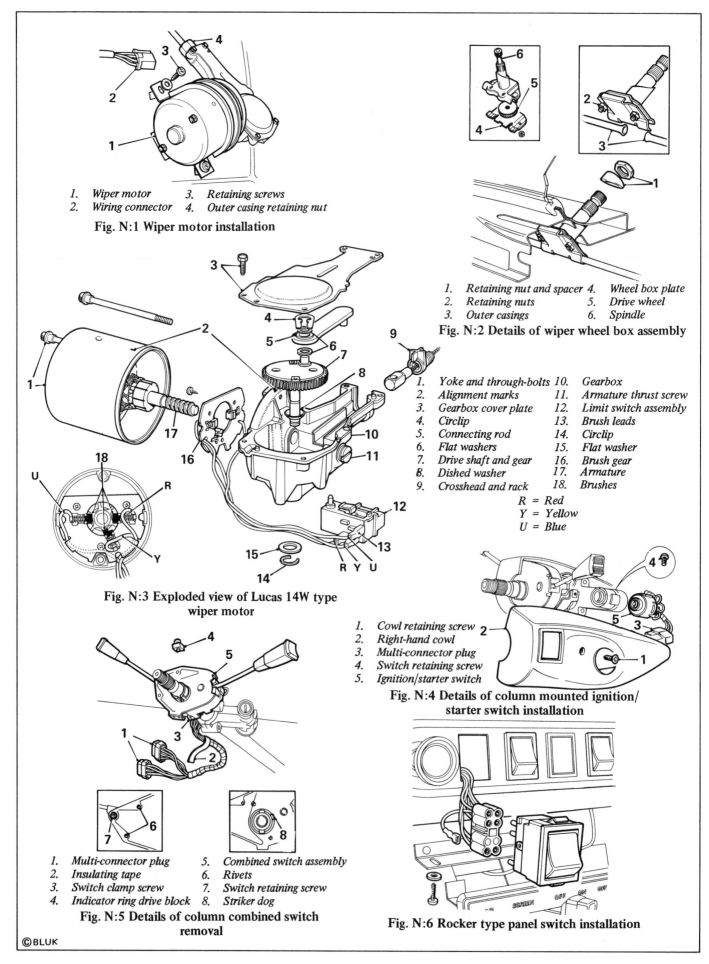

1. Wiper motor   3. Retaining screws
2. Wiring connector   4. Outer casing retaining nut

Fig. N:1 Wiper motor installation

1. Retaining nut and spacer   4. Wheel box plate
2. Retaining nuts   5. Drive wheel
3. Outer casings   6. Spindle

Fig. N:2 Details of wiper wheel box assembly

1. Yoke and through-bolts   10. Gearbox
2. Alignment marks   11. Armature thrust screw
3. Gearbox cover plate   12. Limit switch assembly
4. Circlip   13. Brush leads
5. Connecting rod   14. Circlip
6. Flat washers   15. Flat washer
7. Drive shaft and gear   16. Brush gear
8. Dished washer   17. Armature
9. Crosshead and rack   18. Brushes

R = Red
Y = Yellow
U = Blue

**Fig. N:3 Exploded view of Lucas 14W type
wiper motor**

1. Cowl retaining screw
2. Right-hand cowl
3. Multi-connector plug
4. Switch retaining screw
5. Ignition/starter switch

**Fig. N:4 Details of column mounted ignition/
starter switch installation**

1. Multi-connector plug   5. Combined switch assembly
2. Insulating tape   6. Rivets
3. Switch clamp screw   7. Switch retaining screw
4. Indicator ring drive block   8. Striker dog

**Fig. N:5 Details of column combined switch
removal**

Fig. N:6 Rocker type panel switch installation

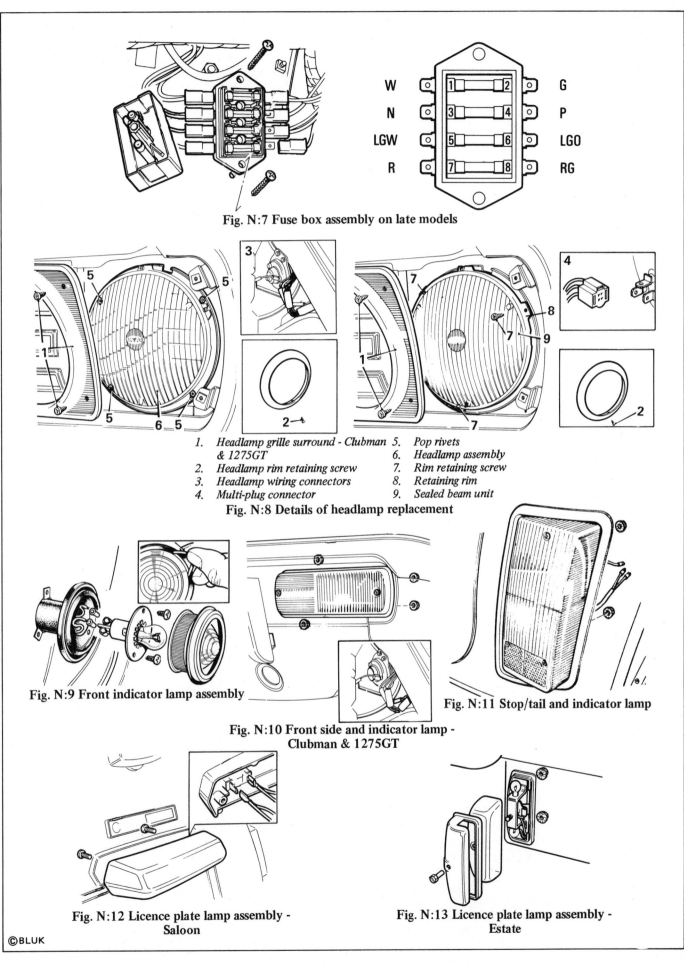

Fig. N:7 Fuse box assembly on late models

1. Headlamp grille surround - Clubman & 1275GT
2. Headlamp rim retaining screw
3. Headlamp wiring connectors
4. Multi-plug connector
5. Pop rivets
6. Headlamp assembly
7. Rim retaining screw
8. Retaining rim
9. Sealed beam unit

Fig. N:8 Details of headlamp replacement

Fig. N:9 Front indicator lamp assembly

Fig. N:10 Front side and indicator lamp - Clubman & 1275GT

Fig. N:11 Stop/tail and indicator lamp

Fig. N:12 Licence plate lamp assembly - Saloon

Fig. N:13 Licence plate lamp assembly - Estate

Replacement (Fig. N:5)

1. Remove the screw from the bottom of the steering column cowl. Also remove the two screws securing the two halves of the cowl to the column bracket and detach the cowl.
2. Prise the hub cover from the centre of the steering wheel and remove the wheel retaining nut and lock washer.
3. Mark the steering wheel hub and the inner column to ensure correct alignment on reassembly, then withdraw the steering wheel off the inner column.
4. Disconnect the column switch wiring connectors.
5. Remove the indicator cancelling ring drive block.
6. Slacken the switch clamp screw and withdraw the switch assembly from the steering column.
7. Remove the insulating tape to separate the wiring harness of the two switches.
8. Drill out the two rivets securing the wiper/washer switch to the mounting plate.
9. Remove the screw and detach the wiper/washer switch from the direction indicator switch mounting plate.
10. Assemble and install the new switch in the reverse order of removal.
11. Ensure that the striker dog on the nylon switch centre is in line with and adjacent to the direction indicator stalk (see illustration).
12. When refitting the steering wheel, align the slots in the switch bush with the steering wheel hub, ensuring that the triangle is pointing towards the horn push. Also ensure that the steering wheels spokes are positioned symmetrically with the front wheels in the straight-ahead position.
13. Set the column cowl to give a clearance of 1/8 in (3 mm) from the steering wheel hub. If necessary, slacken the steering column clamp bolt and reset the position of the outer column to achieve this.

PANEL SWITCHES.................[4]

The switches in the central panel assembly may be of either toggle type, or rocker type on later cars. In either case, the interior heater unit must be lowered to gain access to the rear of the panel and allow the switch to be withdrawn.

Removal & Installation

1. Slacken the nut at the rear of the heater unit.
2. Remove the two screws securing the front of the heater and lower the heater from the fascia.
3. With the toggle type switch, unscrew the switch retaining ring and withdraw the switch from the switch panel. Note the respective positions of the wires and disconnect the connectors from the switch terminals.
4. With the rocker type switch, merely push the switch out of the switch panel and disconnect the multi-connector plug from the switch (Fig. N:6).
5. Install the new switch in the reverse order of removing.

FUSES ....[5]

The main fuse box is mounted on the right-hand side of the engine compartment on the wing valance, and may contain either two or four fuses dependent on model year.

Early models were fitted with only two fuses. The lower fuse protects the auxiliary units, namely the interior lights and the horn, which operate without the ignition being switched on. The top fuse protects the auxiliary units which operate only when the ignition is switched on. The units connected into this circuit include the direction indicators, wiper motor, interior heater blower motor and the brake lights. In addition to the main fuse block, an in-line fuse adjacent to the wiper motor protects the side/tail lighting circuit. All these fuses are rated at 35 amps.

The later four-fuse block protects the following circuits, reading from the top (Fig. N:7):-
Fuse 1-2 (17/35 A) Direction indicators & brake lights
Fuse 3-4 (12/25 A) Headlamp flasher, brake failure warning lamp.
Fuse 5-6 (12/25 A) Screen wipers & washers
Fuse 7-8 (8/15 A) Side/tail lamps

An additional in-line fuse protects the interior lights and the hazard warning flashers, and another the radio when fitted.

HEADLAMPS.....................[6]

The headlamp may either be of the bulb type, or the sealed beam type depending on fitment. It may also incorporate the side lamp on certain models. The headlamp bulb or sealed beam unit can be easily replaced as follows:

Remove the screw securing the headlamp rim and detach the rim from the headlamp unit. On Clubman and 1275 GT models the headlamp grille surround must be removed instead (Fig. N:8).

Remove the three headlamp rim retaining screws and detach the rim. The headlamp unit can then be withdrawn. With the sealed beam type unit, merely withdraw the three pin connector from the back of the unit and remove the lamp unit.

With the bulb type unit, withdraw the three pin connector from the rear of the lamp unit. Disengage the spring clip from the reflector lugs and withdraw the bulb from the rear of the reflector. Fit the new bulb, ensuring that the pip on the bulb flange engages the slot in the reflector. Refit the spring clip ensuring that the coils in the clip are resting on the base of the bulb and that the legs of the clip are fully engaged under the reflector lugs.

In either case, reconnect the three-pin connector and refit the lamp unit in the reverse order of removing.

Where the side lamp is incorporated in the headlamp, the bulb holder may be incorporated in the headlamp three-pin connector or may be a separate push-fit holder which locates in an aperture in the headlamp reflector. In either case, replacement of the bulb is a straight forward procedure after removing the headlamp unit as detailed above.

EXTERIOR LAMPS..................[7]

Replacement of the bulbs in the various exterior lamps is a straight forward procedure, and the illustrations given in Figs. N:9 to N:13 are self-explanatory.

ELECTRICAL

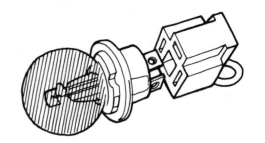

Trouble Shooter

FAULT	CAUSE	CURE
STARTER		
Starter doesn't turn (lights dim)	1. Battery flat or worn. 2. Bad connection in battery circuit	1. Charge or fit new battery. 2. Check all feed and earth connections.
Starter doesn't turn (lights stay bright)	1. Faulty ignition switch 2. Broken starter circuit	1. Check switch. 2. Check starter circuit.
Solenoid switch chatters	1. Flat battery	1. Charge or replace battery.
Starter just spins	1. Bendix gear sticking	1. Remove starter and clean or replace Bendix gear.
CHARGING CIRCUIT		
Low or no charge rate	1. Broken or slipping drive belt 2. Poor connections on or faulty alternator	1. Fit new belt. 2. Check and replace alternator.
LIGHTING CIRCUIT		
No lights (or very dim)	1. Flat or faulty battery, bad battery connections	1. Check battery and connection.
Side and rear lights inoperative although stoplights and flashers work	1. Fuse blown	1. Fit correct value fuse.
One lamp fails	1. Blown bulb 2. Poor bulb contact 3. Bad earth connection. 4. Broken feed	1. Fit new bulb. 2/3. Check connections. 4. Check feed.
Flasher warning bulb stays on or flashers twice as fast	1. Faulty bulb or connection on front or rear of offending side	1. Fit new bulb, make good connection.
Lights dim when idling or at low speed	1. Loose drive belt 2. Flat battery 3. Faulty charging circuit	1. Tighten belt. 2/3. Check charge output and battery.
One dim light	1. Blackened bulb 2. Bad earth 3. Tarnished reflector	1/3. Fit new bulb or sealed-beam. 2. Check earth connections.
WINDSCREEN WIPERS		
Wipers do not work	1. Blown fuse 2. Poor connection 3. Faulty switch 4. Faulty motor	1. Fit fuse. 2. Check connections. 3. Check switch. 4. Remove and examine motor.
Motor operates slowly	1. Excessive resistance in circuit or wiper drive 2. Worn brushes	1. Check wiper circuit. 2. Remove motor and check brushes.

Key to Wiring Diagrams

Several of the components listed in this key may not be fitted to individual models. Some are a special fitment to vehicles exported to certain countries or territories to conform to the mandatory requirements or legislation of those countries.

1. Alternator or dynamo
2. Control box
3. Battery (12 volt)
4. Starter solenoid
5. Starter motor
6. Lighting switch
7. Headlamp dip switch
8. R.H. headlamp
9. L.H. headlamp
10. Main-beam warning lamp
11. R.H. sidelamp/parking lamp
12. L.H. sidelamp/parking lamp
14. Panel lamps
15. Number-plate lamp(s)
16. R.H. stop and tail lamps
17. L.H. stop and tail lamps
18. Stop lamp switch
19. Fuse block
20. Interior light
21. R.H. door switch (and buzzer) when fitted
22. L.H. door switch (and buzzer) when fitted
23. Horn(s)
24. Horn-push
25. Flasher unit
26. Direction indicator, headlamp flasher and dip switch
27. Direction indicator warning lamp(s)
28. R.H. front direction indicator lamp
29. L.H. front direction indicator lamp
30. R.H. rear direction indicator lamp
31. L.H. rear direction indicator lamp
32. Heater or fresh air blower switch
33. Heater or fresh air blower
34. Fuel gauge
35. Fuel gauge tank unit
36. Windscreen wiper switch
37. Windscreen wiper motor
38. Ignition/starter switch
39. Ignition coil
40. Distributor
41. Fuel pump

42. Oil pressure switch
43. Oil pressure gauge or warning lamp
44. Ignition warning lamp
45. Headlamp flasher switch (Mini 1000 Canada)
46. Coolant temperature gauge
47. Coolant temperator transmitter
49. Reverse lamp switch
50. Reverse lamp
64. Bi-metal instrument voltage stablizer
67. Line fuse
75. Automatic transmission safety switch (when fitted)
83. Induction heater and thermostat.
84. Suction chamber heater
95. Tachometer
110. R.H. direction indicator repeater lamp (when fitted)
111. L.H. direction indicator repeater lamp (when fitted)
115. Rear window demister switch
116. Rear window demister unit
139. Alternative connection for two-speed wiper motor and switch
150. Rear window demister warning lamp
153. Hazard warning switch
154. Hazard warning flasher unit
158. Printed circuit instrument panel
159. Brake pressure warning lamp and lamp test switch
160. Brake pressure differential switch
164. Ballast resistor
168. Ignition key audible warning buzzer
170. R.H. front side-marker lamp
171. L.H. front side-marker lamp
172. R.H. rear side-marker lamp
173. L.H. rear side-marker lamp
198. Driver's seat belt switch
199. Passenger's seat belt switch
200. Passenger's seat switch
201. Seat belt warning gearbox switch
202. Seat belt warning lamp
203. Seat belt warning diode

CABLE COLOUR CODE

B.	Black	P.	Purple
G.	Green	R.	Red
K.	Pink	U.	Blue
L.G.	Light Green	W.	White
N.	Brown	Y.	Yellow
O.	Orange		

When a cable has two colour code letters the first denotes the main colour and the second denotes the tracer colour.

Wiring Diagram

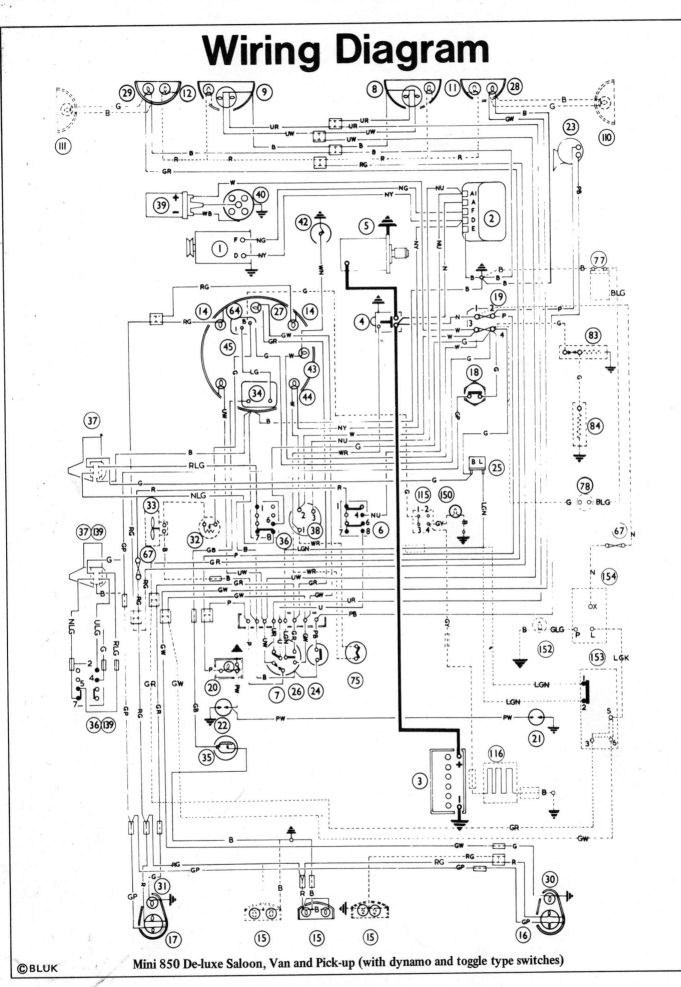

Mini 850 De-luxe Saloon, Van and Pick-up (with dynamo and toggle type switches)

©BLUK

Wiring Diagram

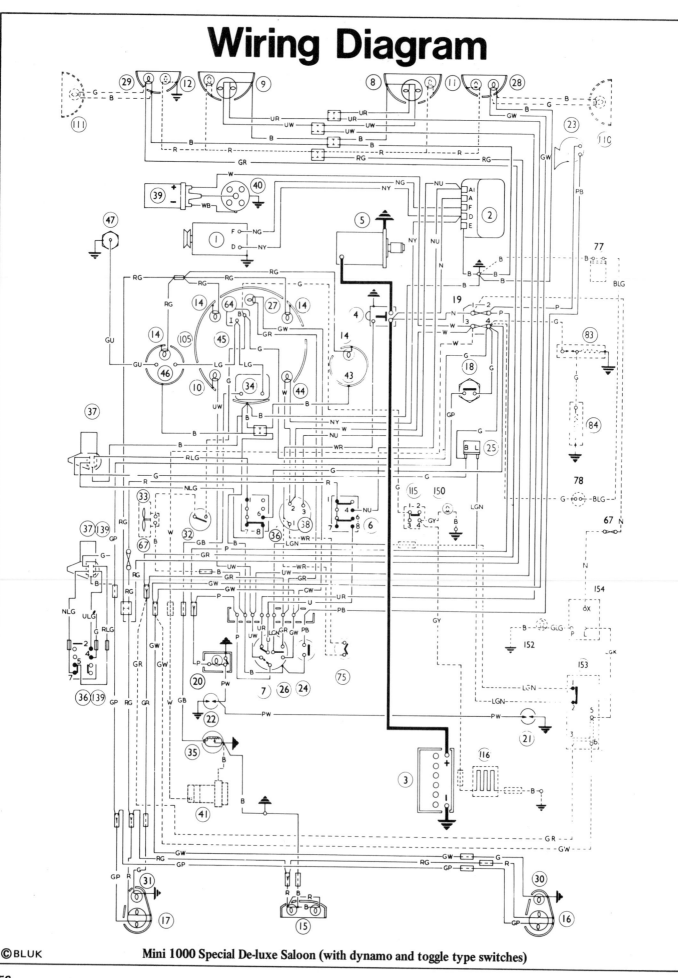

© BLUK — **Mini 1000 Special De-luxe Saloon (with dynamo and toggle type switches)**

Wiring Diagram

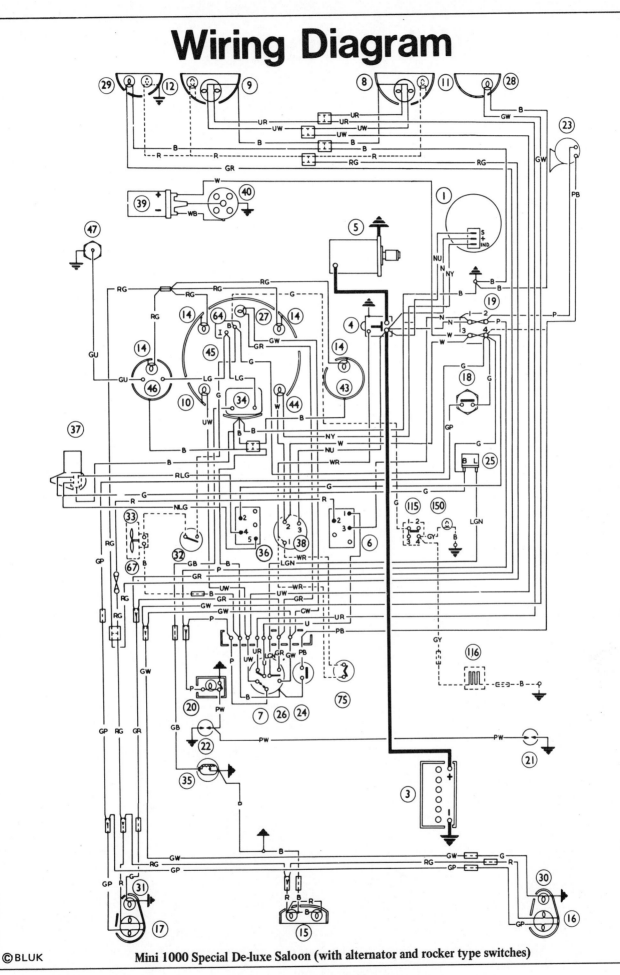

© BLUK

Mini 1000 Special De-luxe Saloon (with alternator and rocker type switches)

Wiring Diagram

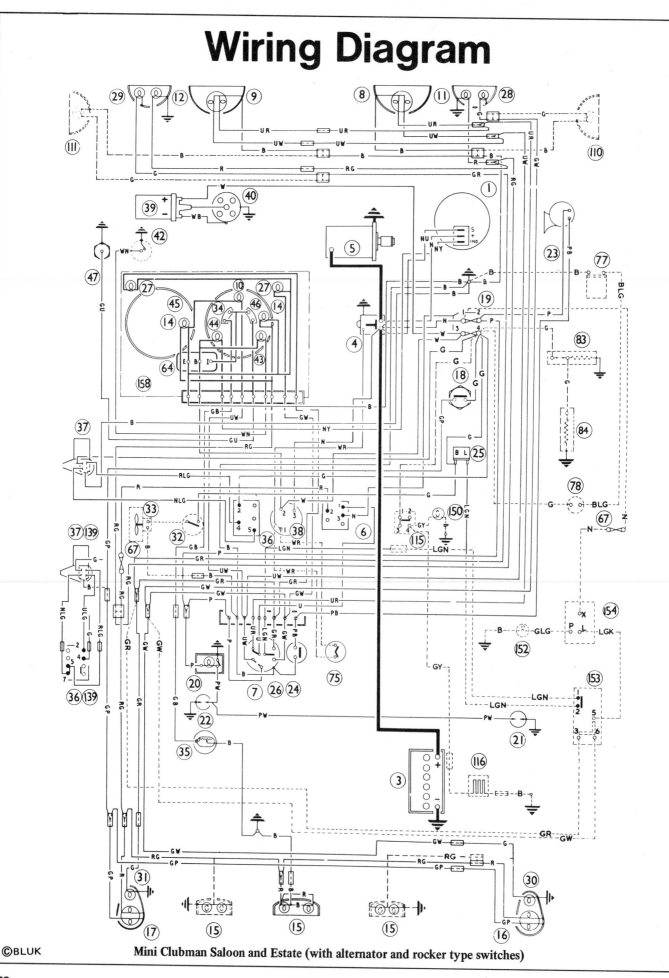

© BLUK

Mini Clubman Saloon and Estate (with alternator and rocker type switches)

Wiring Diagram

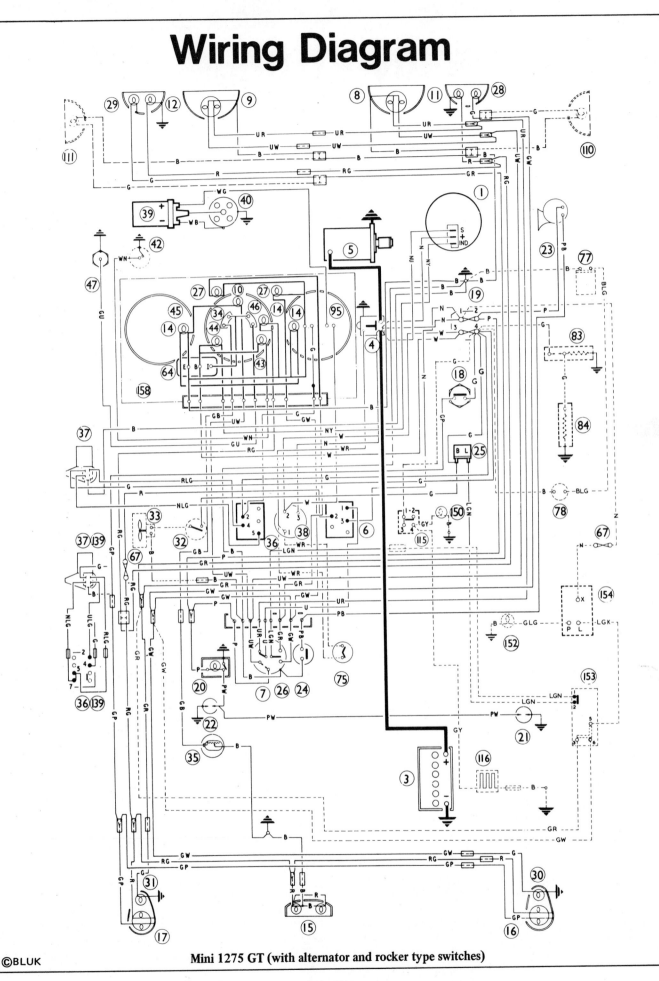

©BLUK

Mini 1275 GT (with alternator and rocker type switches)

Wiring Diagrams

159

Body Fittings

SPEEDOMETER CABLE . . . . [1]
Replacement

On models with the centrally located speedometer, remove the air cleaner assembly and pull back the sound deadening material from the aperture in the centre of the engine compartment bulkhead. Unscrew the knurled nut and disconnect the speedometer cable from the rear of the instrument (Fig. O:1).

On Clubman and 1275 GT models, partially withdraw the instrument panel assembly, as detailed elsewhere in this section, press in the release lever on the speedometer cable and pull the cable out of the rear of the instrument.

Disconnect the knurled nut securing the lower end of the cable to the drive pinion on the gearbox and withdraw the cable. This is not an easy job and may in some cases be done more easily through the aperture above the left-hand drive shaft. If the cable securing nut is too tight to turn by hand, use a suitable tool to release it, or remove the set screw securing the speedometer drive and withdraw the cable complete with the drive assembly and then remove the cable.

Lubricate the new cable lightly with grease except for 8 in (200 mm) at the speedometer end, then install it in the reverse order of removing.

If the speedometer drive was removed, use a new joint washer at the gearbox casing when refitting. Tighten the lower securing nut by hand.

INSTRUMENT PANEL. . . . . [2]

Central Speedo Type

On models with the centrally mounted speedometer, the speedo is located in a housing attached to the centre of the engine compartment bulkhead. De-luxe models have additional instruments located on either side of the speedo and the design of the instrument panel differs dependent on the models.

On Mk I models, the additional instrument panel is attached to brackets on the speedometer housing and is enclosed by a detachable shroud. On later models the instruments are contained in a single nacelle which itself is secured to the bulkhead.

In each case the speedometer can be removed by withdrawing it into the engine compartment after removing the two securing screws and disconnecting the speedo cable (Fig. O:2). On Mk I models the additional instrument panel must first be removed to gain access to these screws. The shroud is secured by four screws in the front face of the panel, and the instrument panel by another

four screws again in the front face of the panel. The panel mounting brackets are attached to the speedometer securing screws in the side of the speedo housing, together with distance pieces.

The fuel gauge is incorporated in the speedometer and once the speedo is removed the fuel gauge can be detached by removing the two securing screws.

The oil and temperature gauges are removed by withdrawing them into the car interior, but this involves removing the instrument panel shroud on Mk I models to gain access to the rear of the instruments. The individual instruments are secured to the panel by a saddle-piece and knurled nuts. In the case of the oil pressure gauge, the oil pressure pipe must also be disconnected from the union on the rear of the instrument. On later models, access to the rear of the instruments is gained through the aperture in the engine compartment.

If the complete instrument panel is required to be removed on these later models with the one-piece nacelle, the trim liner must be detached from the fascia panel sufficiently to allow access to the nacelle securing screws. A retaining tab is also located in the fascia ashtray aperture. In some cases, additional securing screws may be fitted from under the parcel shelf and the interior heater unit must then be lowered to gain access to them.

Clubman & 1275 GT

Clubman and 1275 GT models have a twin or triple instrument panel located directly in front of the driver. The instrument assembly incorporates a printed circuit and, apart from changing the panel warning lights, the instrument panel must be removed before any work can be carried out on it or the individual instruments detached.

Removal and Installation (Fig. O:3)

1. First disconnect the battery earth lead as a safety measure.
2. Remove the air ventilation louvre adjacent to the instrument panel by unscrewing the retaining ring and removing the moulding. Turn the ventilation louvre anti-clockwise and withdraw it (Fig. O: 6).
3. Release the portion of the door seal securing the fascia trim panel, withdraw the trim panel from behind the side panel and remove it.
4. Release the trim panel at the other side of the instrument panel in a similar manner, but do not remove it.
5. The four instrument panel screws will now be accessible and should be removed (two at the top and one at either side).
6. Partially withdraw the instrument panel. Press in the

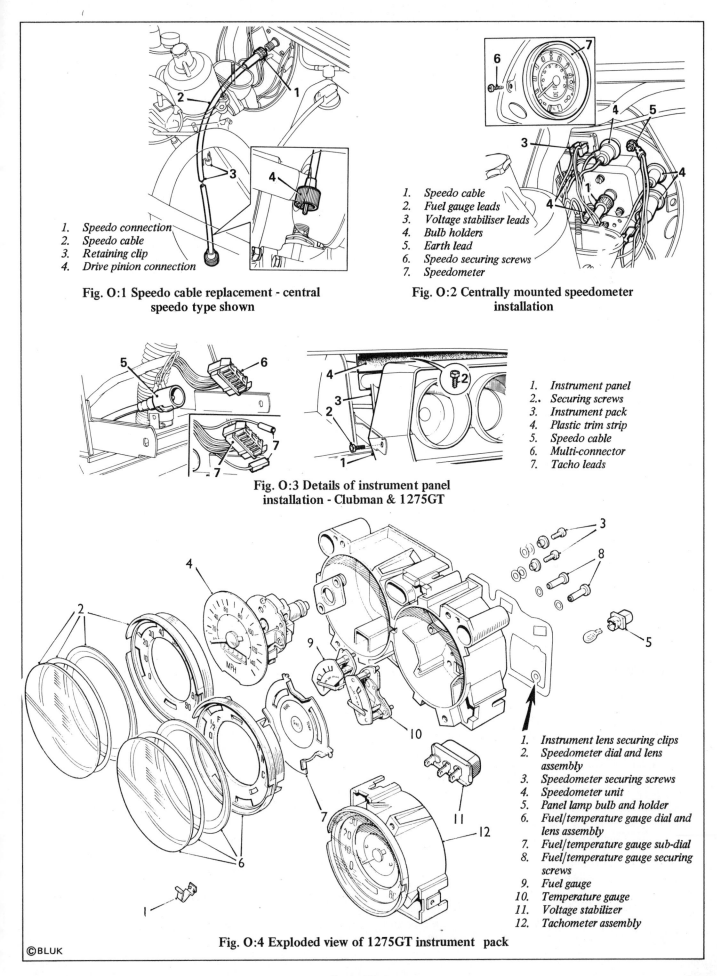

1. Speedo connection
2. Speedo cable
3. Retaining clip
4. Drive pinion connection

Fig. O:1 Speedo cable replacement - central speedo type shown

1. Speedo cable
2. Fuel gauge leads
3. Voltage stabiliser leads
4. Bulb holders
5. Earth lead
6. Speedo securing screws
7. Speedometer

Fig. O:2 Centrally mounted speedometer installation

1. Instrument panel
2. Securing screws
3. Instrument pack
4. Plastic trim strip
5. Speedo cable
6. Multi-connector
7. Tacho leads

Fig. O:3 Details of instrument panel installation - Clubman & 1275GT

1. Instrument lens securing clips
2. Speedometer dial and lens assembly
3. Speedometer securing screws
4. Speedometer unit
5. Panel lamp bulb and holder
6. Fuel/temperature gauge dial and lens assembly
7. Fuel/temperature gauge sub-dial
8. Fuel/temperature gauge securing screws
9. Fuel gauge
10. Temperature gauge
11. Voltage stabilizer
12. Tachometer assembly

Fig. O:4 Exploded view of 1275GT instrument pack

©BLUK

Body Fittings

release lever on the speedometer cable and disconnect the cable from the rear of the speedometer. Pull the multiplug wiring connector from the rear of the instrument panel.

7. On 1275 GT models, disconnect the tachometer connections from the rear of the instrument.

8. Remove the instrument panel assembly from its location.

9. The various instruments can now be detached from the assembly as required, with reference to Fig. O:4.

10. Installation is a reversal of the removal procedure with special attention to the following points.

11. The multi-plug wiring connector will fit only one way round. Ensure that the retaining clips at either side of the plug engage properly.

12. Make sure that the speedometer cable engages fully in the rear of the instrument.

13. Use adhesive to fit the door seal at the outer trim panel if necessary.

14. When installation is completed, check the operation of all the instruments.

HEATER ASSEMBLY . . . . [3]
Removal and Installation (Fig. O:7)

1. Disconnect the battery earth lead as a safety precaution, and drain the cooling system.

2. Pull the demister duct tubes from the outlet on the heater body. On early models it will be necessary to first remove the tube covers to gain access.

3. Slacken the nut securing the rear of the heater unit to its mounting bracket. Also remove the two screws securing the front of the heater to the parcel shelf. Lower the heater and release it from the slotted rear brackets.

4. Disconnect the fan motor switch wires.

5. Pull off the air intake tube from the heater body.

6. Slacken the clips on the heater hose clips and disconnect the hoses from the heater pipes. Plug the pipe and hose ends to prevent water damage to the carpet.

7. Remove the heater unit from the car.

8. Installation is a simple reversal of the removal procedure.

DOOR LOCKS . . . . [4]
Direct-Acting Type

Models with sliding door windows have direct acting door locks, and details of the lock installation is shown in Fig. O:9. To remove the exterior handle, simply remove the retaining screw at the door lock and withdraw the handle from the door panel. The inside door handle will be released as the outer handle spindle is withdraw. On some models the inside handle is secured to the spindle by a clamp screw which must first be released.

The lock itself is secured to the inner door panel by three screws and is easily removed.

Door Locks - Remote Type

On models with wind-up door windows, the door lock is of the remote-acting type, with both the interior handle and the interior lock control connected to it by means of connecting links located behind the door trim panel.

To gain access to the mechanism, the trim panel must first be removed (Fig. O:13). Remove the window winder handle and escutcheon, the door pull and the lock control escutcheon from the door panel. Also remove the door lock interior handle. Lever the trim pad from the retainers at the sides and lower edge, then pull the trim away from the retaining flange at the top and remove the trim panel.

Remove the screws securing the door lock, interior lock control and remote control assembly to the door (Fig. O:10). Pull or carefully prise the bottom of the lock link off the lock operating rod (Fig. O:11). Ease the lock outwards and remove the circlips securing the connecting rods for both the interior lock control and the remote control assembly. Remove the door lock and, if required, withdraw both the remote units from the door panel.

Installation is a reversal of the removal procedure. Ensure that the circlip securing the remote control rod and the interior lock control rod are correctly located and that the lock operating rod is engaged in the spring clip at the exterior handle lock link (Fig. O:11).

Sliding Type

To remove the door glass with the sliding type windows, first remove both the catches from the windows (Fig. O:14). Also remove the channel weather strip fitted to the front edge of the rear glass.

Slide the glasses forward and remove the retaining screws from the window lower channel. Move the glasses to the centre of the window and remove the glasses complete with the lower channel and the glass catch strip from the door. The glasses can then be separated from the lower channel.

Refit the glasses in the reverse order of removing.

DOOR WINDOW GLASS . . . . [5]

Winding Type

To remove the winding type door glass, first detach the trim panel from the door as detailed for lock removal previously.

Remove the four screws securing the window winder mechanism to the door panel (Fig. O:16). Lever the mechanism from the door panel, then wind the mechanism until the arms are at the top of their travel, then wind the mechanism until the arms are at the top of their travel. Slide the mechanism forward and disconnect the rear arm from the door glass channel, then slide it rearwards and disconnect the front arm from the channel. Remove the winder mechanism from the door. Support the door glass with a block of wood, as shown in the illustration.

Pull the door glass outer finisher strip upwards to release it from the clips on the door outer sill. Release the inner finisher from the clips on the door inner sill. Remove the support block, lift the rear end of the door glass and withdraw the door glass from the outer side of the door.

Install the window glass in the reverse order of removing.

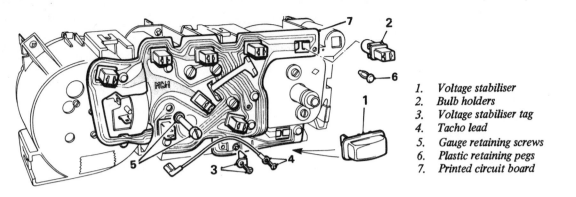

Fig. O:5 Rear view of instrument pack printed circuit panel

1. Voltage stabiliser
2. Bulb holders
3. Voltage stabiliser tag
4. Tacho lead
5. Gauge retaining screws
6. Plastic retaining pegs
7. Printed circuit board

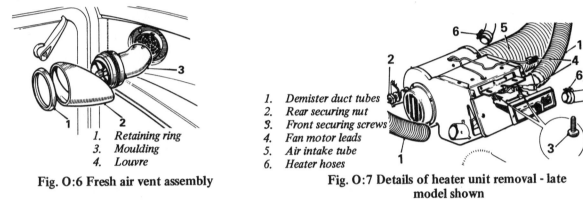

1. Retaining ring
3. Moulding
4. Louvre

Fig. O:6 Fresh air vent assembly

1. Demister duct tubes
2. Rear securing nut
3. Front securing screws
4. Fan motor leads
5. Air intake tube
6. Heater hoses

Fig. O:7 Details of heater unit removal - late model shown

1. Screw, motor to casing
2. Fan motor leads
3. Heater casing
4. Motor assembly
5. Screw, end plate to casing
6. Casing end plate
7. Heater matrix
8. Heater control plate
9. Screw, plate to casing
10. Control mounting plate

Fig. O:8 Exploded view of interior heater unit

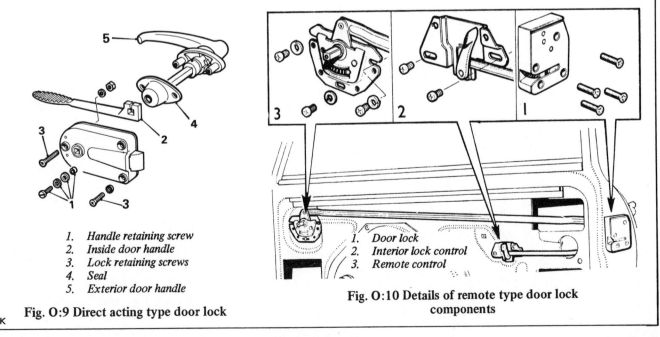

1. Handle retaining screw
2. Inside door handle
3. Lock retaining screws
4. Seal
5. Exterior door handle

Fig. O:9 Direct acting type door lock

1. Door lock
2. Interior lock control
3. Remote control

Fig. O:10 Details of remote type door lock components

©BLUK

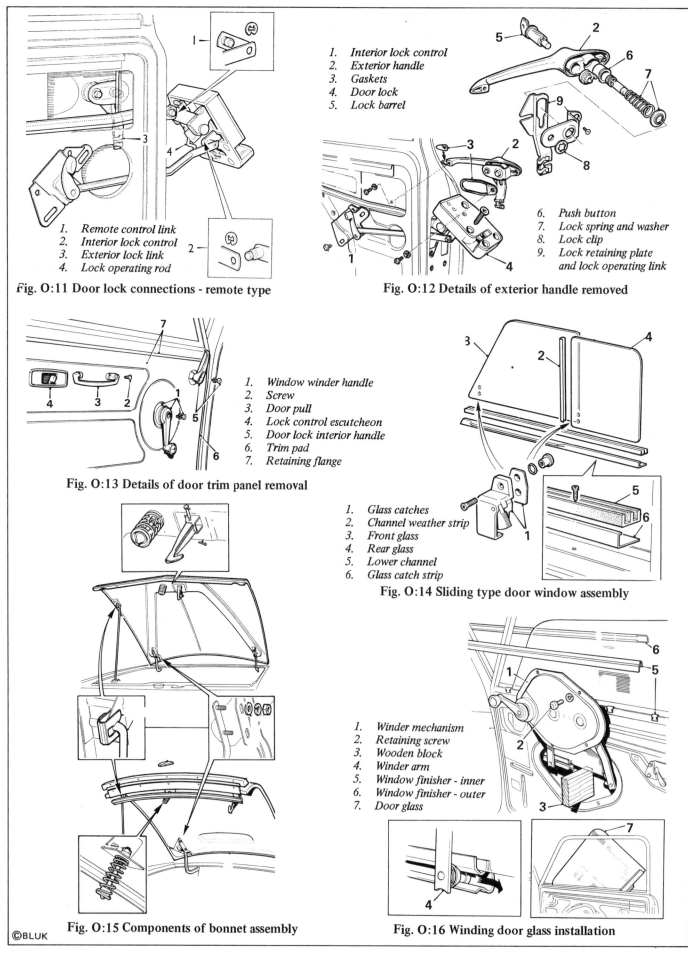

1. Interior lock control
2. Exterior handle
3. Gaskets
4. Door lock
5. Lock barrel

6. Push button
7. Lock spring and washer
8. Lock clip
9. Lock retaining plate and lock operating link

1. Remote control link
2. Interior lock control
3. Exterior lock link
4. Lock operating rod

Fig. O:11 Door lock connections - remote type

Fig. O:12 Details of exterior handle removed

1. Window winder handle
2. Screw
3. Door pull
4. Lock control escutcheon
5. Door lock interior handle
6. Trim pad
7. Retaining flange

Fig. O:13 Details of door trim panel removal

1. Glass catches
2. Channel weather strip
3. Front glass
4. Rear glass
5. Lower channel
6. Glass catch strip

Fig. O:14 Sliding type door window assembly

1. Winder mechanism
2. Retaining screw
3. Wooden block
4. Winder arm
5. Window finisher - inner
6. Window finisher - outer
7. Door glass

Fig. O:15 Components of bonnet assembly

Fig. O:16 Winding door glass installation

©BLUK

SEAT BELTS . . . . [6]

Although seat belts are fitted to a car this doesn't necessarily mean that they are working efficiently or, indeed, that they are capable of doing their job when they are actually needed. This is why the condition of the seat belt is now included in the annual MoT test. There are some simple checks to be made on a regular basis to see that they are in working order. They are as follows:

1. Pull each seat belt against its anchorage to see that it is properly secured to the vehicle structure.
2. Examine carefully the condition of the webbing looking for cuts or obvious signs of deterioration.
3. Fasten each seat belt locking mechanism and then try to pull the locked sections apart. Operate the mechanism, whilst pulling on the belt to determine that the mechanism releases when required.
3. Check the condition of the attachment fittings and adjusting fitting on each belt for distortion or fracture.
5. As far as practicable check the condition of the vehicle structure around the seat belt anchorages - this will be best carried out from below the vehicle.
6. If the seat belt is of the retracting type, pull a section of the webbing from the reel unit and then release it to see that the webbing automatically winds back. Bear in mind that some inertia reel belts require some manual assistance before retraction takes place.

CORROSION . . . . [7]

We all recognise rust when it starts to appear around certain parts of our cars anatomy. Then, before we are aware, it's too late and metal has been replaced by a very poor substitute. The result is costly, can be dangerous and will not win the car any beauty awards!

The only way to beat rust is to prevent it in the first place or at the very least slow it down. To do this, first of all we must realise how rust is formed.

Think of a piece of metal with a bead of water sitting on top. The metal below the water is starved of air and is called anodic. The metal outside this area is known as cathodic. An electrolytic action is formed between these two conditions and it is this process that causes corrosion. There are acceleration factors involved such as dirt, grit or salt. These can be contained in the water and will increase the conductivity. So basically rust is formed by an electro-chemical reaction. Bear in mind that rain needn't necessarily be the water factor involved in the process - condensation plays its role too.

Obviously it doesn't take much logic to understand how rust can be prevented in the first place. The metal work of the car has to be protected from moisture and air. This protection is partly taken care of by the car manufacturer when the car is put together - paint on the outside and special inhibitors used on the inside. However, the rust protection is only as good as the application of these materials and one spot missed means that rust will accelerate all the more in this particular spot.

The importance of regular washing and touching up paintwork play there part in rust protection. For example,

regular hosing down of the underneath of the car can help prevent any build up of mud forming in certain areas. Mud can act like a damp sponge during wet weather so that you have a constant moisture problem even during dry spells. You'll find that common rust problems on particular models usually originate from mud-traps.

You can always go one step further and improve on the manufacturers rust protection by tackling your own rustproofing. This involves applying light viscosity water-dispacing material inside all the box sections and/or applying underbody sealant.

There are various kits on the market designed specifically for the keen DIY motorist and even if you don't treat all the box sections it is worthwhile devoting some time to protecting the rust prone areas of your particular car.

An important part of protection is treating the car with an underbody sealant. Here preparation is of the utmost importance because if the sealant doesn't attach firmly to the car body then the air gap between seal and metal can help accelerate corrosion rather than prevent it.

First of all the car will have to be thoroughly cleaned underneath. A high pressure hose is obviously helpful in removing dirt but better still is to have the car steam cleaned first. Apply an underbody sealant is a dirty job and you should be well prepared with old clothes, gloves and a hat. If you are venturing underneath the car and it has to be jacked up then make certain that it is well supported on axle stands.

After thoroughly cleaning the underside you should go over stubborn dirt or caked mud with a good fine wire brush. The important thing is that the surface to be treated is obsolutely clear of any foreign matter. For good application of underbody sealant use a cheap paint brush. It is important that the sealant used will remain flexible and will not chip or flake at a later date. Obviously care will have to be taken not to cover moving parts such as the drive shafts, handbrake linkages, etc. If necessary then mask these areas first.

The first part of this section on corrosion concentrates on the matter of protection. Which is fine before corrosion takes place. But what happens if corrosion has already taken a hold?

It can be a costly business when corrosion dictates the vehicle being taken off the road through an MoT failure. As already explained in 'Passing the MoT' page at the beginning of this Repair Manual, an MoT tester will check for damage or corrosion in or on a vehicle that is likely to render it unsafe.

With the Mini, the tester will pay special attention to the front and rear sub-frames and the sub-frame mountings, side sills, inner support rib and the floor, the latter especially where the steering rack is mounted. Also he'll check the seat belt mounting areas.

Having checked and identified the important areas, the MoT tester will check the extent or level of suspect corrosion. He should do this by pressing hard against the area and testing the amount of 'give' which results. Often he will also tap the component lightly (it should not be necessary to subject the area to heavy blows), listening for differences in sound which will result from unaffected metal compared with corroded metal.

Accessories

RADIO . . . . [1]

Installation

The following instructions describe the installation of a radio. These are based on information received from Radiomobile Ltd, leading radio and tape player manufacturers.

A retractable aerial must be mounted in the appropriate position in the nearside front wing (see AERIAL later).

Components are provided in the Radiomobile installation kit for suppressing interference from the coil and alternator and details on their fitting is given in the SUPPRESSION section.

WARNING: Before connection to the battery supply it is essential to ensure that the polarity of the radio is suitable for vehicle application. See instruction on underside of unit. Wrong polarity will damage transistors.

850 & 1000 Saloon

1. Disconnect battery.
2. Loosely assemble radio into radio unit mounting bracket as shown in Fig. P:1 inset, using fixings provided.
3. Offer assembly up to underside of drive side front parcel tray between steering column bracket and body side panel.
4. Align assembly under tray so that the front of the radio unit is level with the front under edge of the parcel tray rail as shown in Fig. P:1.
5. Hold assembly steady and mark the position of the radio unit mounting bracket on to underside of parcel tray.
6. Remove the radio unit from the radio unit mounting bracket and offer the bracket up to the previously marked position under parcel tray.
7. Using bracket as a template mark the position of the four fixing holes on underside of parcel tray.
8. Drill fixing holes through metal and trim.
NOTE: Great care must be exercised when drilling rear holes not to allow the drill to run through into the vertical trim finisher panel above parcel tray.
9. Secure radio mounting bracket to parcel tray using fixings provided ensuring the four bronze screws are fitted through tray as shown in Fig. P:1.
10. Assemble radio unit to bracket using fixings provided, adjusting radio in bracket so that the front edge is level with the front underside edge of parcel tray and secure fixings.
11. Connect battery lead to snap connector, green lead/

white tracer located to the rear of heater on right hand side.

Pre March 1976 Models

12. Connect fuse lead with Lucar type blade to main battery connection (brown lead) on ignition switch.

Pre March 1976 Models with Heater

To gain access to ignition switch it is necessary to remove the two fixing screws at the top front edge of the heater unit. The front edge of the heater can then be lowered away from the switch panel. Care should be taken when re-fitting heater to ensure that adjacent wiring is not disturbed.

13. Connect speaker, aerial and fuse leads to radio. Reconnect battery.
14. Switch on radio and adjust aerial trimmer as detailed in car radio operating instructions.

Clubman & 1275 GT

1. Using existing hole 'A' Fig. P:2 in the underside front edge of the parcel tray, temporarily secure the radio mounting bracket to the underside of tray using one of the fixings provided.
NOTE: It may be found necessary to cut away trim material in the area of hole 'A' (underside).
2. Align the mounting bracket so that it lies squarely under tray and using bracket as a template mark off the position of the two remaining fixing holes 'B' Fig. P:2.
3. Remove mounting bracket and drill two holes at marked off positions in parcel tray.
4. Secure mounting bracket to the underside of tray with fixings provided as shown in Fig. P:2.
5. Assemble radio unit into mounting bracket using fixings provided, adjusting radio in bracket so that the front edge is level with the front under side edge of parcel tray and secure fixings.
6. Connect battery lead to snap connector green lead/white tracer located to rear of heater on right hand side.

Pre March 1976 with Column Switch

7. Using the double Lucar termination now provided on radio fuse lead, connect to rear of lighting switch at brown lead/blue tracer. (Pull off brown lead/blue tracer from switch, connect radio lead to switch and then connect brown lead/blue tracer to blade on side of radio lead connector).

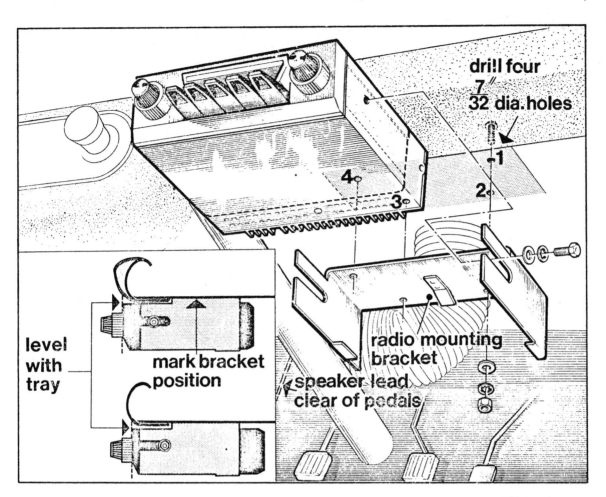

Fig. P:1 Radio installation on 850, 1000 Saloons, Countryman, Traveller, Van and Pick-up

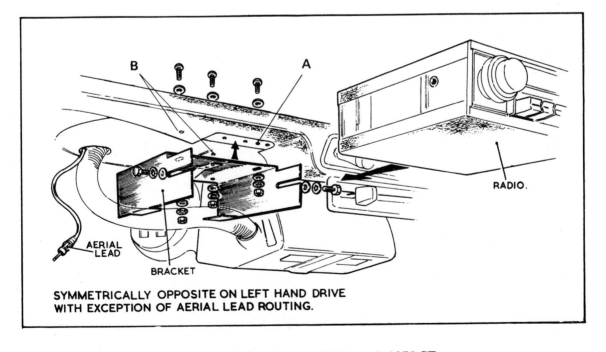

Fig. P:2 Radio installation Clubman & 1275 GT

Pre March 1976 Without Column Switch

Connect fuse lead to the spare 'Lucar' type blade at main battery connection (brown lead) at rear of ignition switch.

NOTE: Vehicles with de luxe heater. To gain access to rear of ignition switch remove the two drive screws at the top flange of heater unit. The heater unit can then be lowered away from switch panel.

8. Connect speaker, aerial and fuse leads to radio.
9. Switch on radio and adjust aerial trimmer as detailed in car radio operating instructions.

Countryman, Traveller, Van & Pick-Up

1. Disconnect battery.
2. Loosely assemble radio unit into radio unit mounting bracket as shown in Fig. P:1 inset, using fixings provided.
3. Offer assembly up to underside of drive side front parcel tray between steering column bracket and body side panel.
4. Align assembly under tray so that the front of the radio unit is level with the front under edge of the parcel tray as shown in Fig. P:1.
5. Hold assembly steady and mark the position of the radio unit mounting bracket on to underside of parcel tray.
6. Remove the radio unit from the radio unit mounting bracket and offer the bracket up to the previously marked position under parcel tray.
7. Using bracket as a template, mark the position of four fixing holes on underside of parcel tray.
8. Drill fixing holes through metal and trim.
NOTE: Great care must be taken when drilling rear holes not to allow the drill to run through into the vertical trim finisher panel above parcel tray.
9. Secure radio mounting bracket to parcel tray using fixings provided ensuring the four bronze screws are fitted through tray as shown in Fig. P:1.
10. Assemble radio unit to bracket using fixings provided, adjusting radio in bracket so that the front edge is level with the front underside edge of parcel tray and secure fixings.
11. Connect fuse lead to spare 'Lucar' type blade at main battery connection (brown lead) on ignition switch.
NOTE: VEHICLES WITH DE-LUXE HEATER. To gain access to ignition switch it is necessary to remove the two fixing screws at the top front edge of the heater unit. The front edge of the heater can then be lowered away from the switch panel. Care should be taken when refitting heater to ensure that adjacent wiring is not disturbed.
12. Connect speaker, aerial and fuse leads to radio. Reconnect battery.
13. Switch on radio, tune to a weak signal on approximately 250 metres (1.2 Mhz.) and adjust aerial trimmer for maximum volume.

SPEAKER(S) . . . . [2]

All Saloon Models - Installation

1. Route speaker lead from radio position to centre line of bulkhead (positioning lead to avoid interference with pedal movements) down to floor tunnel (underneath the floor covering) and along side of the tunnel to the front seat floor stiffener.
2. Route lead under front seat floor stiffener via the shallow pressing in the floor running under the stiffener, and along floor tunnel to rear seat.
NOTE: On some vehicles it may be found necessary to use a fish wire when routing loudspeaker lead.
3. Temporarily lift out rear seat cushion.
4. Drill a 5/8 in dia. hole through front section of the rear seat pan, 5 in to rear of front edge on centre line of car, route speaker lead through this hole using grommet provided .
5. Drill a 5/8 in dia. hole below rear seat squab through rear bulkhead into luggage compartment 1½ in up from seat pan on centre line of car, route speaker lead through this hole using grommet provided.
6. Pass lead through cable clips up the side of petrol tank.
7. Locate holes provided in centre of metal panel of rear parcel shelf. See Fig. P:5.
NOTE: On some vehicle variations a sheet of felt wadding is attached to the underside of the rear shelf. The wadding must be cut away to expose the speaker holes and to clear speaker chassis.
8. Cut away the sections of trimmed pad which are visible through the two larger holes.
9. Pierce through trimmed pad the four holes for speaker bezel studs.
10. Connect lead to speaker.
11. Assemble bezel and speaker to parcel shelf as shown in Fig. P:5, secure with fixings provided.
12. Secure speaker lead to floor, tunnel, seat pan etc. with self adhesive tape provided.
13. Refit rear seat cushion.

Clubman Estate - Installation (Fig. P:3)

1. Remove directional face level air vent from passenger side of fascia by unscrewing the plastic outer rim and removing vent cowling. Disengage vent pipe by twisting half a turn anti-clockwise and withdraw. See Fig. P:3.
2. Unclip section of passenger side rubber door seal, and break adhesive bond between end of parcel tray trim panel and post. Release other end of trim panel by easing side flap out from behind rim of instrument nacelle and remove panel completely by bowing outwards sufficiently to clear the underside of fascia top rail.
3. Mark and cut out a 5 5/8 in dia. hole in trim panel to dimensions shown in Fig. P:3.
4. Pierce four 5/32 in dia. fixing holes in trim panel using speaker as template, see Fig. P:3 for position of holes.
5. Fit the spring clips provided to speaker support board and assemble speaker and mounting components to trim panel as shown in Fig. P:3.
6. Connect speaker lead to speaker and route lead down through demister pipe hole at rear of parcel tray to radio position.
7. Refit the trim panel/speaker assembly and directional face level air vent in a similar reverse manner to that used for removal.

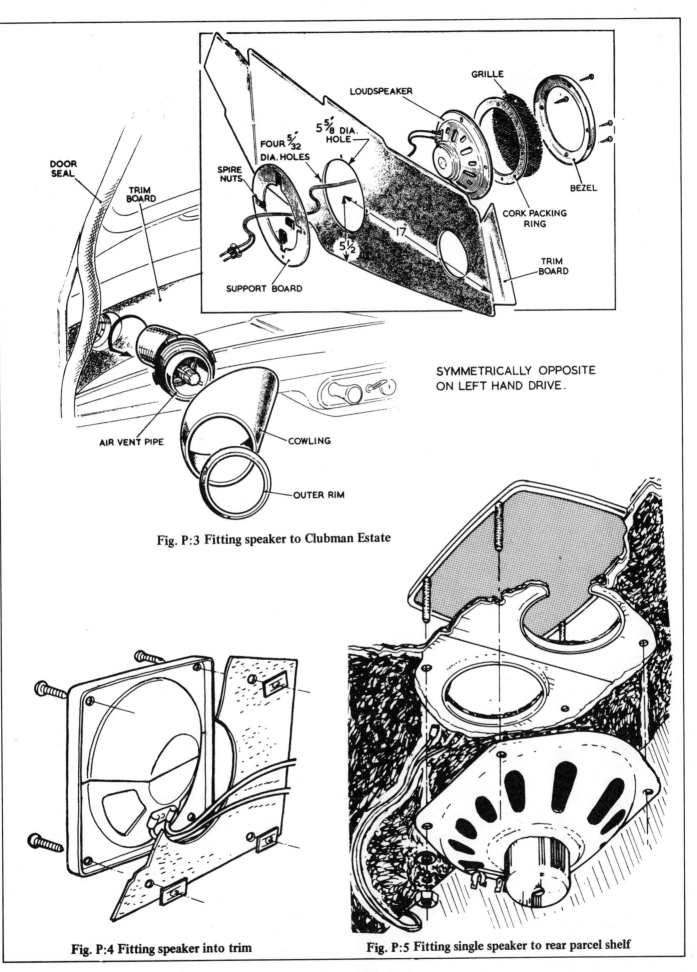

DOOR SEAL

TRIM BOARD

LOUDSPEAKER

GRILLE

$5\frac{5}{8}$ DIA. HOLE

FOUR $\frac{5}{32}$ DIA. HOLES

SPIRE NUTS

$5\frac{1}{2}$

17

BEZEL

CORK PACKING RING

TRIM BOARD

SUPPORT BOARD

SYMMETRICALLY OPPOSITE ON LEFT HAND DRIVE.

AIR VENT PIPE

COWLING

OUTER RIM

Fig. P:3 Fitting speaker to Clubman Estate

Fig. P:4 Fitting speaker into trim

Fig. P:5 Fitting single speaker to rear parcel shelf

Accessories

Stereo Speakers

Installation - General (Fig. P:4)

1. Remove interior trim panel from door or side panel after removing door handle, window winder, etc (see Body Fittings).
2. Where possible, select a position on the trim panel that coincides with a suitable hole in the metal door panel.
3. Ensure that the speaker magnet is clear of the window winding mechanism and that the speaker grille is clear of the window winder and door handles.
4. Using templates, pierce four 1/8 in (3 mm) dia. fixing holes and cut the 5 inch diameter centre hole.
5. When there is a clearance hole in the metal panel behind the fixing holes, secure the speaker to the trim using four No. 6 x 1.25 in screws and flat nuts.
6. If any of the fixing holes are backed by metal, drill a 5/64 in (2 mm) dia. hole and secure the screw to the metal panel without using the flat nut.
7. The water proof cowl must be positioned at the top of the speaker (Motorola type shown).
8. If there is no suitable hole in the metal door panel, cut the door trim panel and using this as a template, cut and drill corresponding holes in the metal door panel.
9. Before securing the speaker, drill a 3/8 in (9 mm) dia. hole in the leading edge of the door and a corresponding hole in the door pillar, unless suitable holes exist.
10. Fit the rubber grommets provided to these holes, and route the speaker lead from the radio or tape player position through these grommets to the speaker position.
11. Attach the leads to the speaker and secure the speaker door trim etc., ensuring that the speaker lead is clear of the window winding mechanism.

AERIAL . . . . [3]

1. Mark and drill a 7/8 in dia. hole in the left hand side front wing to dimensions shown in Figs. P:6 or P:7.
2. Drill a 9/16 in dia. hole through wing valance from engine side of car as indicated in Fig. P:9.
NOTE: Ensure that the air ducting hose under wing is clear of drilling area.
3. Scrape around the underside of the aerial hole to reveal bright metal in order to ensure a good earth connection. Failure to do this may result in aerial-borne interference being transmitted to the receiver.
4. Pass the aerial upward through the aerial hole and secure into position taking care to position any keyhole or locking device for easy access.
4. Route aerial lead through hole in valance to engine compartment and fit grommet provided.
5. Feed aerial lead through grommet 'B' in the engine bulkhead (Fig. P:9). From inside the car locate the aerial plug through demister pipe hole in underside of front parcel tray and draw lead to radio position.
NOTE: On some vehicles it may be found necessary to pull back the sound proofing material to locate grommet 'B' in engine bulkhead.

SUPPRESSION . . . . [4]

It is important in the interests of efficient suppression, to scrape to bare metal each point at which an earth connection is made.
1. Fit a 1 mfd capacitor to the 'SW' terminal on ignition coil. Earth under coil mounting bolt.
ALTERNATOR WITH YELLOW IDENTIFICATION MARK
2. Where alternator is fitted with yellow identification mark on alternator cap no further suppression is required to this component.
ALTERNATOR WITHOUT YELLOW IDENTIFICATION MARK.
Connect a 1 mfd. suppressor capacitor to the output terminal of alternator as follows:
a) Pull off plug connection on alternator back plate.
b) Withdraw the two moulded cover securing screws and cover.
c) Route fly lead of capacitor through slot in moulded cover and, ensuring that associated wiring is not disturbed, connect lead to spare 3/16 in terminal blade attached to the main output terminal on alternator.
d) Refit moulded cover and reconnect plug to alternator.
e) Earth capacitor mounting clip under alternator rear fixing bolt.
VEHICLES FITTED WITH DYNAMO
Fit a 1 mfd. capacitor to the output (large) terminal on the dynamo. Earth under dynamo mounting bolt.
3. Fit a 1 mfd. capacitor to the supply terminal (white lead) on petrol pump. (This unit is located under left hand rear of body). Connect small tag of earthing lead supplied, to earth terminal on petrol pump, earth large tag of lead, and capacitor to bolt on pump mounting bracket.
4. Connect small tag of other earthing lead supplied, to small cheese head screw on terminal end plate (motor body) of the windscreen wiper motor. Earth other end of lead to gusset plate immediately forward of wiper motor where a hole should be provided.

BABY SEAT . . . . [5]

Only by fitting a safety seat or harness, secured firmly to the car structure, can a child have a good chance of surviving a severe road accident without injury. Furthermore with the child safely in position at the rear of the car a driver can concentrate on the road with less distraction, while the child can enjoy the ride in safety and comfort.

There are many types of baby seat and cot restraints on the market and it is essential to the child's safety that a unit be fitted which meets with required safety standards. KL Jeenay Safety Systems are BSI approved, and are generally accepted as being among the best on the market.

Baby or child seats are normally suitable for children aged from 6/9 months to children aged 5 years. KL Jeenay safety seats or harnesses can, if necessary, be fitted 2 or 3 abreast, doubling up anchor plates at anchorage points where necessary.

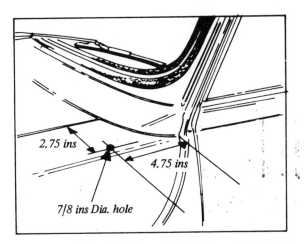

Fig. P:6 Aerial positioning - Mini Clubman/1275 GT

2.75 ins

4.75 ins

7/8 ins Dia. hole

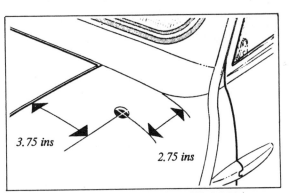

3.75 ins

2.75 ins

Fig. P:7 Aerial positioning - Mini 850/
1000 Saloon, etc.

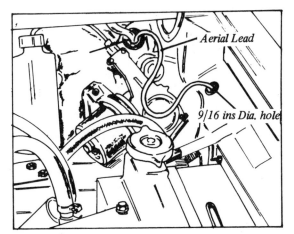

Aerial Lead

9/16 ins Dia. hole

Fig. P:9 Routing aerial lead

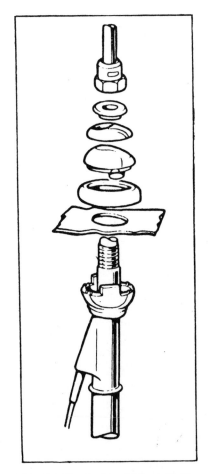

Fig. P:8 Typical aerial installation

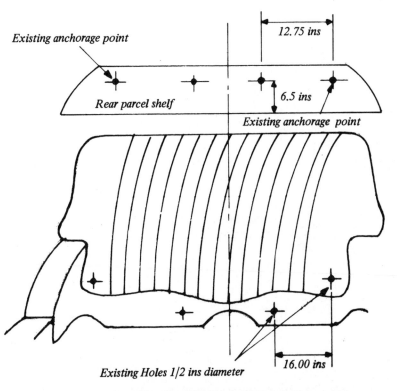

Existing anchorage point

Rear parcel shelf

12.75 ins

6.5 ins

Existing anchorage point

Existing Holes 1/2 ins diameter

16.00 ins

Fig. P:10 Baby seat fitting location points -
Mini Saloon

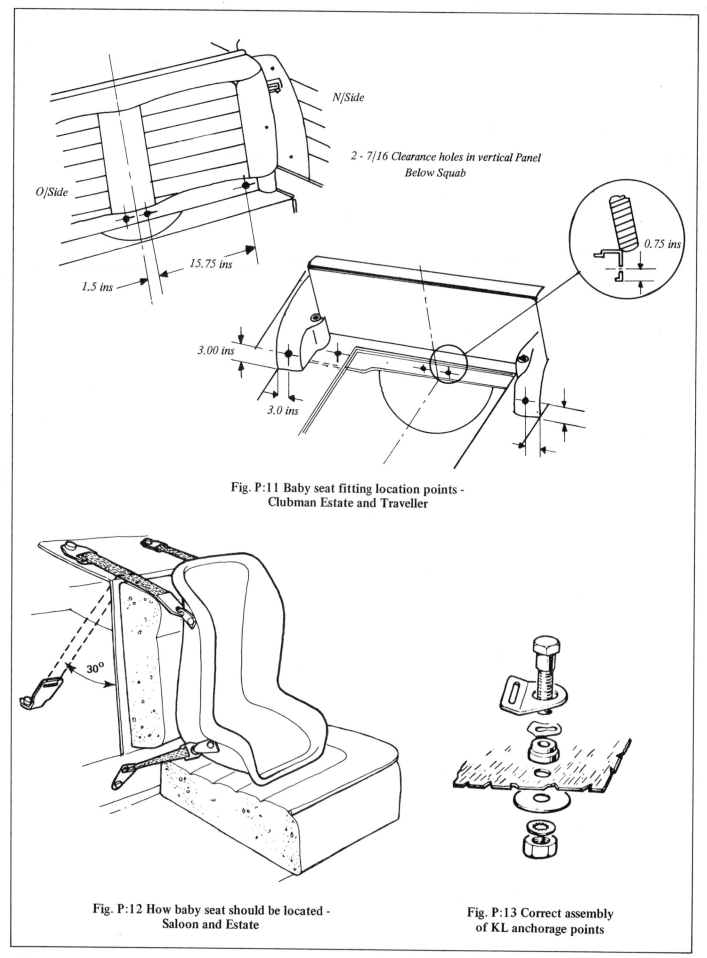

2 - 7/16 Clearance holes in vertical Panel
Below Squab

N/Side

O/Side

15.75 ins

1.5 ins

0.75 ins

3.00 ins

3.0 ins

Fig. P:11 Baby seat fitting location points -
Clubman Estate and Traveller

30°

Fig. P:12 How baby seat should be located -
Saloon and Estate

Fig. P:13 Correct assembly
of KL anchorage points

Most cars have 2 or 3 built-in anchorage points for each seating position. These are usually concealed behind the trim or soundproofing and plugged or grommetted (ses Figs. P:10 and P:11). Always use the existing points, even if it means doubling up on an existing rear adult safety belt, using longer bolts (supplied in KL kit).

A general guide to fitting is as follows:

1. Remove the seat cushion (bottom part). Two points will be found and may be covered in tape or filled with paste.

2. If anchorage points have to be drilled then it should be stressed that only fixed parts of the steel structure should be used. The size of the holes should be 7/16 in (11.5 mm). Always check the position of petrol tank, brake fluid pipes, electrical wiring, spare wheel and other obstructions before drilling.

3. On estate versions the two upper straps must make an angle of at least 30° (Fig. P:12) in side view with the car's back seat. Use both wheel arches if required. Ensure that the 2 slot slide adjuster is near the end of the webbing.

4. When fitting anchorage points refer to Fig. P:13 for correct order of assembly. This is important.

5. Fit the four restraint strap assemblies to the anchorage points using short straps for the bottom of the seat and obviously the long straps for the top.

6. Adjust seat straps to keep the safety seat as high as possible.

7. Attach lower straps to seat and adjust webbing to suit, without overtightening.

8. To remove the seat, press into car squab and remove lower lugs first.

9. Adjust the harness straps to fit as tightly as comfortable. The lap straps should rest low over the bony part of the hip. Always ensure that the crotch strap is used.

SOUNDPROOFING . . . . [6]

In any car, a certain amount of noise is transmitted to the passenger compartment and, if of a high enough level, can not only be annoying, but also tiring on long journeys. Therefore, the elimination or reduction of this noise is desirable for more enjoyable and safer motoring.

The passengers in a car can be subjected to noise from various sources: the wind rushing round the body and blowing round badly sealed doors; mechanical noise from the engine and transmission; the exhaust; tyres drumming on the road; and noise cause by the vibration of the car's sheet metal panels. By insulating the body of the car, it is possible to eliminate or considerably reduce a large proportion of this noise. Sound Service (Oxford) Ltd., of Witney, Oxon, are leading manufacturers of sound proofing materials, and their Autosound kit for the Mini contains a variety of these, each designed specially to reduce or eliminate the various types of noise experienced in the car. The following is based on information supplied by the company.

Before doing anything, the front seats should ideally be removed as well as all the carpets and floor mats. Then the floor should be thoroughly cleaned. Leave in place trim carpet below parcel shelf and on wheel arches.

With the floor/bulkhead area clear, check for any holes and seal them with the mastic sealing strip supplied in the Autosound kit. This should also be applied to all rubber grommets where cables and pipes pass through the bulkhead and to the area at the bottom of the steering column. The object is to obtain an air-tight seal between the engine and passenger compartments.

All the components of the kit are pre-cut to shape and numbered, and the next step should be to lay them out and identify them. Two rigid bitumen and four pliable damper pads are included and these should be stuck in each footwell and in other areas of the floor where vibration is apparent. These can be found by gently tapping with a rubber hammer; if they emit a thumping sound, they should be treated. Each damper pad is self-adhesive on one side, allowing it to be stuck in place and it acts as a stiffener. As the panel vibrates, the board is alternately stretched and compressed and thus acts to slow down the vibration reducing the noise level.

The next job is to fit pre-cut pieces of Sound Barrier Mat to both sides of the bulkhead. These are made from a grey foam material with a stiff rubber-like facing on one side. The material is glued in place on the panels, using the adhesive supplied in the kit, the foam being placed against the steel panel. In practice, this allows the sound waves to pass through the panel, into the foam where some of the energy of the vibrating air particles is dissipated as they pass through its tiny passages, and then bounce back from the stiff outer layer. In this way much of the sound is trapped between the two layers and gradually losses its energy as it bounces to and fro.

For the under-bonnet area, the Autosound kit includes some items in Neoprene faced felt. These are glued in place in the same manner as the Sound Barrier Mat, the smooth surface outermost. Like the foam material, the felt has tiny passages between its fibres that help dissipate energy of the vibrating air particles. This material cuts down multiple reflections of sounds within the engine compartment, preventing the build up of noise.

One further item provided is a roll of Weatherseal tape for sealing doors, etc. Rather than placing this along the entire opening, it is often more effective simply to place it where the air is actually leaking through the seal, and to find this is a simple matter. It is necessary to drive the car with a passenger who should have a section of normal garden hose. By holding one end of the hose to his ear and the other to the door seal, he can determine exactly where the seal is deficient. By marking the extremities of the leak with chalk or some similar means, it is a simple matter to cut the Weatherseal tape to size and install it exactly where needed.

The final job is to replace the carpets and seats and check the operation of all instruments and lights, etc., in case any wires have been displaced during the operation.

Tightening Torques

ENGINE

Cylinder head nuts. . . . . 50 lb ft (7.0 kg m)
    Additional nut & bolt (1275 GT) . . 25 lb ft (3.5 kg m)
    Emission control engines. . . . . . . 40 lb ft (5.5 kg m)
Rocker pedestal nuts . . . . 24 lb ft (3.2 kg m)
Rocker cover . . . . .3.5 lb ft (0.5 kg m)
Manifold to cylinder head . . . . 14 lb ft (1.9 kg m)
Heater control to cyl head. . . . . .8 lb ft (1.1 kg m)
Water outlet elbow. . . . . .8 lb ft (1.1 kg m)
Temperature sender unit. . . . . 16 lb ft (2.2 kg m)
Spark plugs . . . . 18 lb ft (2.5 kg m)
Main bearing cap bolts . . . . 63 lb ft (8.7 kg m)
Connecting rod big end cap:
    Bolts. . . . . 37 lb ft (5.1 kg m)
    Nuts (1275 GT) . . . . 33 lb ft (4.6 kg m)
Piston pin clamp bolts (848 cc) . . . . 24 lb ft (3.2 kg m)
Camshaft nut . . . . 65 lb ft (8.9 kg m)
Crankshaft pulley nut. . . . . 75 lb ft (10.3 kg m)
Timing cover and front plate:
    1/4 in UNF bolts. . . . . .5 lb ft (0.7 kg m)
    5/16 in UNF bolts. . . . . 12 lb ft (1.7 kg m)
Water pump . . . . 16 lb ft (2.2 kg m)
Cylinder side covers. . . . . .3.5 lb ft (0.5 kg m)
Clutch cover to pressure plate
    (driving pins) . . . . 16 lb ft (2.2 kg m)
Drive strap to flywheel. . . . . 16 lb ft (2.2 kg m)
Flywheel centre bolt . . . . 112 lb ft (15.5 kg m)
Flywheel housing bolts & stud nuts. . 18 lb ft (2.5 kg m)
Oil pump. .8 lb ft (1.1 kg m)
Oil pipe banjo. . . . . 38 lb ft (5.3 kg m)
Oil filter head nuts. . . . . 14 lb ft (1.9 kg m)
Oil filter bowl centre bolt . . . . 14 lb ft (1.9 kg m)
Oil filter head nuts. . . . . 14 lb ft (1.9 kg m)
Oil pressure relief valve - dome nut . . 43 lb ft (5.9 kg m)

MANUAL TRANSMISSION

Drain plug . . . . 25 lb ft (3.5 kg m)
Transmission case to crankcase. . . . . . 6 lb ft (0.8 kg m)
Transmission case studs
    3/8 UNC . . . . .8 lb ft (1.1 kg m)
    5/16 UNC . . . . .6 lb ft (0.8 kg m)
Transmission case stud units:
    3/8 in UNF . . . . 25 lb ft (3.5 kg m)
    5/16 in UNF. . . . . 18 lb ft (2.5 kg m)
Gearchange extension bottom
    cover plate. . . . . .6 lb ft (0.8 kg m)
Input shaft nut . . . . 150 lb ft (20.7 kg m)
Mainshaft nut . . . . 150 lb ft (20.7 kg m)
Crownwheel to differential case . . . . 60 lb ft (8.3 kg m)
Final drive housing end cover bolts . . .18 lb ft (2.5 kg m)
Drive flange to final drive shaft nuts . . 70 lb ft (9.6 kg m)
Speedometer drive housing nuts. . . . . 18 lb ft (2.5 kg m)

AUTOMATIC TRANSMISSION

Converter centre bolt. . . . . 112 lb ft (15.5 kg m)
Converter, six central bolts . . . . 21 lb ft (2.9 kg m)
Converter drain plugs. . . . . 20 lb ft (2.8 kg m)
Converter housing bolts . . . . 18 lb ft (2.5 kg m)
Transmission case to crankcase nut . . 12 lb ft (1.7 kg m)
Input shaft nut . . . . 70 lb ft (9.7 kg m)
Kickdown control assembly to trans.

casing (on nylon housing) . . . . .5 lb ft (0.7 kg m)
Drive flange to find drive shaft bolts . . 43 lb ft (5.9 kg m)
Oil filter bowl. . . . . 14 lb ft (1.9 kg m)

FRONT SUSPENSION

Drive shaft nut (front hub):
    Drum front brakes. . . . . 60 lb ft (8.3 kg m)
    Disc front brakes (1275 GT) . . . 150 lb ft (20.7 kg m)
Swivel hub ball joint nuts . . . . 38 lb ft (5.3 kg m)
Swivel joint ball pin retainer . . . . . 75 lb ft (10.3 kg m)
Steering arm to swivel hub . . . . 35 lb ft (4.8 kg m)
Upper suspension arm pivot shaft nuts. 53 lb ft (7.3 kg m)
Lower suspension arm pivot shaft nuts 33 lb ft (4.5 kg m)
Tie-rod to lower arm . . . . 19 lb ft (2.6 kg m)
Tie-rod to body bracket . . . . 22 lb ft (3.0 kg m)
Drive shaft coupling 'U' bolt nuts. . . . 10 lb ft (1.4 kg m)
Road wheel nuts . . . . 45 lb ft (6.4 kg m)

REAR SUSPENSION

Hub nut. 60 lb ft (8.3 kg m)
Radius arm pivot shaft nuts. . . . . . . 53 lb ft (7.3 kg m)

STEERING

Track rod to steering arm . . . . 22 lb ft (3.0 kg m)
Steering arm to swivel hub . . . . 33 lb ft (4.5 kg m)
Steering rack 'U' bolts . . . . 11 lb ft (1.5 kg m)
Steering column to pinion shaft
    clamp bolt . . . . 12 lb ft (1.7 kg m)
Steering column upper support bracket.14 lb ft (1.9 kg m)
Steering wheel retaining nut . . . . 35 lb ft (4.8 kg m)

BRAKES

Caliper retaining bolts . . . . 38 lb ft (5.3 kg m)
Brake disc to driving flange . . . . 42 lb ft (5.8 kg m)
Rear backplate to radius arm . . . . . . 20 lb ft (2.8 kg m)
Split braking system: Tandem master cyl. reservoir
    flange screws . . . . .5 lb ft (0.7 kg m)
    Master cylinder body outlet
        connections . . . . 28 lb ft (3.9 kg m)
    Inbuilt PDWA end plug. . . . . 33 lb ft (4.5 kg m)
    PDWA end plug. . . . . 26 lb ft (3.6 kg m)
    Nylon switch to PDWA. . . . . 14 lb ft (1.9 kg m)
    Inertia valve end plug. . . . . 45 lb ft (6.4 kg m)

ELECTRICAL EQUIPMENT

Dynamo pulley nut . . . . 16 lb ft (2.2 kg m)
Dynamo mounting bolts. . . . . 17 lb ft (2.3 kg m)
Dynamo mounting bracket . . . . 25 lb ft (3.5 kg m)
11 AC Alternator:
    Through bolts. . . . . 50 lb in (0.57 kg m)
    Brush box fixing screws . . . . 10 lb in (0.12 kg m)
16 ACR Alternator:
    Pulley nut . . . . 28 lb ft (3.9 kg m)
Starter motor mounting bolts . . . . . . 25 lb ft (3.5 kg m)
Distributor, plate retaining screws. . . . .8 lb ft (1.1 kg m)
Distributor clamp bolt:
    Fixed nut type . . . . 50 lb in (0.58 kg m)
    Fixed bolt type. . . . . 30 lb in (0.35 kg m)

Index

Brief History

September 1959	Austin 7 and Morris Mini-Minor Mk I Saloons introduced with rubber cone suspension and 848 cc engine, drum brakes all round and sliding side windows.
September 1960	Estate car versions announced, known as Austin 7 Countryman (with an all metal body) and Morris Mini-Traveller, (with exterior wood framework).
September 1961	Mini Cooper Mk I introduced with front disc brakes, 997 cc engine, twin S.U. carbs and three-branch exhaust system, remote control gear lever.
October 1961	Wolseley Hornet and Riley Elf Mk I versions announced. Distinguished by extended rear boot compartment and revised front grill panel arrangement.
January 1962	All models Austin and Morris saloons now known as MINI.
October 1962	Revised gearbox introduced with bulk-ring synchromesh on upper 3 gears.
February 1963	MK 2 versions of Wolseley Hornet and Riley Elf introduced with larger 998 cc engine.
March 1963	Mini-Cooper 'S' version introduced, similar to Mini-Cooper but with 1071 cc engine.
January 1964	Mini-Cooper now fitted with larger 998 cc engine.
March 1964	1071 cc Mini-Cooper 'S' version discontinued.
April 1964	Mini-Cooper 'S 1275' Mk I introduced with 1275 cc engine.
June 1964	Mini-Cooper 'S 1000' introduced with 1071 cc engine.
September 1964	Hydrolastic suspension introduced on all saloon models. Revised gear lever and modified gearbox. Diaphragm spring clutch now fitted and revised front drum brakes.
January 1965	Mini-Cooper 'S 1000' model discontinued.
October 1965	Automatic transmission now available as optional extra - except Hornet and Elf.
October 1966	Mk 3 version of Wolseley Hornet and Riley Elf announced with remote gear lever and revised interior.
October 1967	Automatic transmission now available on Hornet and Elf. Mk 2 versions of MINI 848 cc, Traveller and Countryman estate cars, Mini-Cooper and Mini-Cooper 'S 1275' announced. Mk 2 Mini-Cooper now known as 'Mk 2 1000'. New 998 cc, 'MINI 1000' model introduced.
August 1968	New all-synchromesh gearbox now fitted to all models.
May 1969	MINI 'CLUBMAN' Saloon and Estate cars introduced.
October 1969	MINI 850 and MINI 1000 models introduced. Austin and Morris badges discontinued. Hornet and Elf versions discontinued.
November 1969	Mk 2 versions of Traveller and Countryman estate cars discontinued. Replaced by MINI Estate car. MINI 1275 GT version introduced with Clubman-shaped body. All saloons now have 'dry' cone rubber suspension and wind-up windows.
March 1970	Mk 2 Mini-Cooper 'S 1275' discontinued. Replaced by MINI-COOPER 'S' Mk 3.
December 1970	Steering column lock now fitted as standard on all models.
June 1971	'Dry' cone rubber suspension replaces 'Hydrolastic' on CLUBMAN models.
July 1974	Revised specifications on all models with improved carpets.
October 1975	Revised seats and styling trim. 1098 cc engine now fitted to CLUBMAN manual models.
May 1976	Revised instrument panel with rocker switches and face level vents.
August 1977	Revised, more luxurious interior. Denovo safety tyres standard on 1275 GT.
August 1978	Automatic transmission option discontinued.